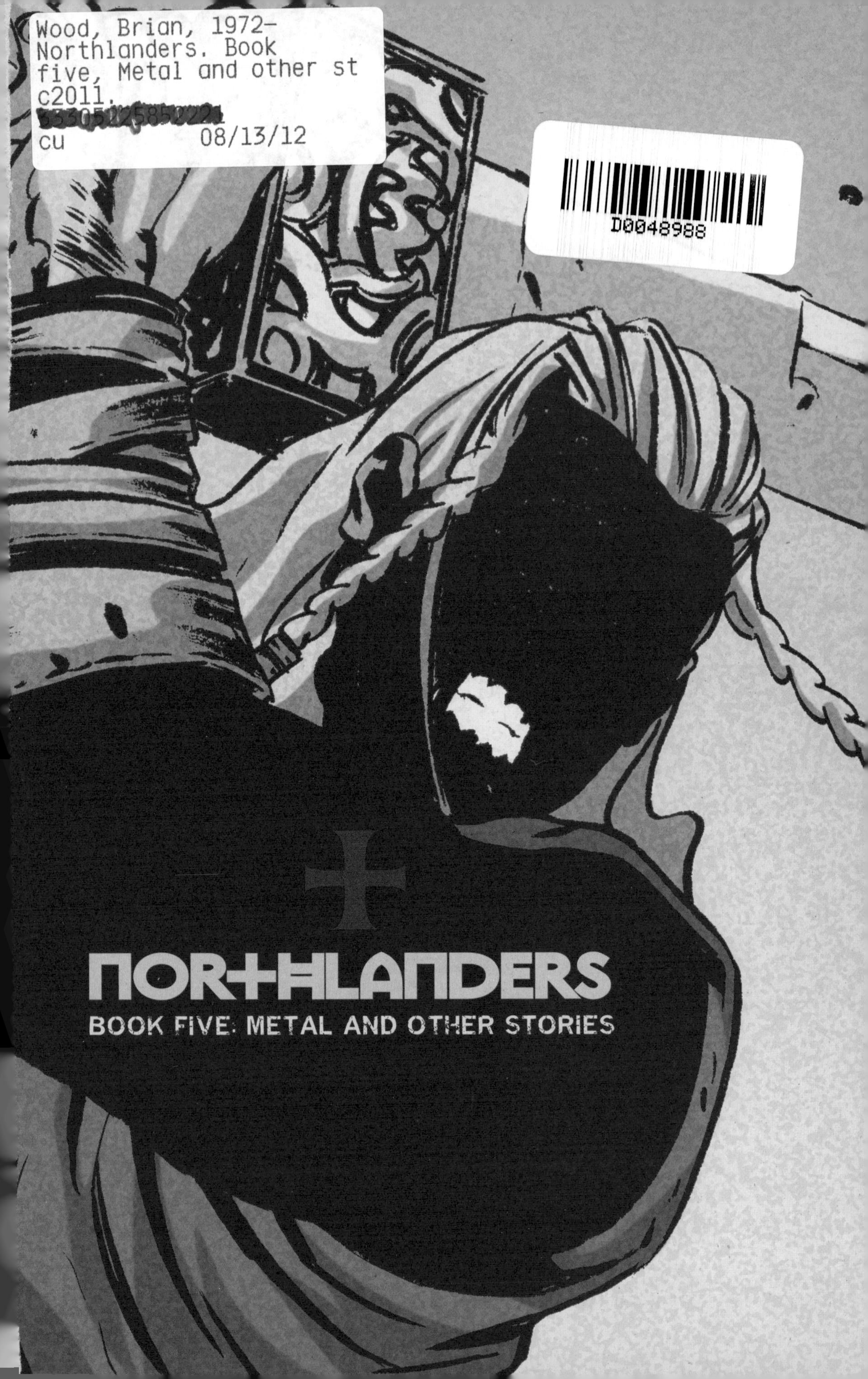
NORTHLANDERS
BOOK FIVE: METAL AND OTHER STORIES

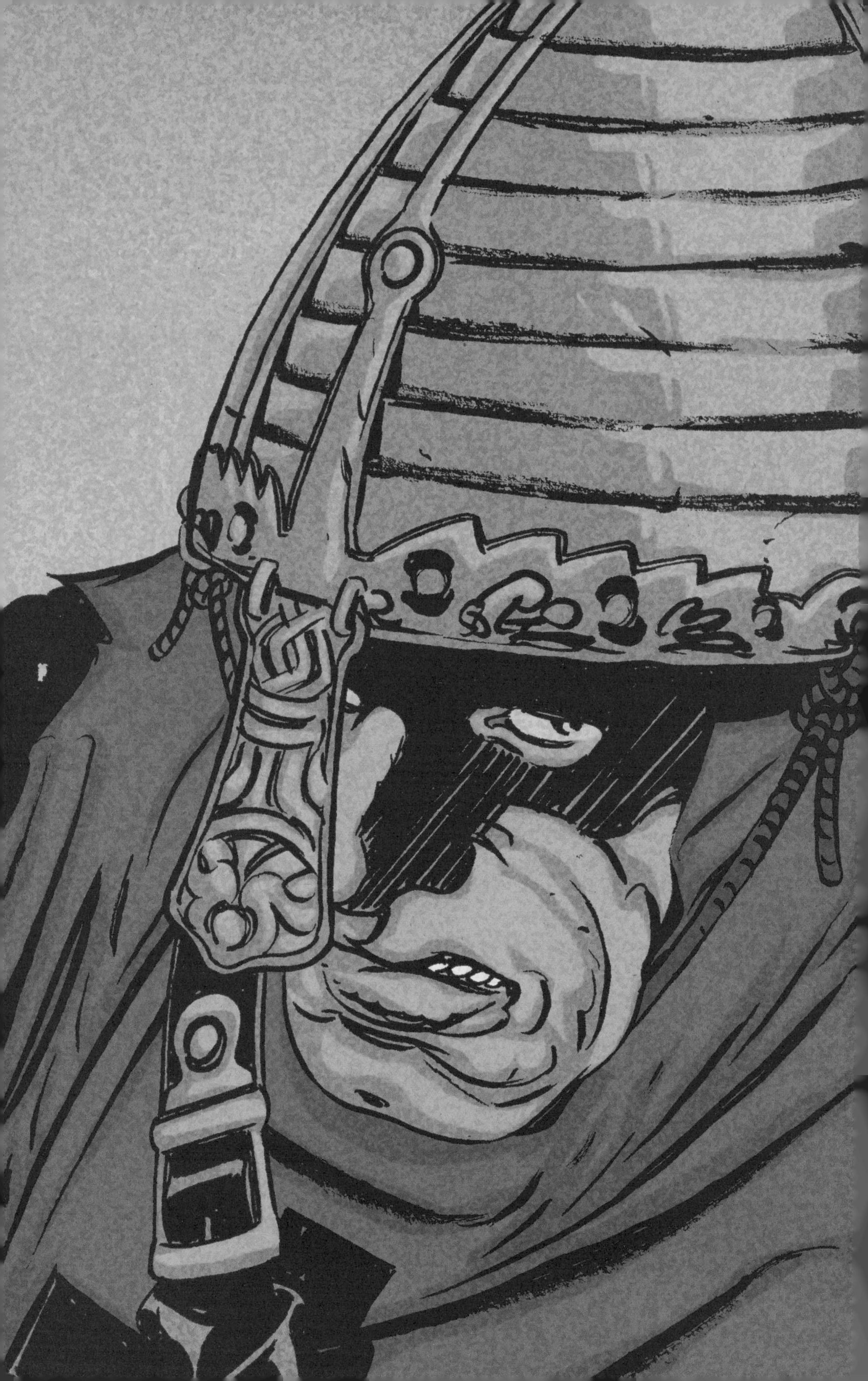

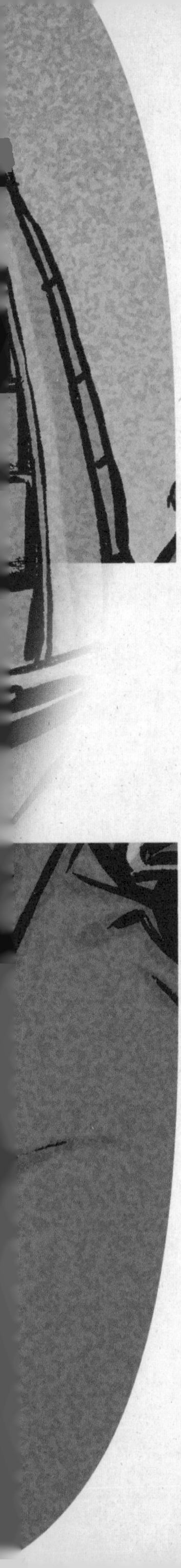

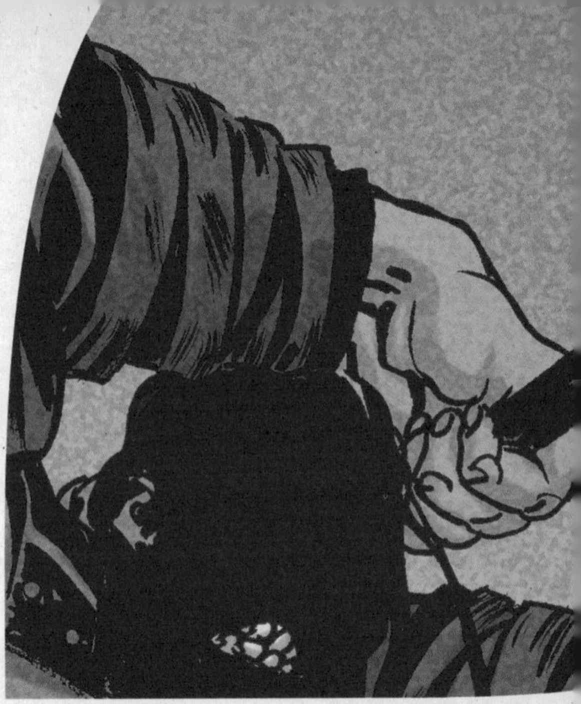

NORTHLANDERS

BOOK FIVE: METAL AND OTHER STORIES

Brian Wood Writer

Riccardo Burchielli
Fiona Staples
Becky Cloonan Artists

Dave McCaig Colorist

Travis Lanham Letterer

Cover Art and
Original Series Covers by
Massimo Carnevale

Cover design by **Brian Wood**

Northlanders created by
Brian Wood

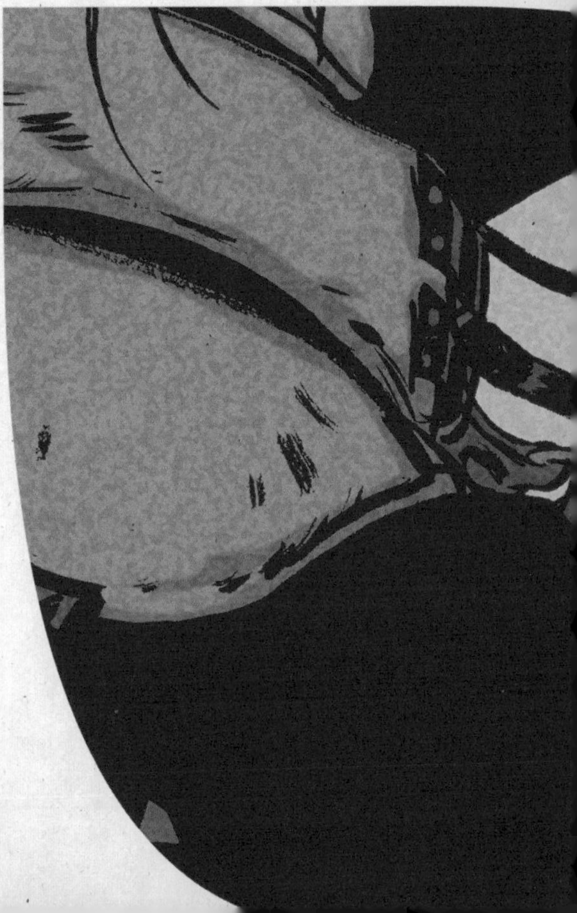

NORTHLANDERS: METAL AND OTHER STORIES

Published by DC Comics. Cover and compilation Copyright © 2011 Brian Wood and DC Comics.
All Rights Reserved.

Originally published as NORTHLANDERS 29-36. Copyright © 2010, 2011 Brian Wood and
DC Comics. All Rights Reserved. VERTIGO and all characters, their distinctive likenesses
and related elements featured in this publication are trademarks of DC Comics. The stories,
characters and incidents featured in this publication are entirely fictional. DC Comics does
not read or accept unsolicited submissions of ideas, stories or artwork.

DC Comics, 1700 Broadway, New York, NY 10019. A Warner Bros. Entertainment Company
Printed in the USA. First Printing. ISBN: 978-1-4012-3160-6

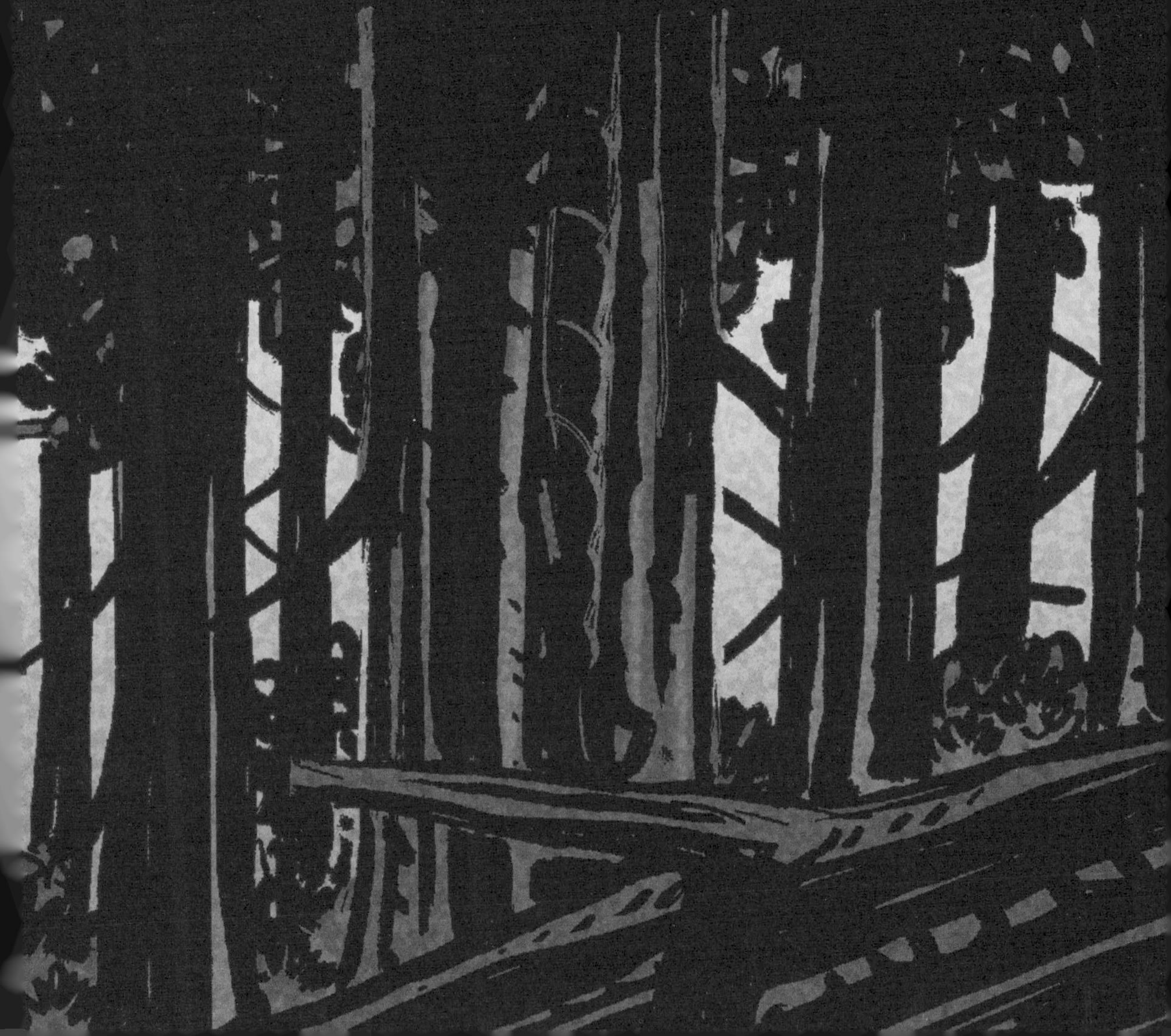

The Sea Road

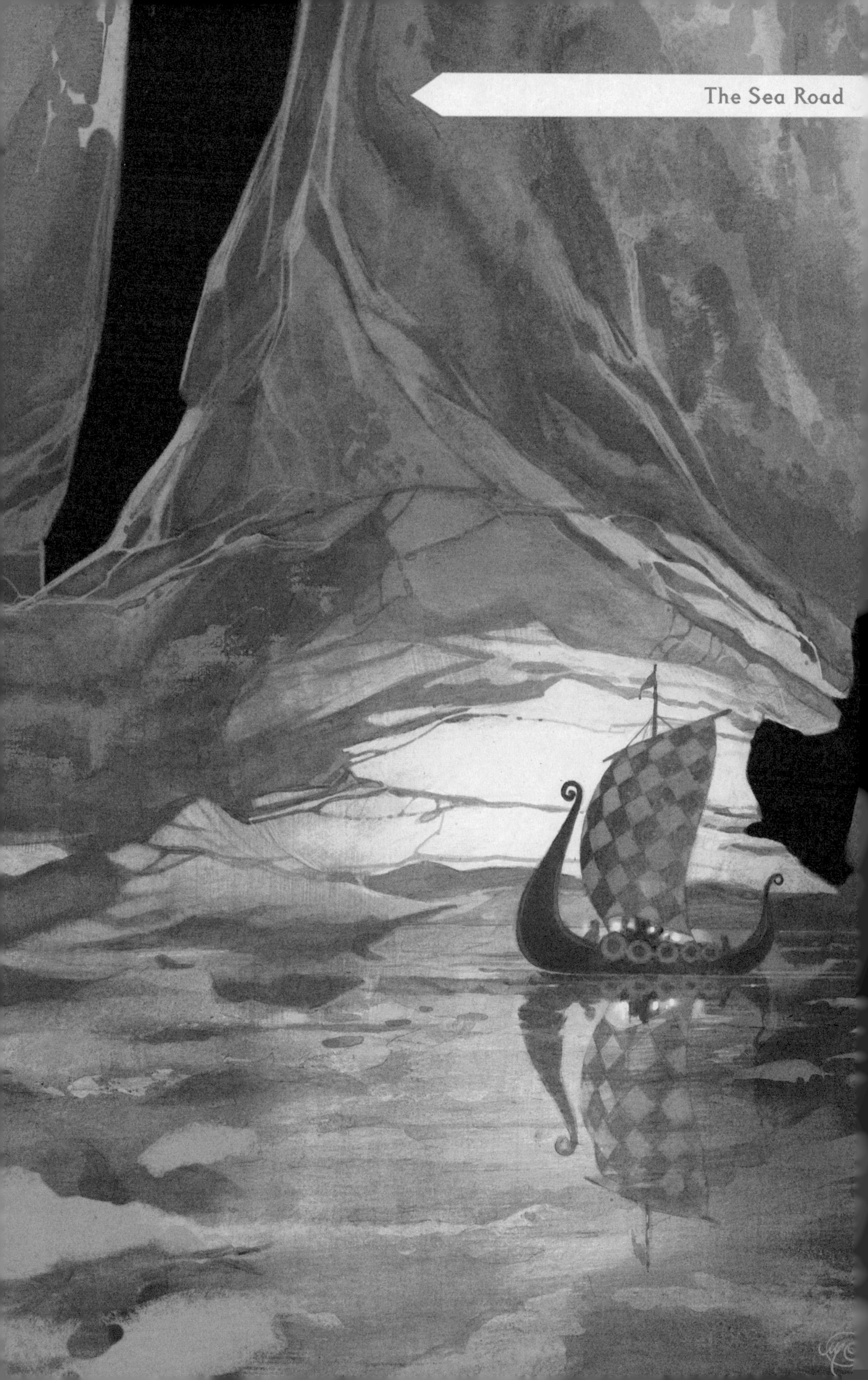

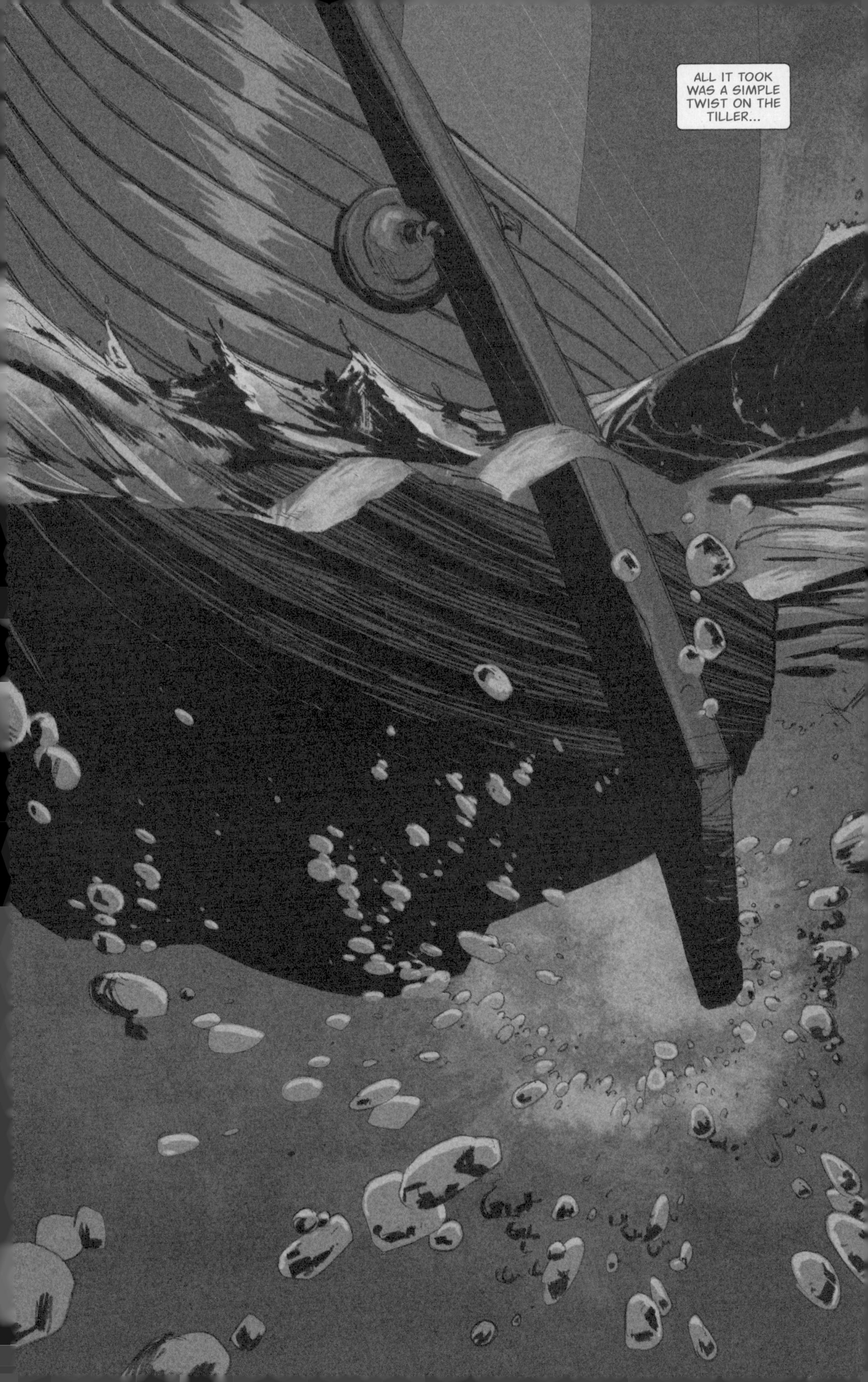
ALL IT TOOK WAS A SIMPLE TWIST ON THE TILLER...

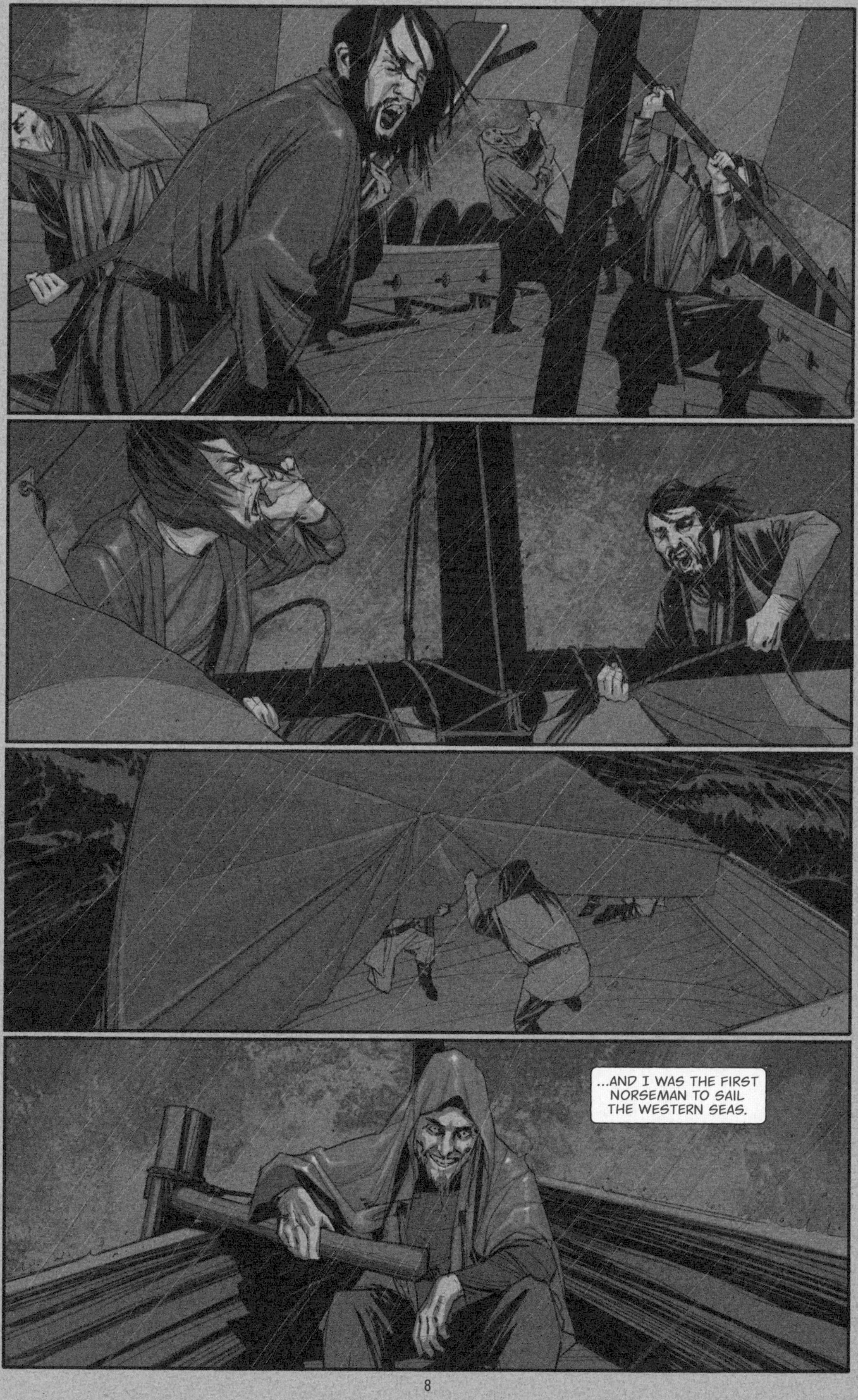
...AND I WAS THE FIRST NORSEMAN TO SAIL THE WESTERN SEAS.

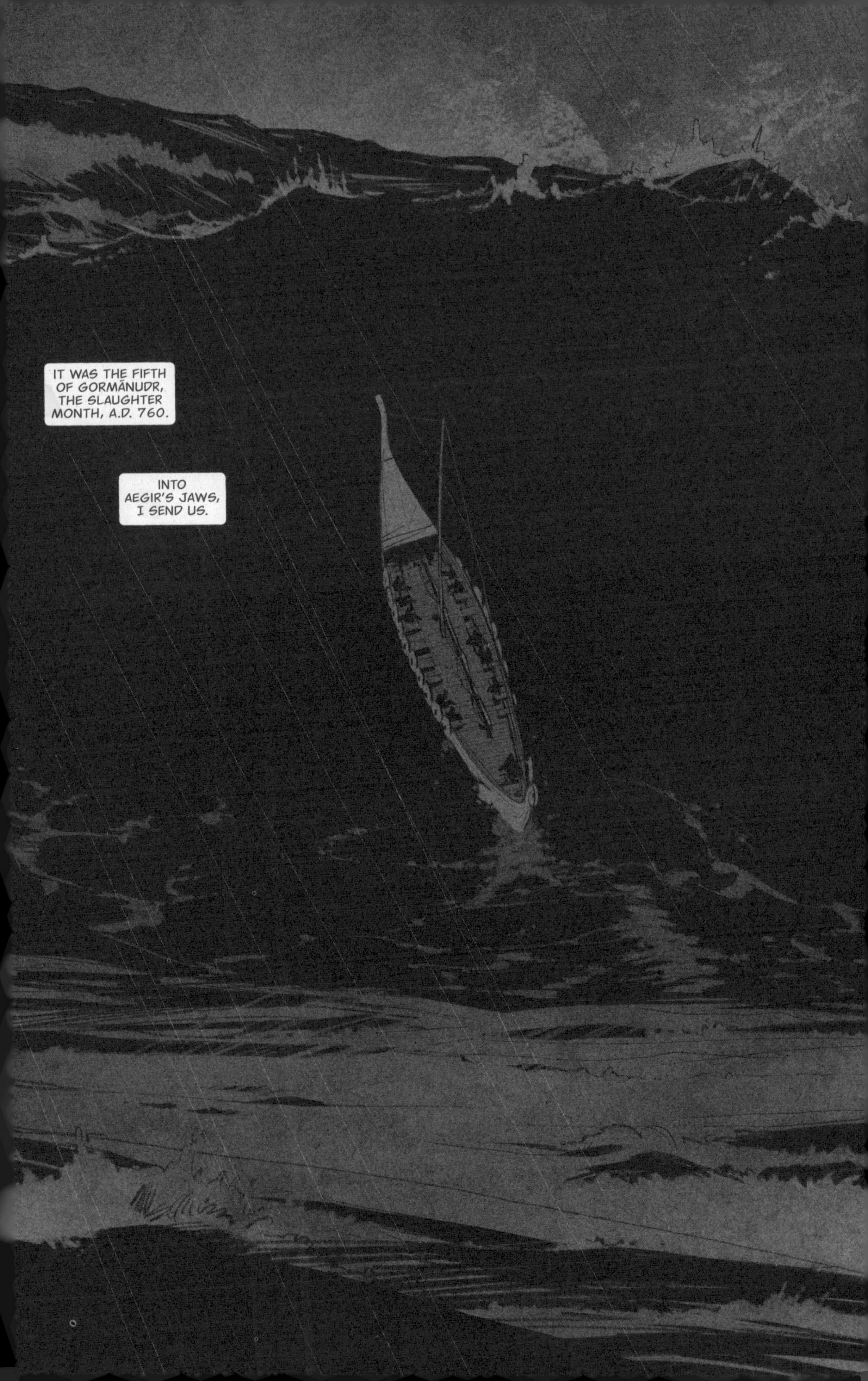
IT WAS THE FIFTH OF GORMÁNUDR, THE SLAUGHTER MONTH, A.D. 760.
INTO AEGIR'S JAWS, I SEND US.

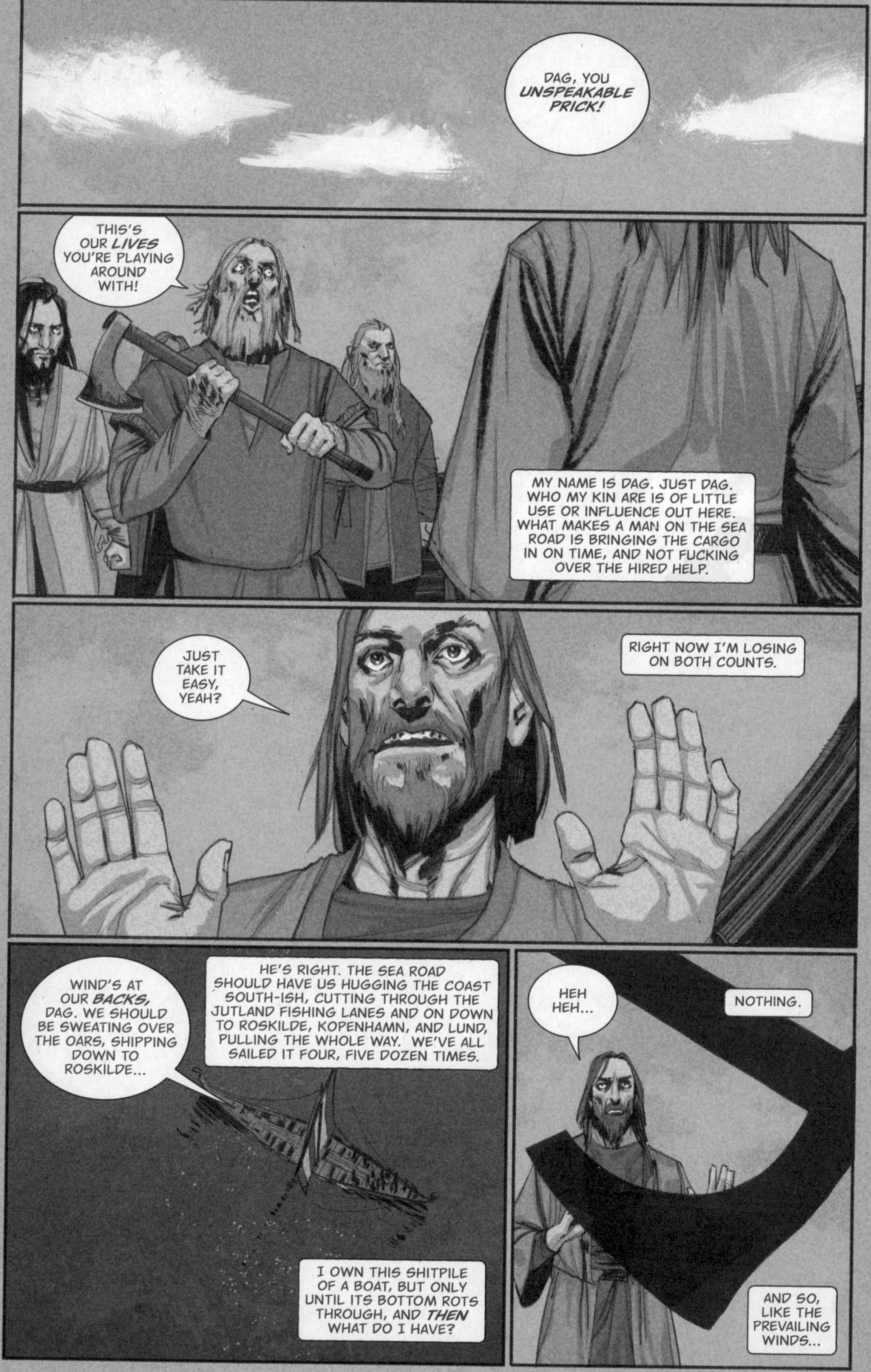
DAG, YOU *UNSPEAKABLE PRICK!*
THIS'S OUR *LIVES* YOU'RE PLAYING AROUND WITH!
MY NAME IS DAG. JUST DAG. WHO MY KIN ARE IS OF LITTLE USE OR INFLUENCE OUT HERE. WHAT MAKES A MAN ON THE SEA ROAD IS BRINGING THE CARGO IN ON TIME, AND NOT FUCKING OVER THE HIRED HELP.
JUST TAKE IT EASY, YEAH?
RIGHT NOW I'M LOSING ON BOTH COUNTS.
WIND'S AT OUR *BACKS,* DAG. WE SHOULD BE SWEATING OVER THE OARS, SHIPPING DOWN TO ROSKILDE...
HE'S RIGHT. THE SEA ROAD SHOULD HAVE US HUGGING THE COAST SOUTH-ISH, CUTTING THROUGH THE JUTLAND FISHING LANES AND ON DOWN TO ROSKILDE, KOPENHAMN, AND LUND, PULLING THE WHOLE WAY. WE'VE ALL SAILED IT FOUR, FIVE DOZEN TIMES.
I OWN THIS SHITPILE OF A BOAT, BUT ONLY UNTIL ITS BOTTOM ROTS THROUGH, AND *THEN* WHAT DO I HAVE?
HEH HEH...
NOTHING.
AND SO, LIKE THE PREVAILING WINDS...

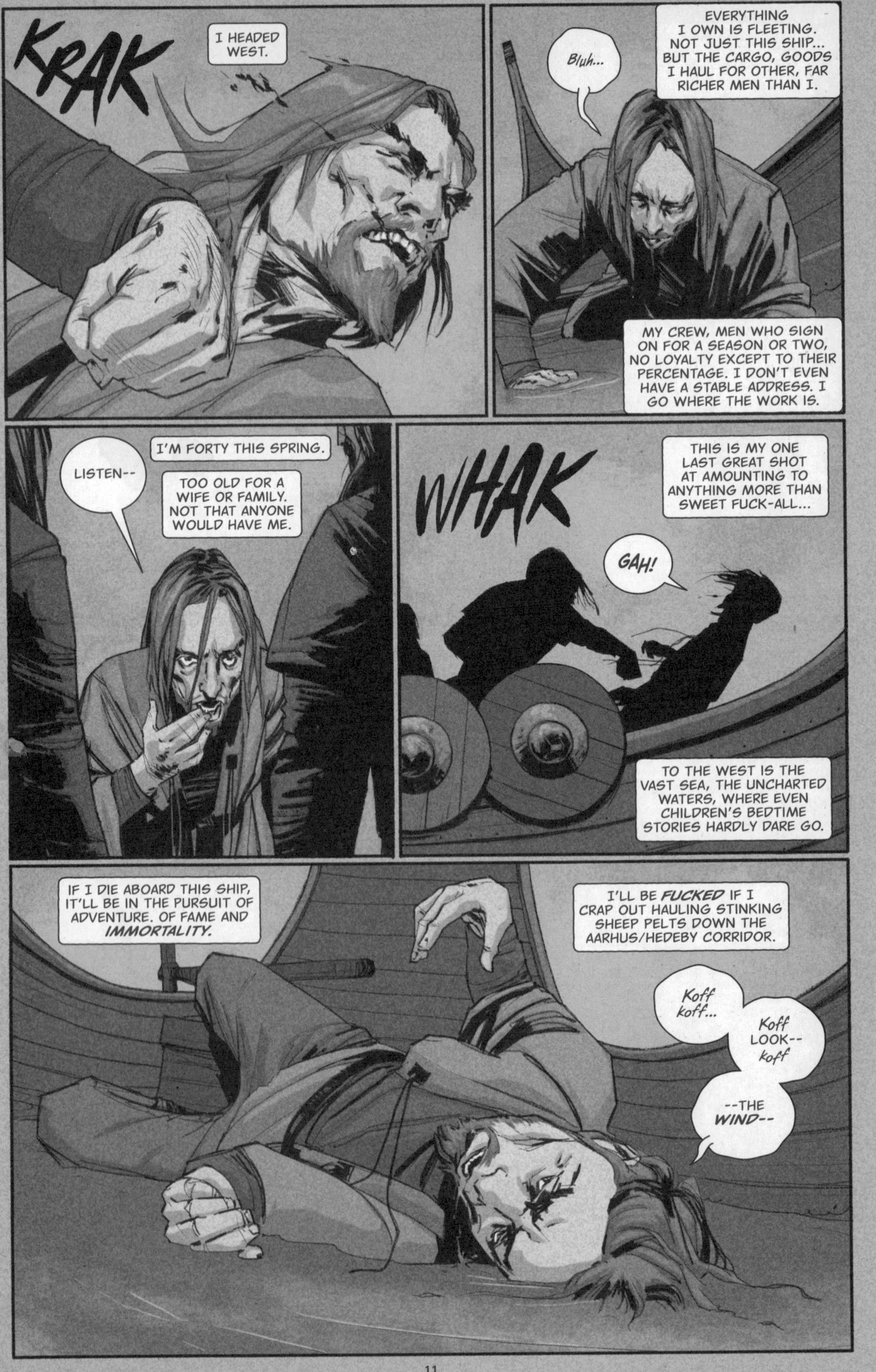
KRAK
I HEADED WEST.
EVERYTHING I OWN IS FLEETING. NOT JUST THIS SHIP... BUT THE CARGO, GOODS I HAUL FOR OTHER, FAR RICHER MEN THAN I.
Bluh...
MY CREW, MEN WHO SIGN ON FOR A SEASON OR TWO, NO LOYALTY EXCEPT TO THEIR PERCENTAGE. I DON'T EVEN HAVE A STABLE ADDRESS. I GO WHERE THE WORK IS.
I'M FORTY THIS SPRING.
LISTEN--
TOO OLD FOR A WIFE OR FAMILY. NOT THAT ANYONE WOULD HAVE ME.
WHAK
THIS IS MY ONE LAST GREAT SHOT AT AMOUNTING TO ANYTHING MORE THAN SWEET FUCK-ALL...
GAH!
TO THE WEST IS THE VAST SEA, THE UNCHARTED WATERS, WHERE EVEN CHILDREN'S BEDTIME STORIES HARDLY DARE GO.
IF I DIE ABOARD THIS SHIP, IT'LL BE IN THE PURSUIT OF ADVENTURE. OF FAME AND ***IMMORTALITY.***
I'LL BE ***FUCKED*** IF I CRAP OUT HAULING STINKING SHEEP PELTS DOWN THE AARHUS/HEDEBY CORRIDOR.
Koff koff...
Koff LOOK-- koff
--THE ***WIND--***

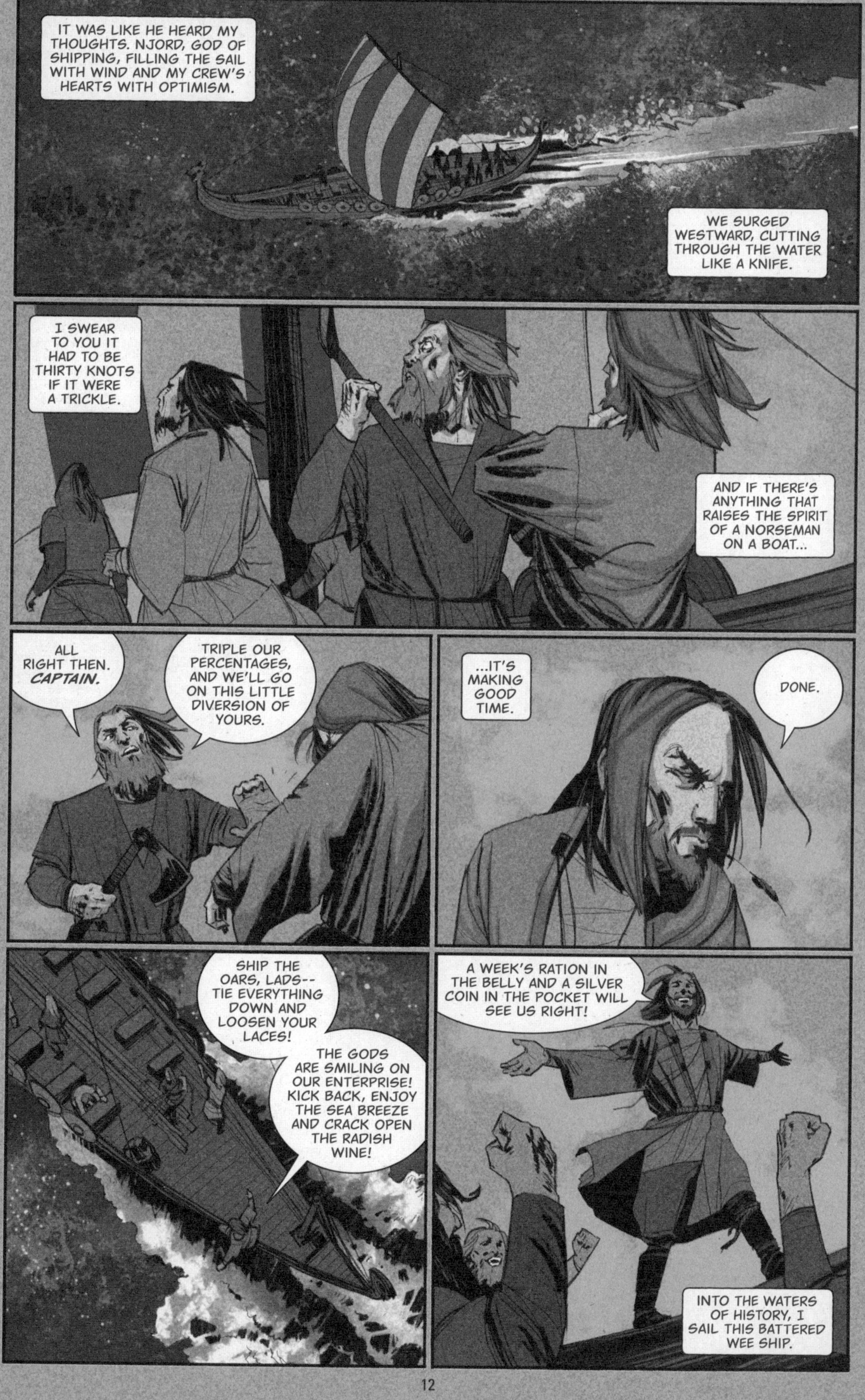
IT WAS LIKE HE HEARD MY THOUGHTS. NJORD, GOD OF SHIPPING, FILLING THE SAIL WITH WIND AND MY CREW'S HEARTS WITH OPTIMISM.
WE SURGED WESTWARD, CUTTING THROUGH THE WATER LIKE A KNIFE.
I SWEAR TO YOU IT HAD TO BE THIRTY KNOTS IF IT WERE A TRICKLE.
AND IF THERE'S ANYTHING THAT RAISES THE SPIRIT OF A NORSEMAN ON A BOAT...
ALL RIGHT THEN. *CAPTAIN.*
TRIPLE OUR PERCENTAGES, AND WE'LL GO ON THIS LITTLE DIVERSION OF YOURS.
...IT'S MAKING GOOD TIME.
DONE.
SHIP THE OARS, LADS-- TIE EVERYTHING DOWN AND LOOSEN YOUR LACES!
THE GODS ARE SMILING ON OUR ENTERPRISE! KICK BACK, ENJOY THE SEA BREEZE AND CRACK OPEN THE RADISH WINE!
A WEEK'S RATION IN THE BELLY AND A SILVER COIN IN THE POCKET WILL SEE US RIGHT!
INTO THE WATERS OF HISTORY, I SAIL THIS BATTERED WEE SHIP.

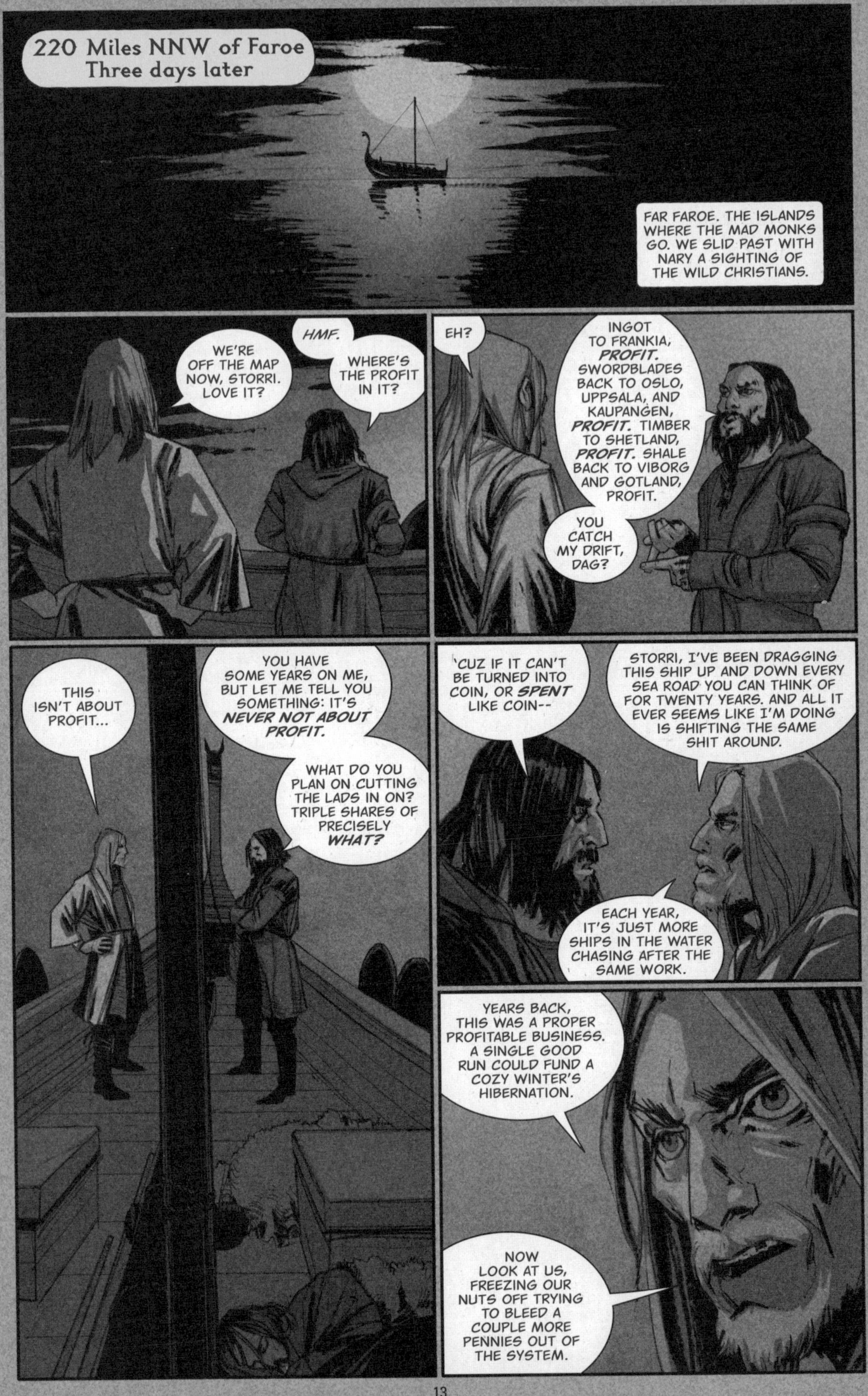
220 Miles NNW of Faroe
Three days later
FAR FAROE. THE ISLANDS WHERE THE MAD MONKS GO. WE SLID PAST WITH NARY A SIGHTING OF THE WILD CHRISTIANS.
WE'RE OFF THE MAP NOW, STORRI. LOVE IT?
HMF.
WHERE'S THE PROFIT IN IT?
EH?
INGOT TO FRANKIA, PROFIT. SWORDBLADES BACK TO OSLO, UPPSALA, AND KAUPANGEN, PROFIT. TIMBER TO SHETLAND, PROFIT. SHALE BACK TO VIBORG AND GOTLAND, PROFIT.
YOU CATCH MY DRIFT, DAG?
THIS ISN'T ABOUT PROFIT...
YOU HAVE SOME YEARS ON ME, BUT LET ME TELL YOU SOMETHING: IT'S NEVER NOT ABOUT PROFIT.
WHAT DO YOU PLAN ON CUTTING THE LADS IN ON? TRIPLE SHARES OF PRECISELY WHAT?
'CUZ IF IT CAN'T BE TURNED INTO COIN, OR SPENT LIKE COIN--
STORRI, I'VE BEEN DRAGGING THIS SHIP UP AND DOWN EVERY SEA ROAD YOU CAN THINK OF FOR TWENTY YEARS. AND ALL IT EVER SEEMS LIKE I'M DOING IS SHIFTING THE SAME SHIT AROUND.
EACH YEAR, IT'S JUST MORE SHIPS IN THE WATER CHASING AFTER THE SAME WORK.
YEARS BACK, THIS WAS A PROPER PROFITABLE BUSINESS. A SINGLE GOOD RUN COULD FUND A COZY WINTER'S HIBERNATION.
NOW LOOK AT US, FREEZING OUR NUTS OFF TRYING TO BLEED A COUPLE MORE PENNIES OUT OF THE SYSTEM.

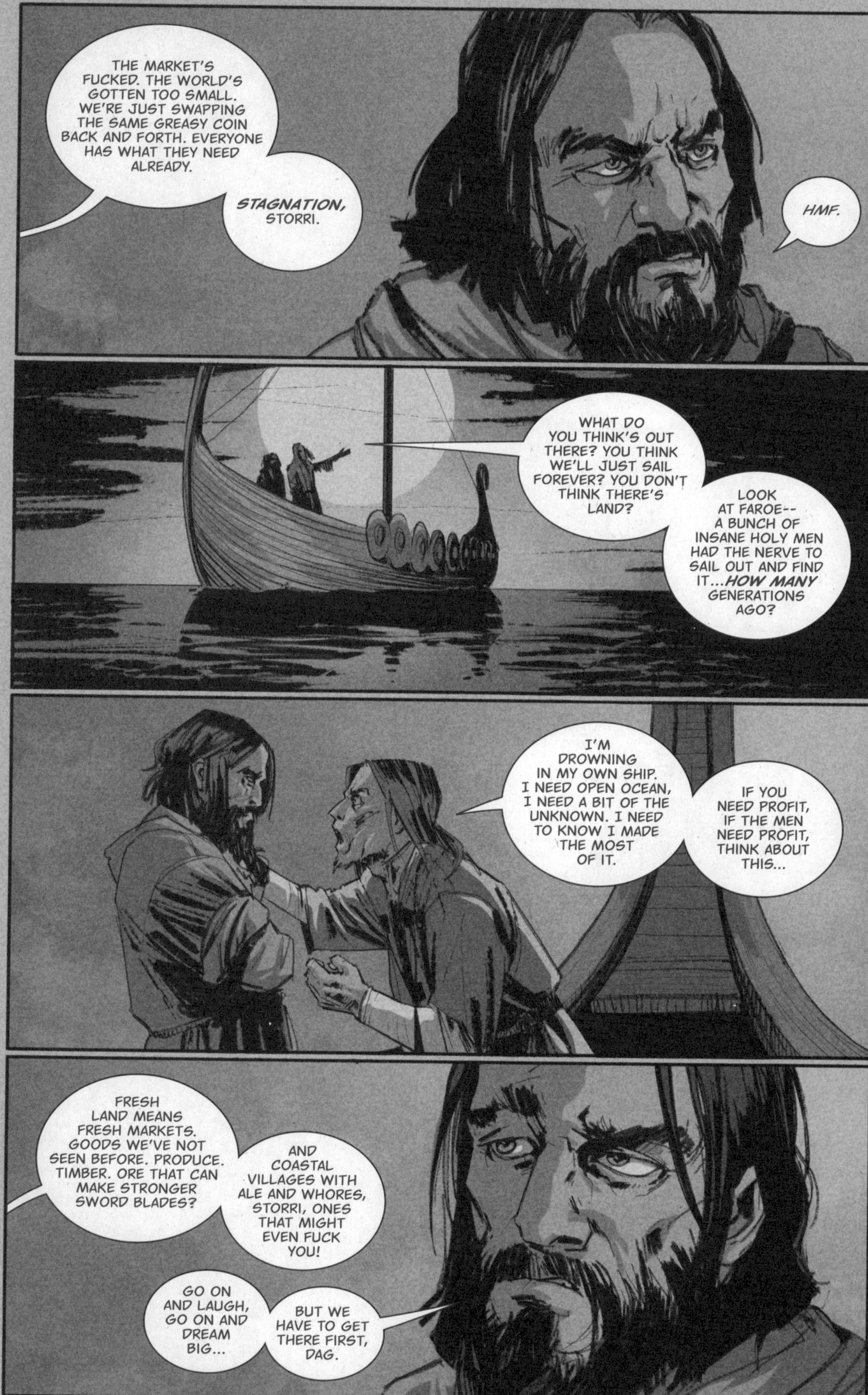
THE MARKET'S FUCKED. THE WORLD'S GOTTEN TOO SMALL. WE'RE JUST SWAPPING THE SAME GREASY COIN BACK AND FORTH. EVERYONE HAS WHAT THEY NEED ALREADY.
STAGNATION, STORRI.
HMF.
WHAT DO YOU THINK'S OUT THERE? YOU THINK WE'LL JUST SAIL FOREVER? YOU DON'T THINK THERE'S LAND?
LOOK AT FAROE-- A BUNCH OF INSANE HOLY MEN HAD THE NERVE TO SAIL OUT AND FIND IT...HOW MANY GENERATIONS AGO?
I'M DROWNING IN MY OWN SHIP. I NEED OPEN OCEAN, I NEED A BIT OF THE UNKNOWN. I NEED TO KNOW I MADE THE MOST OF IT.
IF YOU NEED PROFIT, IF THE MEN NEED PROFIT, THINK ABOUT THIS...
FRESH LAND MEANS FRESH MARKETS. GOODS WE'VE NOT SEEN BEFORE. PRODUCE. TIMBER. ORE THAT CAN MAKE STRONGER SWORD BLADES?
AND COASTAL VILLAGES WITH ALE AND WHORES, STORRI, ONES THAT MIGHT EVEN FUCK YOU!
GO ON AND LAUGH, GO ON AND DREAM BIG...
BUT WE HAVE TO GET THERE FIRST, DAG.

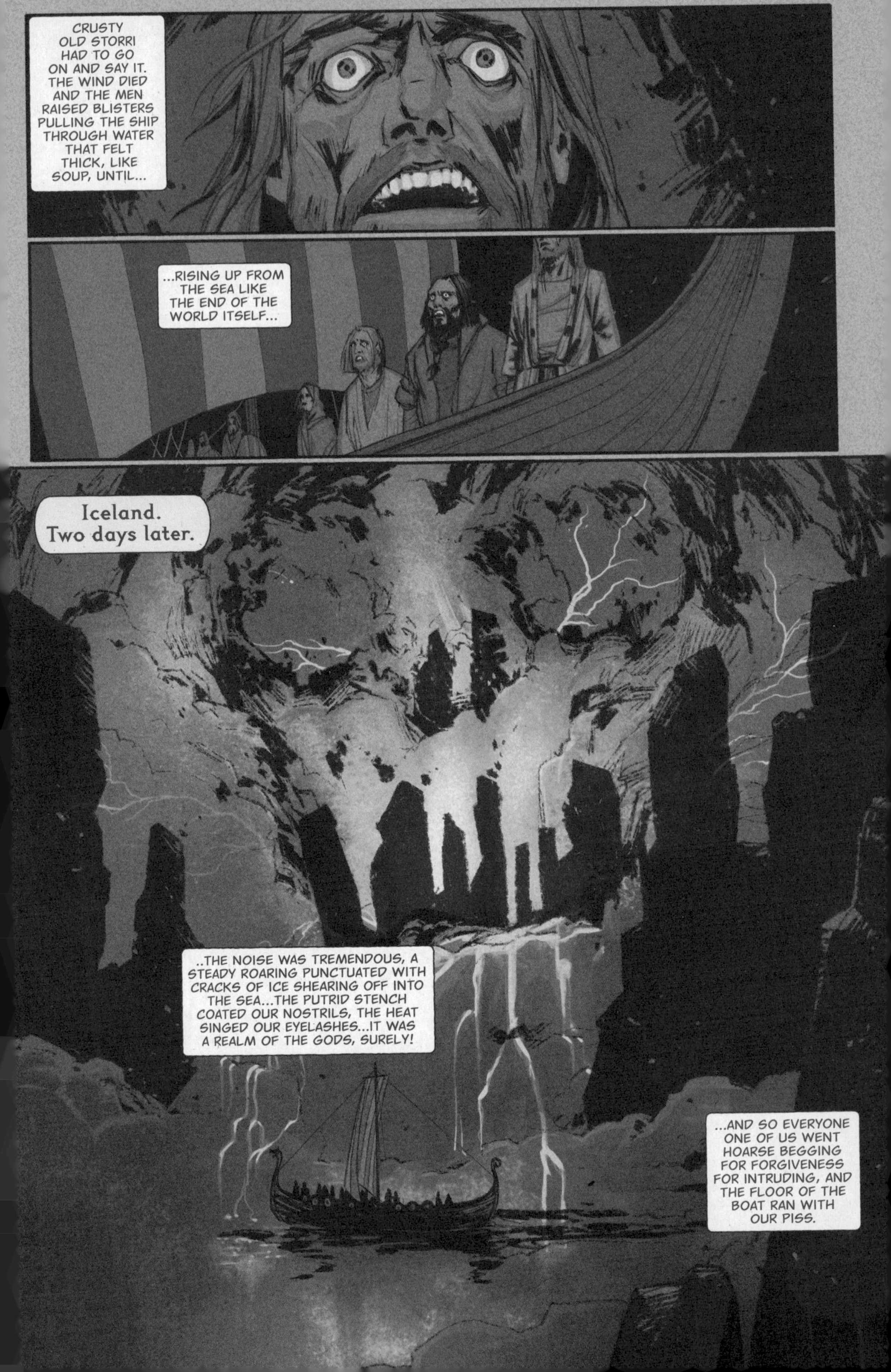
CRUSTY OLD STORRI HAD TO GO ON AND SAY IT. THE WIND DIED AND THE MEN RAISED BLISTERS PULLING THE SHIP THROUGH WATER THAT FELT THICK, LIKE SOUP, UNTIL...
...RISING UP FROM THE SEA LIKE THE END OF THE WORLD ITSELF...
Iceland. Two days later.
..THE NOISE WAS TREMENDOUS, A STEADY ROARING PUNCTUATED WITH CRACKS OF ICE SHEARING OFF INTO THE SEA...THE PUTRID STENCH COATED OUR NOSTRILS, THE HEAT SINGED OUR EYELASHES...IT WAS A REALM OF THE GODS, SURELY!
...AND SO EVERYONE ONE OF US WENT HOARSE BEGGING FOR FORGIVENESS FOR INTRUDING, AND THE FLOOR OF THE BOAT RAN WITH OUR PISS.

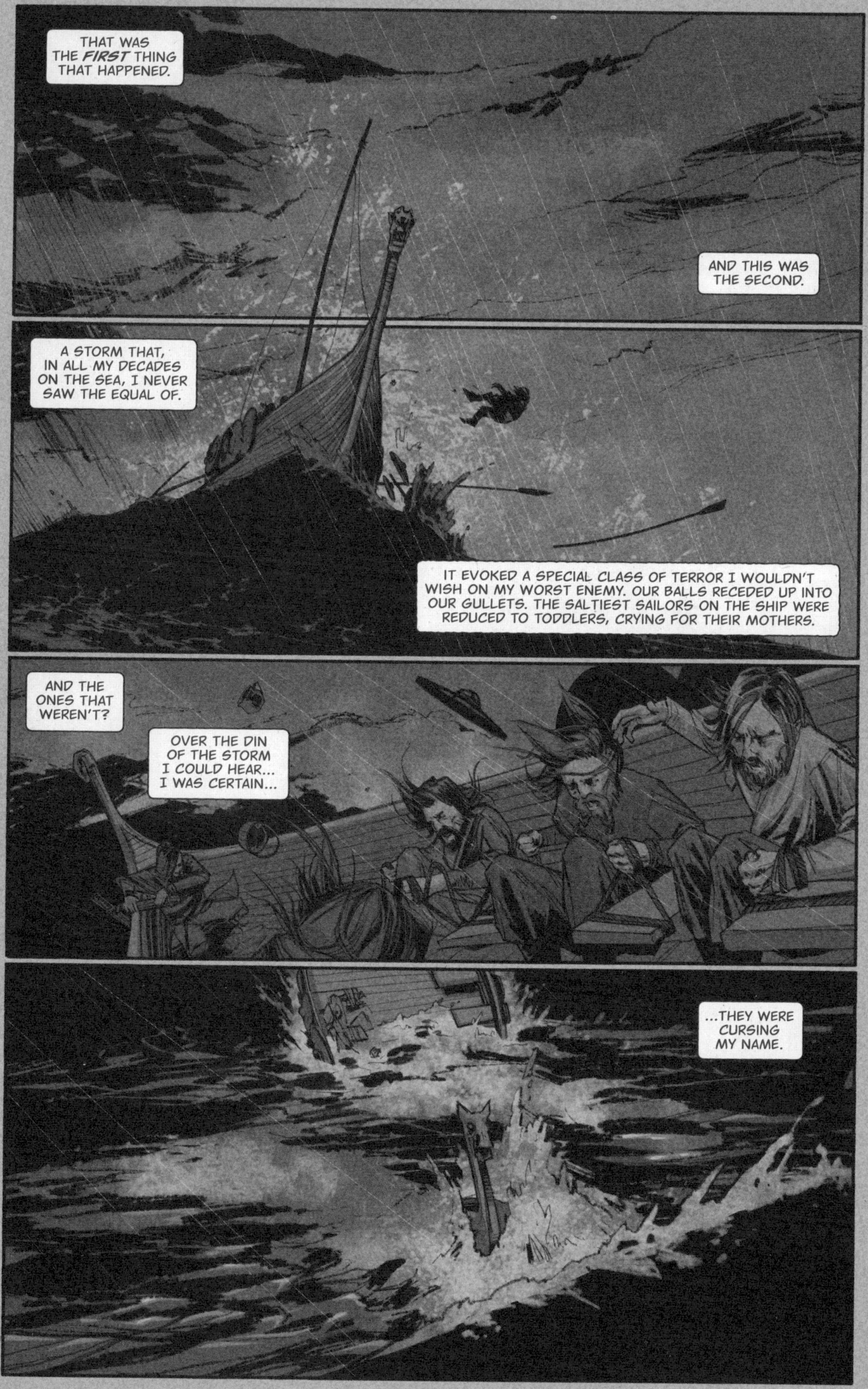
THAT WAS THE FIRST THING THAT HAPPENED.
AND THIS WAS THE SECOND.
A STORM THAT, IN ALL MY DECADES ON THE SEA, I NEVER SAW THE EQUAL OF.
IT EVOKED A SPECIAL CLASS OF TERROR I WOULDN'T WISH ON MY WORST ENEMY. OUR BALLS RECEDED UP INTO OUR GULLETS. THE SALTIEST SAILORS ON THE SHIP WERE REDUCED TO TODDLERS, CRYING FOR THEIR MOTHERS.
AND THE ONES THAT WEREN'T?
OVER THE DIN OF THE STORM I COULD HEAR... I WAS CERTAIN...
...THEY WERE CURSING MY NAME.

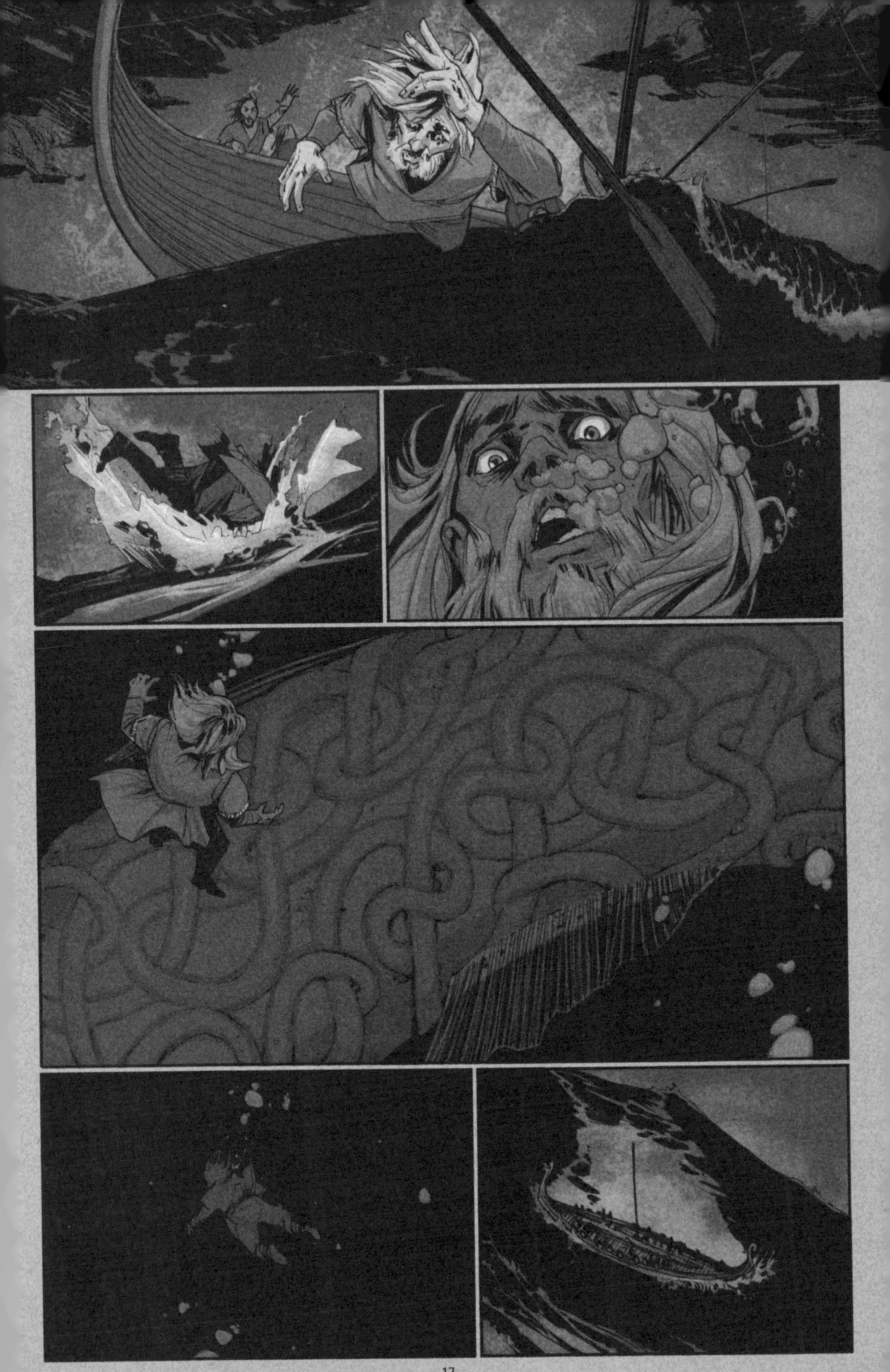

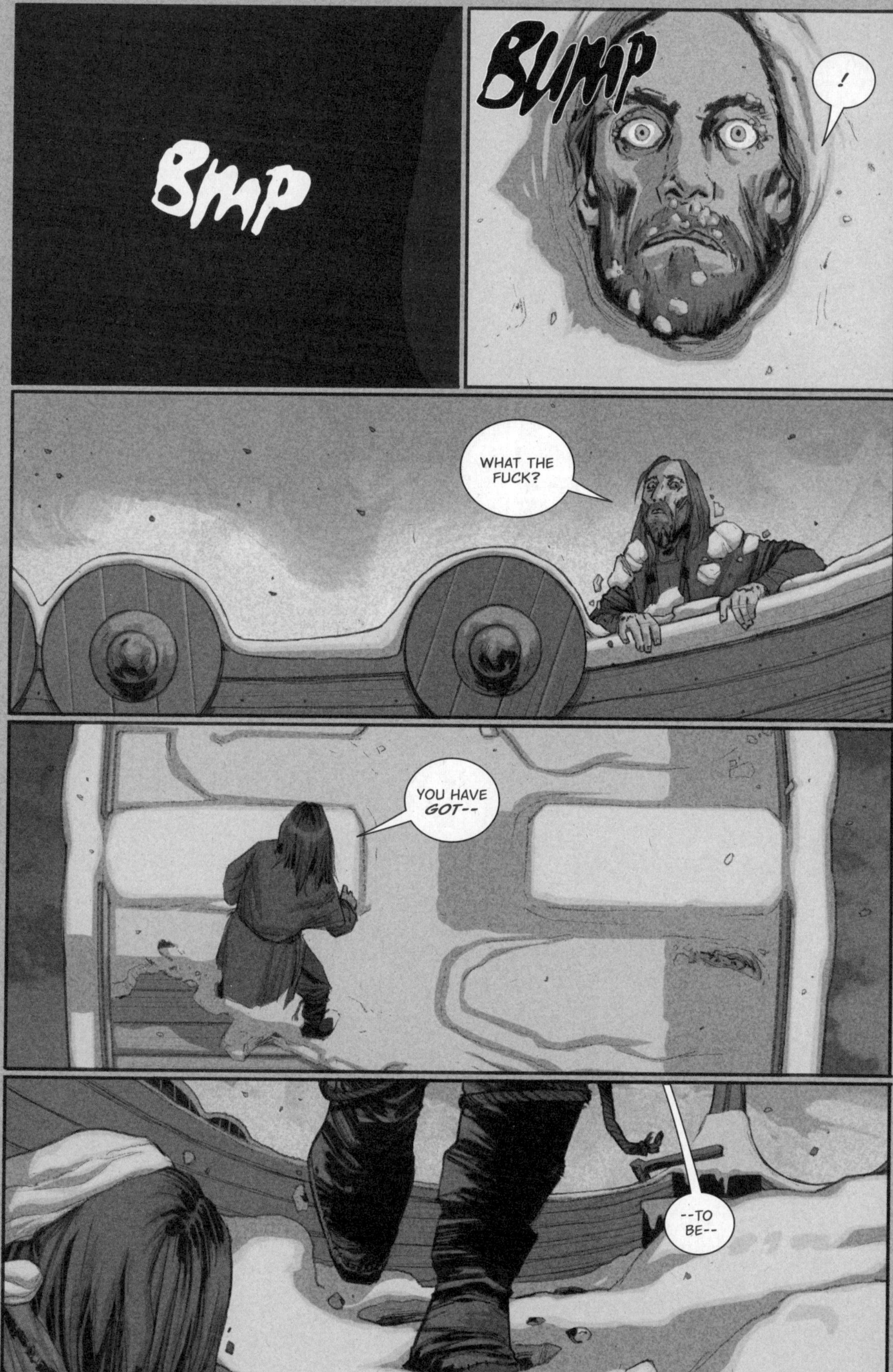
BMP
BUMP
!
WHAT THE FUCK?
YOU HAVE *GOT*--
--TO BE--

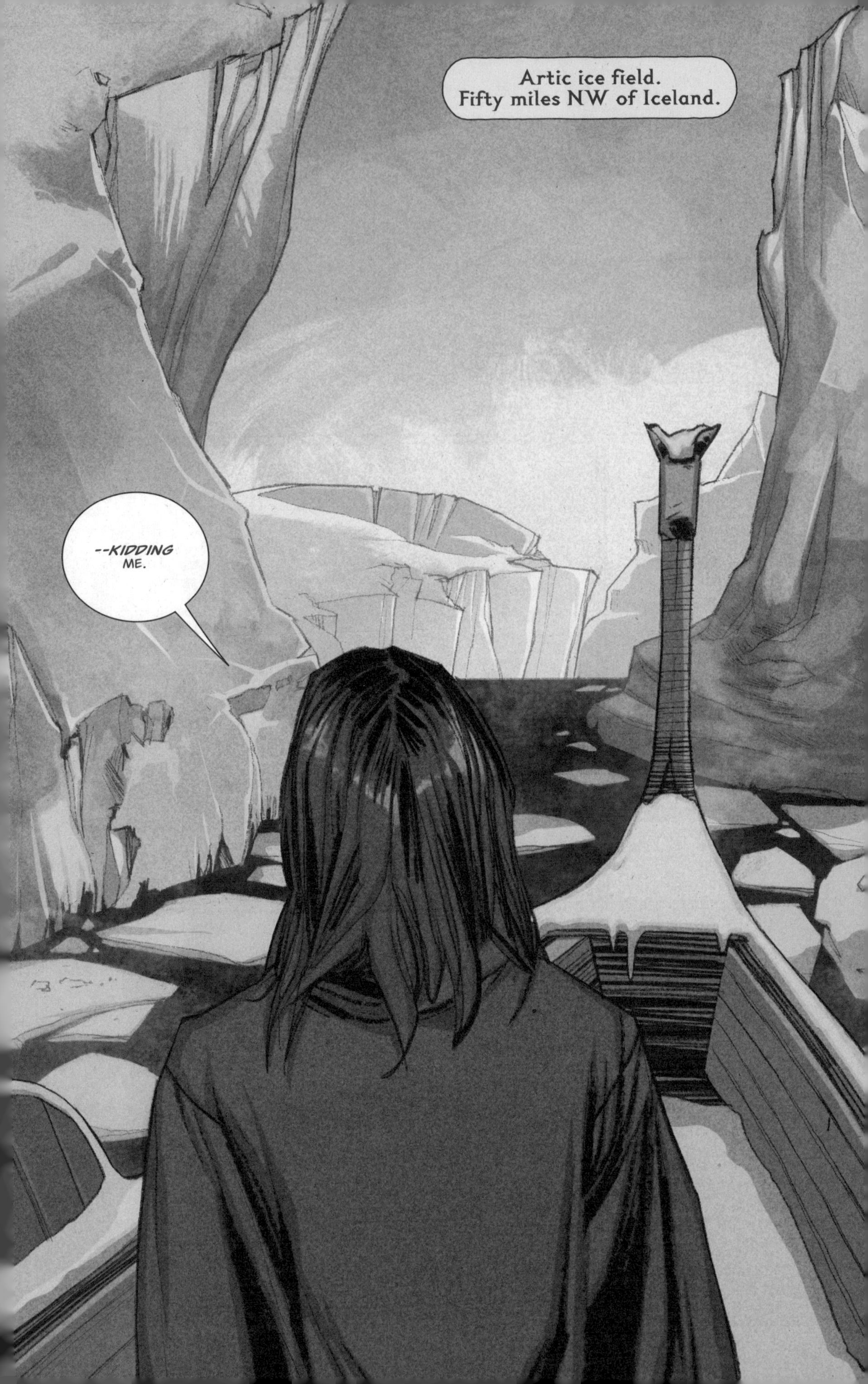
Artic ice field.
Fifty miles NW of Iceland.
--KIDDING ME.

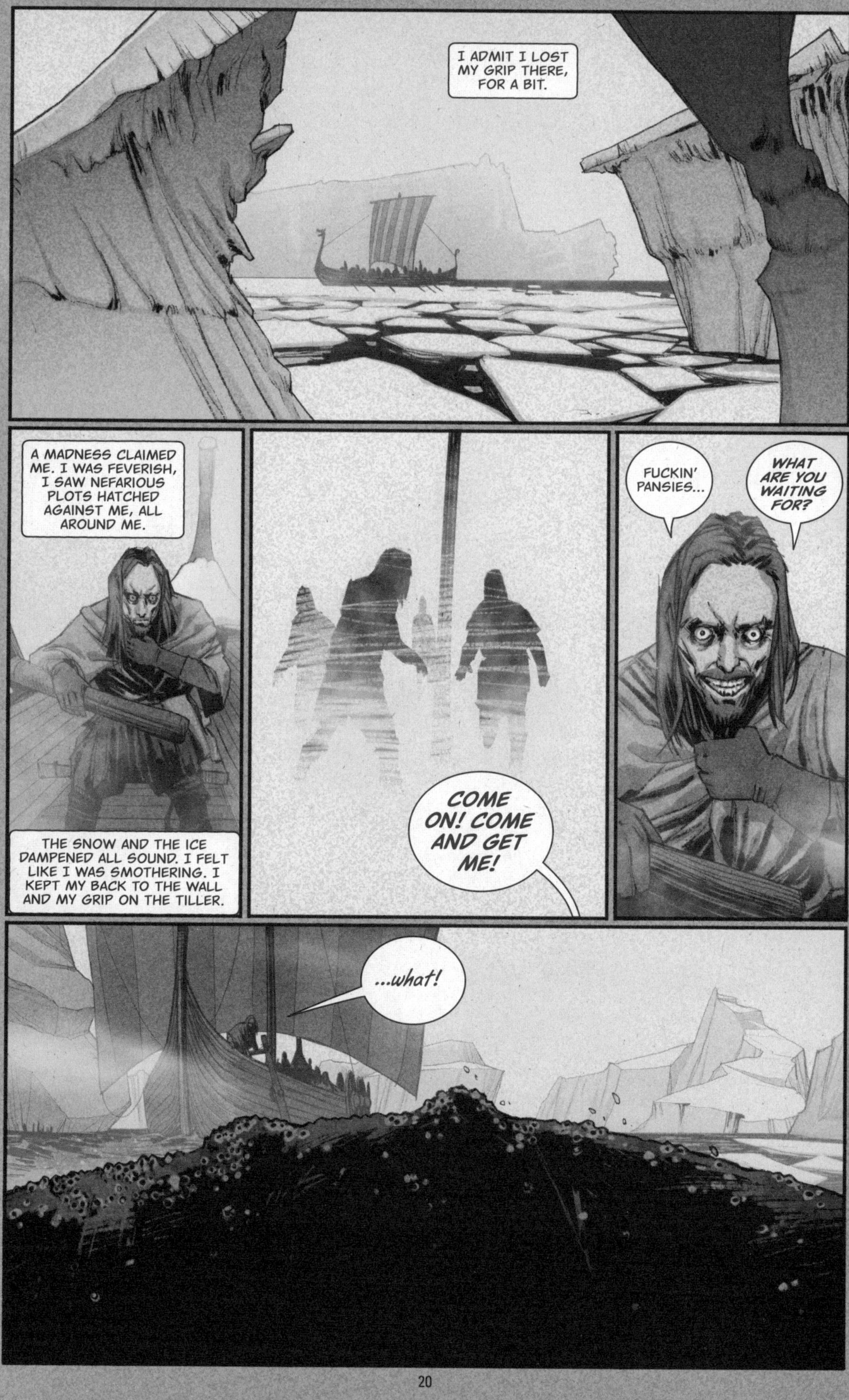
I ADMIT I LOST MY GRIP THERE, FOR A BIT.
A MADNESS CLAIMED ME. I WAS FEVERISH, I SAW NEFARIOUS PLOTS HATCHED AGAINST ME, ALL AROUND ME.
THE SNOW AND THE ICE DAMPENED ALL SOUND. I FELT LIKE I WAS SMOTHERING. I KEPT MY BACK TO THE WALL AND MY GRIP ON THE TILLER.
COME ON! COME AND GET ME!
FUCKIN' PANSIES...
WHAT ARE YOU WAITING FOR?
...what!

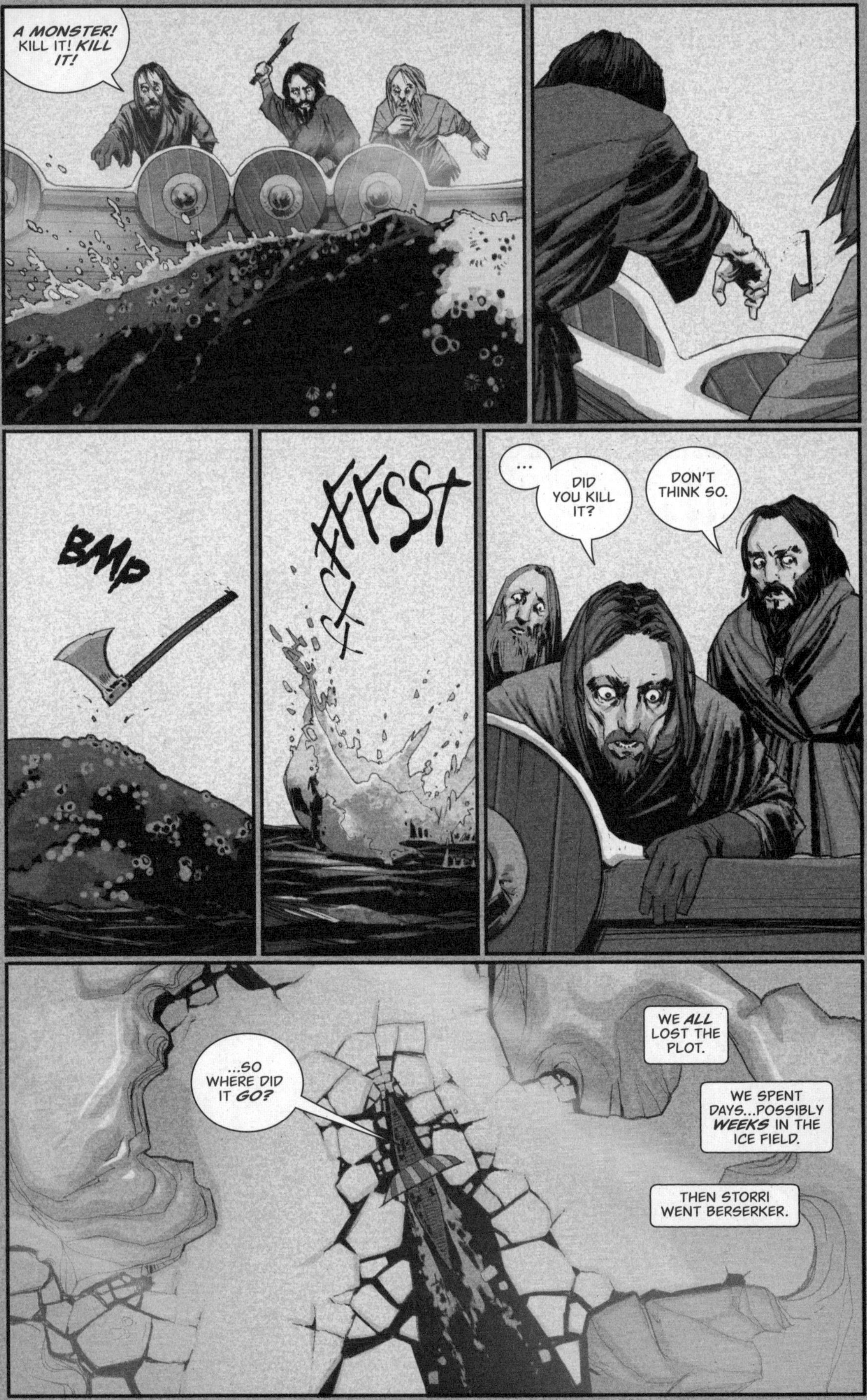
A MONSTER! KILL IT! KILL IT!
BMP
FFFSST
...
DID YOU KILL IT?
DON'T THINK SO.
WE ALL LOST THE PLOT.
WE SPENT DAYS...POSSIBLY WEEKS IN THE ICE FIELD.
THEN STORRI WENT BERSERKER.
...SO WHERE DID IT GO?

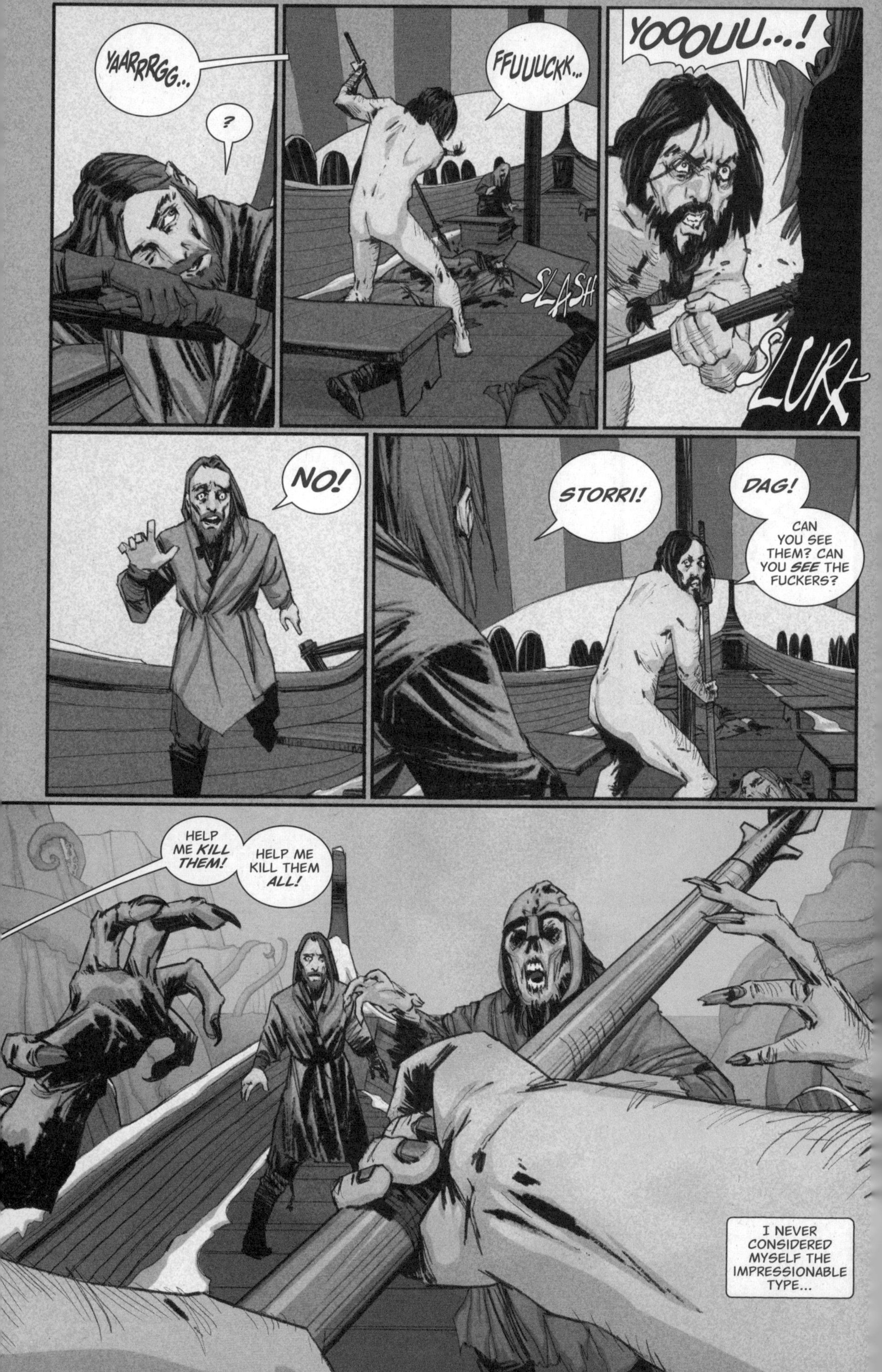
YAARRRGG...
?
FFUUUCKK...
SLASH
YOOOUU...!
SLURK
NO!
STORRI!
DAG!
CAN YOU SEE THEM? CAN YOU SEE THE FUCKERS?
HELP ME KILL THEM!
HELP ME KILL THEM ALL!
I NEVER CONSIDERED MYSELF THE IMPRESSIONABLE TYPE...

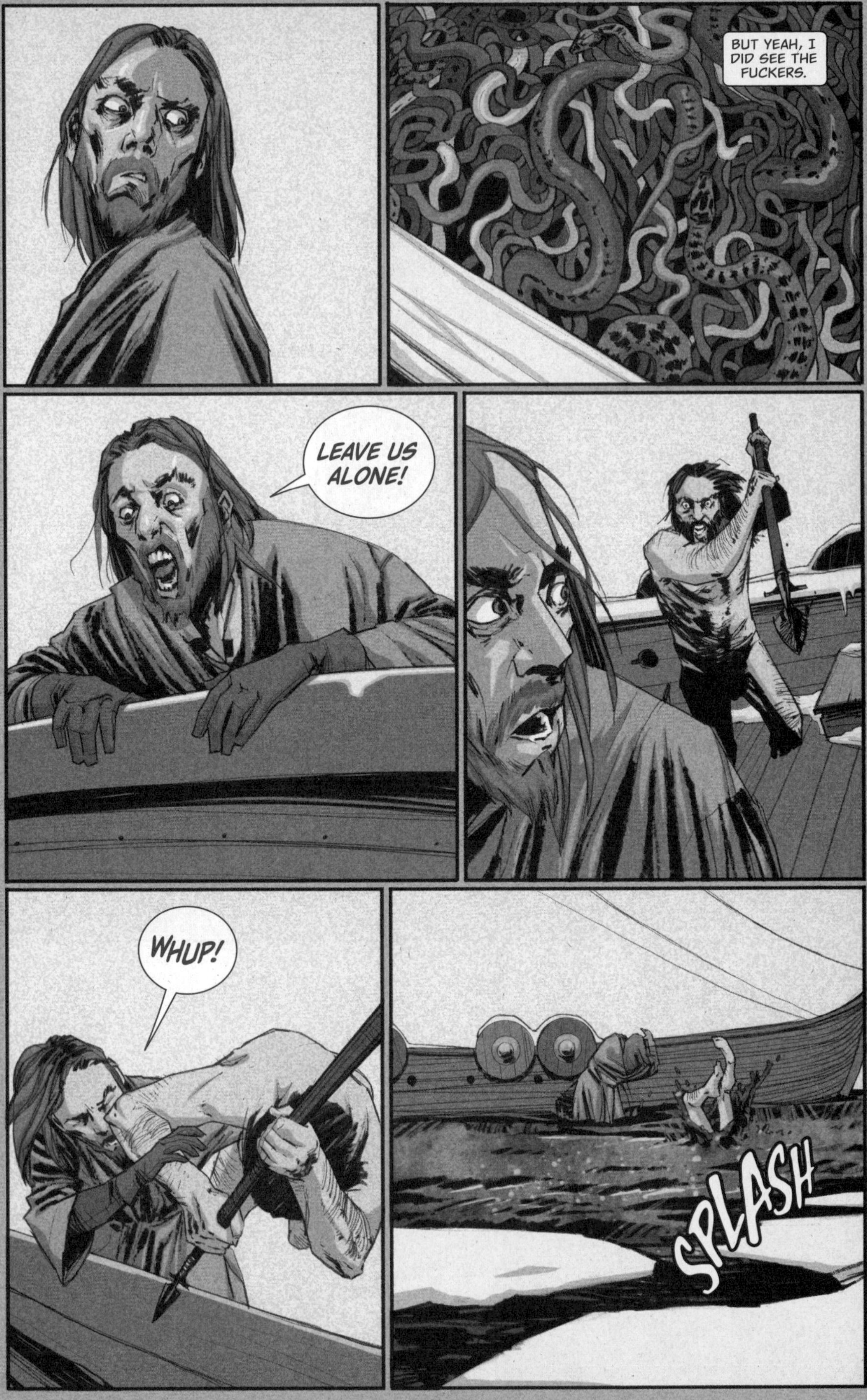
BUT YEAH, I DID SEE THE FUCKERS.
LEAVE US ALONE!
WHUP!
SPLASH

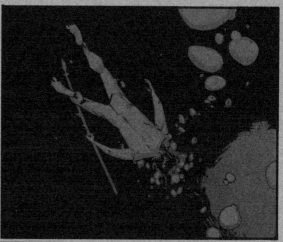

I'D FUCK YOUR MOTHER, YOU UGLY BASTARD FISHIE...

...TO BE BACK ON THE AARHUS/HEDEBY CORRIDOR, HAULING STINKING SHEEP PELTS.

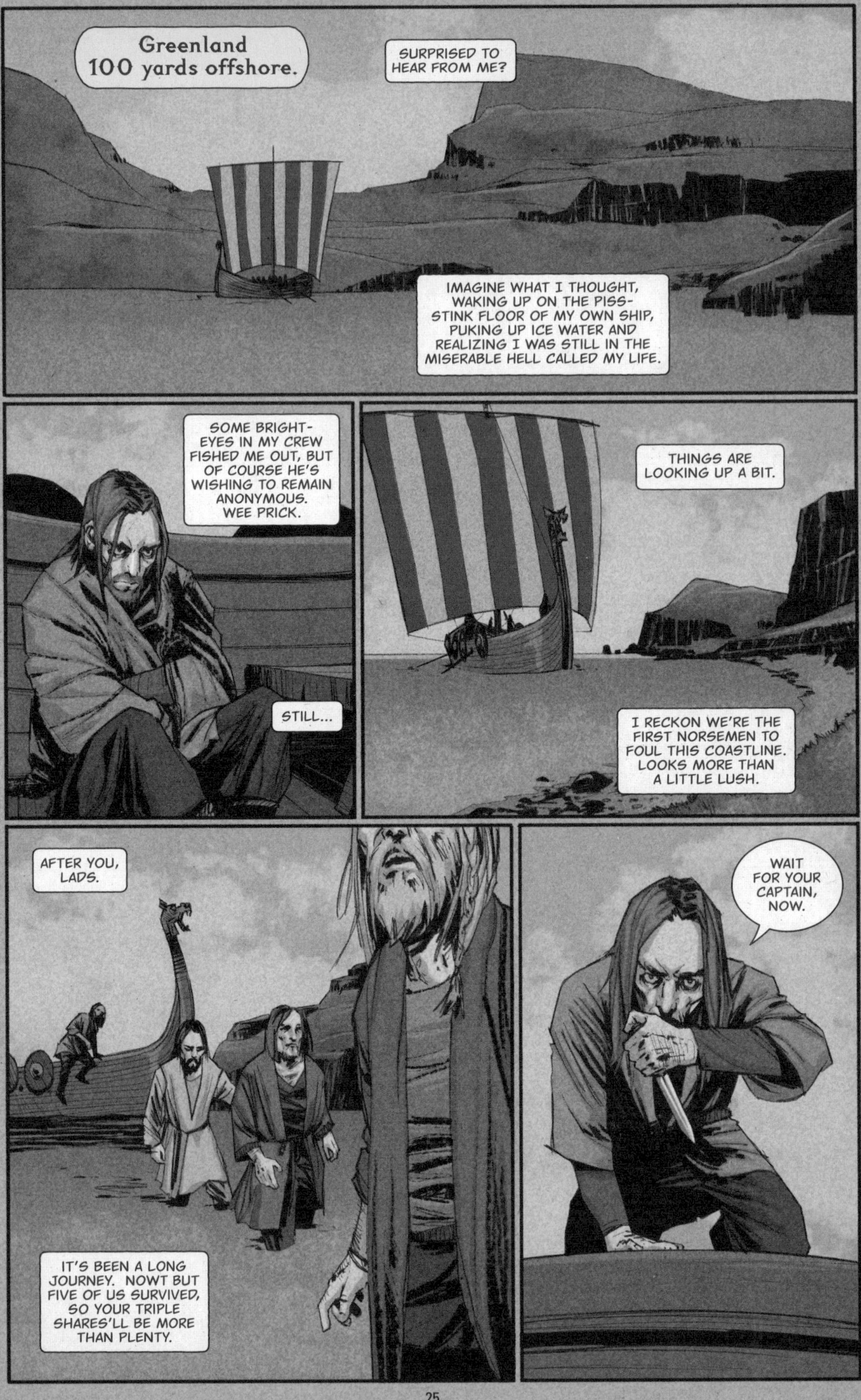
Greenland
100 yards offshore.
SURPRISED TO HEAR FROM ME?
IMAGINE WHAT I THOUGHT, WAKING UP ON THE PISS-STINK FLOOR OF MY OWN SHIP, PUKING UP ICE WATER AND REALIZING I WAS STILL IN THE MISERABLE HELL CALLED MY LIFE.
SOME BRIGHT-EYES IN MY CREW FISHED ME OUT, BUT OF COURSE HE'S WISHING TO REMAIN ANONYMOUS. WEE PRICK.
STILL...
THINGS ARE LOOKING UP A BIT.
I RECKON WE'RE THE FIRST NORSEMEN TO FOUL THIS COASTLINE. LOOKS MORE THAN A LITTLE LUSH.
AFTER YOU, LADS.
IT'S BEEN A LONG JOURNEY. NOWT BUT FIVE OF US SURVIVED, SO YOUR TRIPLE SHARES'LL BE MORE THAN PLENTY.
WAIT FOR YOUR CAPTAIN, NOW.

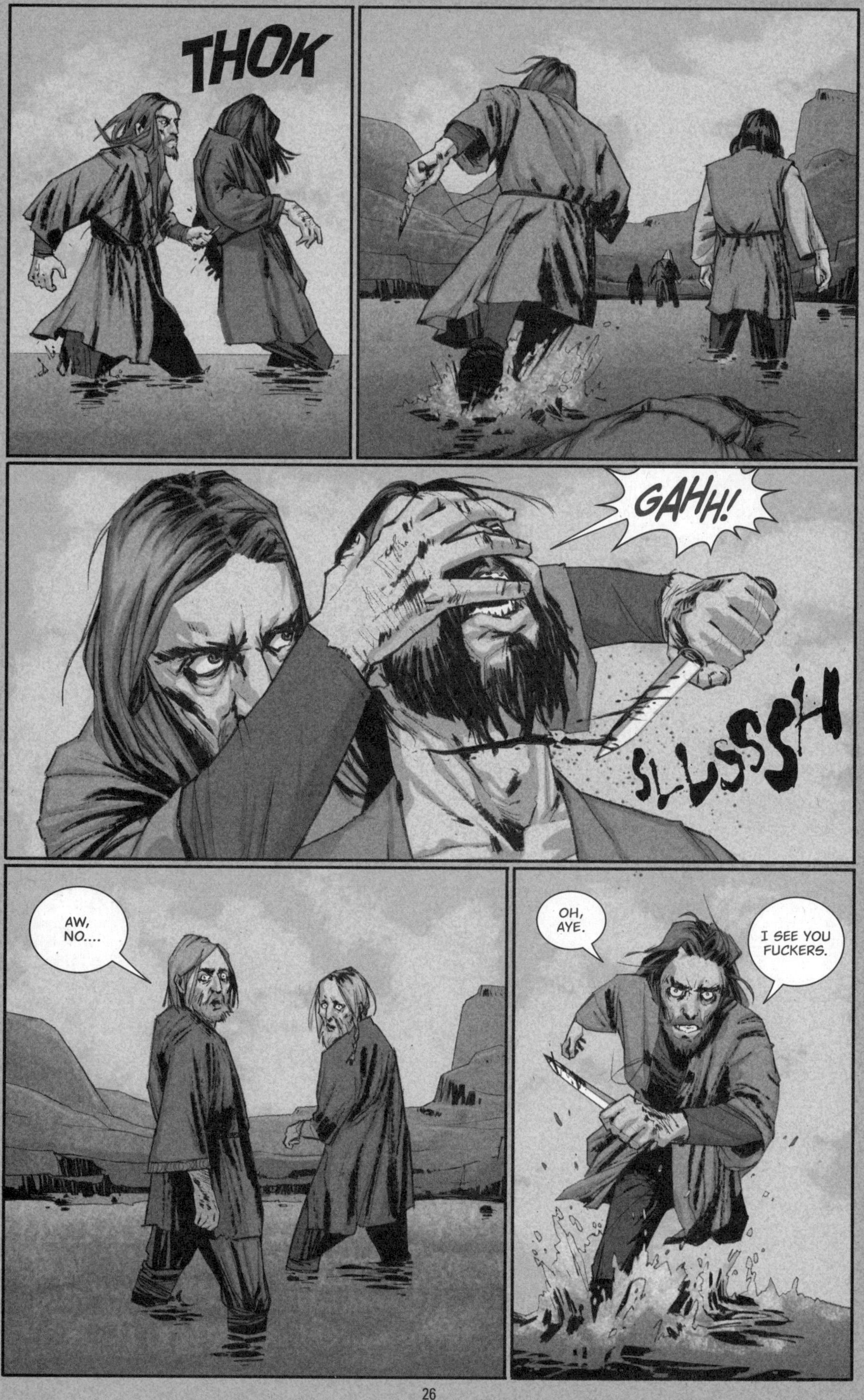
THOK
GAHH!
SLLSSSH
AW, NO....
OH, AYE.
I SEE YOU FUCKERS.

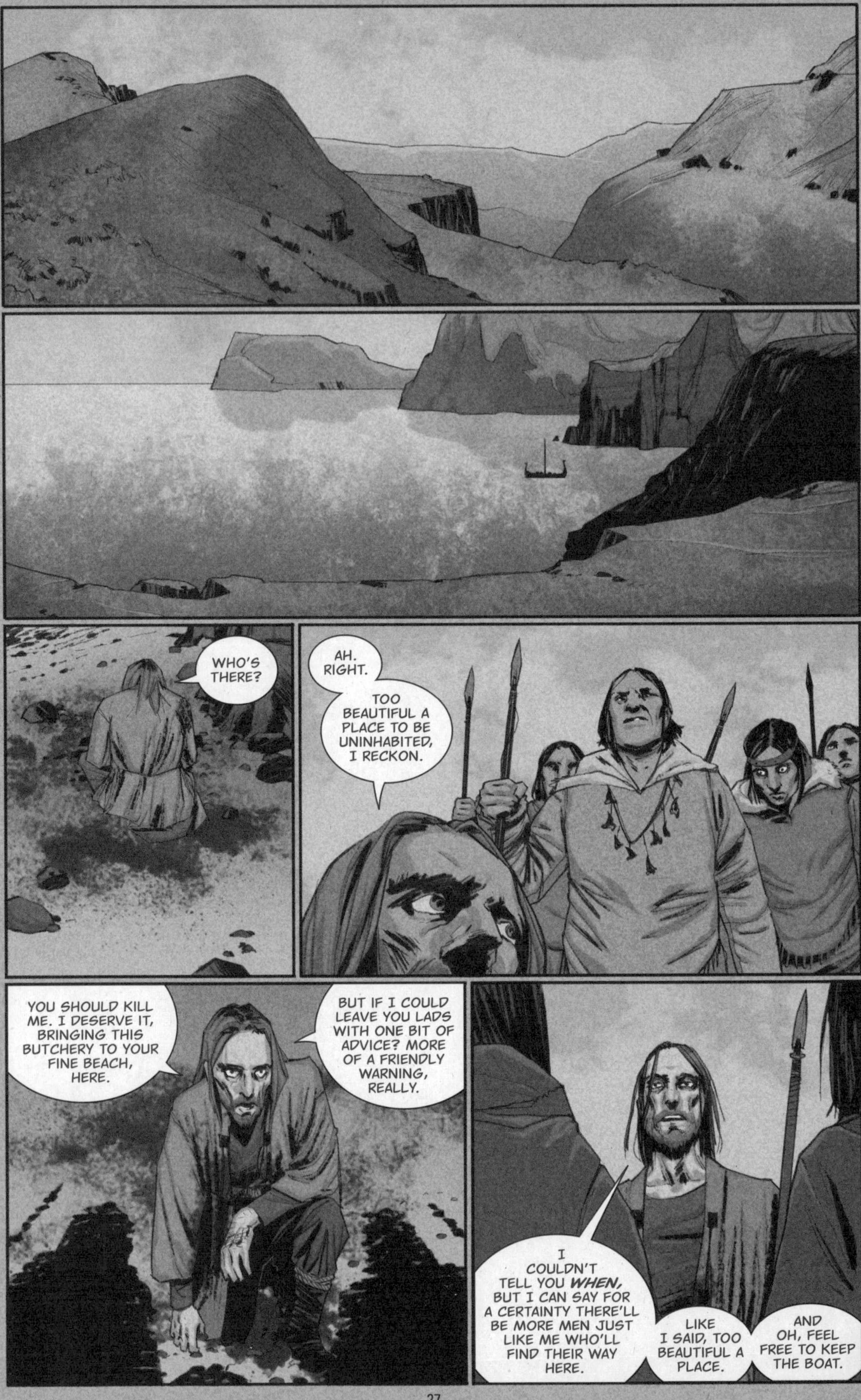
WHO'S THERE?
AH. RIGHT.
TOO BEAUTIFUL A PLACE TO BE UNINHABITED, I RECKON.
YOU SHOULD KILL ME. I DESERVE IT, BRINGING THIS BUTCHERY TO YOUR FINE BEACH, HERE.
BUT IF I COULD LEAVE YOU LADS WITH ONE BIT OF ADVICE? MORE OF A FRIENDLY WARNING, REALLY.
I COULDN'T TELL YOU *WHEN,* BUT I CAN SAY FOR A CERTAINTY THERE'LL BE MORE MEN JUST LIKE ME WHO'LL FIND THEIR WAY HERE.
LIKE I SAID, TOO BEAUTIFUL A PLACE.
AND OH, FEEL FREE TO KEEP THE BOAT.

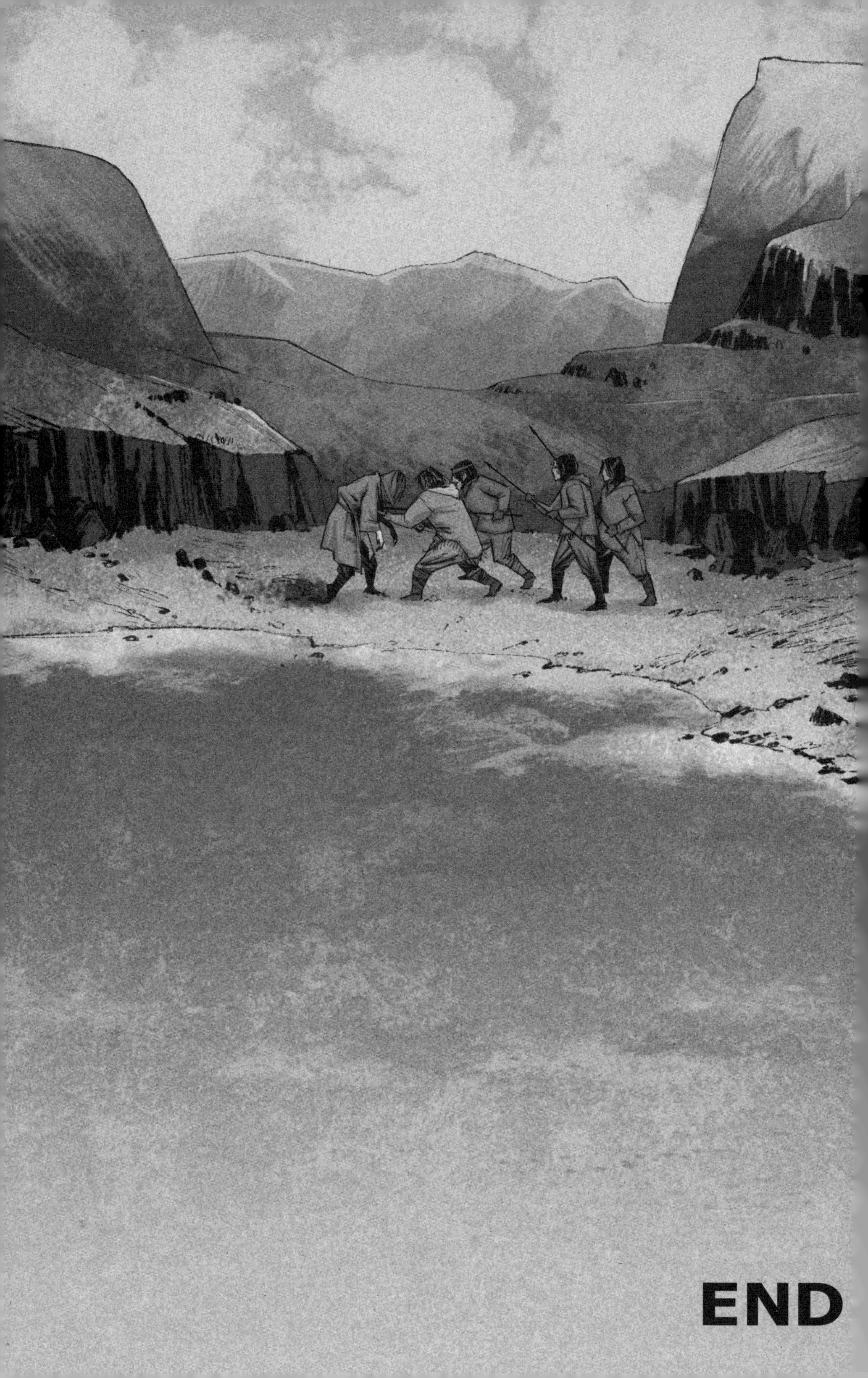
END

Metal Part One: The Old Ways

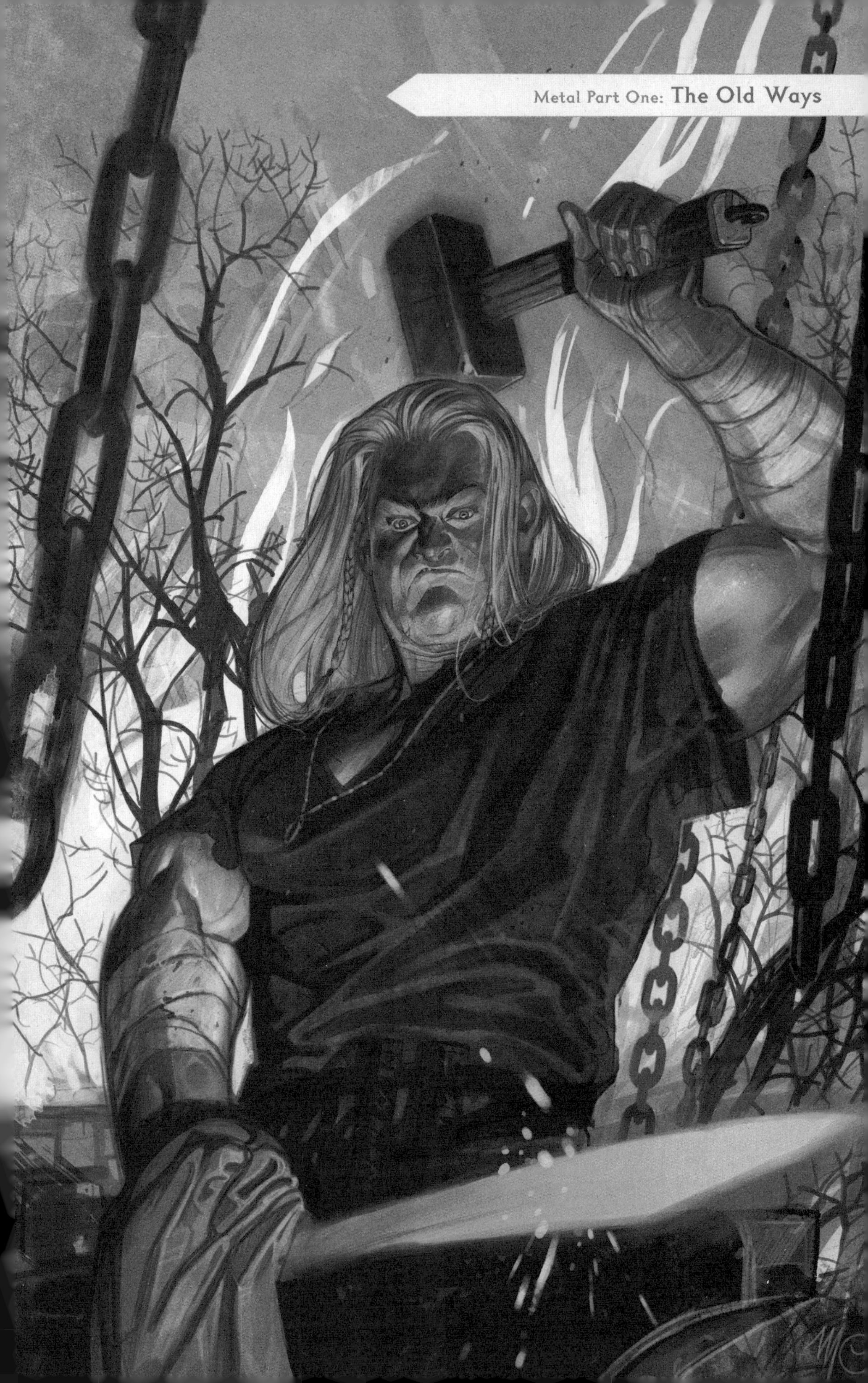

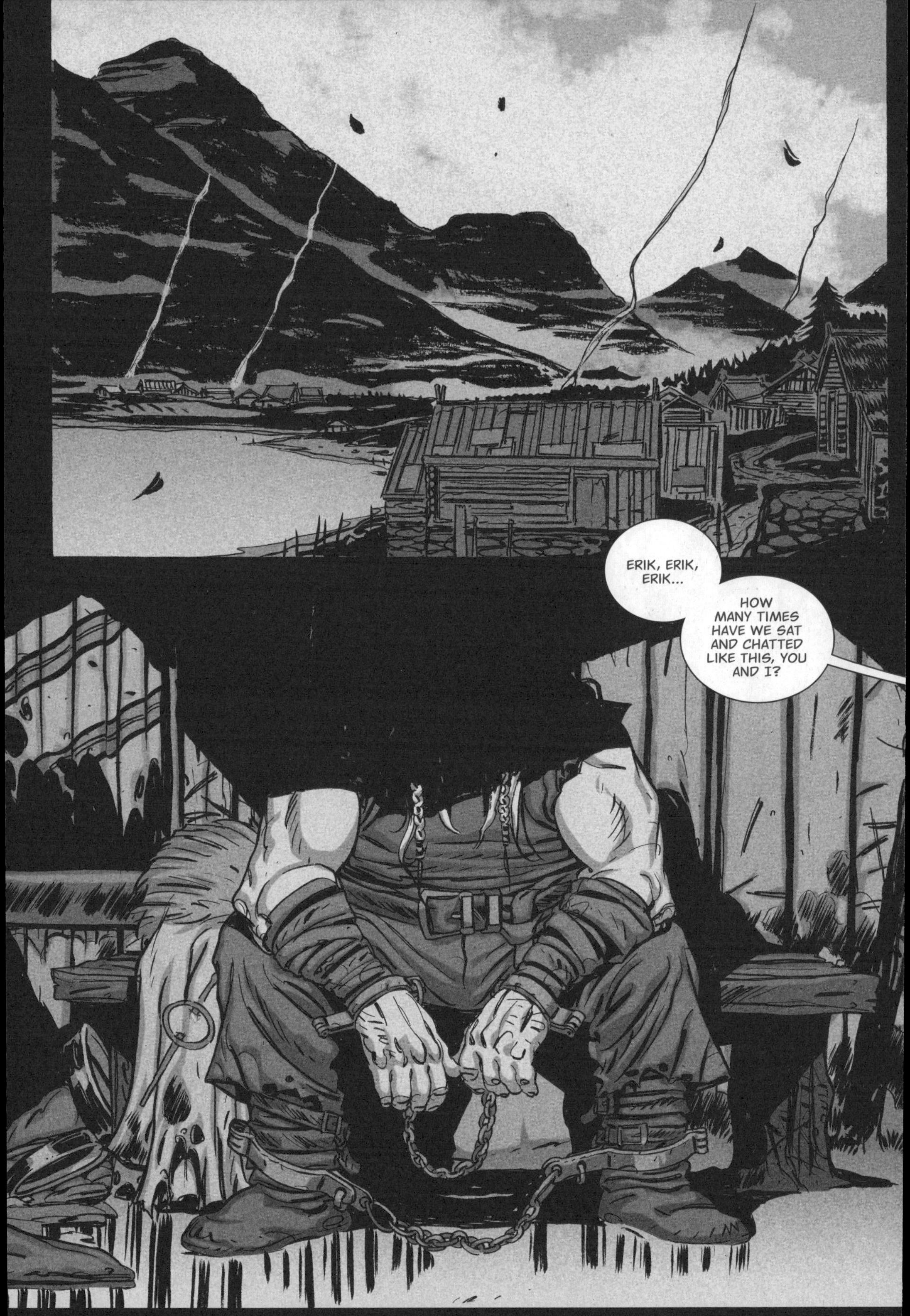
ERIK, ERIK, ERIK...
HOW MANY TIMES HAVE WE SAT AND CHATTED LIKE THIS, YOU AND I?

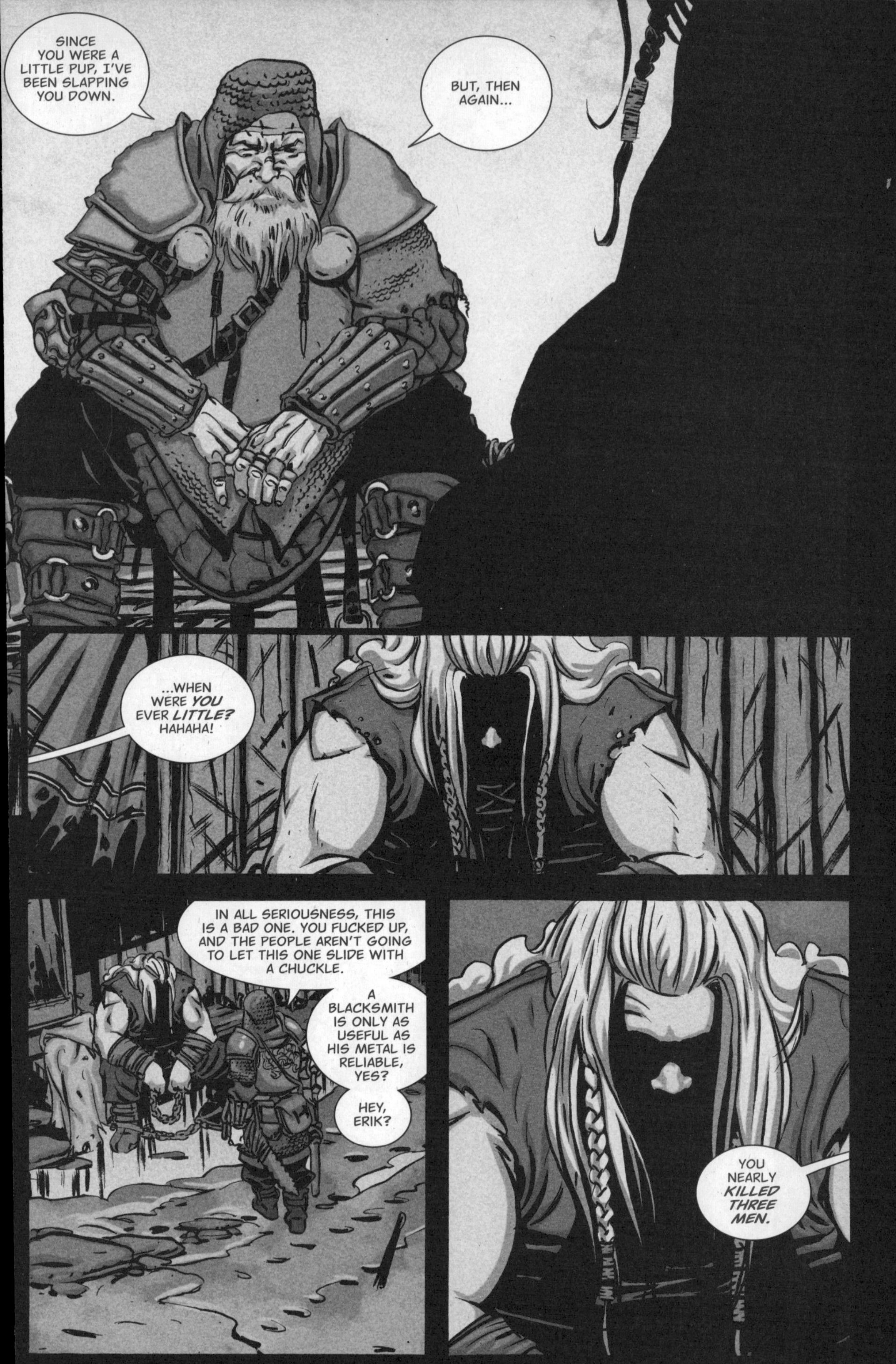
SINCE YOU WERE A LITTLE PUP, I'VE BEEN SLAPPING YOU DOWN.
BUT, THEN AGAIN...
...WHEN WERE *YOU* EVER *LITTLE?* HAHAHA!
IN ALL SERIOUSNESS, THIS IS A BAD ONE. YOU FUCKED UP, AND THE PEOPLE AREN'T GOING TO LET THIS ONE SLIDE WITH A CHUCKLE.
A BLACKSMITH IS ONLY AS USEFUL AS HIS METAL IS RELIABLE, YES?
HEY, ERIK?
YOU NEARLY *KILLED THREE MEN.*

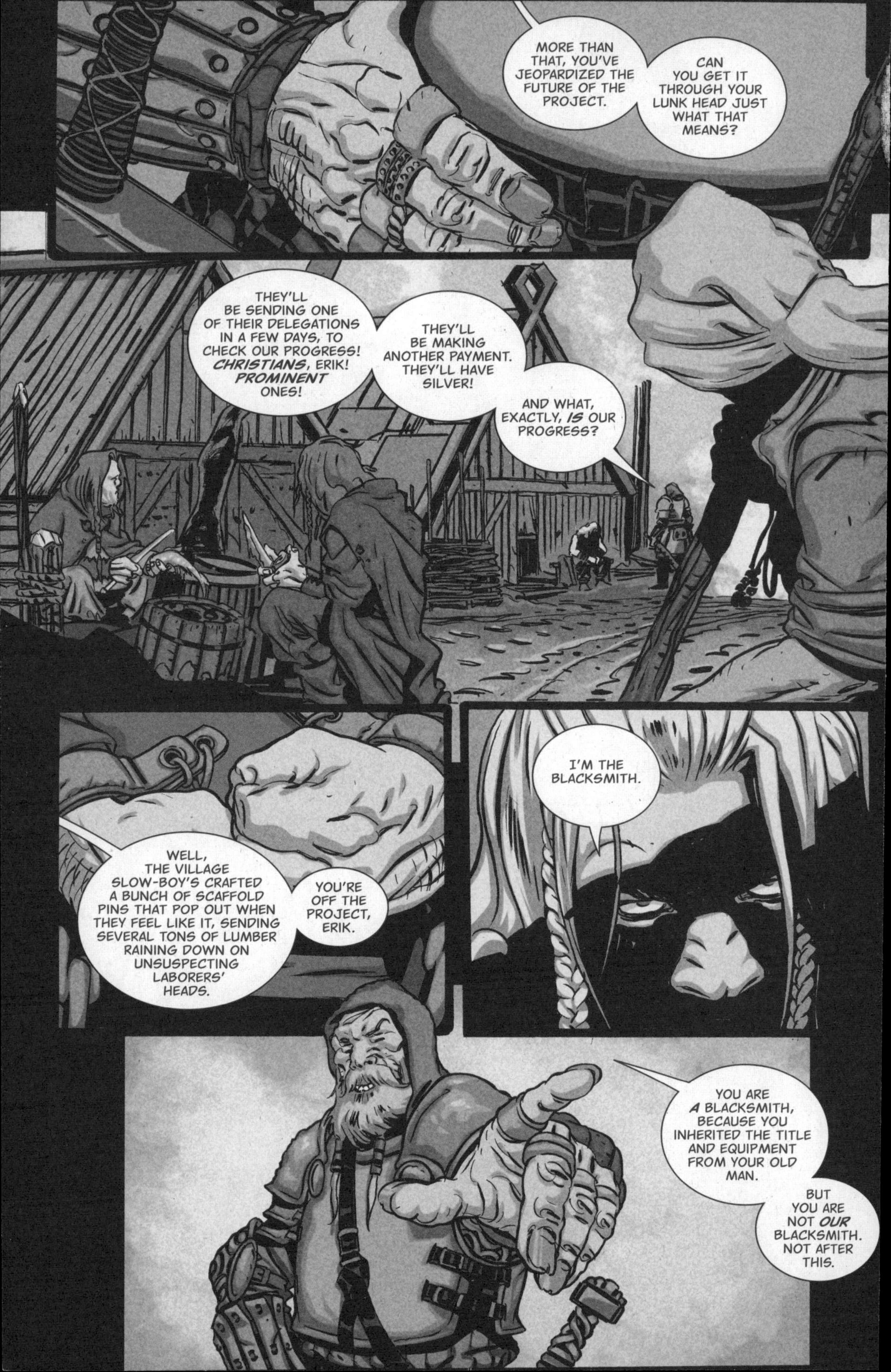
MORE THAN THAT, YOU'VE JEOPARDIZED THE FUTURE OF THE PROJECT.
CAN YOU GET IT THROUGH YOUR LUNK HEAD JUST WHAT THAT MEANS?
THEY'LL BE SENDING ONE OF THEIR DELEGATIONS IN A FEW DAYS, TO CHECK OUR PROGRESS! CHRISTIANS, ERIK! PROMINENT ONES!
THEY'LL BE MAKING ANOTHER PAYMENT. THEY'LL HAVE SILVER!
AND WHAT, EXACTLY, IS OUR PROGRESS?
WELL, THE VILLAGE SLOW-BOY'S CRAFTED A BUNCH OF SCAFFOLD PINS THAT POP OUT WHEN THEY FEEL LIKE IT, SENDING SEVERAL TONS OF LUMBER RAINING DOWN ON UNSUSPECTING LABORERS' HEADS.
YOU'RE OFF THE PROJECT, ERIK.
I'M THE BLACKSMITH.
YOU ARE A BLACKSMITH, BECAUSE YOU INHERITED THE TITLE AND EQUIPMENT FROM YOUR OLD MAN.
BUT YOU ARE NOT OUR BLACKSMITH. NOT AFTER THIS.

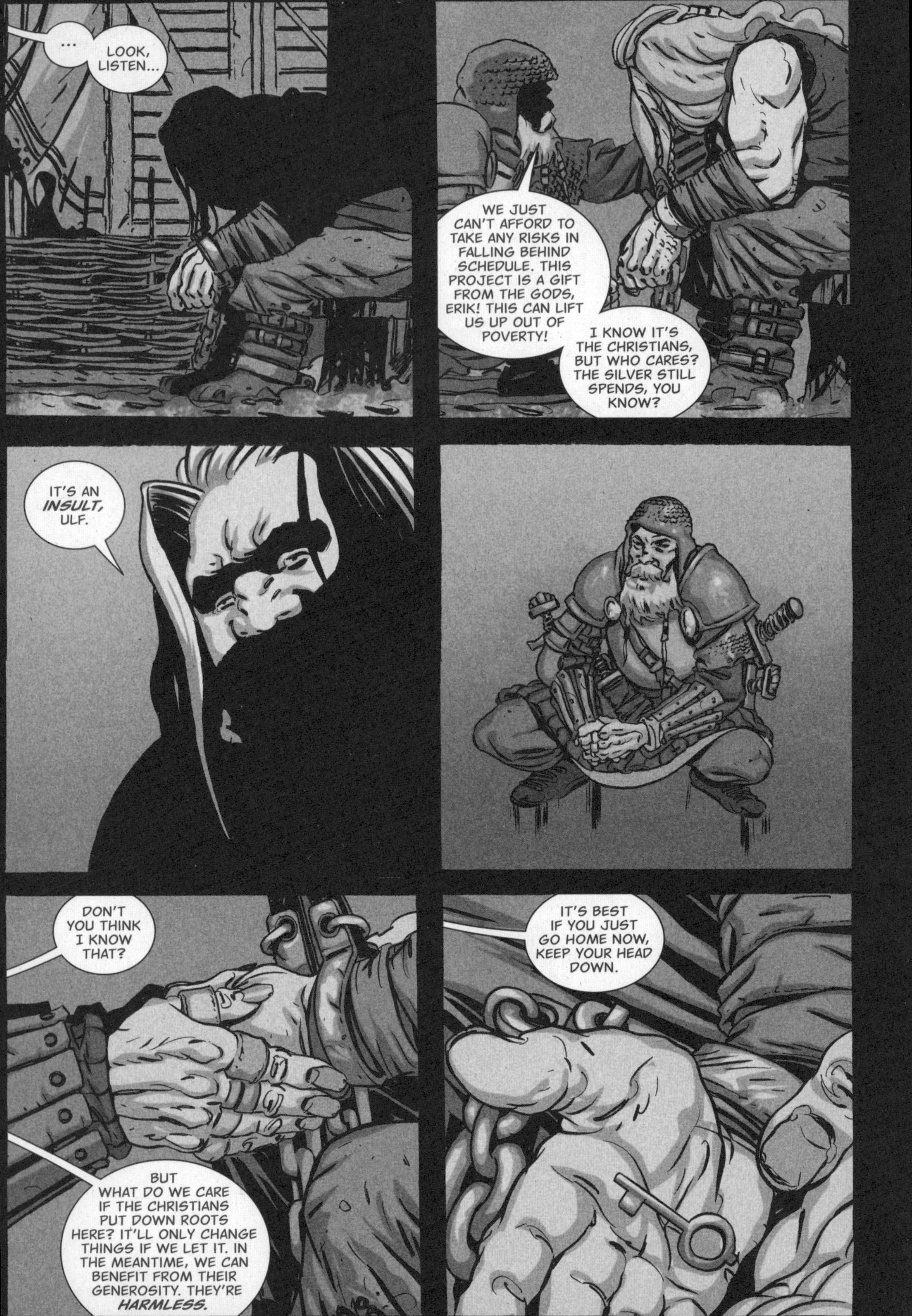

... LOOK, LISTEN...
WE JUST CAN'T AFFORD TO TAKE ANY RISKS IN FALLING BEHIND SCHEDULE. THIS PROJECT IS A GIFT FROM THE GODS, ERIK! THIS CAN LIFT US UP OUT OF POVERTY!
I KNOW IT'S THE CHRISTIANS, BUT WHO CARES? THE SILVER STILL SPENDS, YOU KNOW?
IT'S AN INSULT, ULF.
DON'T YOU THINK I KNOW THAT?
BUT WHAT DO WE CARE IF THE CHRISTIANS PUT DOWN ROOTS HERE? IT'LL ONLY CHANGE THINGS IF WE LET IT. IN THE MEANTIME, WE CAN BENEFIT FROM THEIR GENEROSITY. THEY'RE HARMLESS.
IT'S BEST IF YOU JUST GO HOME NOW, KEEP YOUR HEAD DOWN.

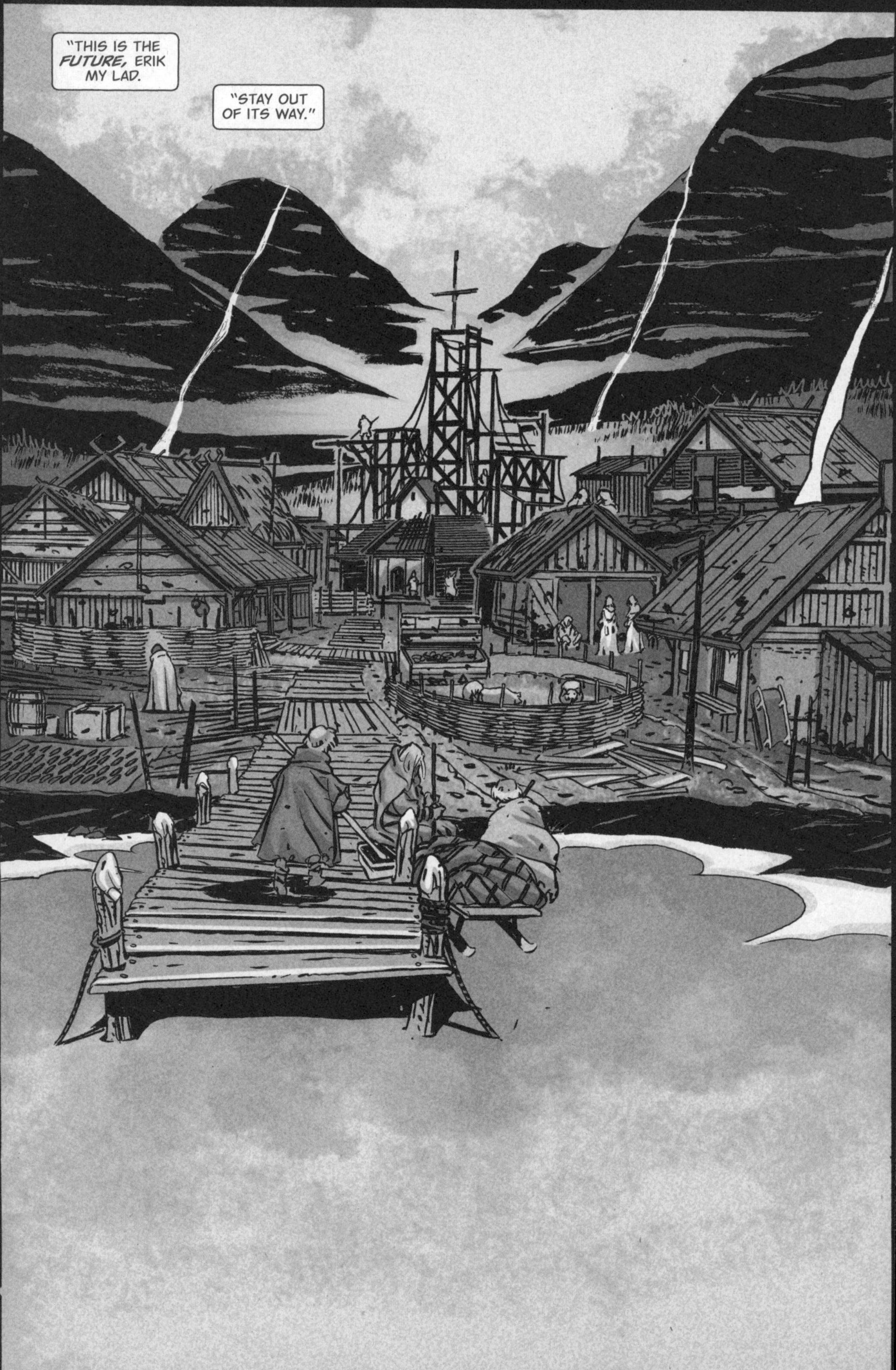
"THIS IS THE FUTURE, ERIK MY LAD.
"STAY OUT OF ITS WAY."

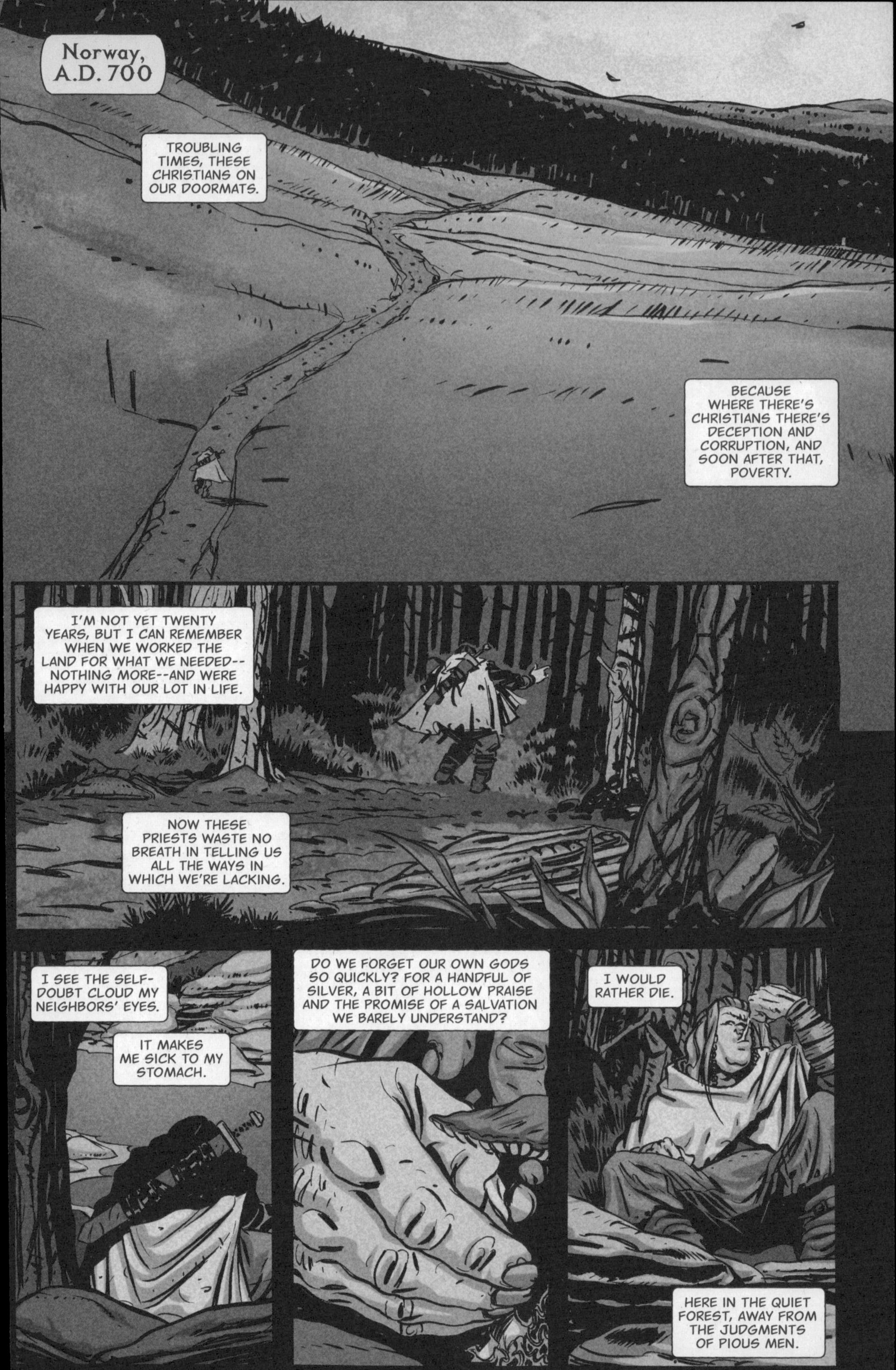
Norway, A.D. 700
TROUBLING TIMES, THESE CHRISTIANS ON OUR DOORMATS.
BECAUSE WHERE THERE'S CHRISTIANS THERE'S DECEPTION AND CORRUPTION, AND SOON AFTER THAT, POVERTY.
I'M NOT YET TWENTY YEARS, BUT I CAN REMEMBER WHEN WE WORKED THE LAND FOR WHAT WE NEEDED--NOTHING MORE--AND WERE HAPPY WITH OUR LOT IN LIFE.
NOW THESE PRIESTS WASTE NO BREATH IN TELLING US ALL THE WAYS IN WHICH WE'RE LACKING.
I SEE THE SELF-DOUBT CLOUD MY NEIGHBORS' EYES.
IT MAKES ME SICK TO MY STOMACH.
DO WE FORGET OUR OWN GODS SO QUICKLY? FOR A HANDFUL OF SILVER, A BIT OF HOLLOW PRAISE AND THE PROMISE OF A SALVATION WE BARELY UNDERSTAND?
I WOULD RATHER DIE.
HERE IN THE QUIET FOREST, AWAY FROM THE JUDGMENTS OF PIOUS MEN.

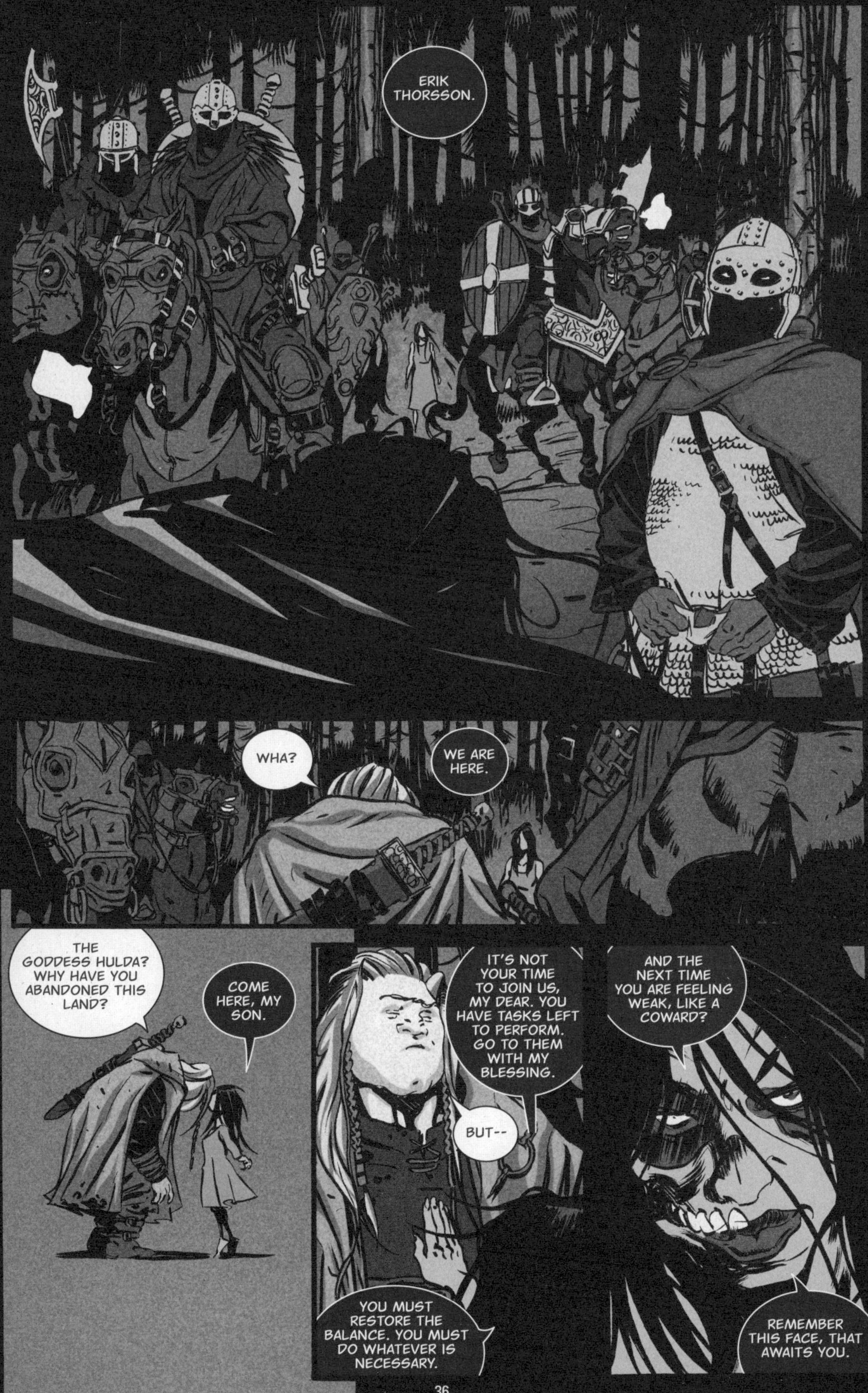
ERIK THORSSON.
WHA?
WE ARE HERE.
THE GODDESS HULDA? WHY HAVE YOU ABANDONED THIS LAND?
COME HERE, MY SON.
IT'S NOT YOUR TIME TO JOIN US, MY DEAR. YOU HAVE TASKS LEFT TO PERFORM. GO TO THEM WITH MY BLESSING.
BUT--
YOU MUST RESTORE THE BALANCE. YOU MUST DO WHATEVER IS NECESSARY.
AND THE NEXT TIME YOU ARE FEELING WEAK, LIKE A COWARD?
REMEMBER THIS FACE, THAT AWAITS YOU.

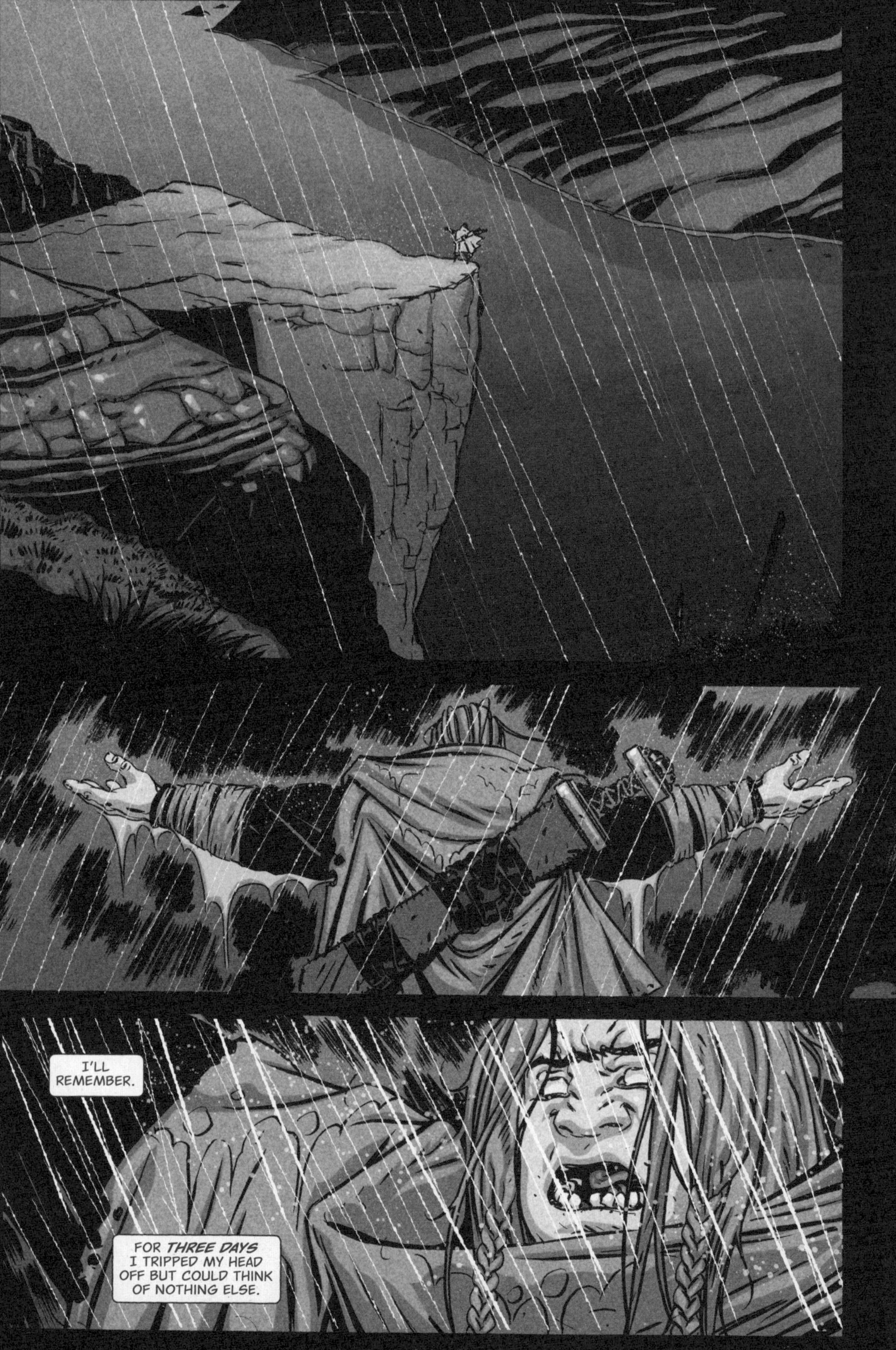
I'LL REMEMBER.
FOR THREE DAYS I TRIPPED MY HEAD OFF BUT COULD THINK OF NOTHING ELSE.

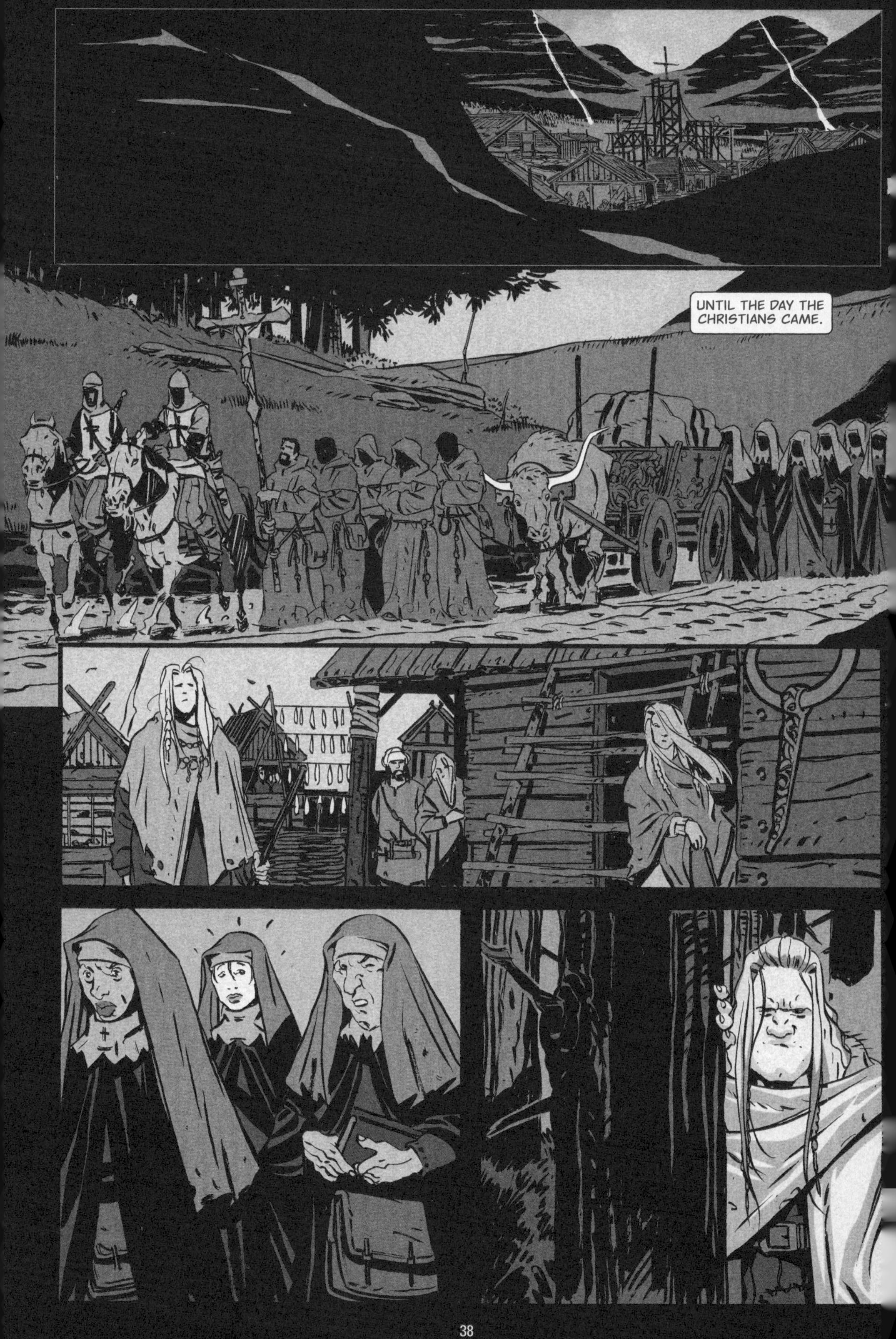
UNTIL THE DAY THE CHRISTIANS CAME.

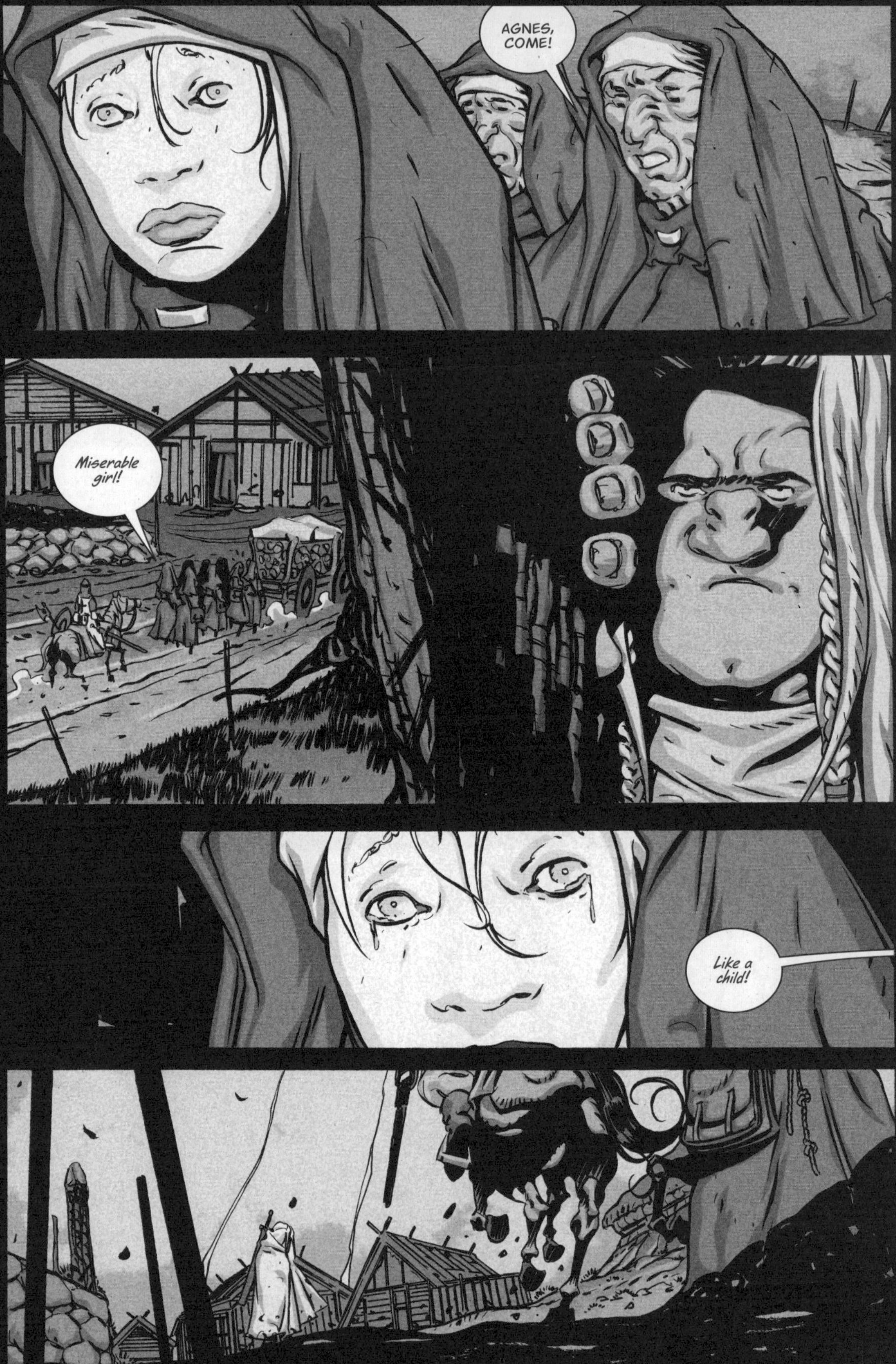
AGNES, COME!
Miserable girl!
Like a child!

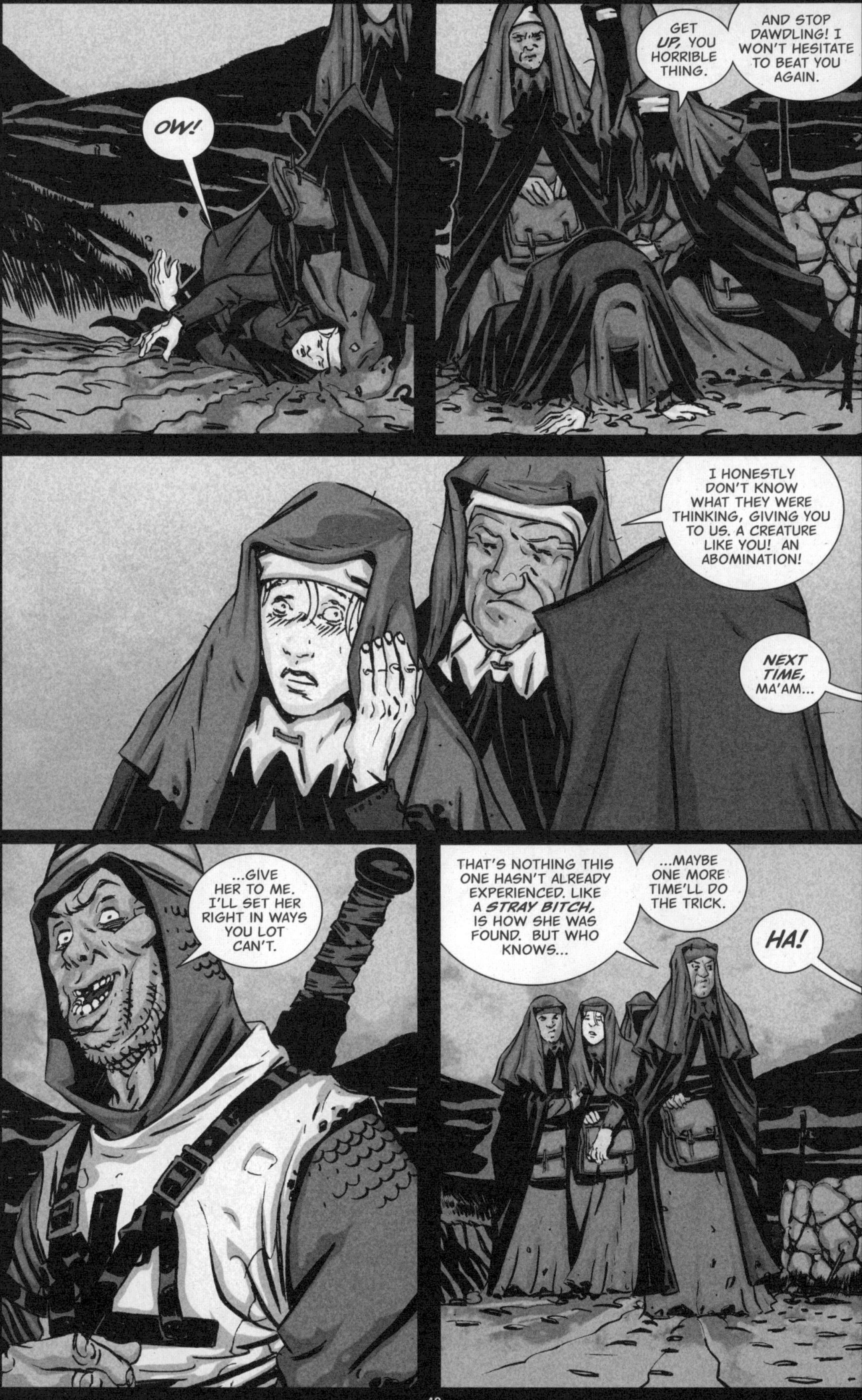
OW!
GET UP, YOU HORRIBLE THING.
AND STOP DAWDLING! I WON'T HESITATE TO BEAT YOU AGAIN.
I HONESTLY DON'T KNOW WHAT THEY WERE THINKING, GIVING YOU TO US. A CREATURE LIKE YOU! AN ABOMINATION!
NEXT TIME, MA'AM...
...GIVE HER TO ME. I'LL SET HER RIGHT IN WAYS YOU LOT CAN'T.
THAT'S NOTHING THIS ONE HASN'T ALREADY EXPERIENCED. LIKE A STRAY BITCH, IS HOW SHE WAS FOUND. BUT WHO KNOWS...
...MAYBE ONE MORE TIME'LL DO THE TRICK.
HA!

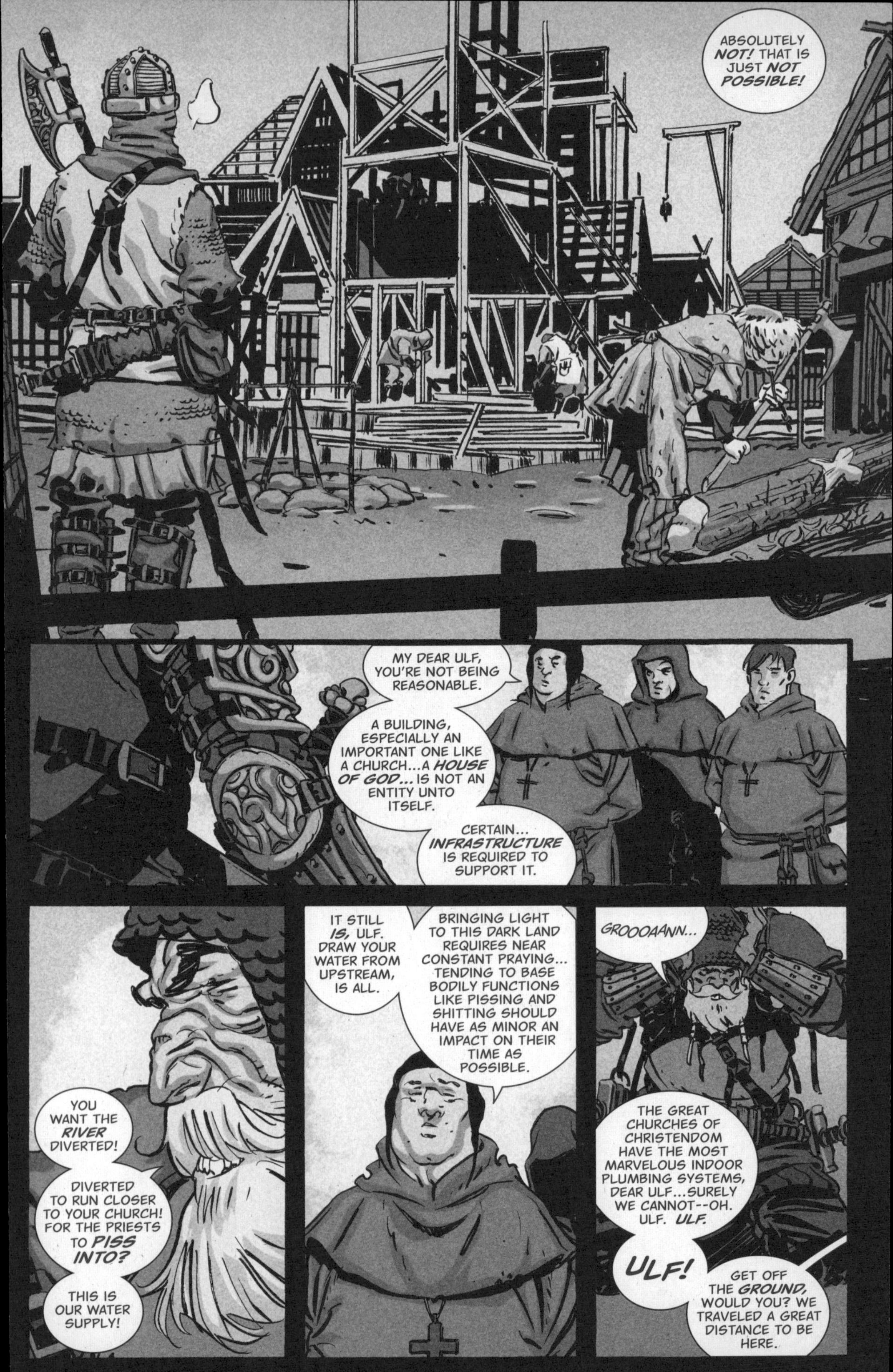
ABSOLUTELY *NOT!* THAT IS JUST *NOT POSSIBLE!*
MY DEAR ULF, YOU'RE NOT BEING REASONABLE.
A BUILDING, ESPECIALLY AN IMPORTANT ONE LIKE A CHURCH...A *HOUSE OF GOD...* IS NOT AN ENTITY UNTO ITSELF.
CERTAIN... *INFRASTRUCTURE* IS REQUIRED TO SUPPORT IT.
YOU WANT THE *RIVER* DIVERTED!
DIVERTED TO RUN CLOSER TO YOUR CHURCH! FOR THE PRIESTS TO *PISS INTO?*
THIS IS OUR WATER SUPPLY!
IT STILL *IS,* ULF. DRAW YOUR WATER FROM UPSTREAM, IS ALL.
BRINGING LIGHT TO THIS DARK LAND REQUIRES NEAR CONSTANT PRAYING... TENDING TO BASE BODILY FUNCTIONS LIKE PISSING AND SHITTING SHOULD HAVE AS MINOR AN IMPACT ON THEIR TIME AS POSSIBLE.
GROOOAANN...
THE GREAT CHURCHES OF CHRISTENDOM HAVE THE MOST MARVELOUS INDOOR PLUMBING SYSTEMS, DEAR ULF...SURELY WE CANNOT--OH. ULF. *ULF.*
ULF!
GET OFF THE *GROUND,* WOULD YOU? WE TRAVELED A GREAT DISTANCE TO BE HERE.

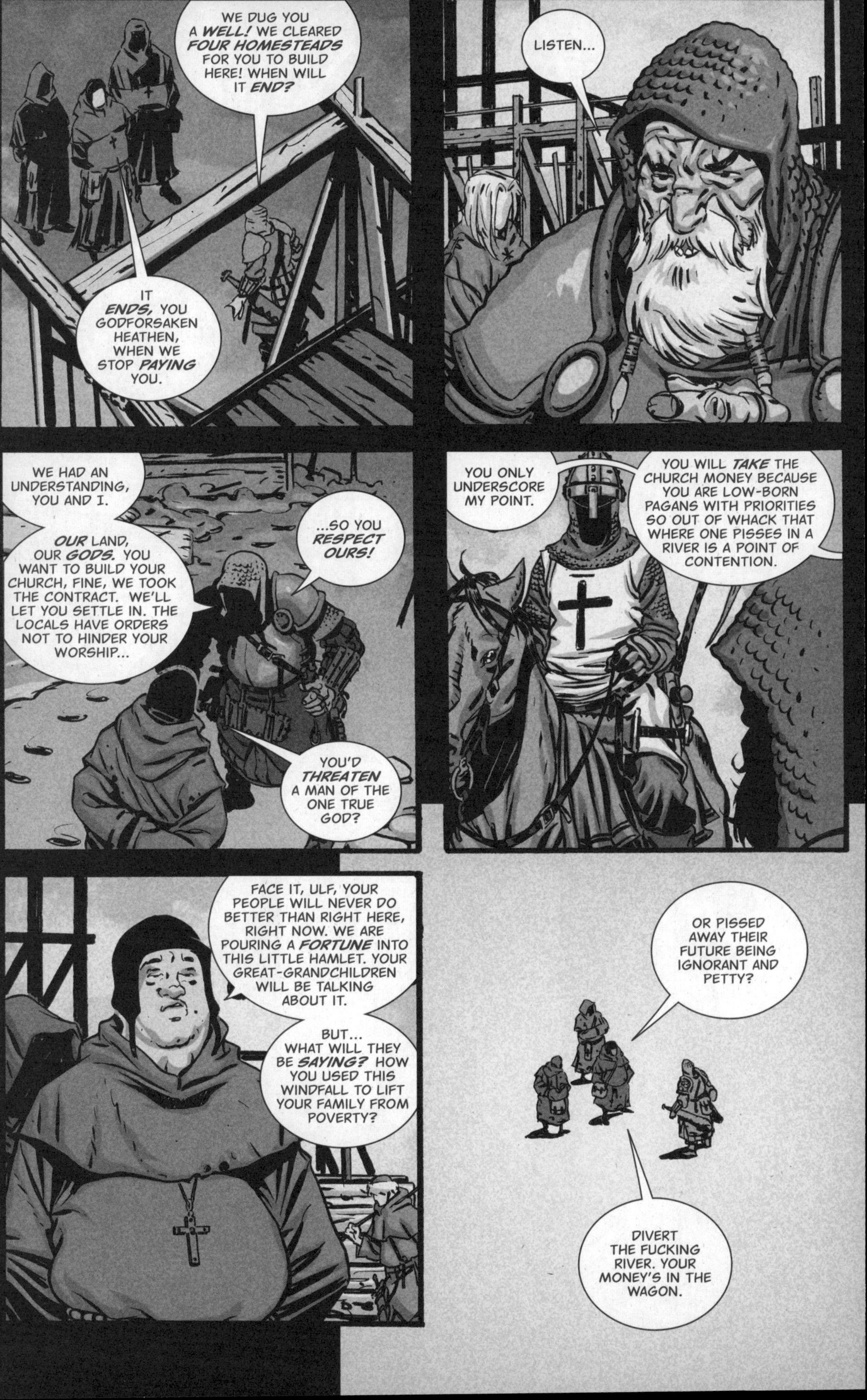
WE DUG YOU A WELL! WE CLEARED FOUR HOMESTEADS FOR YOU TO BUILD HERE! WHEN WILL IT END?
IT ENDS, YOU GODFORSAKEN HEATHEN, WHEN WE STOP PAYING YOU.
LISTEN...
WE HAD AN UNDERSTANDING, YOU AND I.
OUR LAND, OUR GODS. YOU WANT TO BUILD YOUR CHURCH, FINE, WE TOOK THE CONTRACT. WE'LL LET YOU SETTLE IN. THE LOCALS HAVE ORDERS NOT TO HINDER YOUR WORSHIP...
...SO YOU RESPECT OURS!
YOU'D THREATEN A MAN OF THE ONE TRUE GOD?
YOU ONLY UNDERSCORE MY POINT.
YOU WILL TAKE THE CHURCH MONEY BECAUSE YOU ARE LOW-BORN PAGANS WITH PRIORITIES SO OUT OF WHACK THAT WHERE ONE PISSES IN A RIVER IS A POINT OF CONTENTION.
FACE IT, ULF, YOUR PEOPLE WILL NEVER DO BETTER THAN RIGHT HERE, RIGHT NOW. WE ARE POURING A FORTUNE INTO THIS LITTLE HAMLET. YOUR GREAT-GRANDCHILDREN WILL BE TALKING ABOUT IT.
BUT... WHAT WILL THEY BE SAYING? HOW YOU USED THIS WINDFALL TO LIFT YOUR FAMILY FROM POVERTY?
OR PISSED AWAY THEIR FUTURE BEING IGNORANT AND PETTY?
DIVERT THE FUCKING RIVER. YOUR MONEY'S IN THE WAGON.

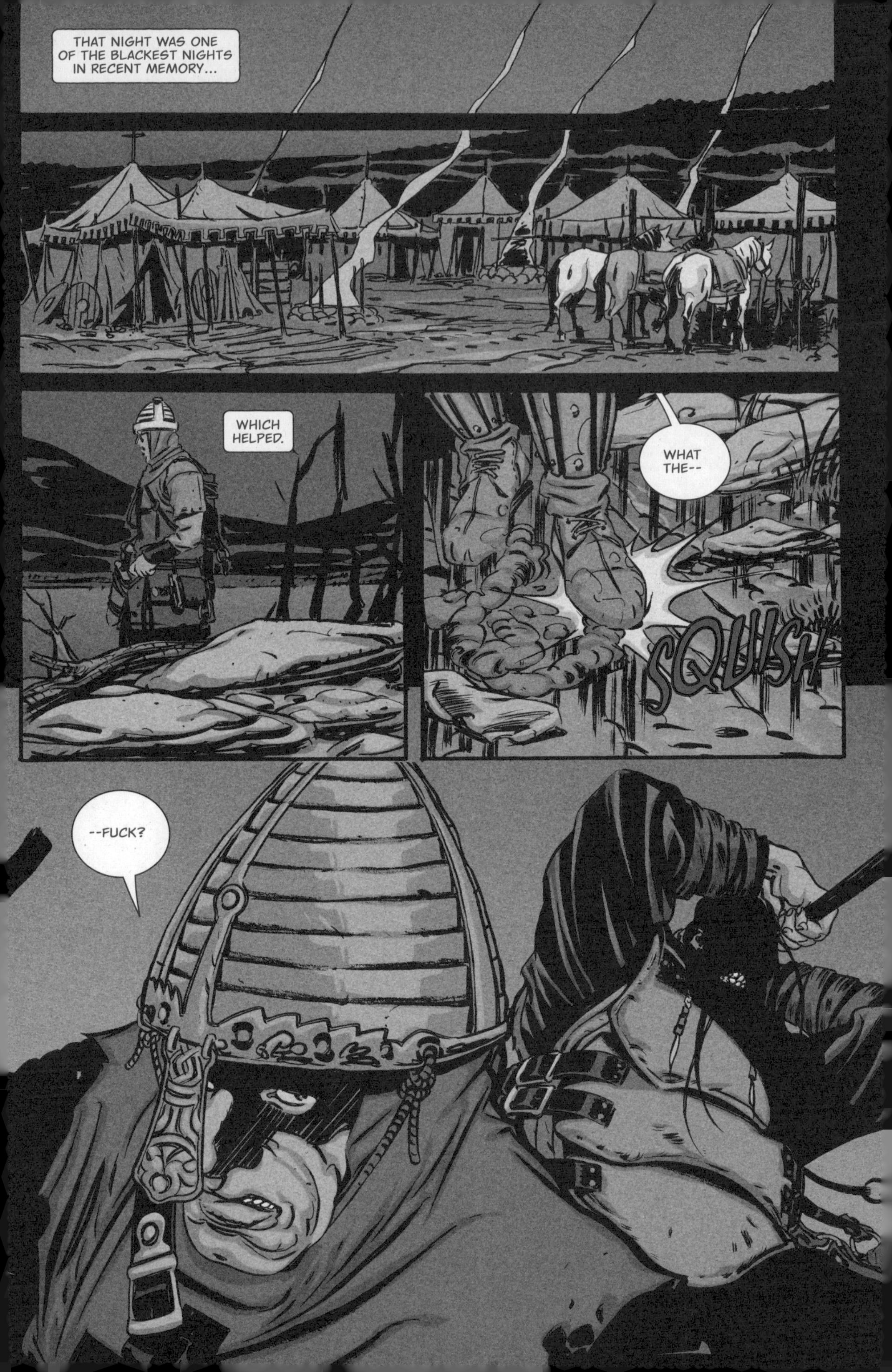
THAT NIGHT WAS ONE OF THE BLACKEST NIGHTS IN RECENT MEMORY...
WHICH HELPED.
WHAT THE--
SQUISH
--FUCK?

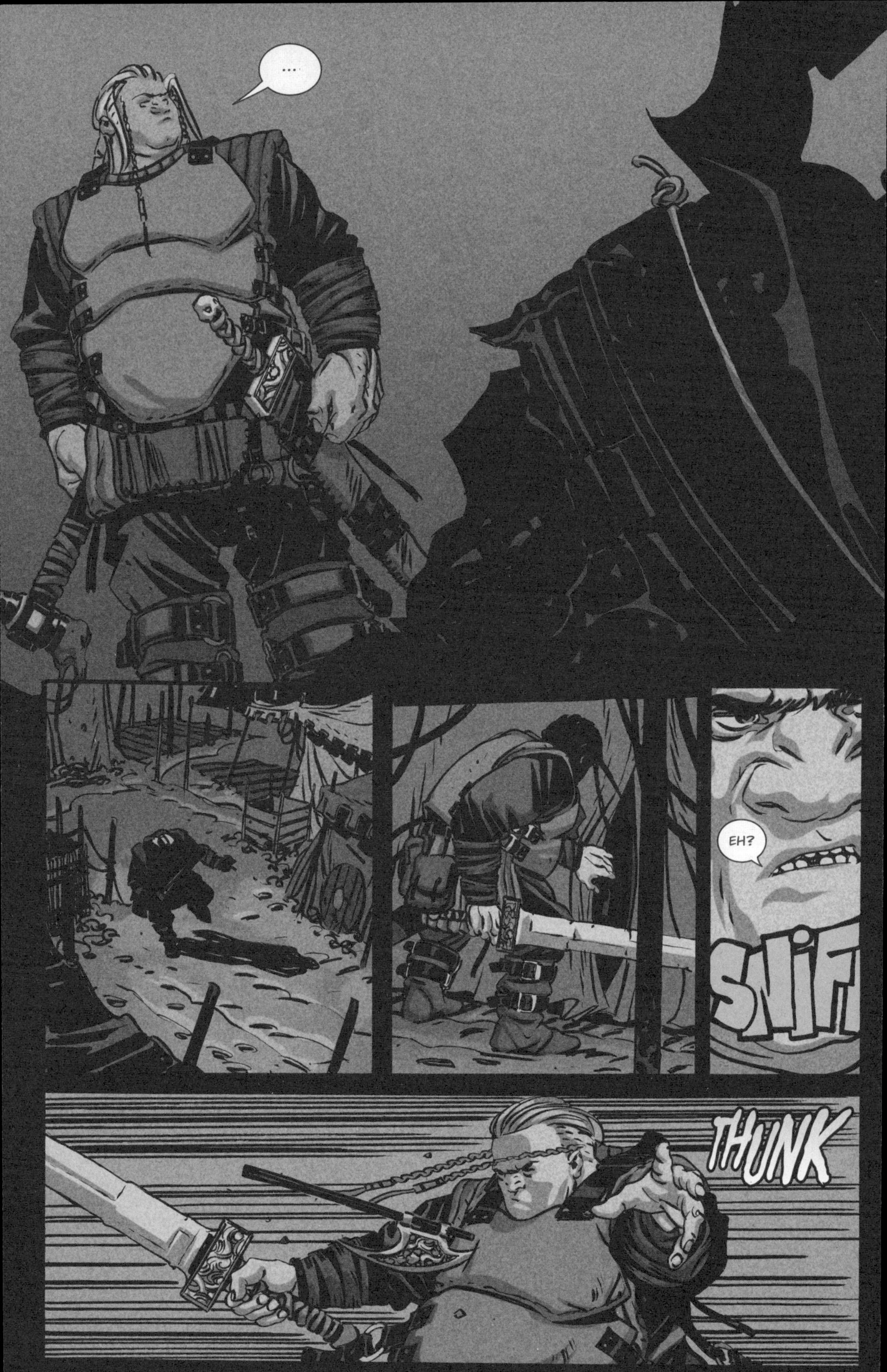
...
EH?
SNIF
THUNK

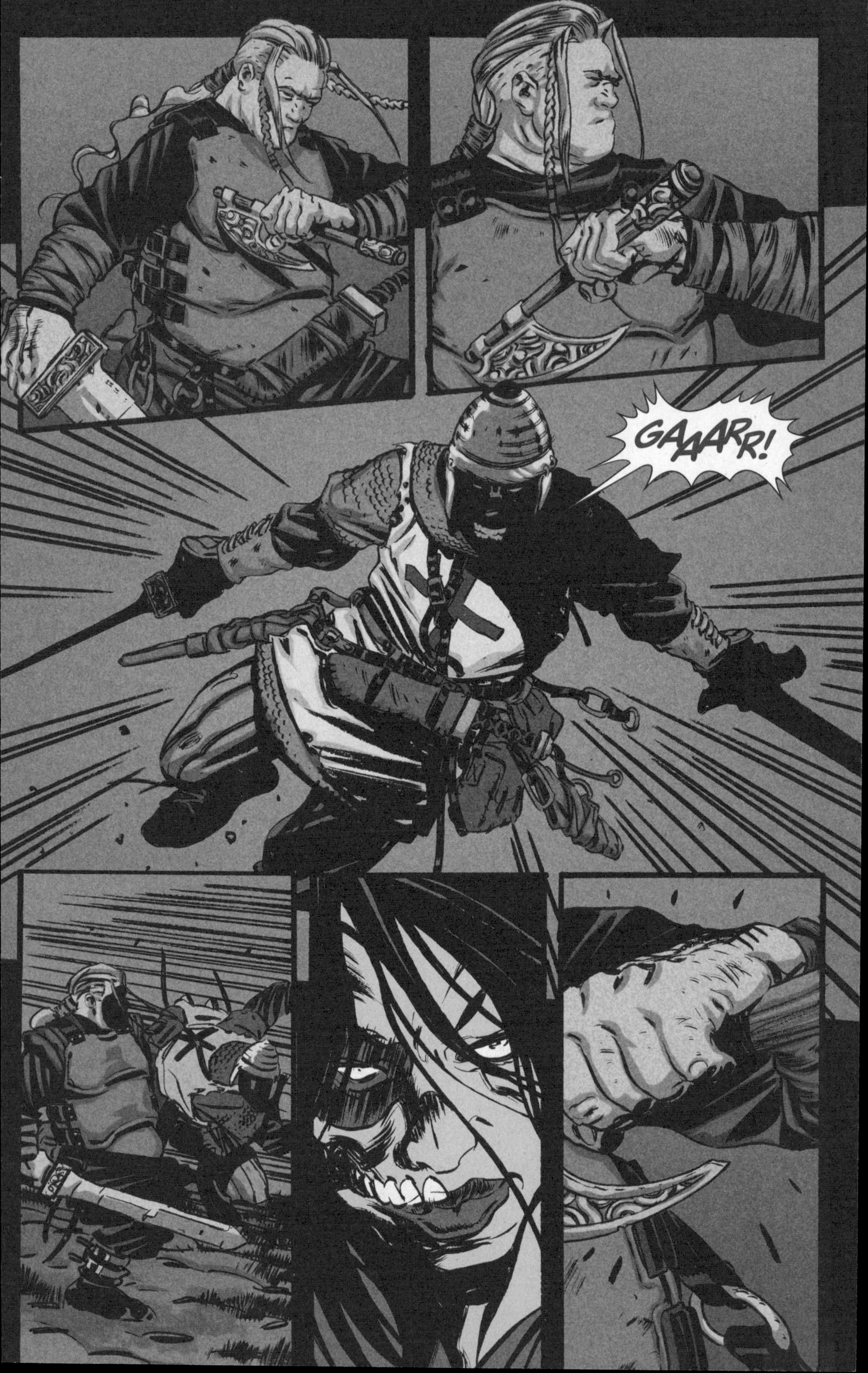
GAAARR!

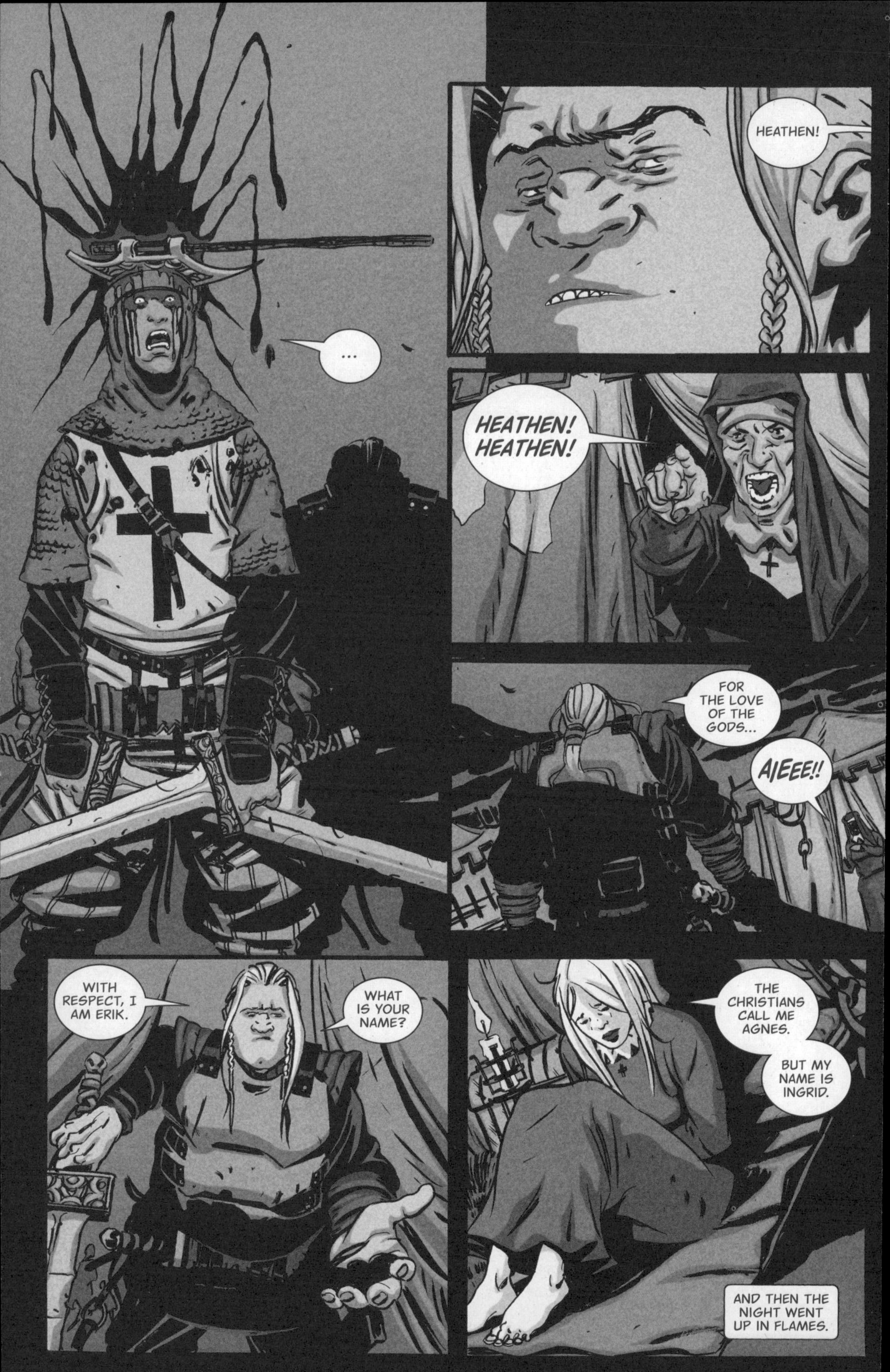
...
HEATHEN!
HEATHEN! HEATHEN!
FOR THE LOVE OF THE GODS...
AIEEE!!
WITH RESPECT, I AM ERIK.
WHAT IS YOUR NAME?
THE CHRISTIANS CALL ME AGNES.
BUT MY NAME IS INGRID.
AND THEN THE NIGHT WENT UP IN FLAMES.

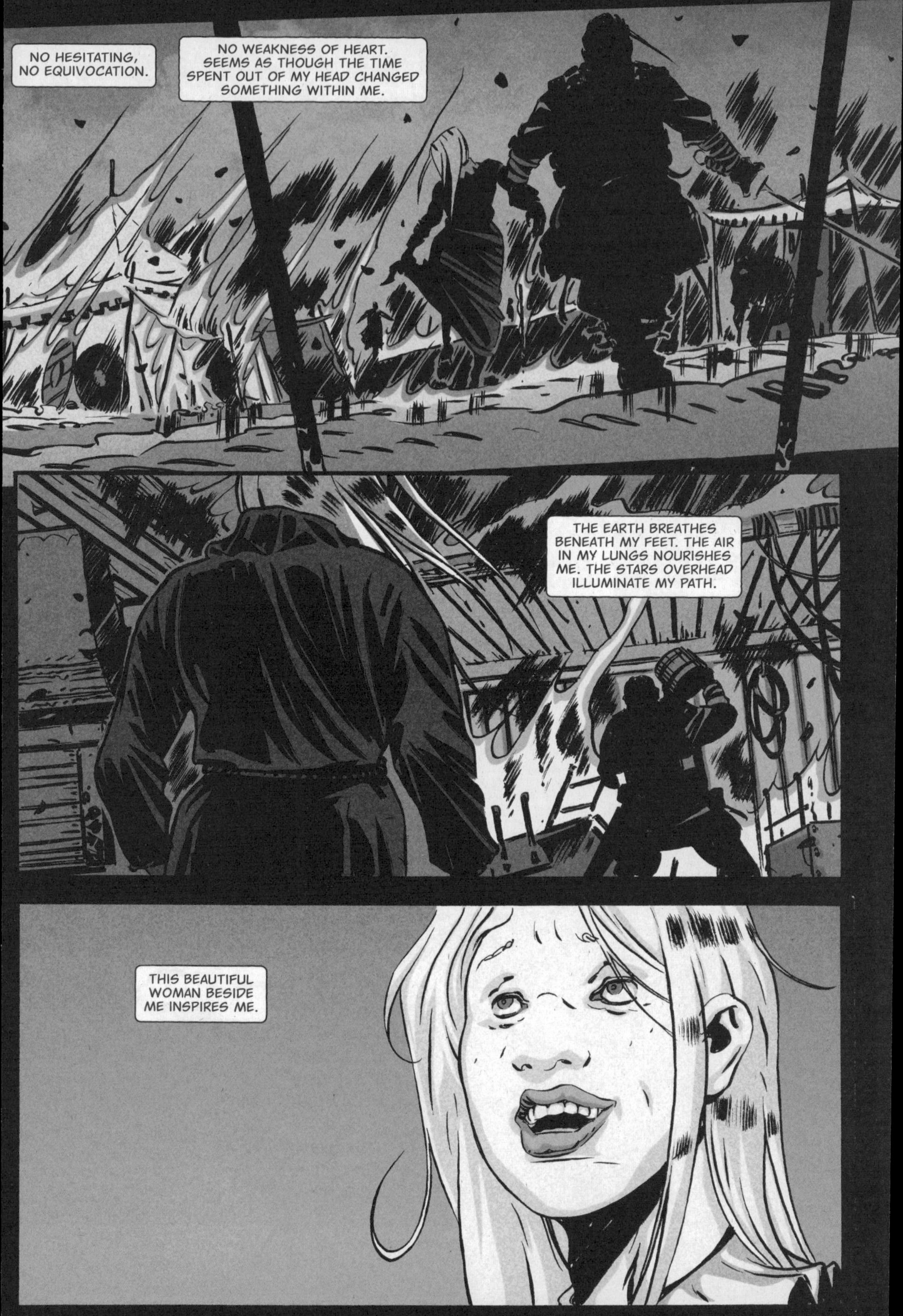
NO HESITATING, NO EQUIVOCATION.
NO WEAKNESS OF HEART. SEEMS AS THOUGH THE TIME SPENT OUT OF MY HEAD CHANGED SOMETHING WITHIN ME.
THE EARTH BREATHES BENEATH MY FEET. THE AIR IN MY LUNGS NOURISHES ME. THE STARS OVERHEAD ILLUMINATE MY PATH.
THIS BEAUTIFUL WOMAN BESIDE ME INSPIRES ME.

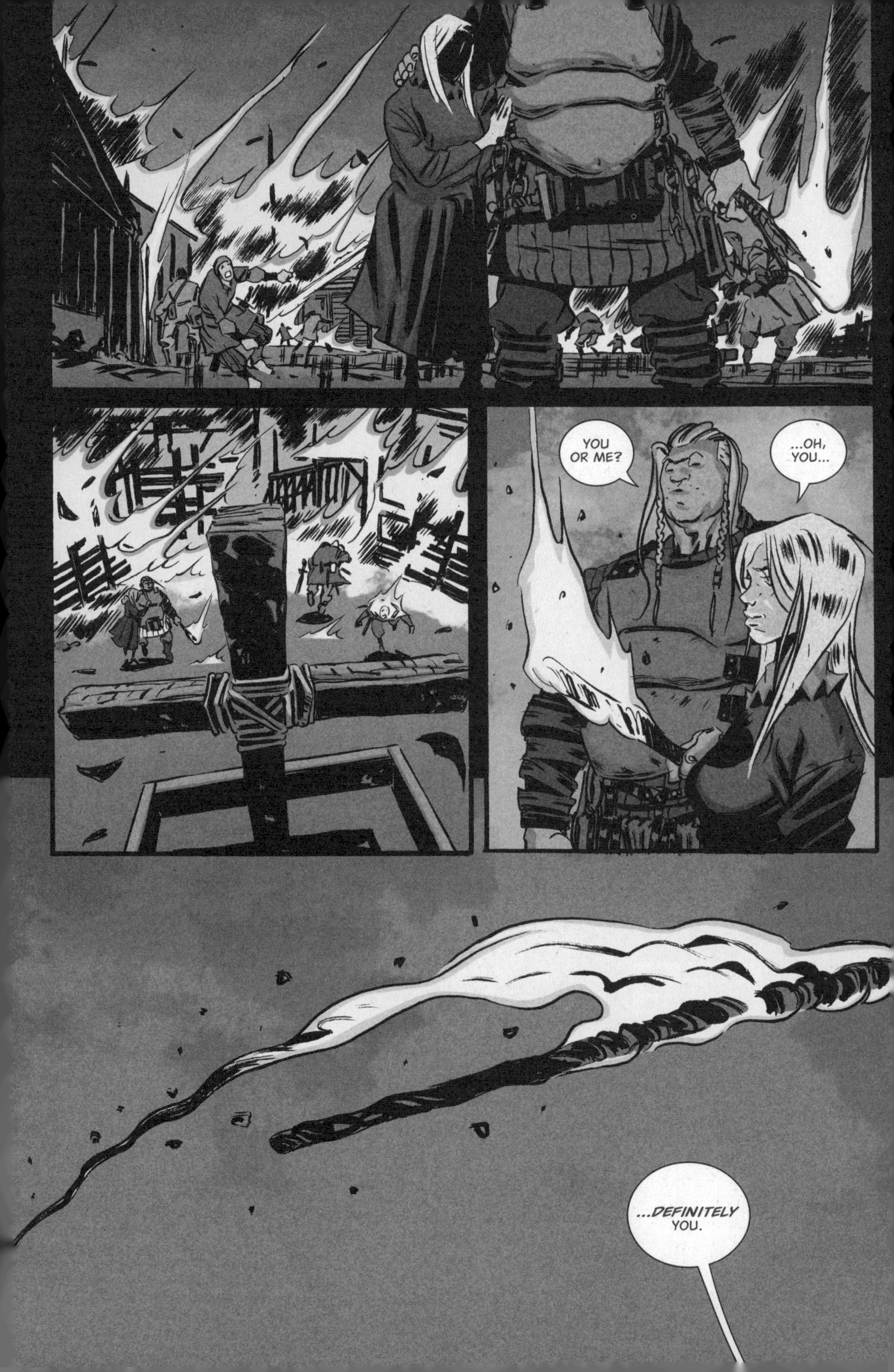
YOU OR ME?
...OH, YOU...
...DEFINITELY YOU.

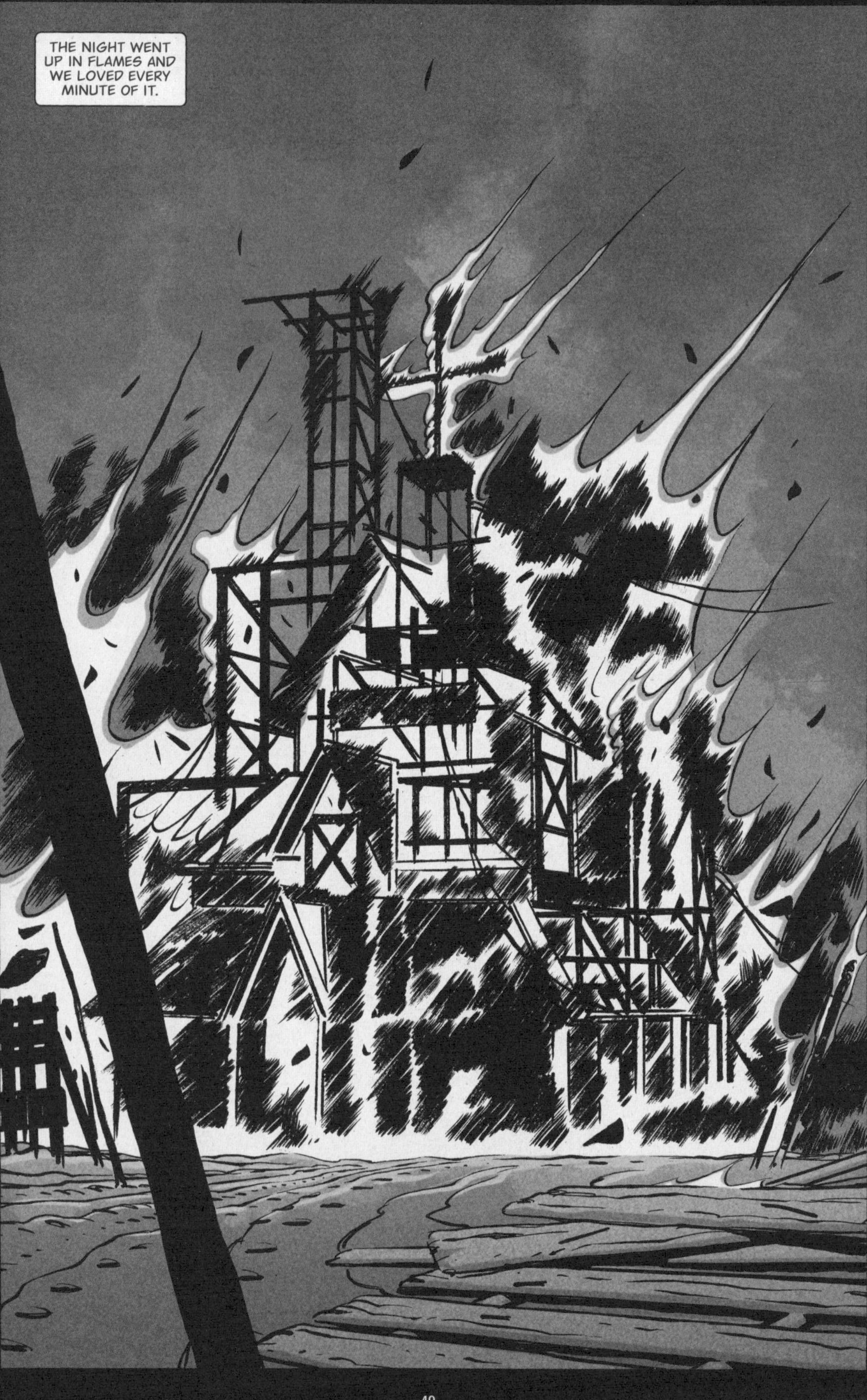
THE NIGHT WENT UP IN FLAMES AND WE LOVED EVERY MINUTE OF IT.

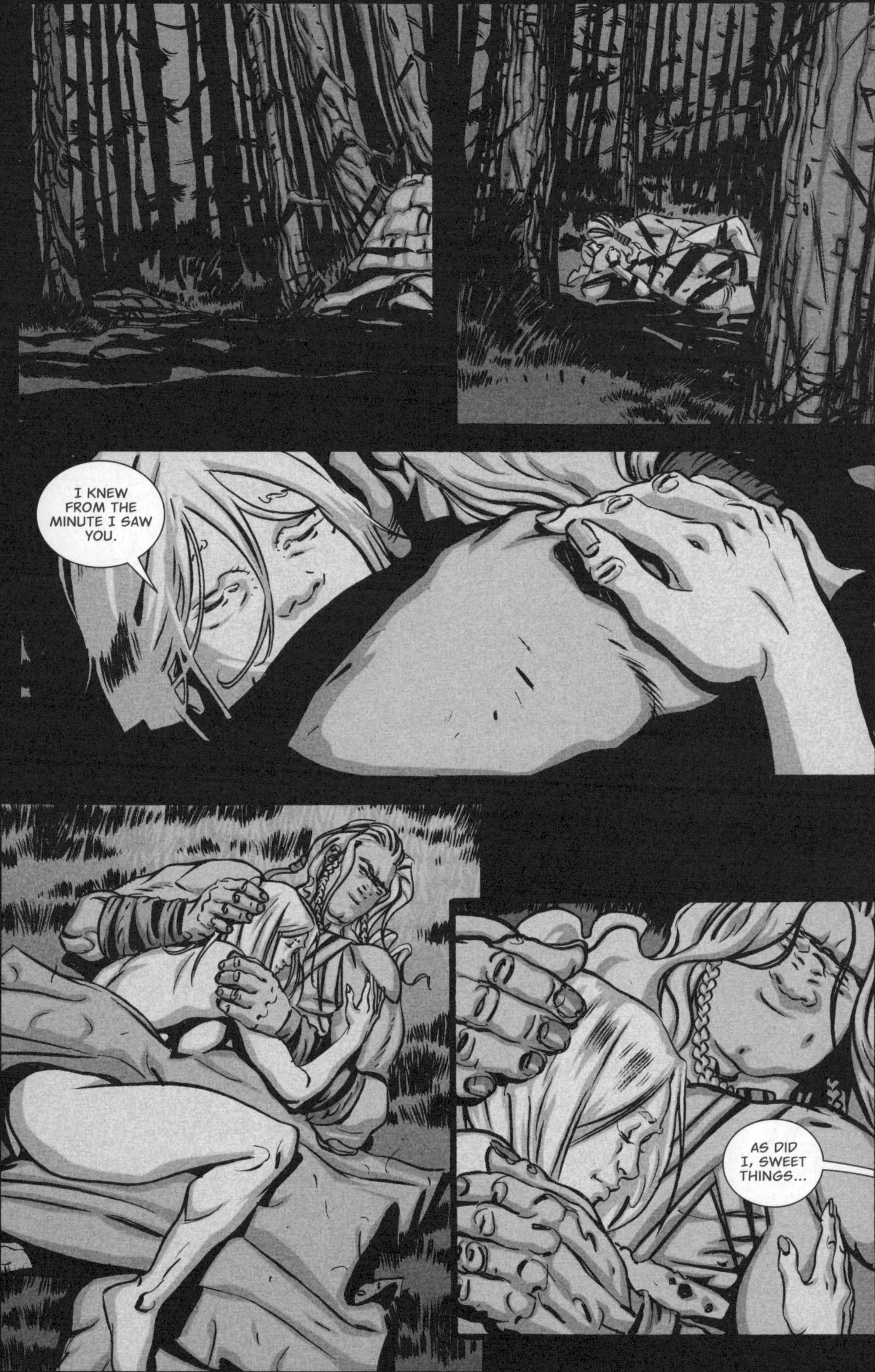
I KNEW FROM THE MINUTE I SAW YOU.
AS DID I, SWEET THINGS...

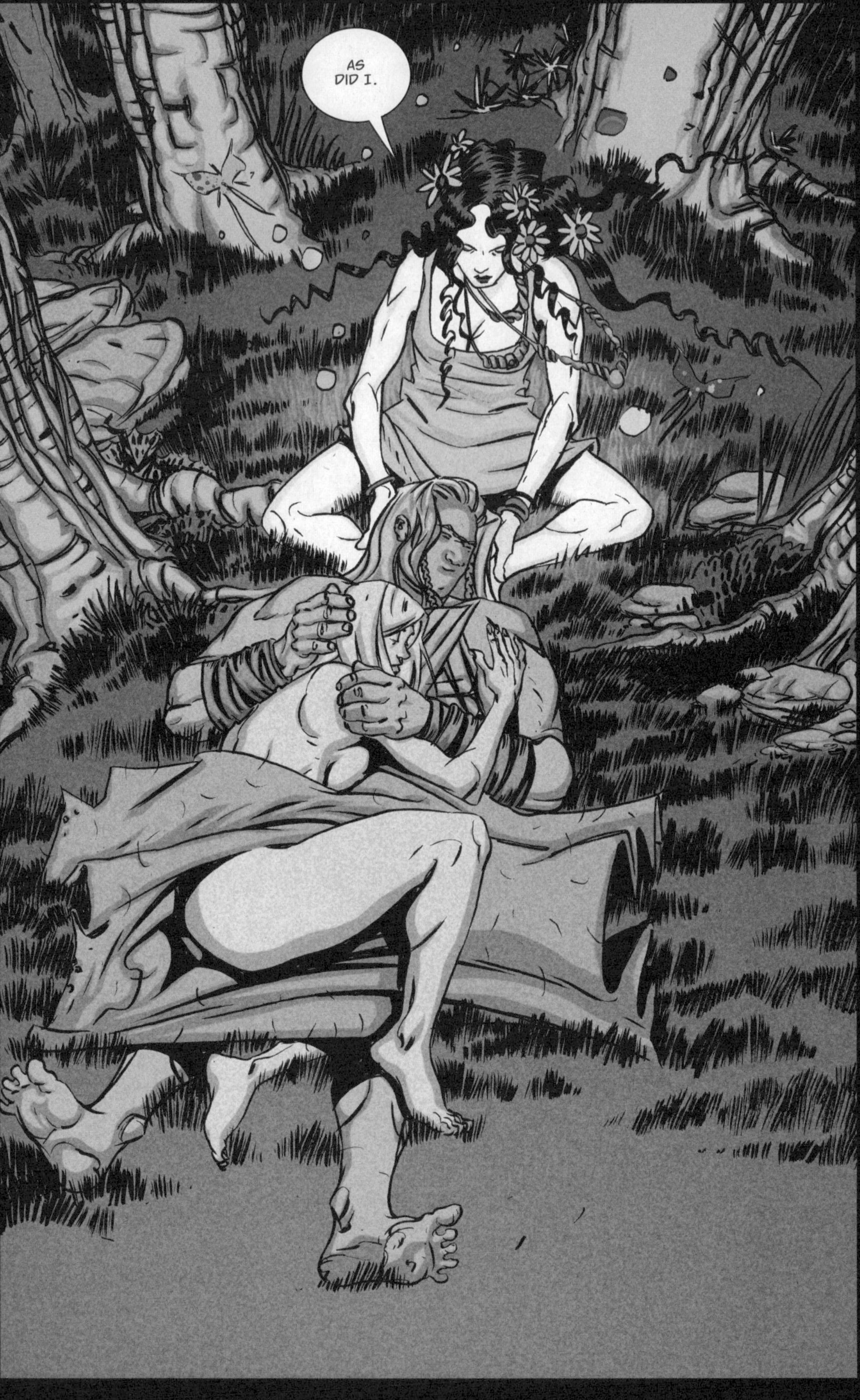
AS DID I.

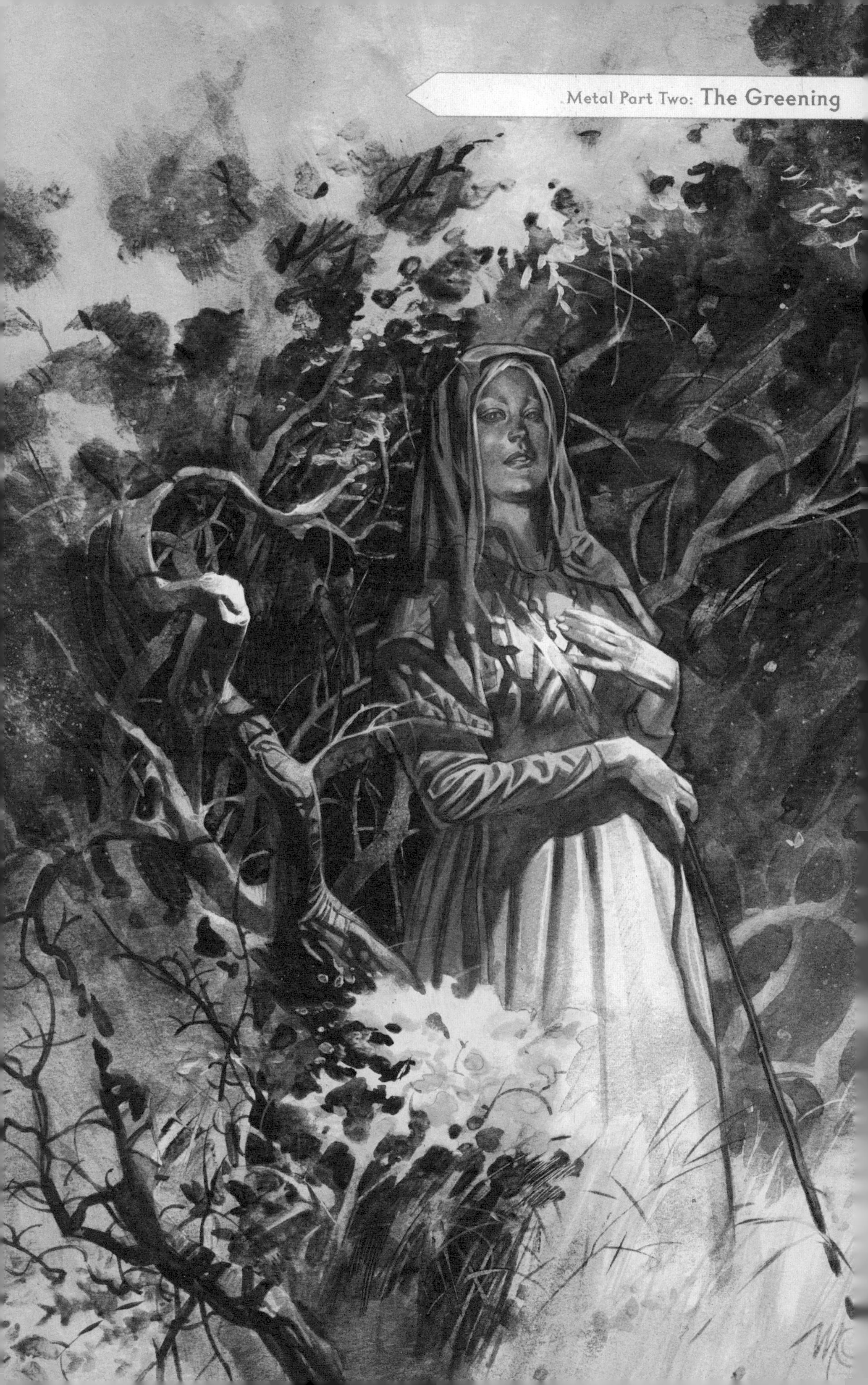

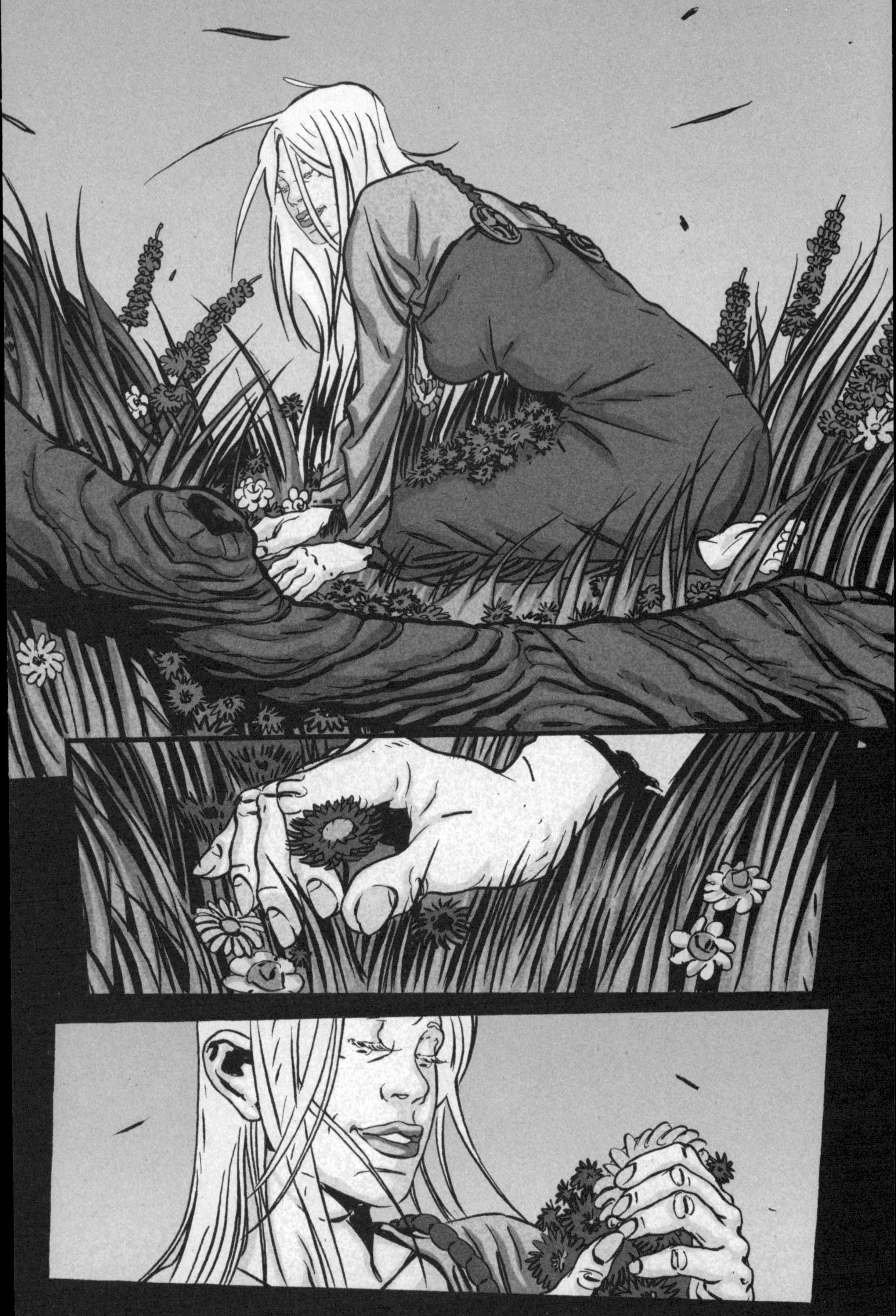

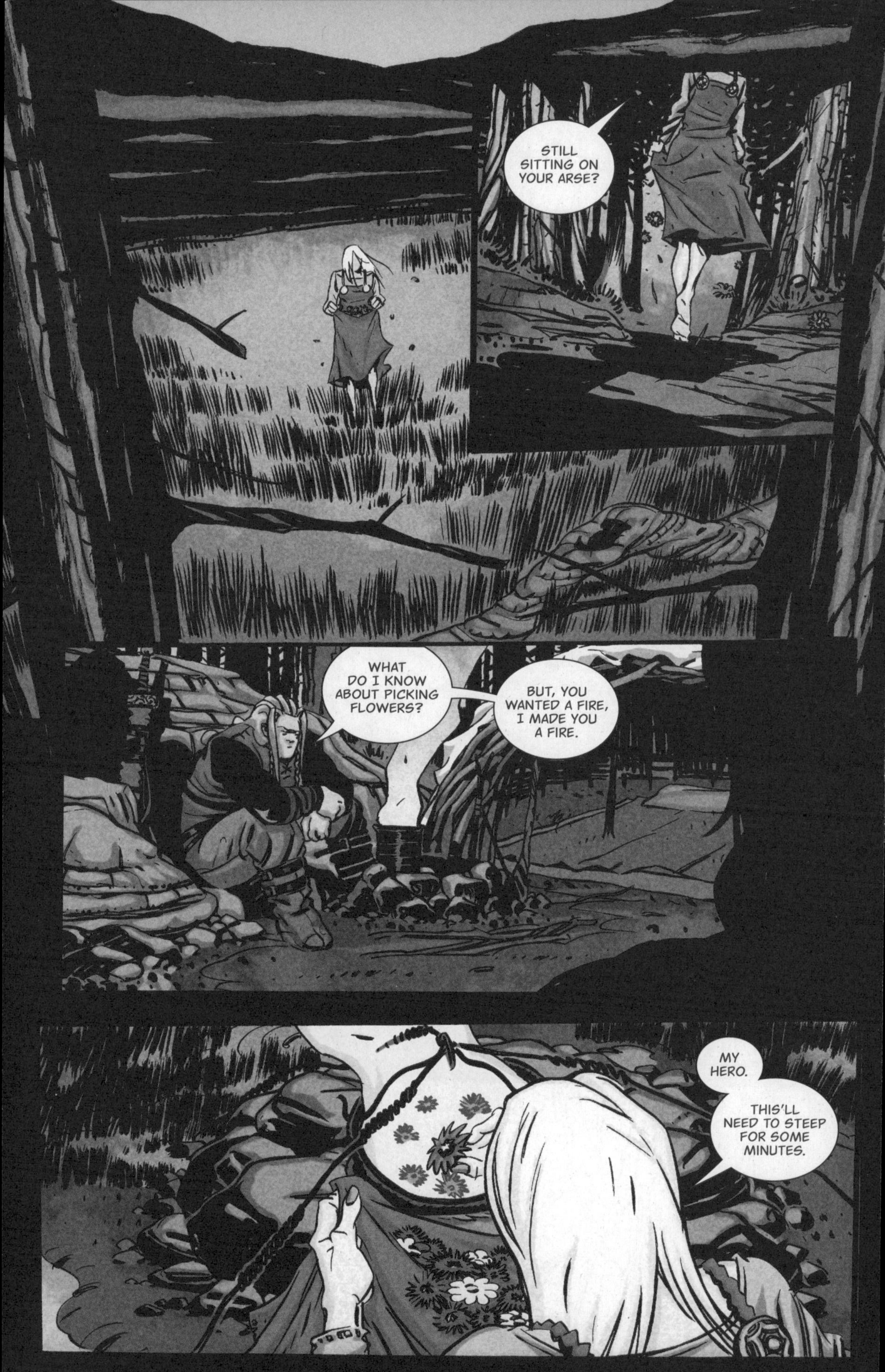

STILL SITTING ON YOUR ARSE?
WHAT DO I KNOW ABOUT PICKING FLOWERS?
BUT, YOU WANTED A FIRE, I MADE YOU A FIRE.
MY HERO.
THIS'LL NEED TO STEEP FOR SOME MINUTES.

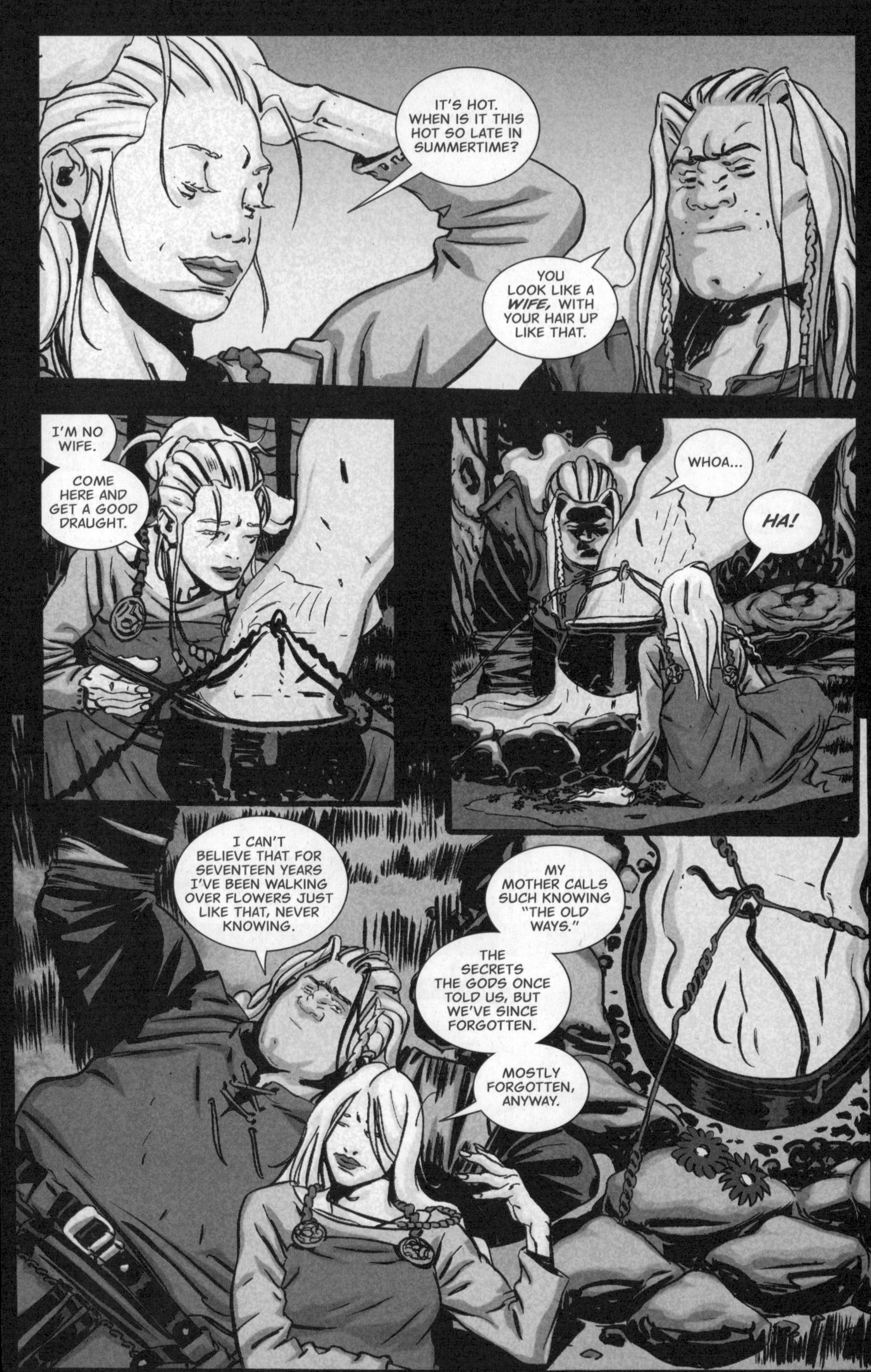
IT'S HOT. WHEN IS IT THIS HOT SO LATE IN SUMMERTIME?
YOU LOOK LIKE A *WIFE,* WITH YOUR HAIR UP LIKE THAT.
I'M NO WIFE.
COME HERE AND GET A GOOD DRAUGHT.
WHOA...
HA!
I CAN'T BELIEVE THAT FOR SEVENTEEN YEARS I'VE BEEN WALKING OVER FLOWERS JUST LIKE THAT, NEVER KNOWING.
MY MOTHER CALLS SUCH KNOWING "THE OLD WAYS."
THE SECRETS THE GODS ONCE TOLD US, BUT WE'VE SINCE FORGOTTEN.
MOSTLY FORGOTTEN, ANYWAY.

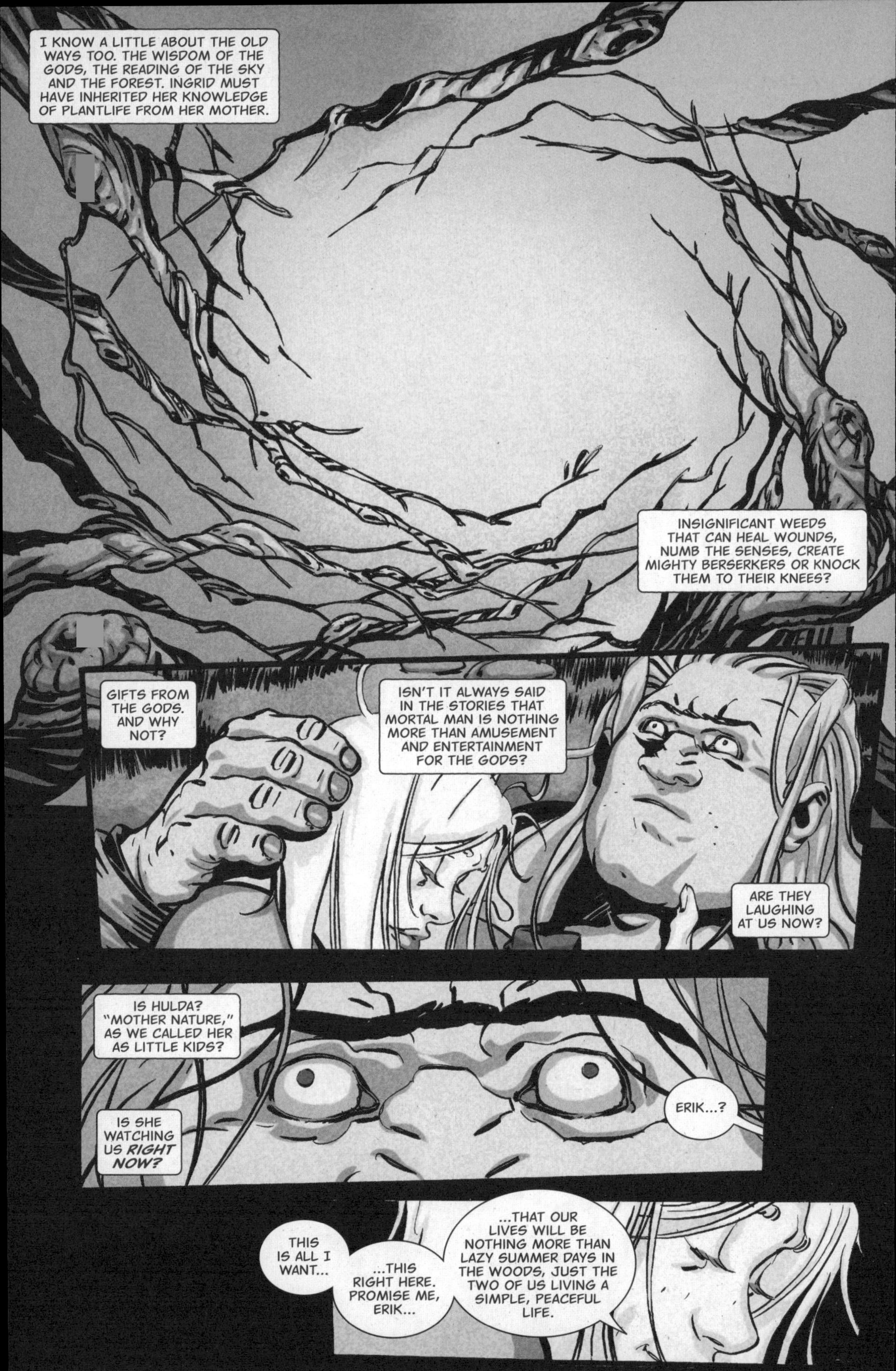
I KNOW A LITTLE ABOUT THE OLD WAYS TOO. THE WISDOM OF THE GODS, THE READING OF THE SKY AND THE FOREST. INGRID MUST HAVE INHERITED HER KNOWLEDGE OF PLANTLIFE FROM HER MOTHER.
INSIGNIFICANT WEEDS THAT CAN HEAL WOUNDS, NUMB THE SENSES, CREATE MIGHTY BERSERKERS OR KNOCK THEM TO THEIR KNEES?
GIFTS FROM THE GODS. AND WHY NOT?
ISN'T IT ALWAYS SAID IN THE STORIES THAT MORTAL MAN IS NOTHING MORE THAN AMUSEMENT AND ENTERTAINMENT FOR THE GODS?
ARE THEY LAUGHING AT US NOW?
IS HULDA? "MOTHER NATURE," AS WE CALLED HER AS LITTLE KIDS?
IS SHE WATCHING US *RIGHT NOW?*
ERIK...?
THIS IS ALL I WANT...
...THIS RIGHT HERE. PROMISE ME, ERIK...
...THAT OUR LIVES WILL BE NOTHING MORE THAN LAZY SUMMER DAYS IN THE WOODS, JUST THE TWO OF US LIVING A SIMPLE, PEACEFUL LIFE.

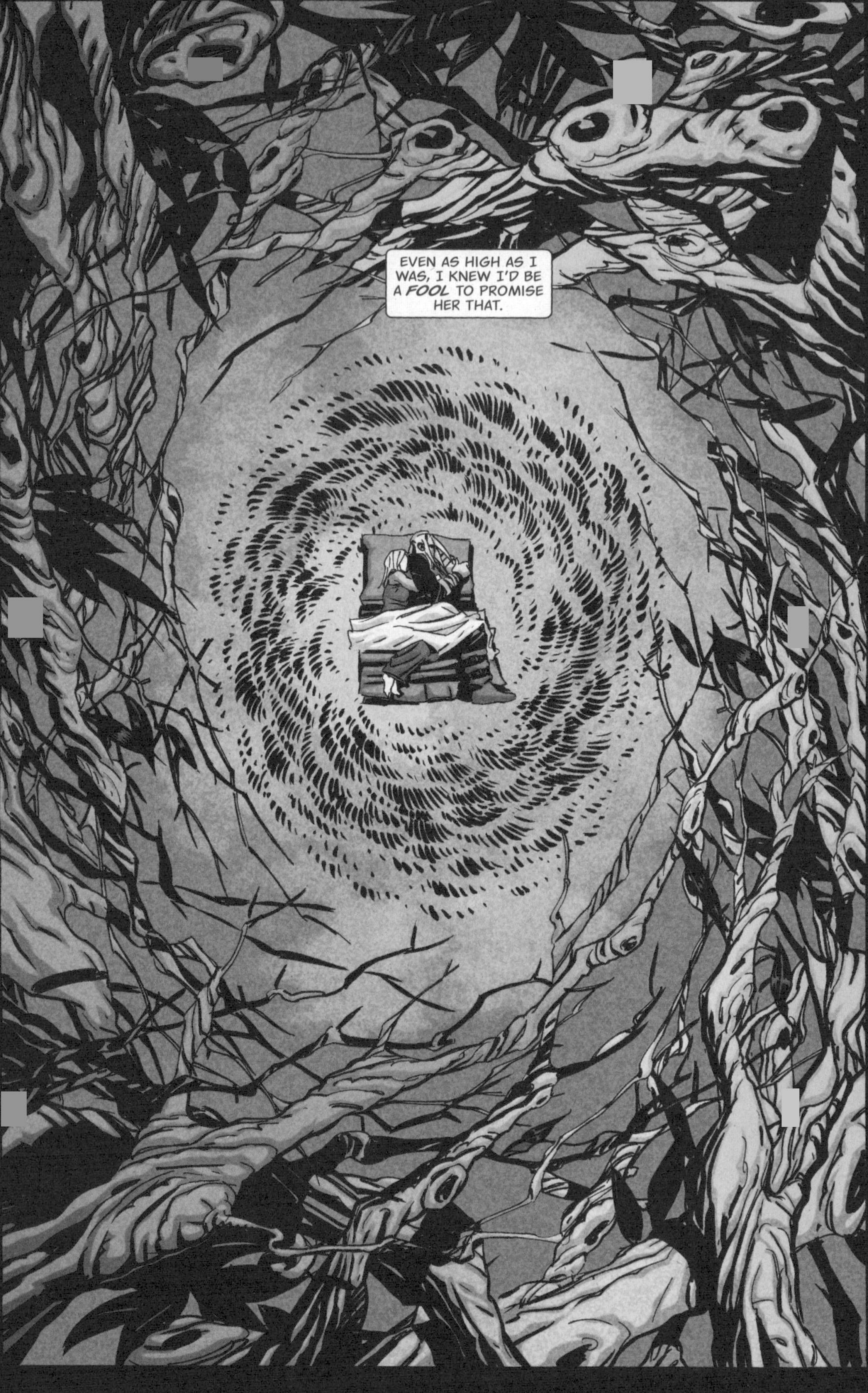
EVEN AS HIGH AS I WAS, I KNEW I'D BE A FOOL TO PROMISE HER THAT.

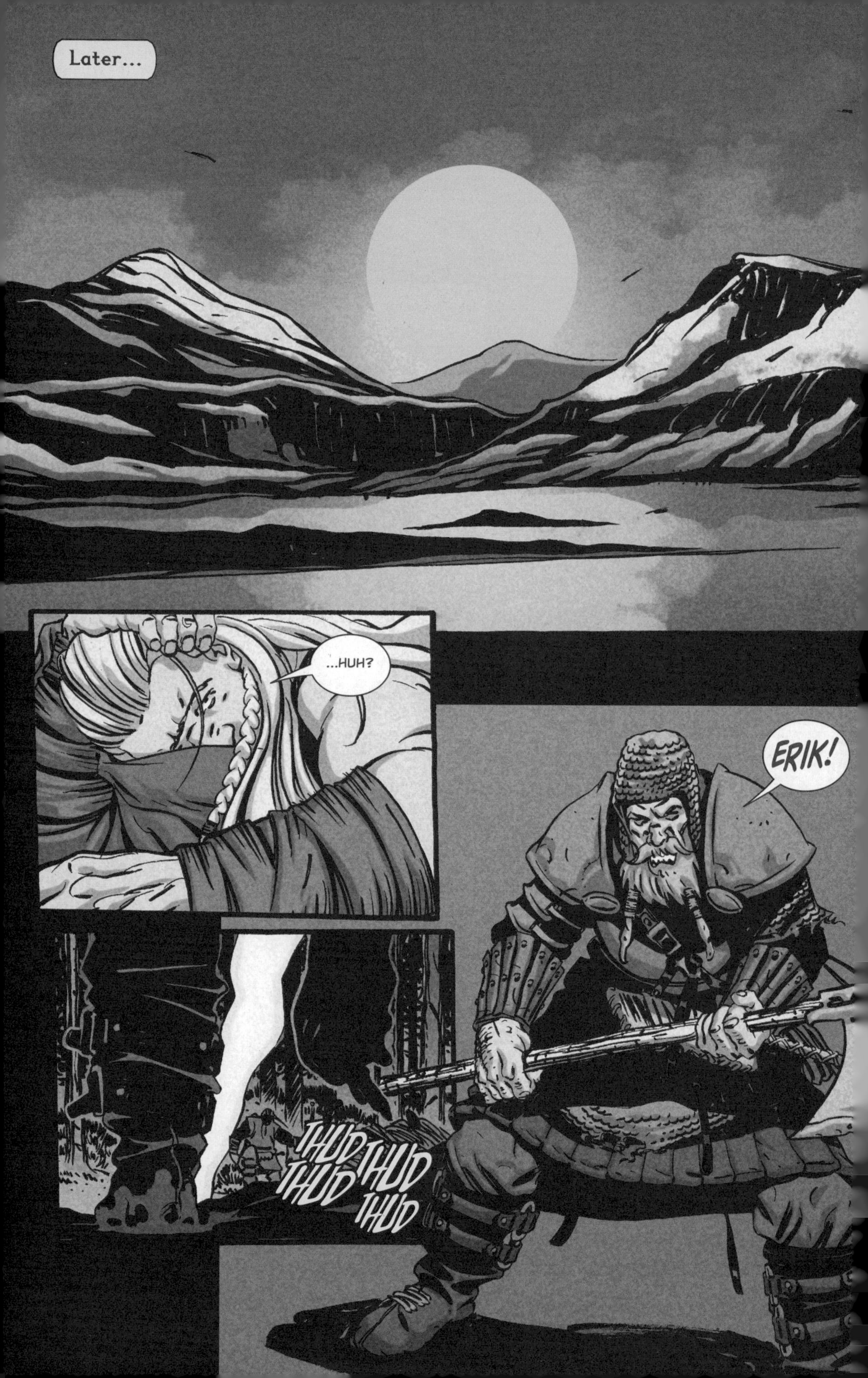
Later...
...HUH?
THUD THUD THUD THUD
ERIK!

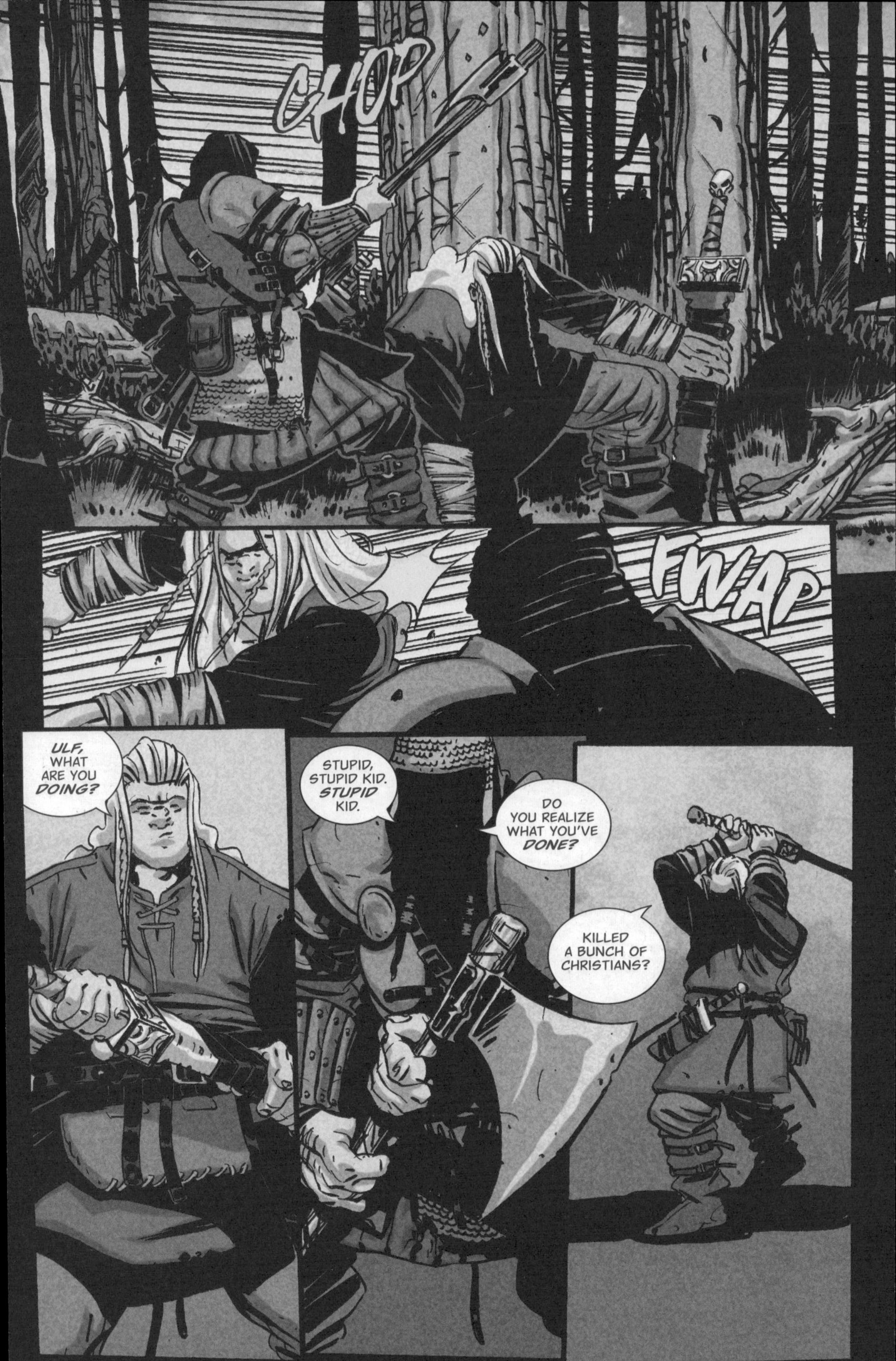
CHOP
FWAP
ULF, WHAT ARE YOU DOING?
STUPID, STUPID KID. STUPID KID.
DO YOU REALIZE WHAT YOU'VE DONE?
KILLED A BUNCH OF CHRISTIANS?

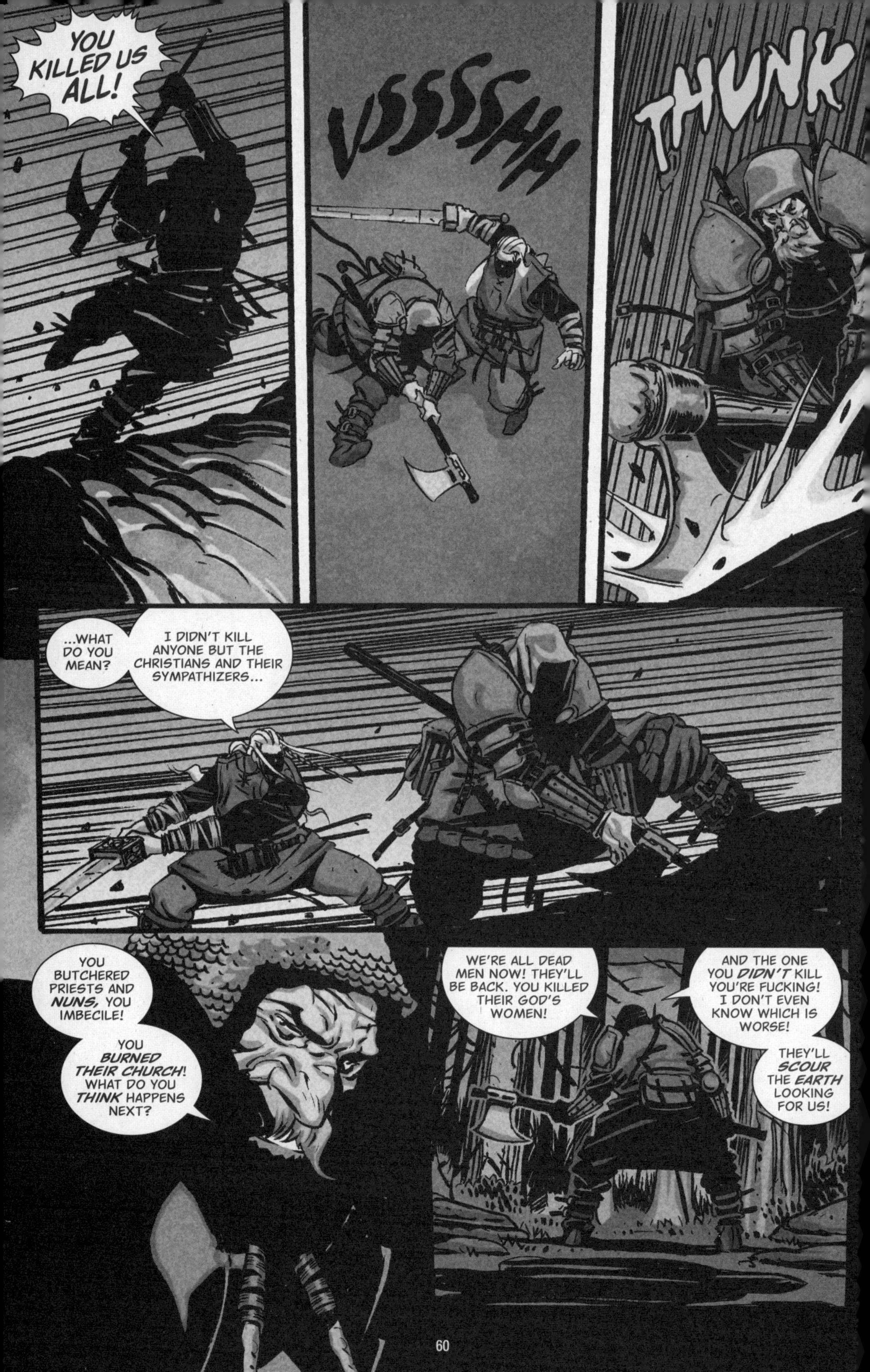
YOU KILLED US ALL!
VSSSSAHH
THUNK
...WHAT DO YOU MEAN?
I DIDN'T KILL ANYONE BUT THE CHRISTIANS AND THEIR SYMPATHIZERS...
YOU BUTCHERED PRIESTS AND *NUNS,* YOU IMBECILE!
YOU *BURNED THEIR CHURCH!* WHAT DO YOU *THINK* HAPPENS NEXT?
WE'RE ALL DEAD MEN NOW! THEY'LL BE BACK. YOU KILLED THEIR GOD'S WOMEN!
AND THE ONE YOU *DIDN'T* KILL YOU'RE FUCKING! I DON'T EVEN KNOW WHICH IS WORSE!
THEY'LL *SCOUR* THE *EARTH* LOOKING FOR US!

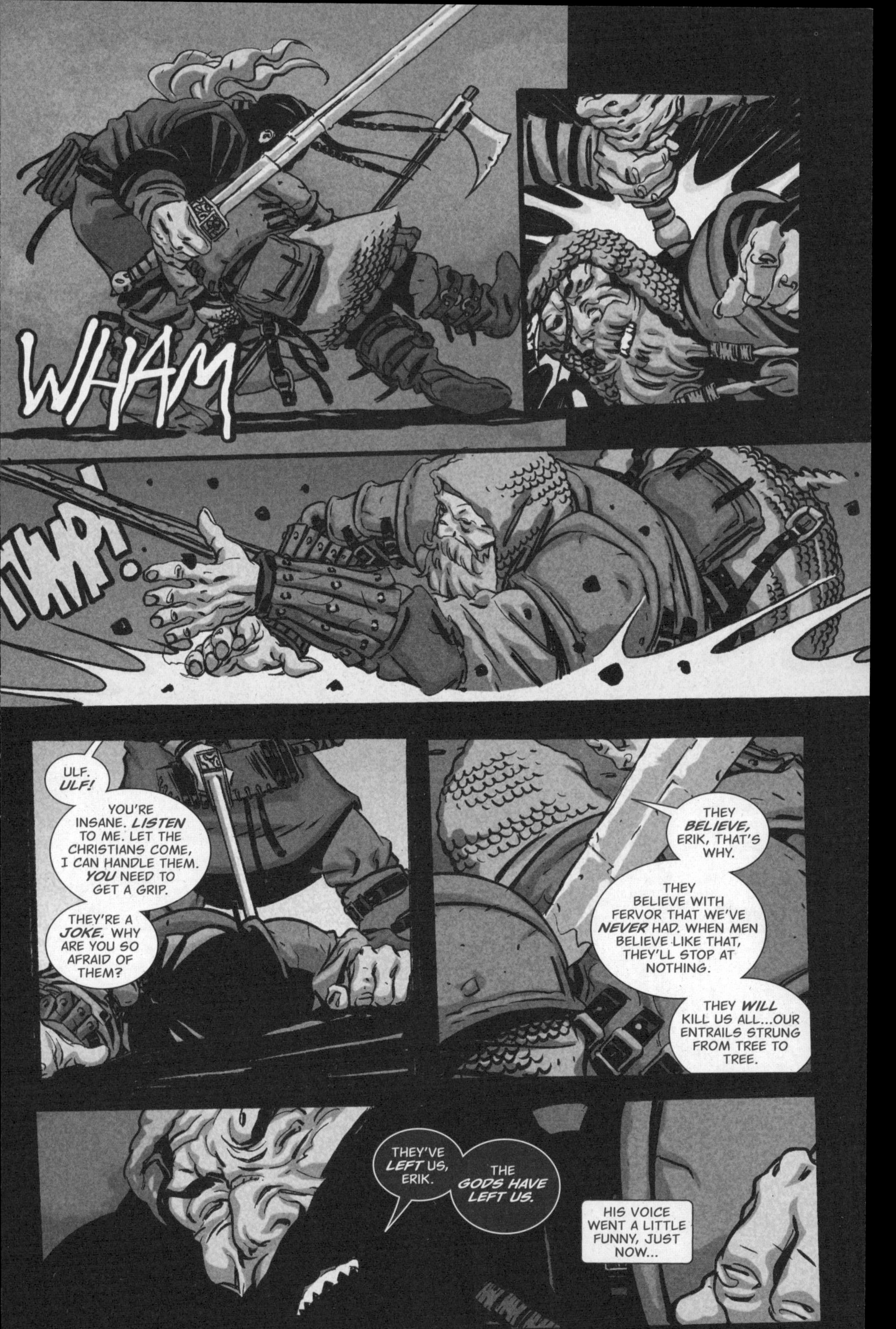

WHAM
THWP!
ULF. ULF!
YOU'RE INSANE. LISTEN TO ME. LET THE CHRISTIANS COME, I CAN HANDLE THEM. YOU NEED TO GET A GRIP.
THEY'RE A JOKE. WHY ARE YOU SO AFRAID OF THEM?
THEY BELIEVE, ERIK, THAT'S WHY.
THEY BELIEVE WITH FERVOR THAT WE'VE NEVER HAD. WHEN MEN BELIEVE LIKE THAT, THEY'LL STOP AT NOTHING.
THEY WILL KILL US ALL...OUR ENTRAILS STRUNG FROM TREE TO TREE.
THEY'VE LEFT US, ERIK.
THE GODS HAVE LEFT US.
HIS VOICE WENT A LITTLE FUNNY, JUST NOW...

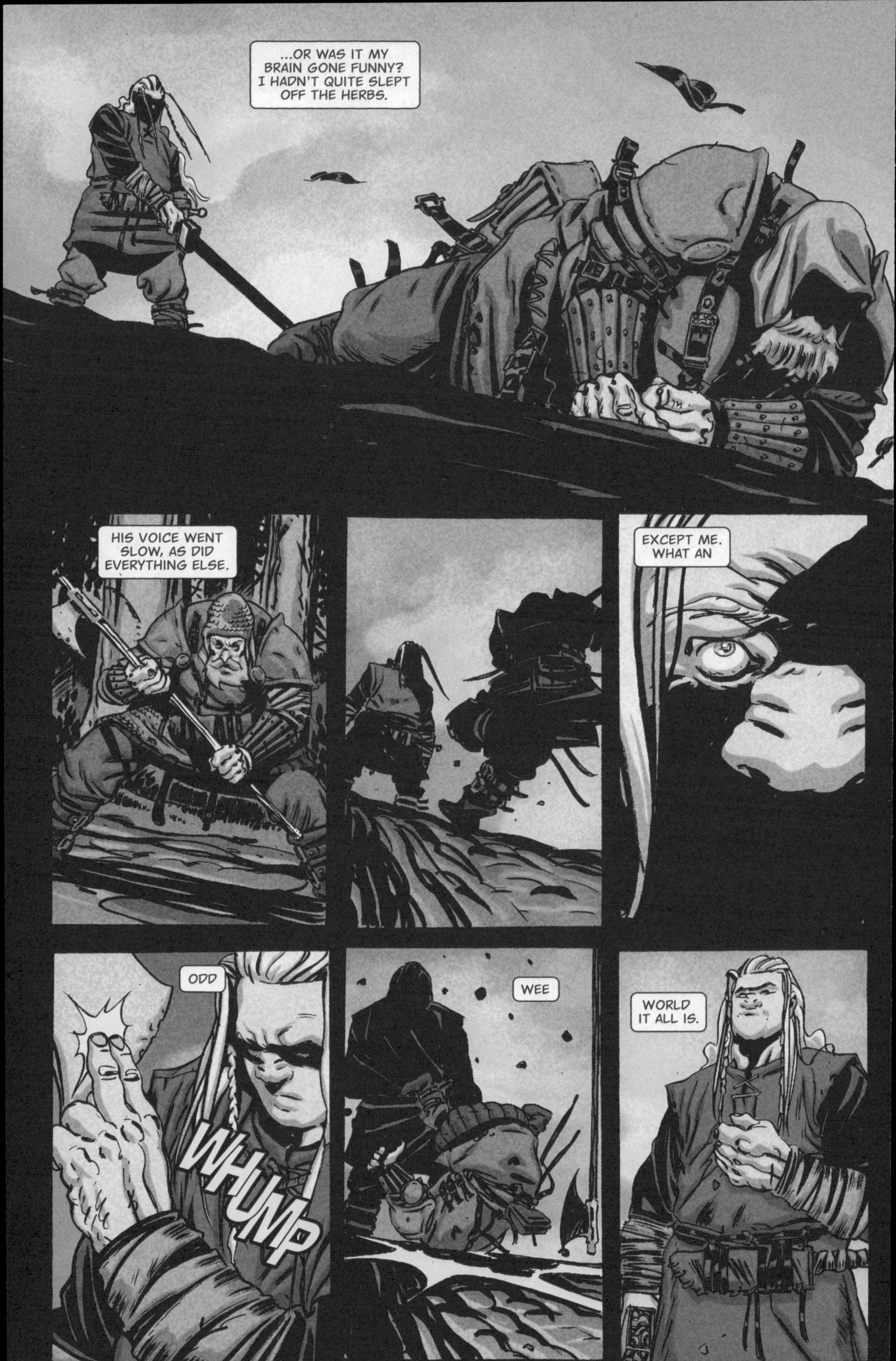
...OR WAS IT MY BRAIN GONE FUNNY? I HADN'T QUITE SLEPT OFF THE HERBS.
HIS VOICE WENT SLOW, AS DID EVERYTHING ELSE.
EXCEPT ME. WHAT AN
ODD
WHUMP
WEE
WORLD IT ALL IS.

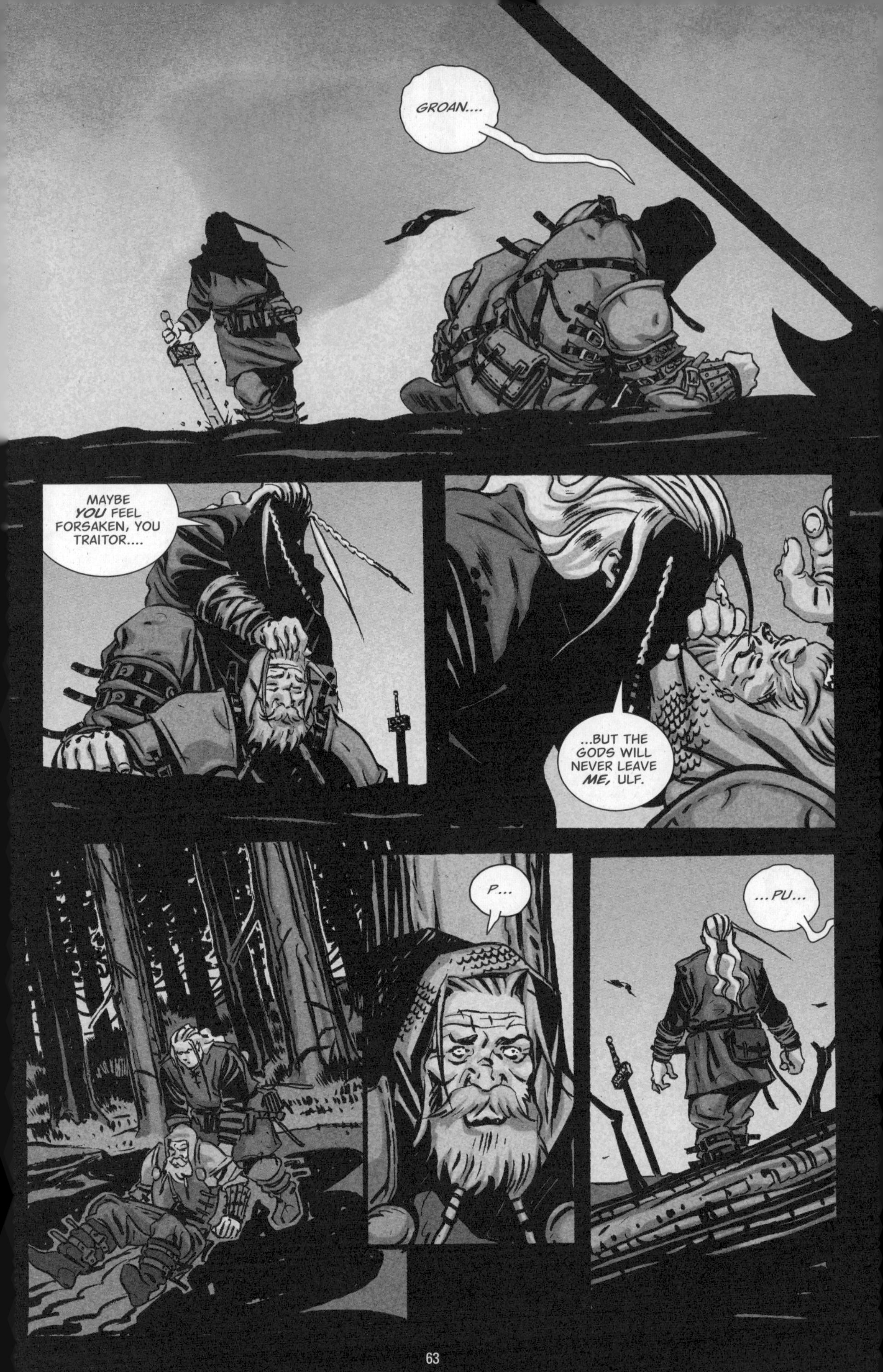
GROAN....
MAYBE YOU FEEL FORSAKEN, YOU TRAITOR....
...BUT THE GODS WILL NEVER LEAVE ME, ULF.
P...
...PU...

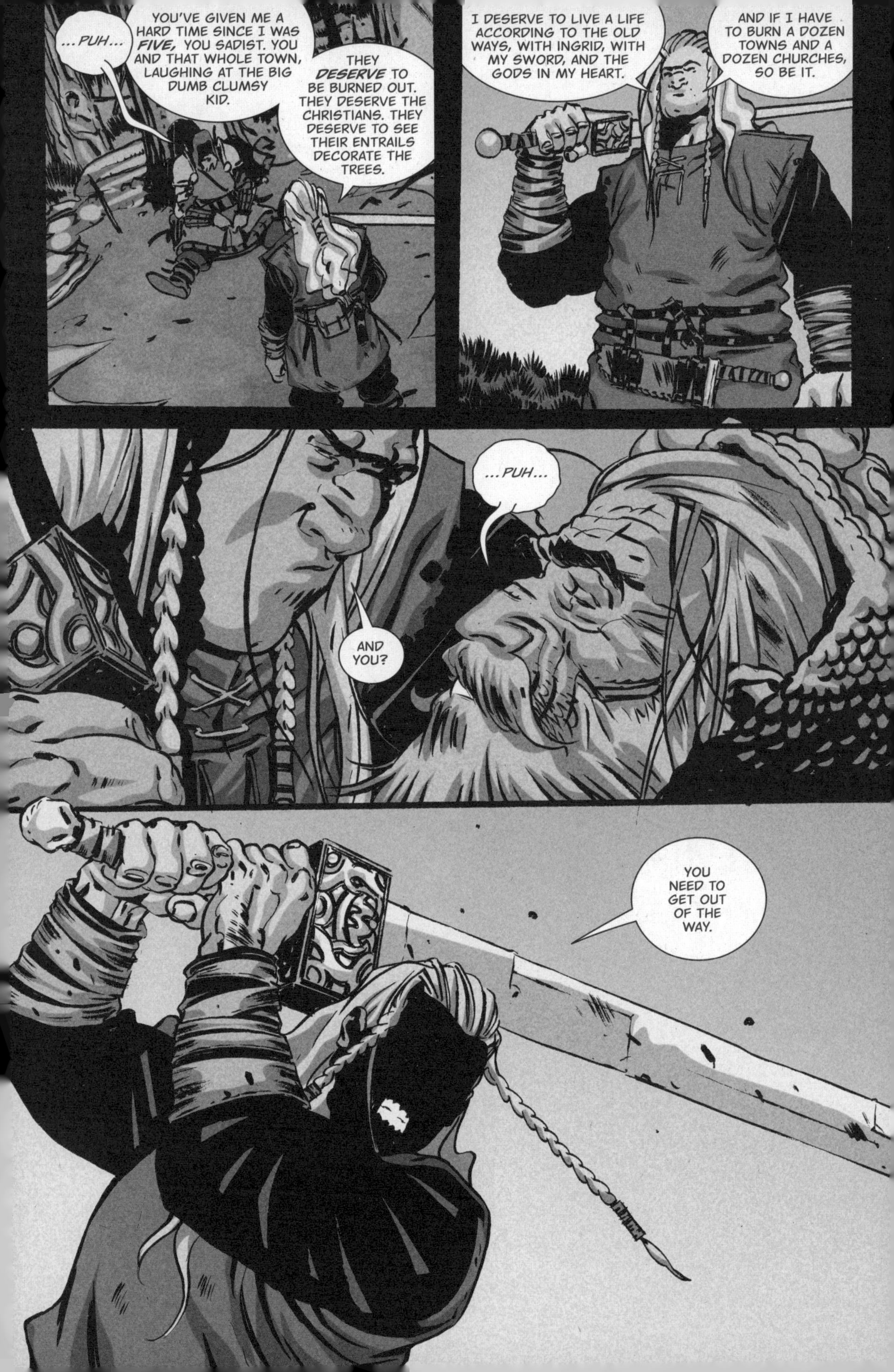
...PUH...
YOU'VE GIVEN ME A HARD TIME SINCE I WAS *FIVE,* YOU SADIST. YOU AND THAT WHOLE TOWN, LAUGHING AT THE BIG DUMB CLUMSY KID.
THEY *DESERVE* TO BE BURNED OUT. THEY DESERVE THE CHRISTIANS. THEY DESERVE TO SEE THEIR ENTRAILS DECORATE THE TREES.
I DESERVE TO LIVE A LIFE ACCORDING TO THE OLD WAYS, WITH INGRID, WITH MY SWORD, AND THE GODS IN MY HEART.
AND IF I HAVE TO BURN A DOZEN TOWNS AND A DOZEN CHURCHES, SO BE IT.
...PUH...
AND YOU?
YOU NEED TO GET OUT OF THE WAY.

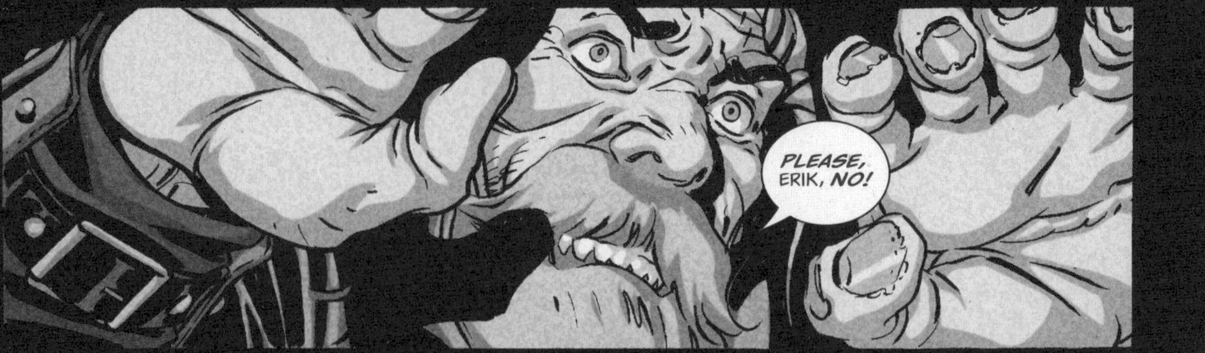
PLEASE, ERIK, NO!

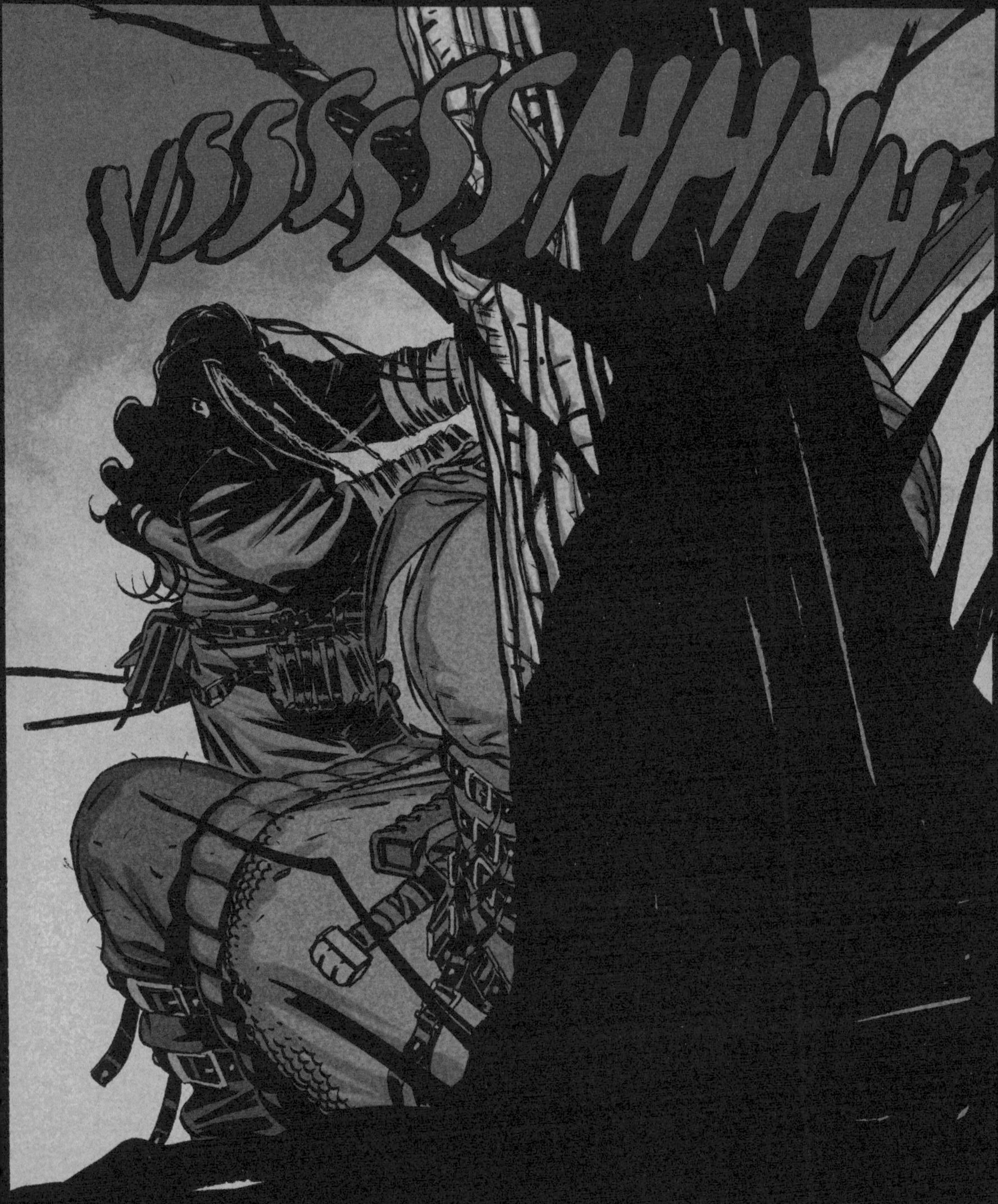
VSSSSSSHHHHH

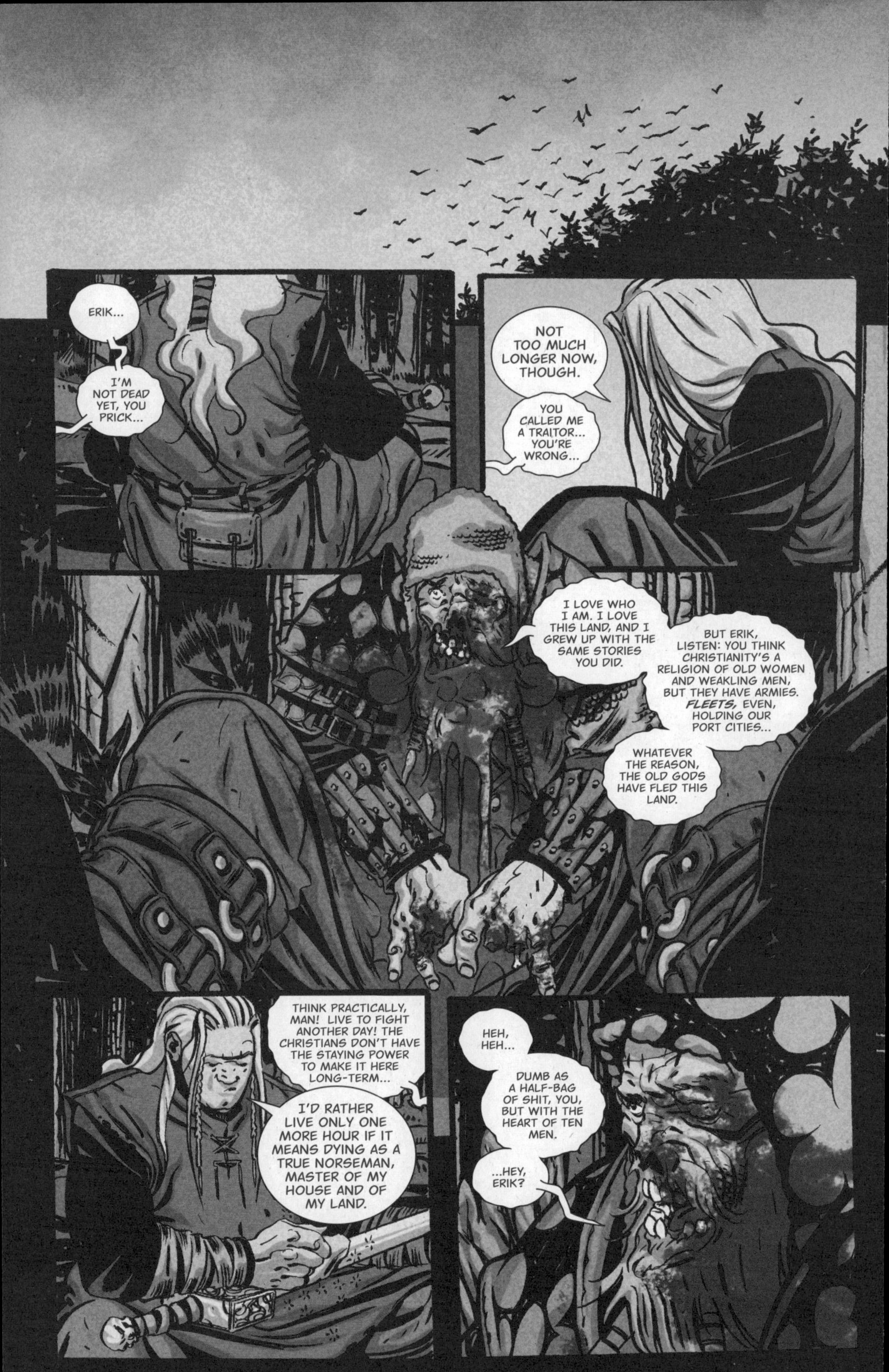
ERIK...
I'M NOT DEAD YET, YOU PRICK...
NOT TOO MUCH LONGER NOW, THOUGH.
YOU CALLED ME A TRAITOR... YOU'RE WRONG...
I LOVE WHO I AM. I LOVE THIS LAND, AND I GREW UP WITH THE SAME STORIES YOU DID.
BUT ERIK, LISTEN: YOU THINK CHRISTIANITY'S A RELIGION OF OLD WOMEN AND WEAKLING MEN, BUT THEY HAVE ARMIES. *FLEETS,* EVEN, HOLDING OUR PORT CITIES...
WHATEVER THE REASON, THE OLD GODS HAVE FLED THIS LAND.
THINK PRACTICALLY, MAN! LIVE TO FIGHT ANOTHER DAY! THE CHRISTIANS DON'T HAVE THE STAYING POWER TO MAKE IT HERE LONG-TERM...
I'D RATHER LIVE ONLY ONE MORE HOUR IF IT MEANS DYING AS A TRUE NORSEMAN, MASTER OF MY HOUSE AND OF MY LAND.
HEH, HEH...
DUMB AS A HALF-BAG OF SHIT, YOU, BUT WITH THE HEART OF TEN MEN.
...HEY, ERIK?

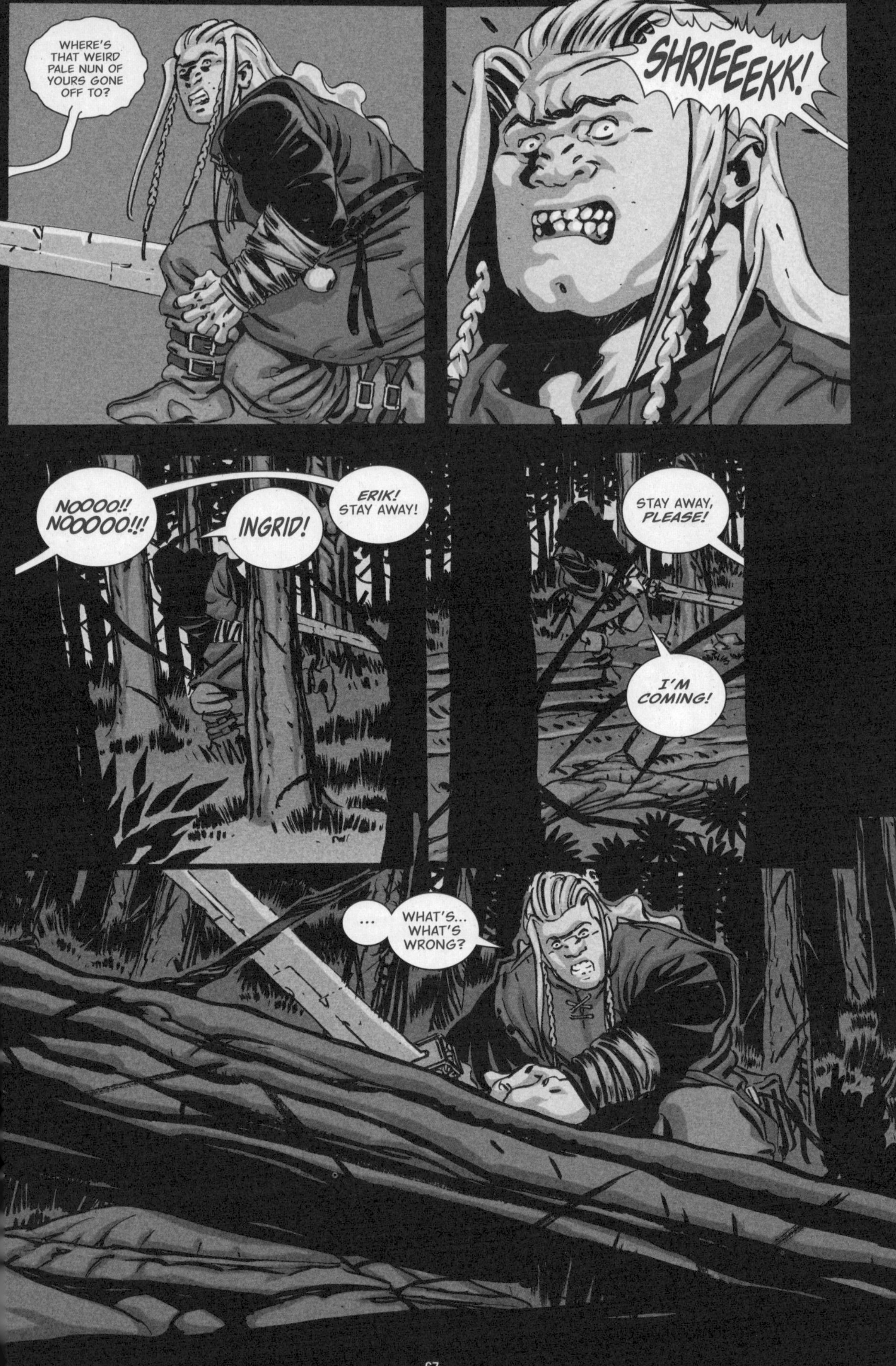
WHERE'S THAT WEIRD PALE NUN OF YOURS GONE OFF TO?
SHRIEEEKK!
NOOOO!! NOOOOO!!!
INGRID!
ERIK! STAY AWAY!
STAY AWAY, PLEASE!
I'M COMING!
...
WHAT'S... WHAT'S WRONG?

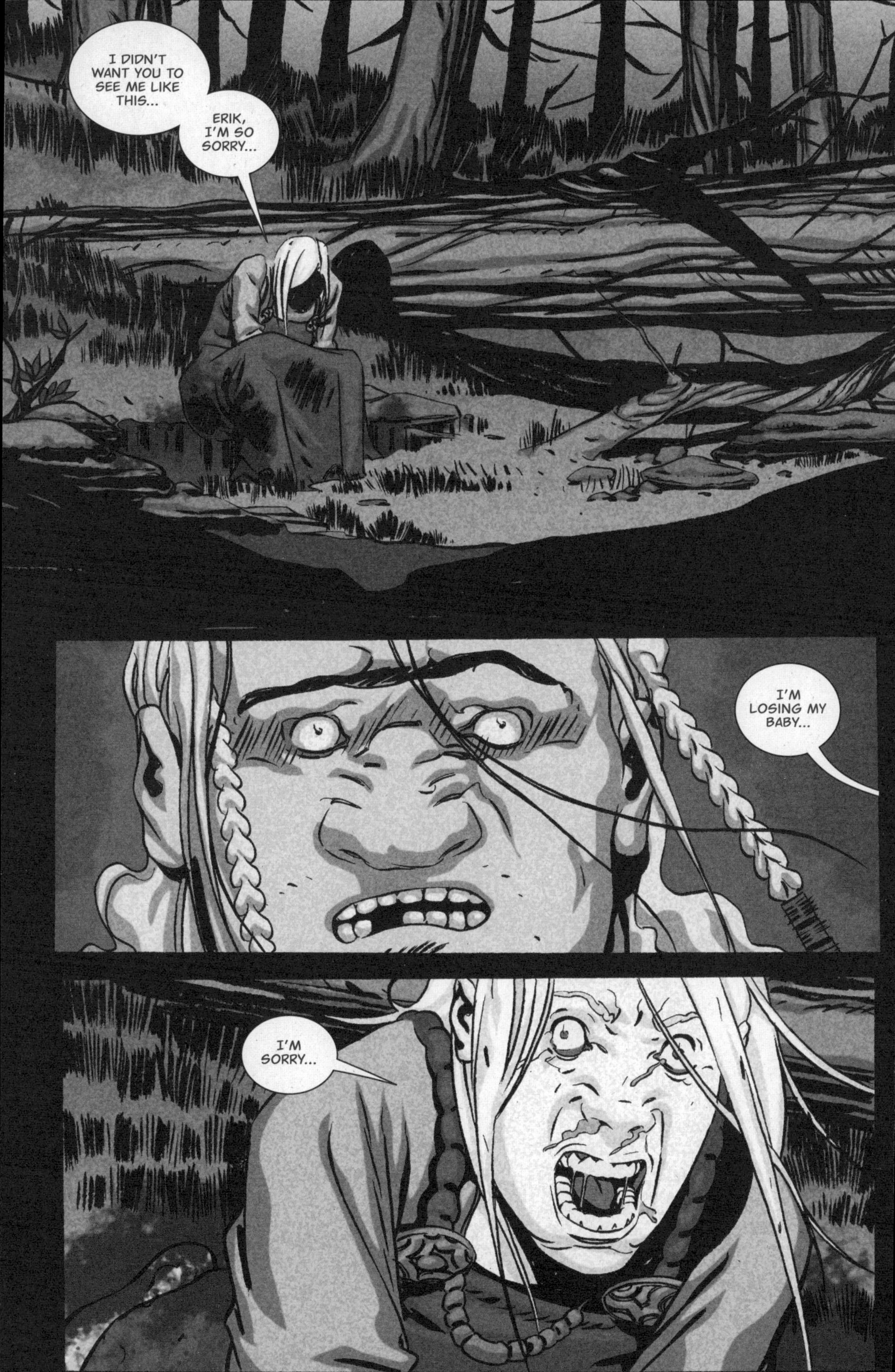
I DIDN'T WANT YOU TO SEE ME LIKE THIS...
ERIK, I'M SO SORRY...
I'M LOSING MY BABY...
I'M SORRY...

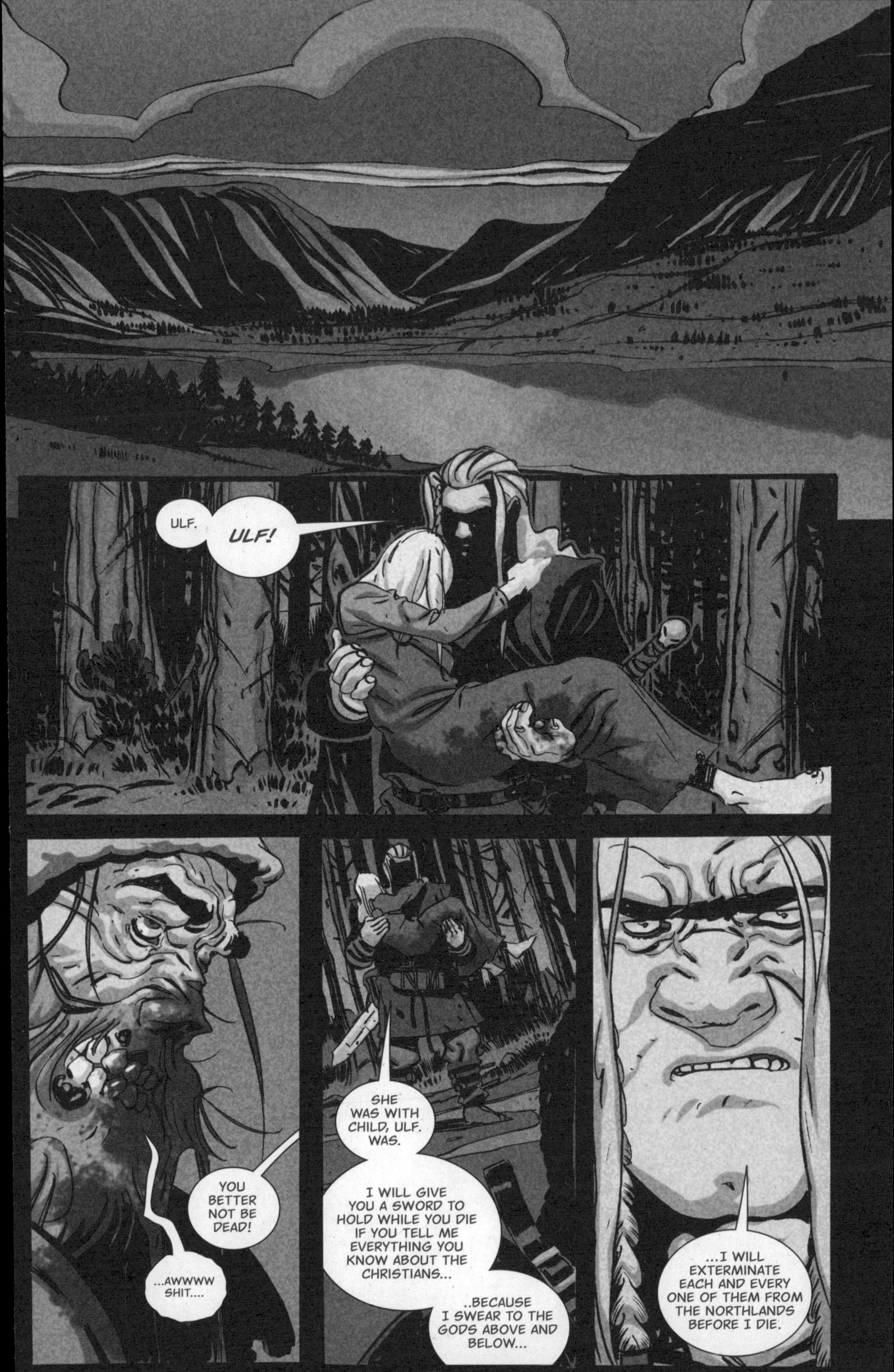
ULF.
ULF!
YOU BETTER NOT BE DEAD!
...AWWWW SHIT....
SHE WAS WITH CHILD, ULF. WAS.
I WILL GIVE YOU A SWORD TO HOLD WHILE YOU DIE IF YOU TELL ME EVERYTHING YOU KNOW ABOUT THE CHRISTIANS...
..BECAUSE I SWEAR TO THE GODS ABOVE AND BELOW...
...I WILL EXTERMINATE EACH AND EVERY ONE OF THEM FROM THE NORTHLANDS BEFORE I DIE.

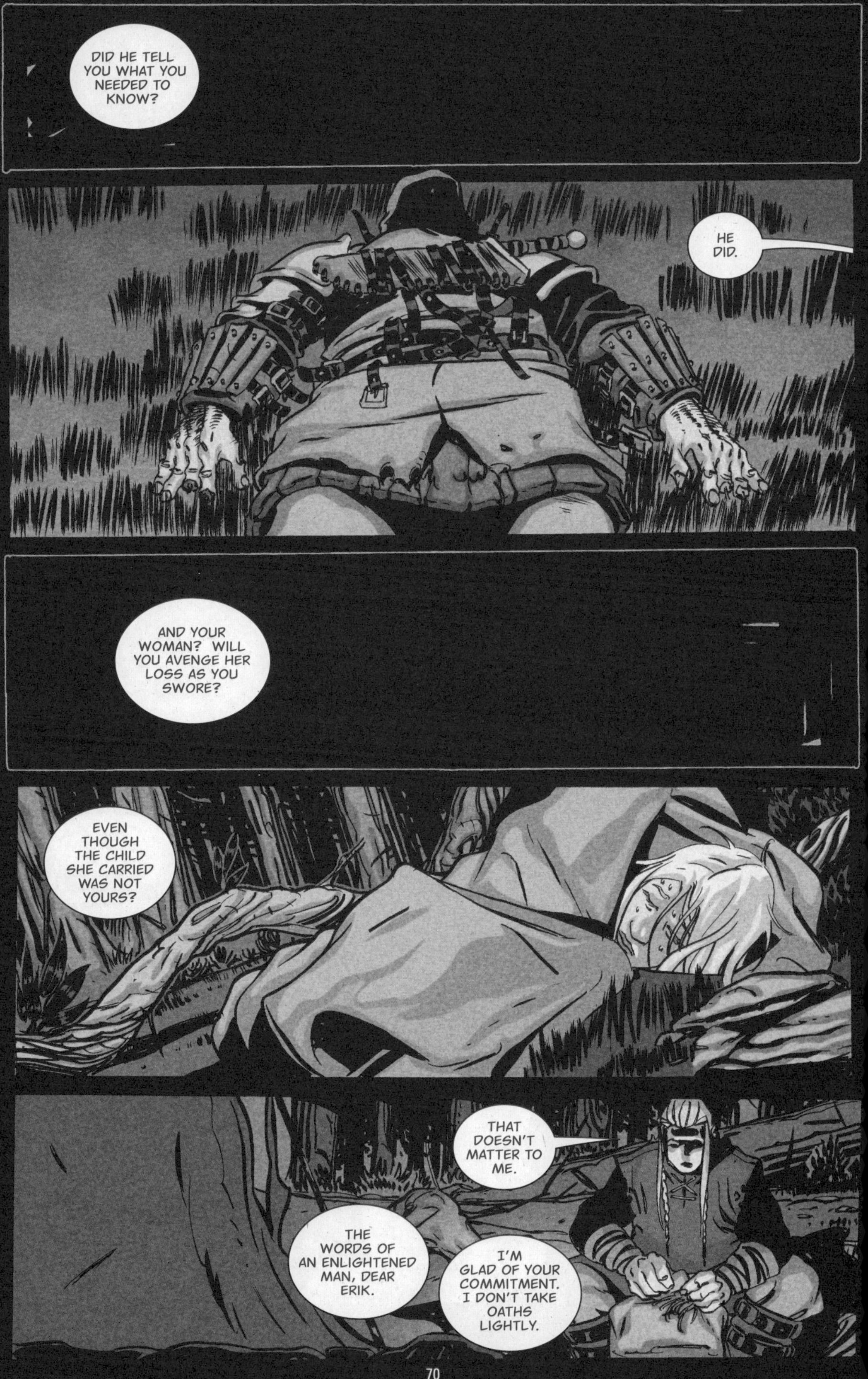
DID HE TELL YOU WHAT YOU NEEDED TO KNOW?
HE DID.
AND YOUR WOMAN? WILL YOU AVENGE HER LOSS AS YOU SWORE?
EVEN THOUGH THE CHILD SHE CARRIED WAS NOT YOURS?
THAT DOESN'T MATTER TO ME.
THE WORDS OF AN ENLIGHTENED MAN, DEAR ERIK.
I'M GLAD OF YOUR COMMITMENT. I DON'T TAKE OATHS LIGHTLY.

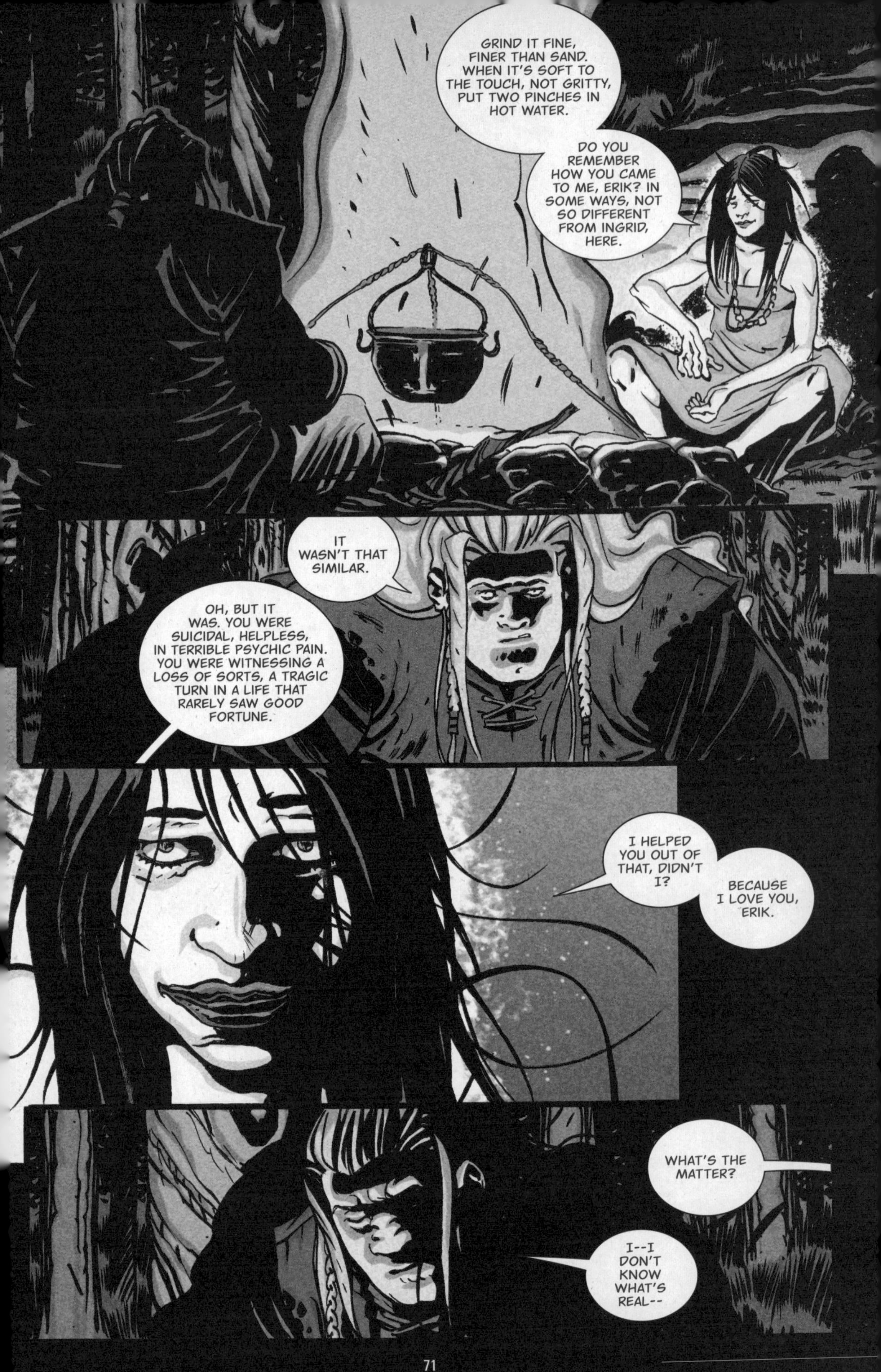
GRIND IT FINE, FINER THAN SAND. WHEN IT'S SOFT TO THE TOUCH, NOT GRITTY, PUT TWO PINCHES IN HOT WATER.
DO YOU REMEMBER HOW YOU CAME TO ME, ERIK? IN SOME WAYS, NOT SO DIFFERENT FROM INGRID, HERE.
IT WASN'T THAT SIMILAR.
OH, BUT IT WAS. YOU WERE SUICIDAL, HELPLESS, IN TERRIBLE PSYCHIC PAIN. YOU WERE WITNESSING A LOSS OF SORTS, A TRAGIC TURN IN A LIFE THAT RARELY SAW GOOD FORTUNE.
I HELPED YOU OUT OF THAT, DIDN'T I?
BECAUSE I LOVE YOU, ERIK.
WHAT'S THE MATTER?
I--I DON'T KNOW WHAT'S REAL--

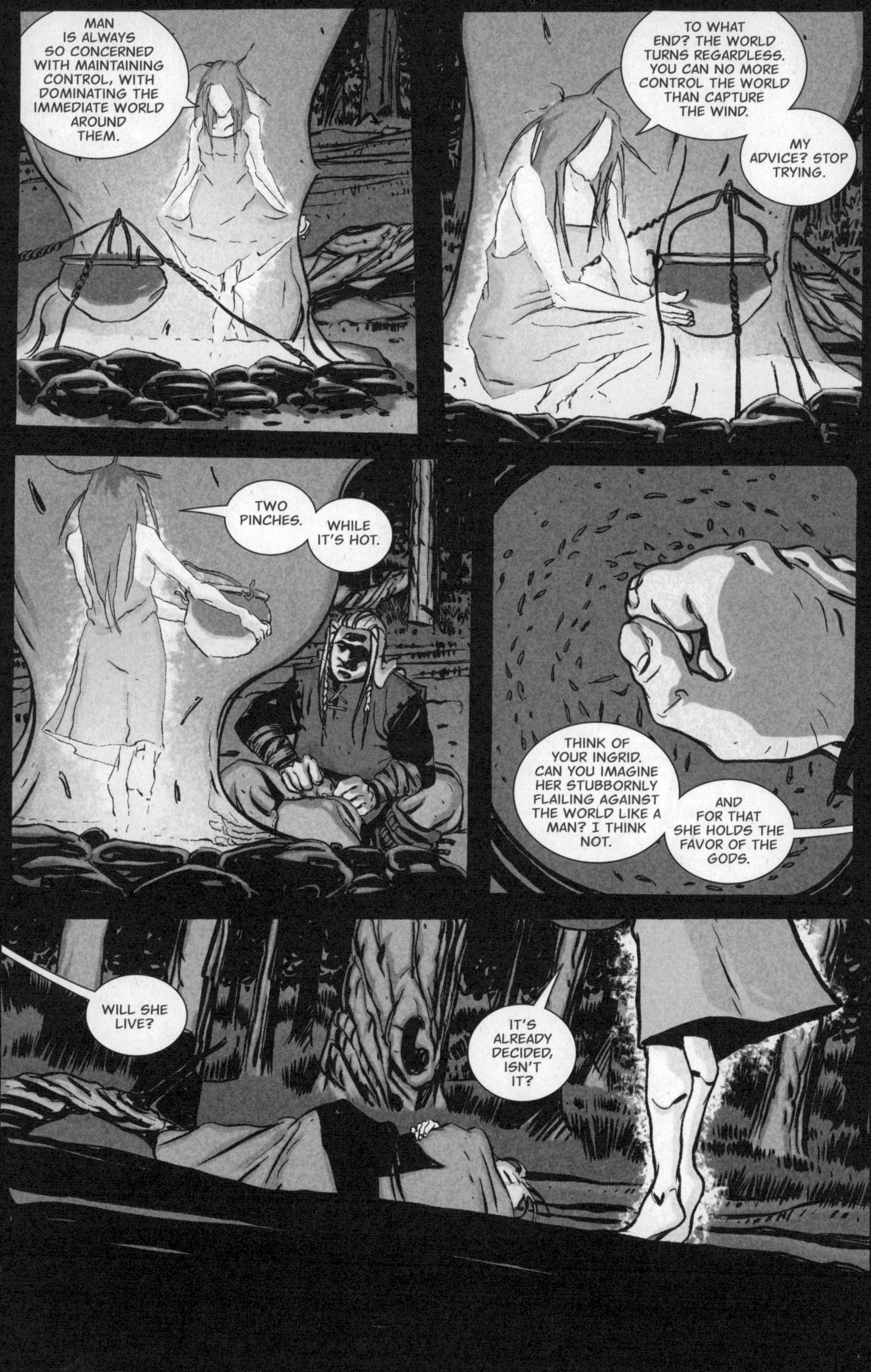
MAN IS ALWAYS SO CONCERNED WITH MAINTAINING CONTROL, WITH DOMINATING THE IMMEDIATE WORLD AROUND THEM.
TO WHAT END? THE WORLD TURNS REGARDLESS. YOU CAN NO MORE CONTROL THE WORLD THAN CAPTURE THE WIND.
MY ADVICE? STOP TRYING.
TWO PINCHES.
WHILE IT'S HOT.
THINK OF YOUR INGRID. CAN YOU IMAGINE HER STUBBORNLY FLAILING AGAINST THE WORLD LIKE A MAN? I THINK NOT.
AND FOR THAT SHE HOLDS THE FAVOR OF THE GODS.
WILL SHE LIVE?
IT'S ALREADY DECIDED, ISN'T IT?

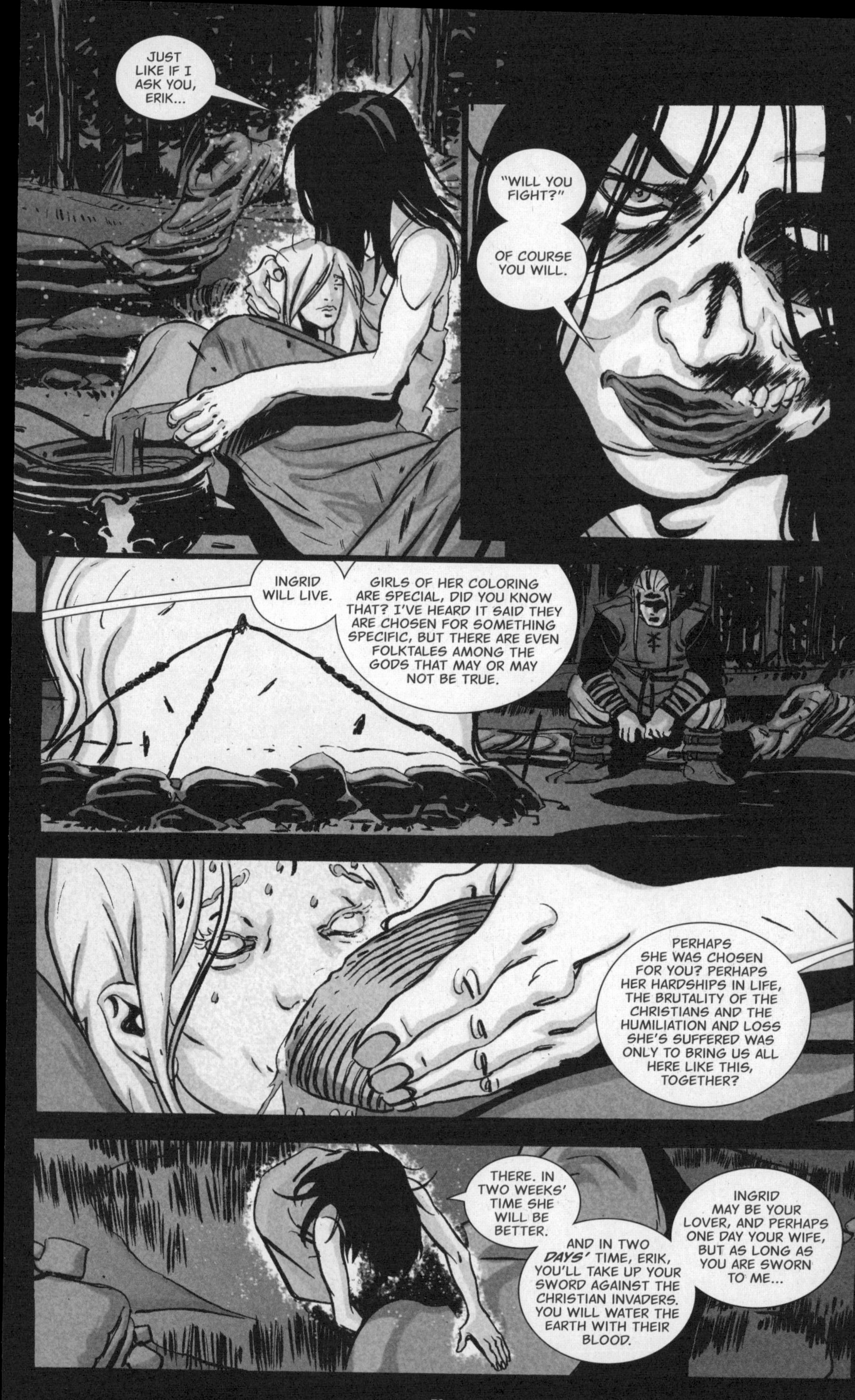
JUST LIKE IF I ASK YOU, ERIK...
"WILL YOU FIGHT?"
OF COURSE YOU WILL.
INGRID WILL LIVE.
GIRLS OF HER COLORING ARE SPECIAL, DID YOU KNOW THAT? I'VE HEARD IT SAID THEY ARE CHOSEN FOR SOMETHING SPECIFIC, BUT THERE ARE EVEN FOLKTALES AMONG THE GODS THAT MAY OR MAY NOT BE TRUE.
PERHAPS SHE WAS CHOSEN FOR YOU? PERHAPS HER HARDSHIPS IN LIFE, THE BRUTALITY OF THE CHRISTIANS AND THE HUMILIATION AND LOSS SHE'S SUFFERED WAS ONLY TO BRING US ALL HERE LIKE THIS, TOGETHER?
THERE. IN TWO WEEKS' TIME SHE WILL BE BETTER.
AND IN TWO *DAYS'* TIME, ERIK, YOU'LL TAKE UP YOUR SWORD AGAINST THE CHRISTIAN INVADERS. YOU WILL WATER THE EARTH WITH THEIR BLOOD.
INGRID MAY BE YOUR LOVER, AND PERHAPS ONE DAY YOUR WIFE, BUT AS LONG AS YOU ARE SWORN TO ME...

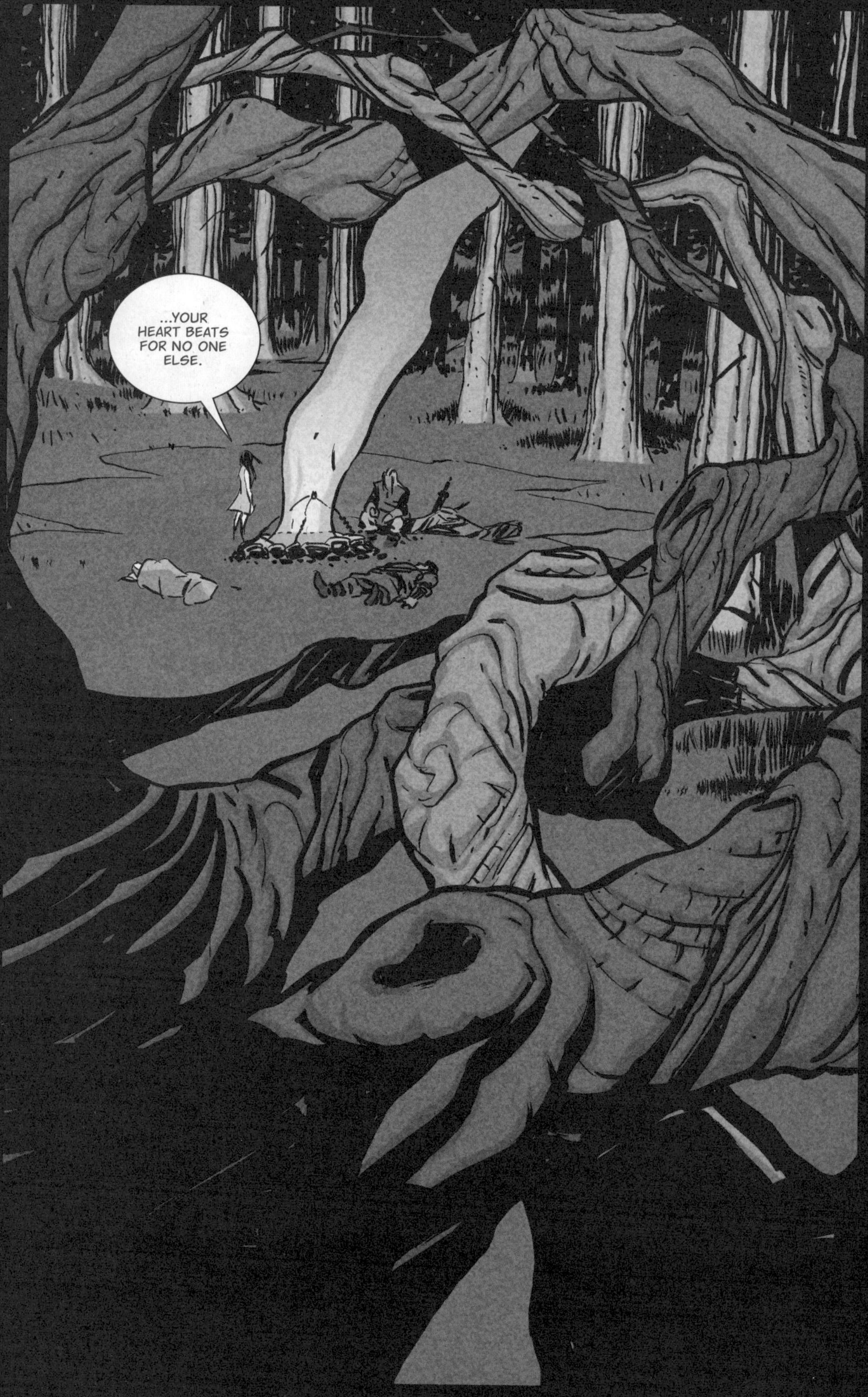
...YOUR HEART BEATS FOR NO ONE ELSE.

Metal Part Three: Holy War

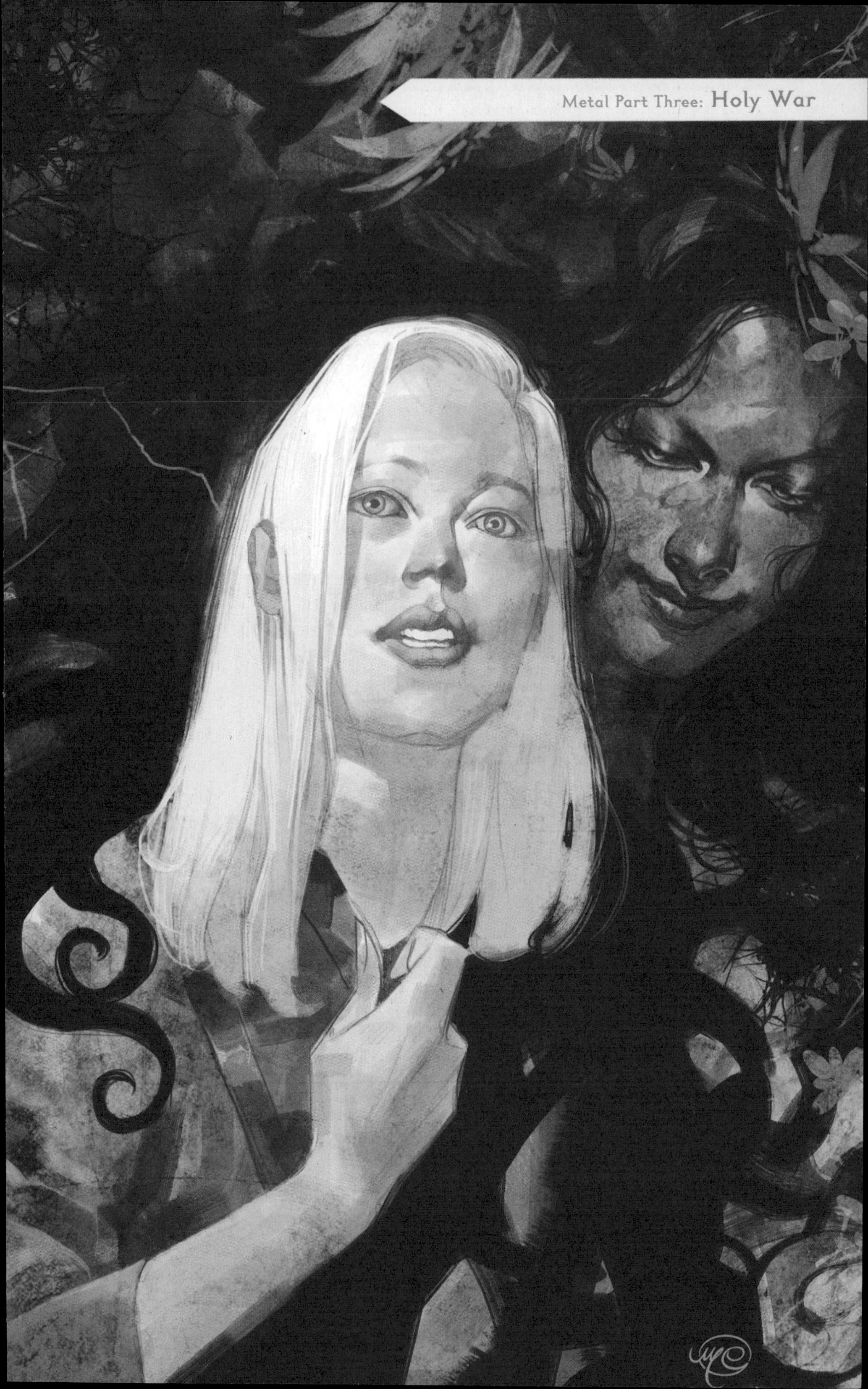

MY LORD! YOU CANNOT TREAT THE DEAD LIKE THAT! EVEN IN DEATH, THEY ARE GOD'S PRECIOUS CHILDREN!
THEY MUST BE PRAYED OVER, BLESSED, THEIR SOULS PURIFIED BEFORE THEY CAN BE WELCOMED INTO HIS HOLY CELESTIAL BOSOM!
IT'S JUST NOT *RIGHT!*
YOU'RE A *PRIEST.*
YOU CAN *MAKE* IT RIGHT.
AHEM...
KRNCH
KRNCH KRNCH KRNCH

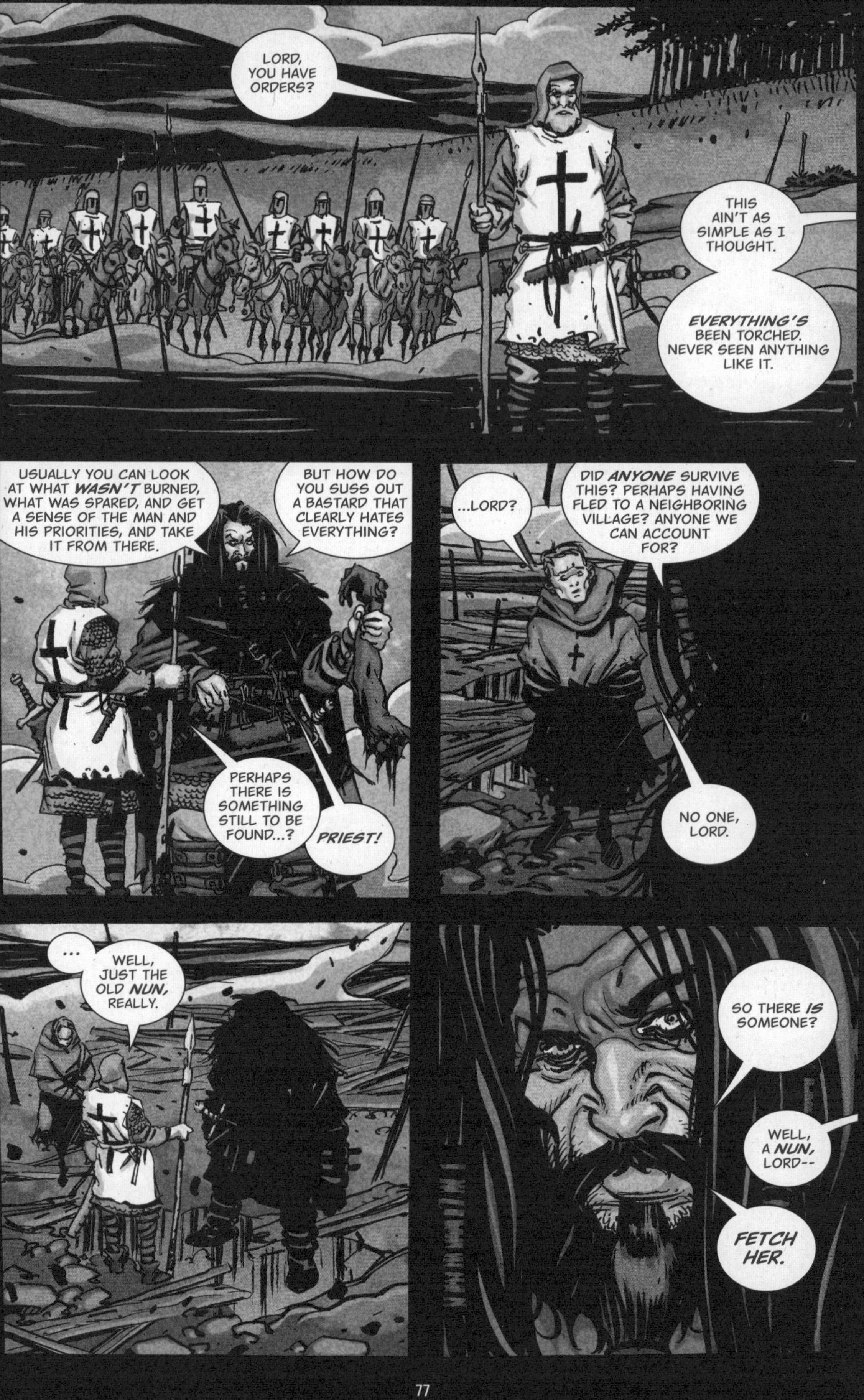

LORD, YOU HAVE ORDERS?
THIS AIN'T AS SIMPLE AS I THOUGHT.
EVERYTHING'S BEEN TORCHED. NEVER SEEN ANYTHING LIKE IT.
USUALLY YOU CAN LOOK AT WHAT WASN'T BURNED, WHAT WAS SPARED, AND GET A SENSE OF THE MAN AND HIS PRIORITIES, AND TAKE IT FROM THERE.
BUT HOW DO YOU SUSS OUT A BASTARD THAT CLEARLY HATES EVERYTHING?
PERHAPS THERE IS SOMETHING STILL TO BE FOUND...?
PRIEST!
...LORD?
DID ANYONE SURVIVE THIS? PERHAPS HAVING FLED TO A NEIGHBORING VILLAGE? ANYONE WE CAN ACCOUNT FOR?
NO ONE, LORD.
...
WELL, JUST THE OLD NUN, REALLY.
SO THERE IS SOMEONE?
WELL, A NUN, LORD--
FETCH HER.

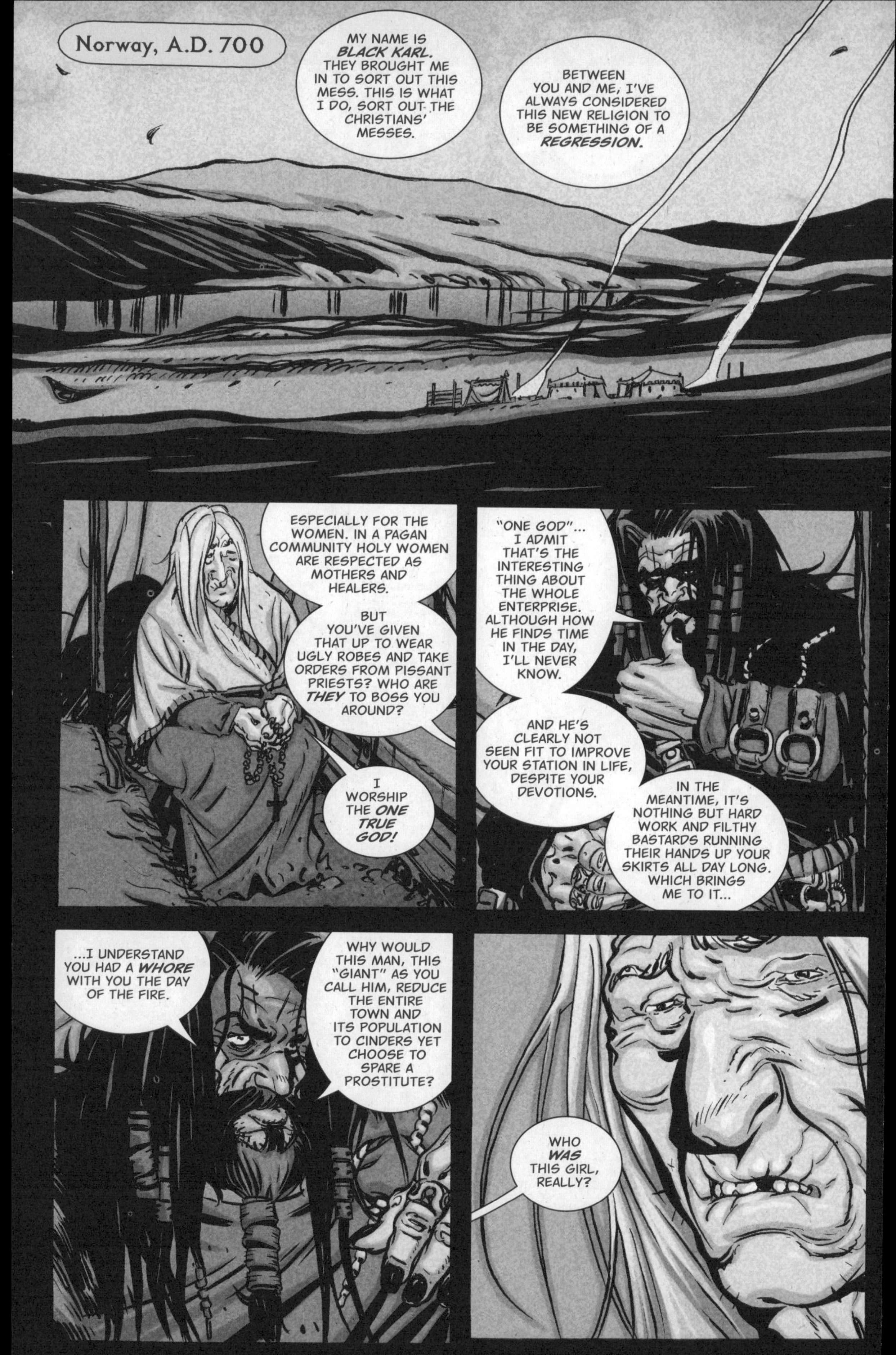

Norway, A.D. 700
MY NAME IS BLACK KARL. THEY BROUGHT ME IN TO SORT OUT THIS MESS. THIS IS WHAT I DO, SORT OUT THE CHRISTIANS' MESSES.
BETWEEN YOU AND ME, I'VE ALWAYS CONSIDERED THIS NEW RELIGION TO BE SOMETHING OF A REGRESSION.
ESPECIALLY FOR THE WOMEN. IN A PAGAN COMMUNITY HOLY WOMEN ARE RESPECTED AS MOTHERS AND HEALERS.
BUT YOU'VE GIVEN THAT UP TO WEAR UGLY ROBES AND TAKE ORDERS FROM PISSANT PRIESTS? WHO ARE THEY TO BOSS YOU AROUND?
I WORSHIP THE ONE TRUE GOD!
"ONE GOD"... I ADMIT THAT'S THE INTERESTING THING ABOUT THE WHOLE ENTERPRISE. ALTHOUGH HOW HE FINDS TIME IN THE DAY, I'LL NEVER KNOW.
AND HE'S CLEARLY NOT SEEN FIT TO IMPROVE YOUR STATION IN LIFE, DESPITE YOUR DEVOTIONS.
IN THE MEANTIME, IT'S NOTHING BUT HARD WORK AND FILTHY BASTARDS RUNNING THEIR HANDS UP YOUR SKIRTS ALL DAY LONG. WHICH BRINGS ME TO IT...
...I UNDERSTAND YOU HAD A WHORE WITH YOU THE DAY OF THE FIRE.
WHY WOULD THIS MAN, THIS "GIANT" AS YOU CALL HIM, REDUCE THE ENTIRE TOWN AND ITS POPULATION TO CINDERS YET CHOOSE TO SPARE A PROSTITUTE?
WHO WAS THIS GIRL, REALLY?

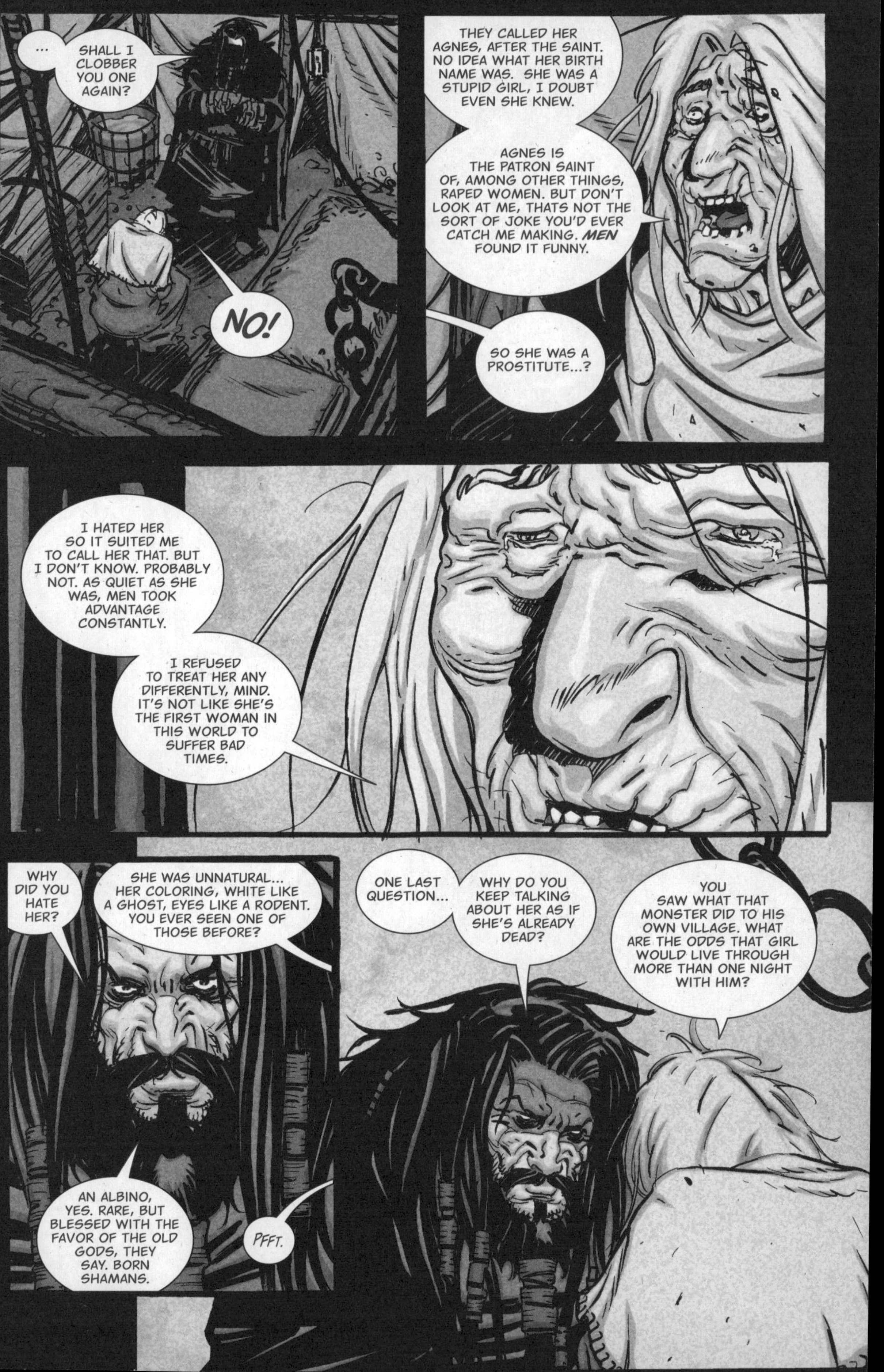
...
SHALL I CLOBBER YOU ONE AGAIN?
NO!
THEY CALLED HER AGNES, AFTER THE SAINT. NO IDEA WHAT HER BIRTH NAME WAS. SHE WAS A STUPID GIRL, I DOUBT EVEN SHE KNEW.
AGNES IS THE PATRON SAINT OF, AMONG OTHER THINGS, RAPED WOMEN. BUT DON'T LOOK AT ME, THATS NOT THE SORT OF JOKE YOU'D EVER CATCH ME MAKING. MEN FOUND IT FUNNY.
SO SHE WAS A PROSTITUTE...?
I HATED HER SO IT SUITED ME TO CALL HER THAT. BUT I DON'T KNOW. PROBABLY NOT. AS QUIET AS SHE WAS, MEN TOOK ADVANTAGE CONSTANTLY.
I REFUSED TO TREAT HER ANY DIFFERENTLY, MIND. IT'S NOT LIKE SHE'S THE FIRST WOMAN IN THIS WORLD TO SUFFER BAD TIMES.
WHY DID YOU HATE HER?
SHE WAS UNNATURAL... HER COLORING, WHITE LIKE A GHOST, EYES LIKE A RODENT. YOU EVER SEEN ONE OF THOSE BEFORE?
AN ALBINO, YES. RARE, BUT BLESSED WITH THE FAVOR OF THE OLD GODS, THEY SAY. BORN SHAMANS.
PFFT.
ONE LAST QUESTION...
WHY DO YOU KEEP TALKING ABOUT HER AS IF SHE'S ALREADY DEAD?
YOU SAW WHAT THAT MONSTER DID TO HIS OWN VILLAGE. WHAT ARE THE ODDS THAT GIRL WOULD LIVE THROUGH MORE THAN ONE NIGHT WITH HIM?

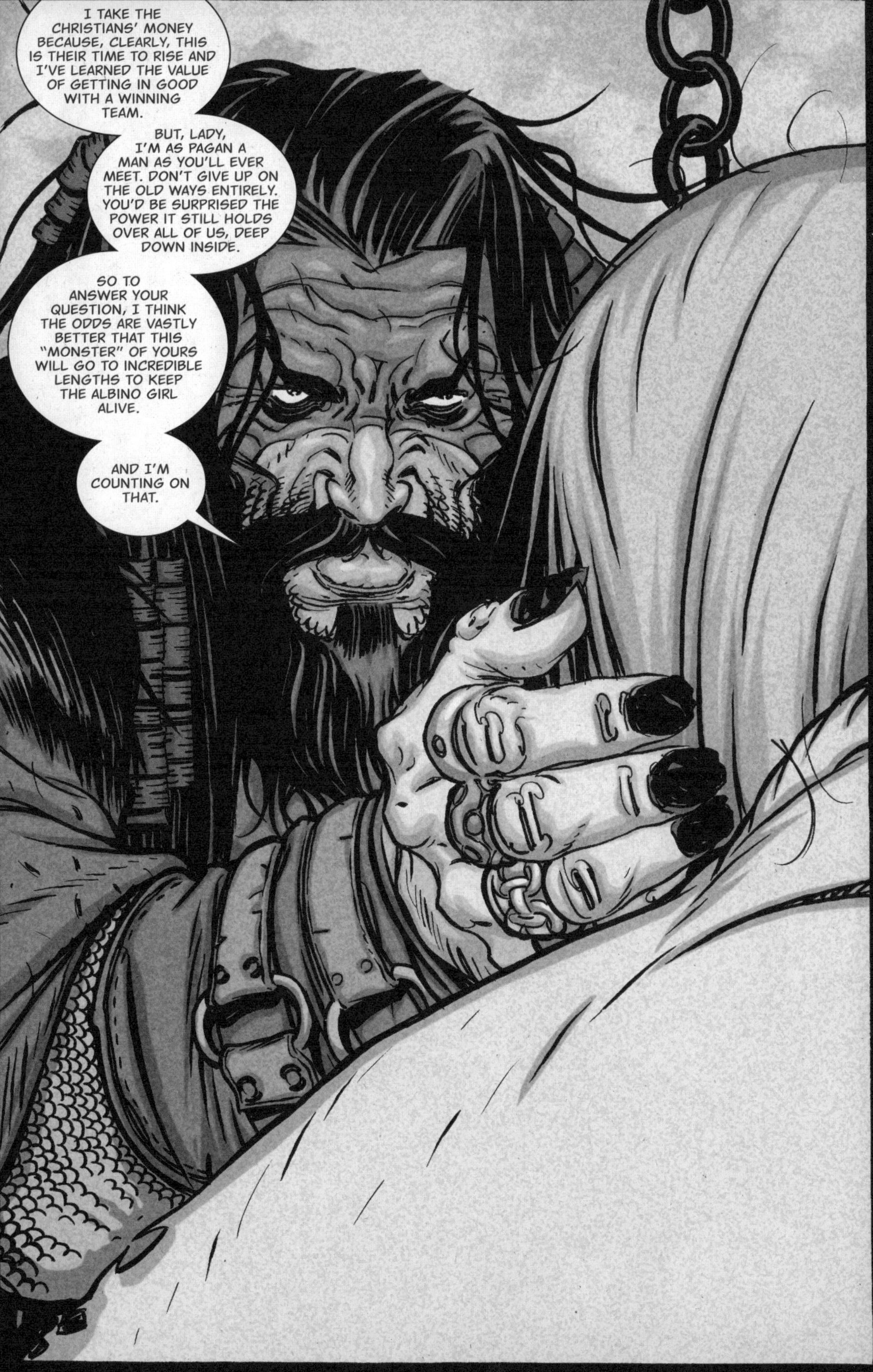
I TAKE THE CHRISTIANS' MONEY BECAUSE, CLEARLY, THIS IS THEIR TIME TO RISE AND I'VE LEARNED THE VALUE OF GETTING IN GOOD WITH A WINNING TEAM.
BUT, LADY, I'M AS PAGAN A MAN AS YOU'LL EVER MEET. DON'T GIVE UP ON THE OLD WAYS ENTIRELY. YOU'D BE SURPRISED THE POWER IT STILL HOLDS OVER ALL OF US, DEEP DOWN INSIDE.
SO TO ANSWER YOUR QUESTION, I THINK THE ODDS ARE VASTLY BETTER THAT THIS "MONSTER" OF YOURS WILL GO TO INCREDIBLE LENGTHS TO KEEP THE ALBINO GIRL ALIVE.
AND I'M COUNTING ON THAT.

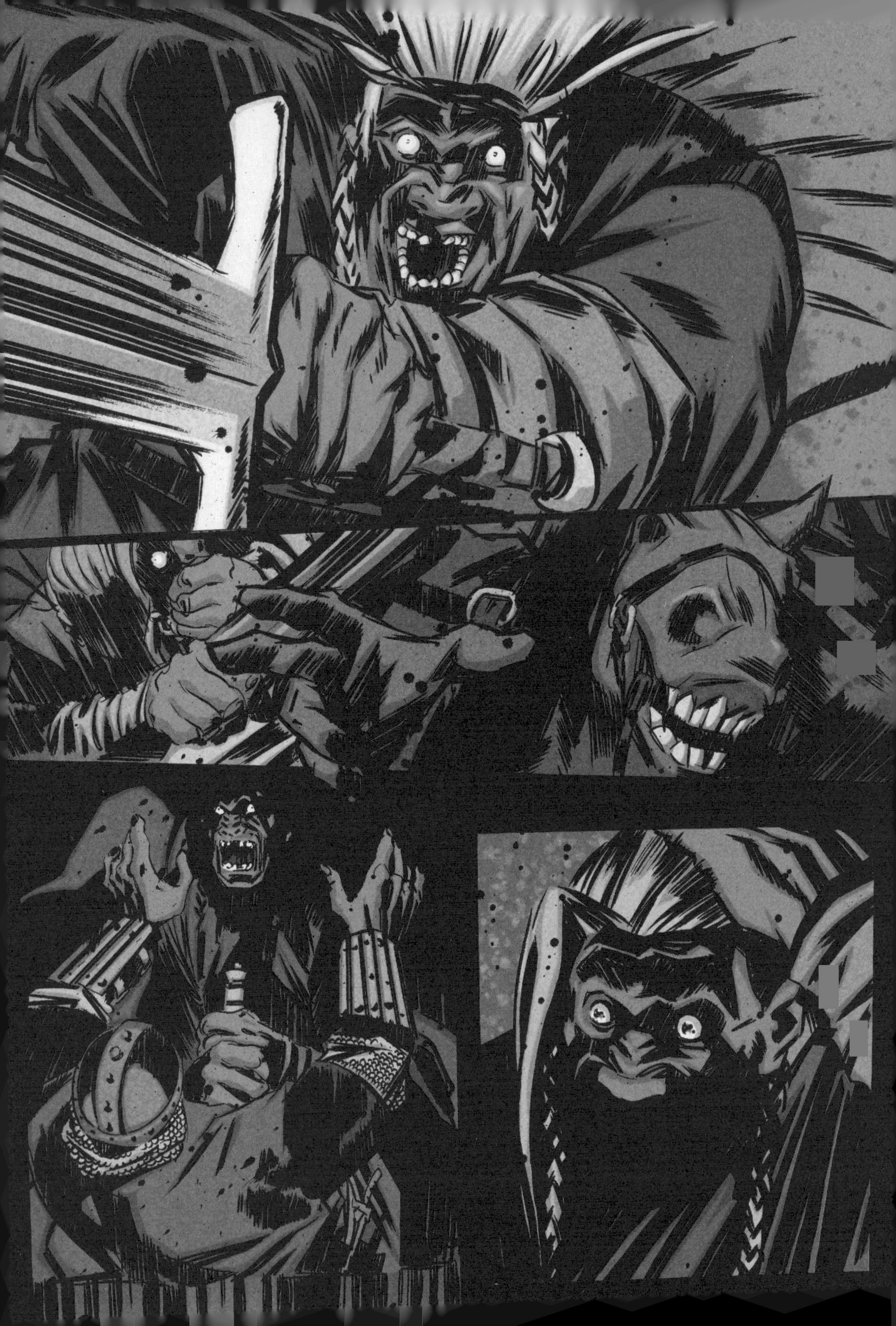

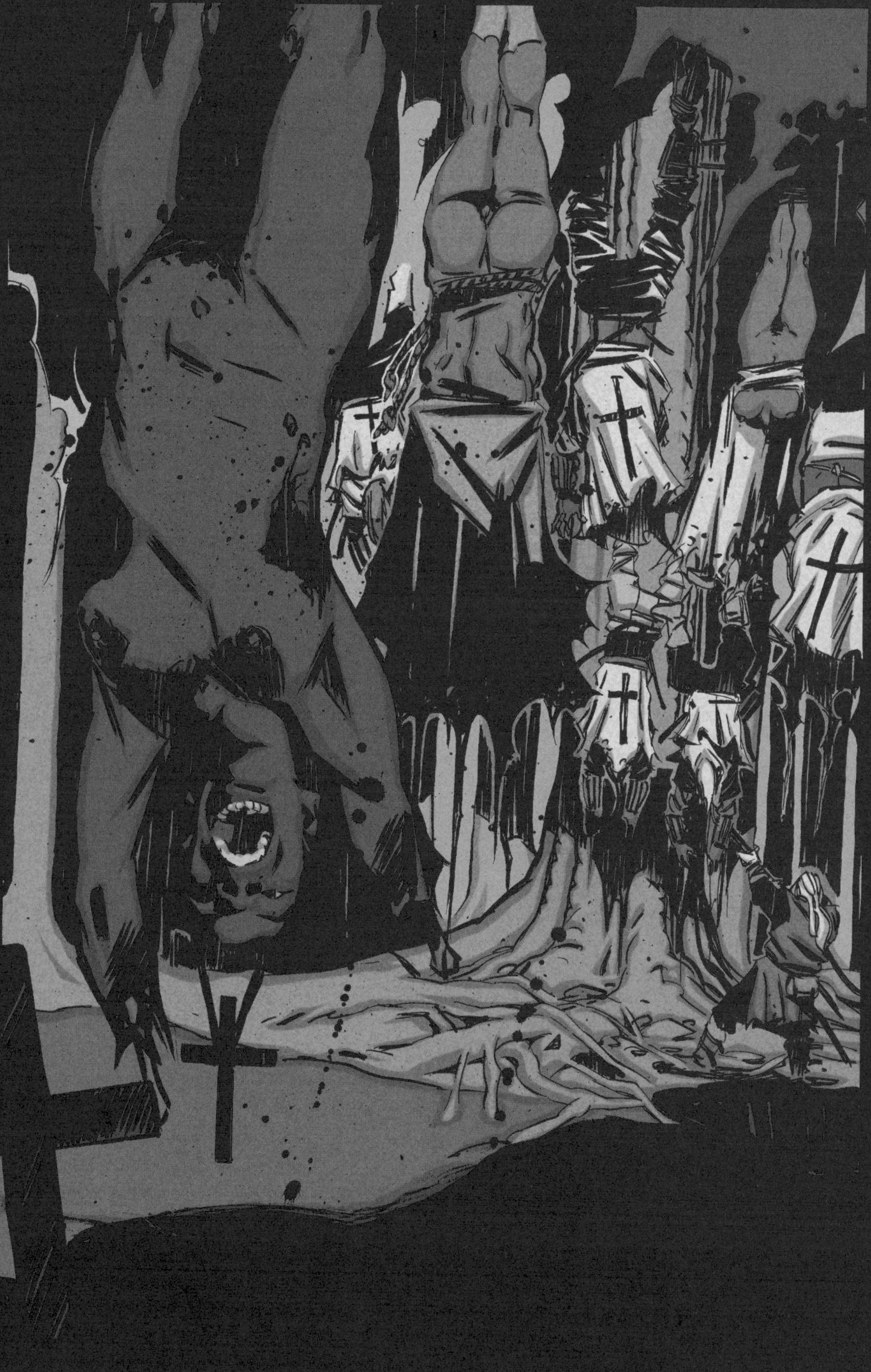

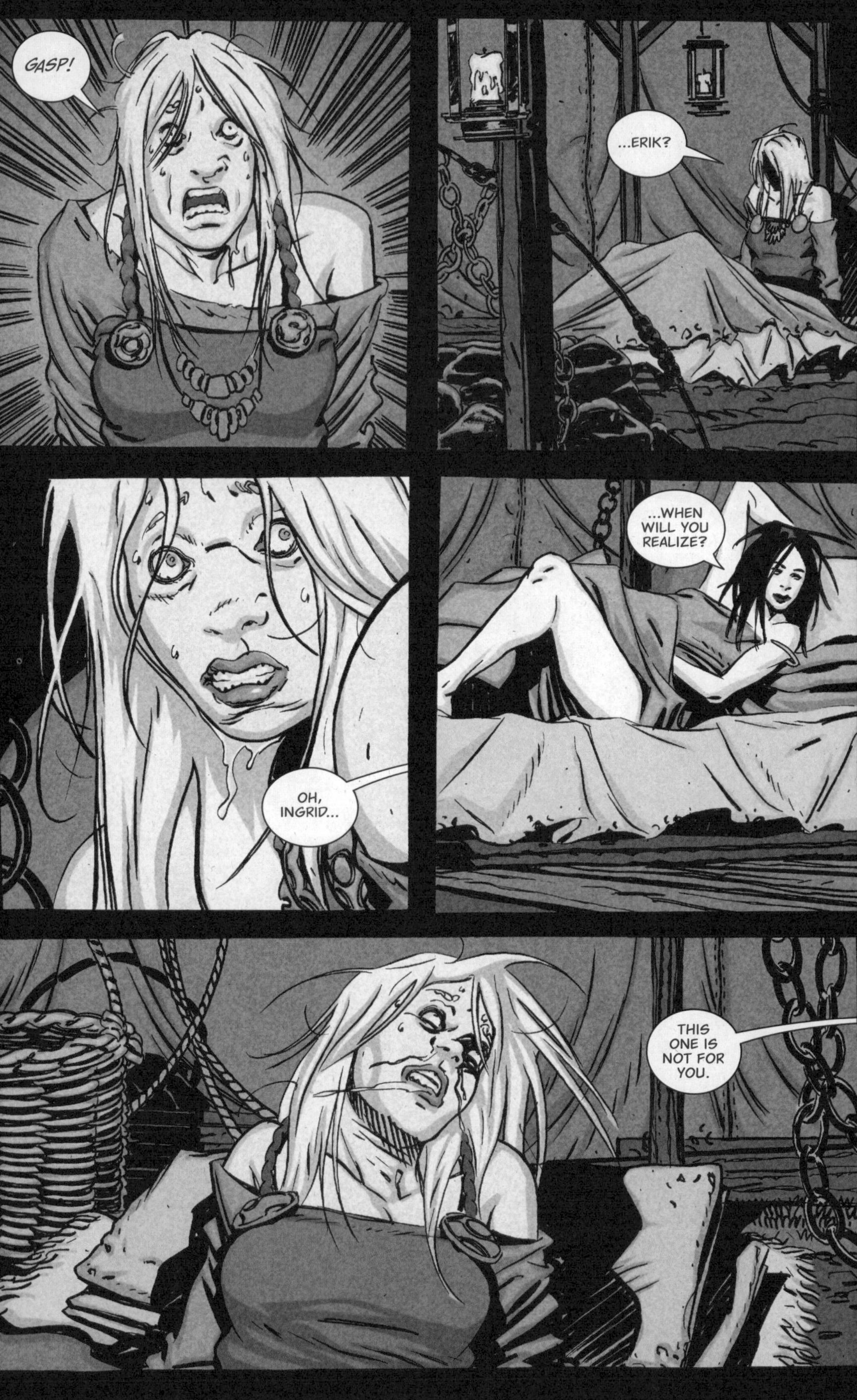
GASP!
...ERIK?
...WHEN WILL YOU REALIZE?
OH, INGRID...
THIS ONE IS NOT FOR YOU.

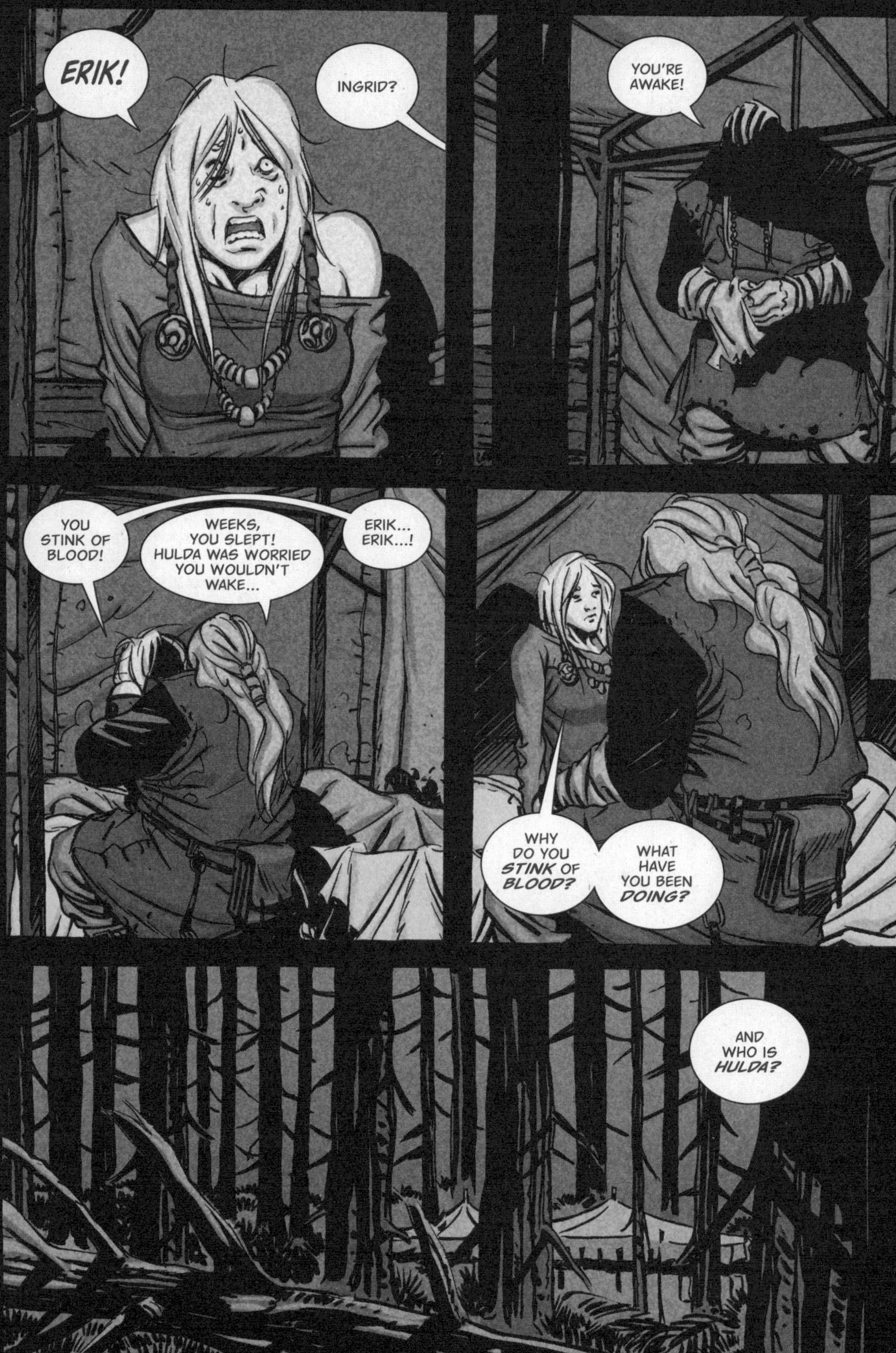
ERIK!
INGRID?
YOU'RE AWAKE!
YOU STINK OF BLOOD!
WEEKS, YOU SLEPT! HULDA WAS WORRIED YOU WOULDN'T WAKE...
ERIK... ERIK...!
WHY DO YOU STINK OF BLOOD?
WHAT HAVE YOU BEEN DOING?
AND WHO IS HULDA?

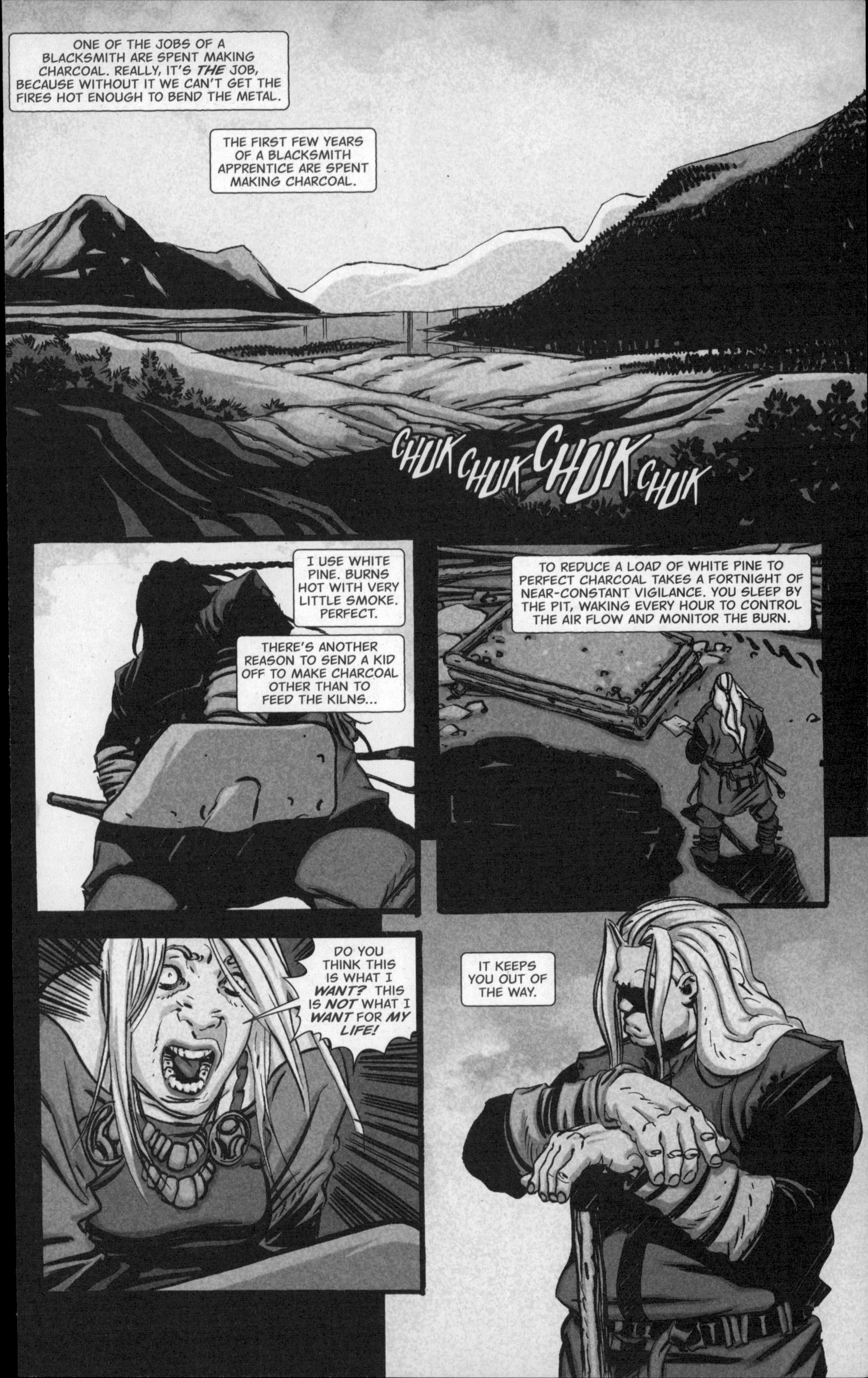
ONE OF THE JOBS OF A BLACKSMITH ARE SPENT MAKING CHARCOAL. REALLY, IT'S *THE* JOB, BECAUSE WITHOUT IT WE CAN'T GET THE FIRES HOT ENOUGH TO BEND THE METAL.
THE FIRST FEW YEARS OF A BLACKSMITH APPRENTICE ARE SPENT MAKING CHARCOAL.
CHUK CHUK CHUK CHUK
I USE WHITE PINE. BURNS HOT WITH VERY LITTLE SMOKE. PERFECT.
THERE'S ANOTHER REASON TO SEND A KID OFF TO MAKE CHARCOAL OTHER THAN TO FEED THE KILNS...
TO REDUCE A LOAD OF WHITE PINE TO PERFECT CHARCOAL TAKES A FORTNIGHT OF NEAR-CONSTANT VIGILANCE. YOU SLEEP BY THE PIT, WAKING EVERY HOUR TO CONTROL THE AIR FLOW AND MONITOR THE BURN.
DO YOU THINK THIS IS WHAT I *WANT?* THIS IS *NOT* WHAT I *WANT* FOR *MY LIFE!*
IT KEEPS YOU OUT OF THE WAY.

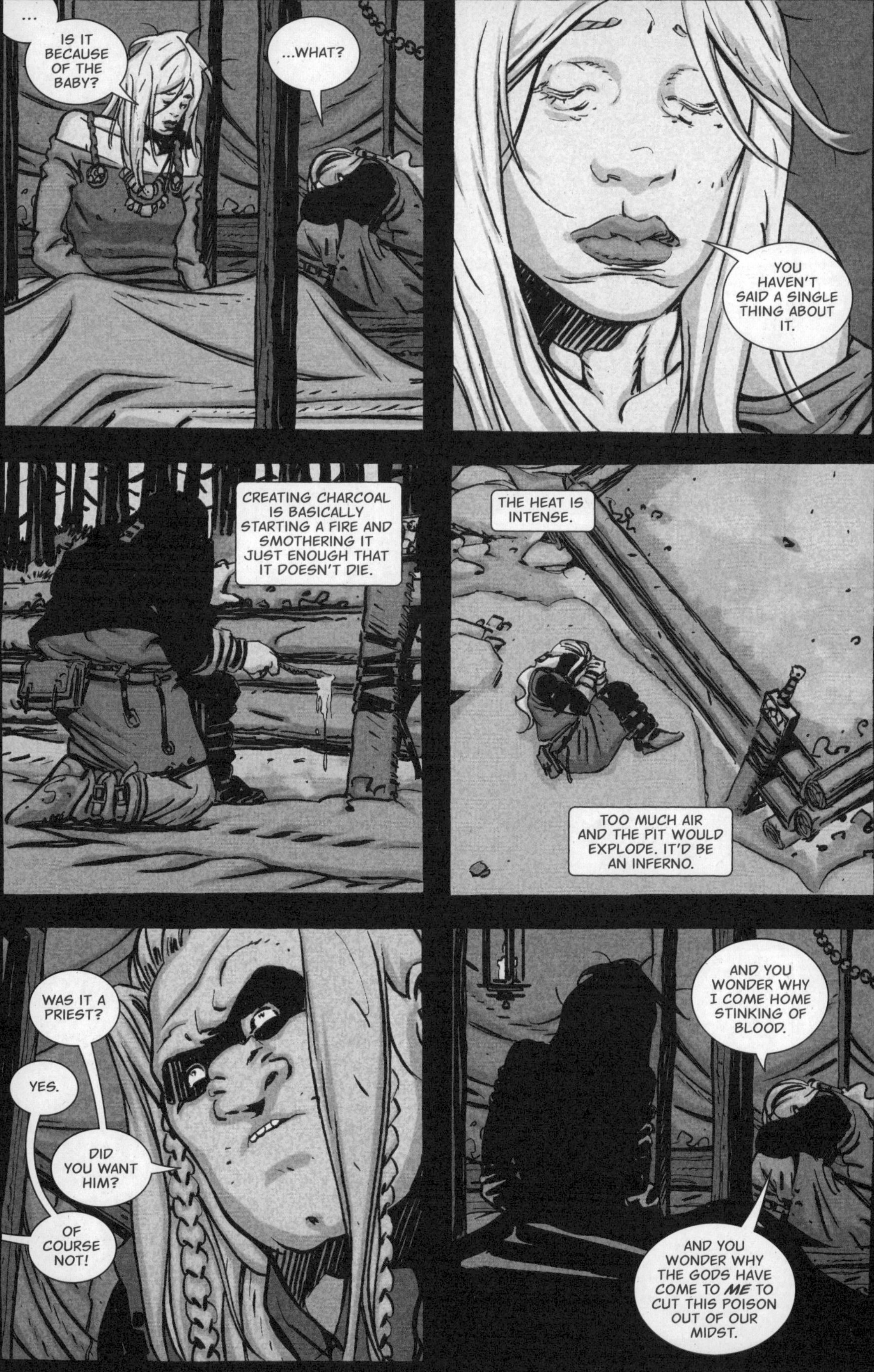
...
IS IT BECAUSE OF THE BABY?
...WHAT?
YOU HAVEN'T SAID A SINGLE THING ABOUT IT.
CREATING CHARCOAL IS BASICALLY STARTING A FIRE AND SMOTHERING IT JUST ENOUGH THAT IT DOESN'T DIE.
THE HEAT IS INTENSE.
TOO MUCH AIR AND THE PIT WOULD EXPLODE. IT'D BE AN INFERNO.
WAS IT A PRIEST?
YES.
DID YOU WANT HIM?
OF COURSE NOT!
AND YOU WONDER WHY I COME HOME STINKING OF BLOOD.
AND YOU WONDER WHY THE GODS HAVE COME TO *ME* TO CUT THIS POISON OUT OF OUR MIDST.

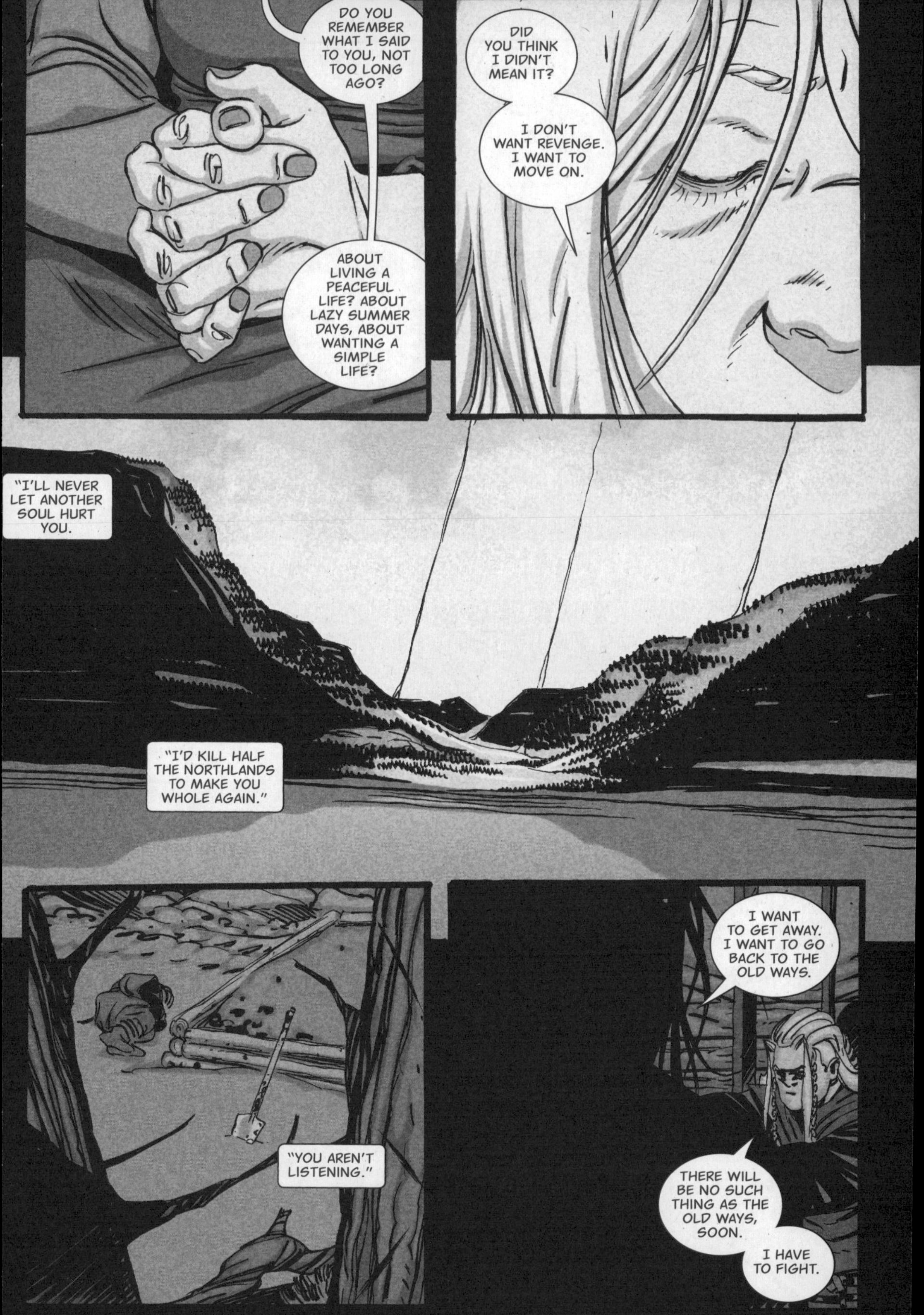
DO YOU REMEMBER WHAT I SAID TO YOU, NOT TOO LONG AGO?
ABOUT LIVING A PEACEFUL LIFE? ABOUT LAZY SUMMER DAYS, ABOUT WANTING A SIMPLE LIFE?
DID YOU THINK I DIDN'T MEAN IT?
I DON'T WANT REVENGE. I WANT TO MOVE ON.
"I'LL NEVER LET ANOTHER SOUL HURT YOU.
"I'D KILL HALF THE NORTHLANDS TO MAKE YOU WHOLE AGAIN."
"YOU AREN'T LISTENING."
I WANT TO GET AWAY. I WANT TO GO BACK TO THE OLD WAYS.
THERE WILL BE NO SUCH THING AS THE OLD WAYS, SOON.
I HAVE TO FIGHT.

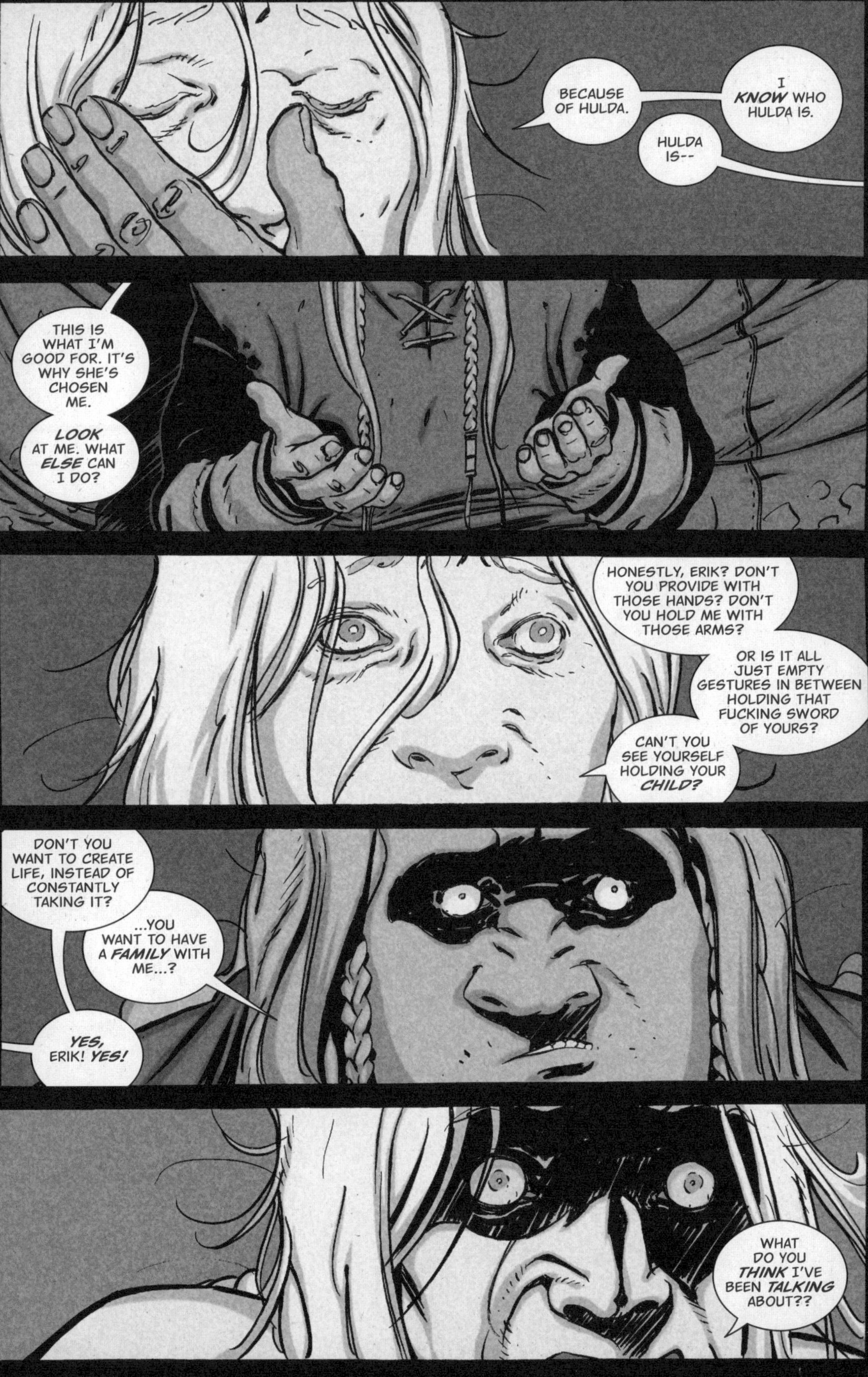
BECAUSE OF HULDA.
I KNOW WHO HULDA IS.
HULDA IS--
THIS IS WHAT I'M GOOD FOR. IT'S WHY SHE'S CHOSEN ME.
LOOK AT ME. WHAT ELSE CAN I DO?
HONESTLY, ERIK? DON'T YOU PROVIDE WITH THOSE HANDS? DON'T YOU HOLD ME WITH THOSE ARMS?
OR IS IT ALL JUST EMPTY GESTURES IN BETWEEN HOLDING THAT FUCKING SWORD OF YOURS?
CAN'T YOU SEE YOURSELF HOLDING YOUR CHILD?
DON'T YOU WANT TO CREATE LIFE, INSTEAD OF CONSTANTLY TAKING IT?
...YOU WANT TO HAVE A FAMILY WITH ME...?
YES, ERIK! YES!
WHAT DO YOU THINK I'VE BEEN TALKING ABOUT??

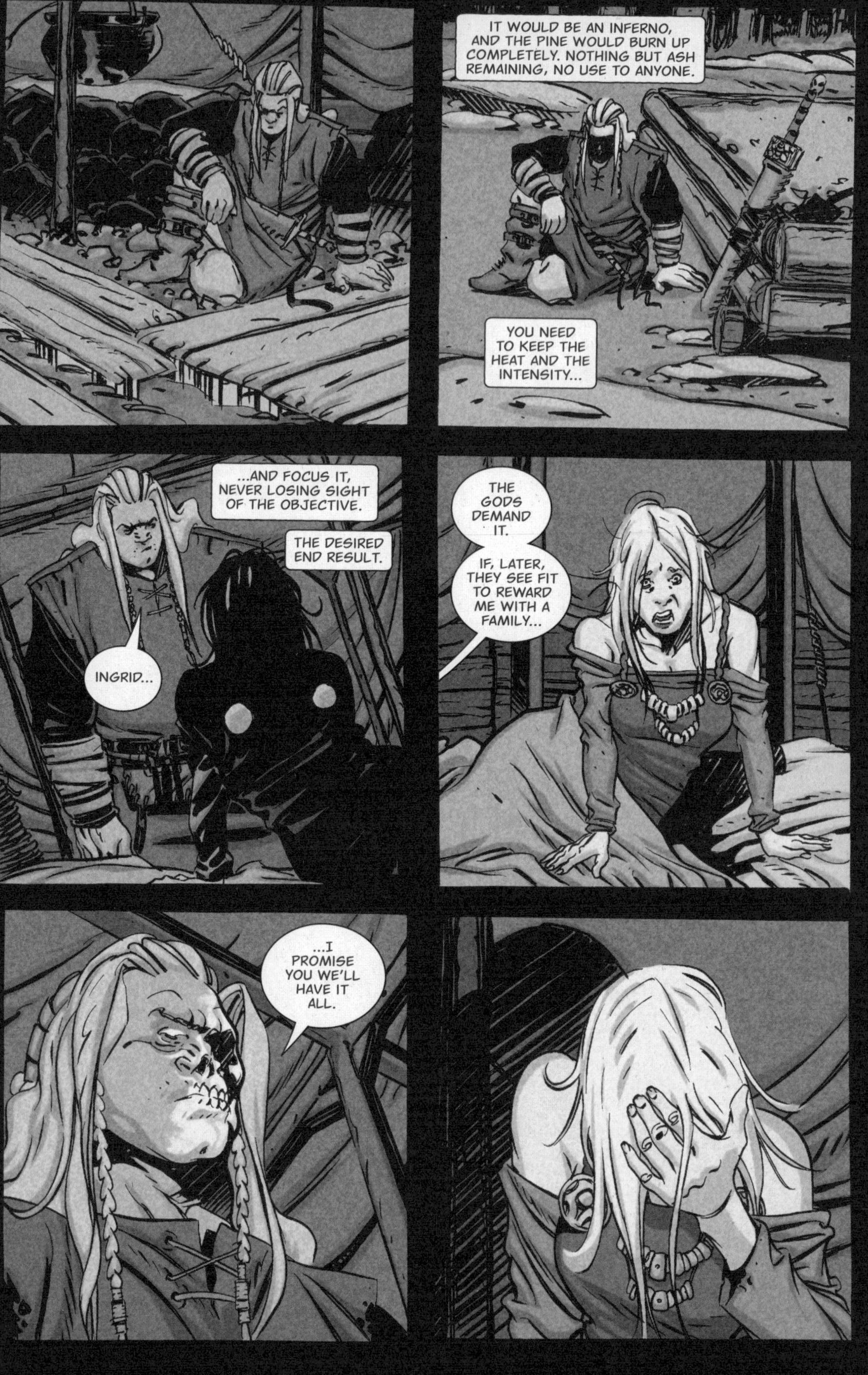
IT WOULD BE AN INFERNO, AND THE PINE WOULD BURN UP COMPLETELY. NOTHING BUT ASH REMAINING, NO USE TO ANYONE.
YOU NEED TO KEEP THE HEAT AND THE INTENSITY...
...AND FOCUS IT, NEVER LOSING SIGHT OF THE OBJECTIVE.
THE DESIRED END RESULT.
INGRID...
THE GODS DEMAND IT.
IF, LATER, THEY SEE FIT TO REWARD ME WITH A FAMILY...
...I PROMISE YOU WE'LL HAVE IT ALL.

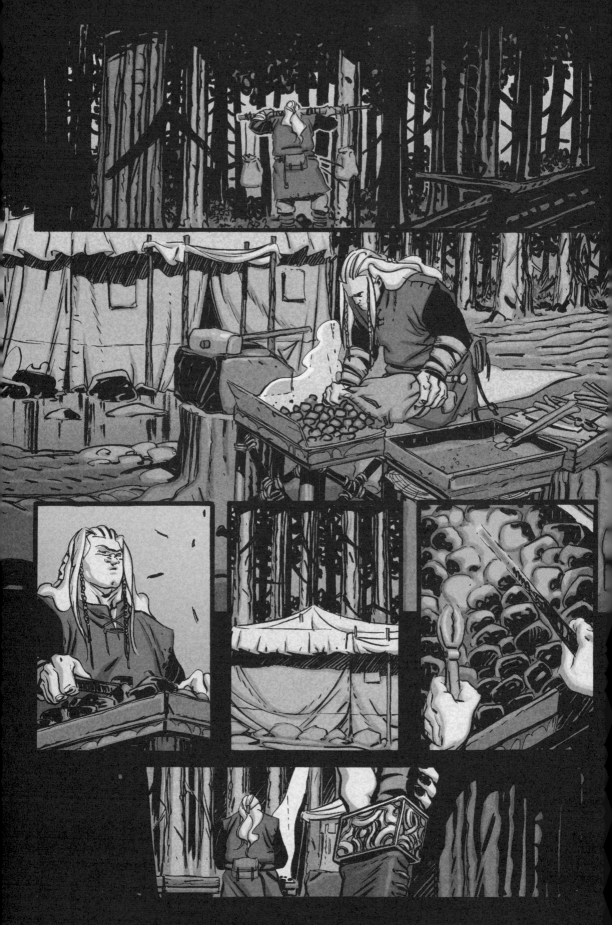

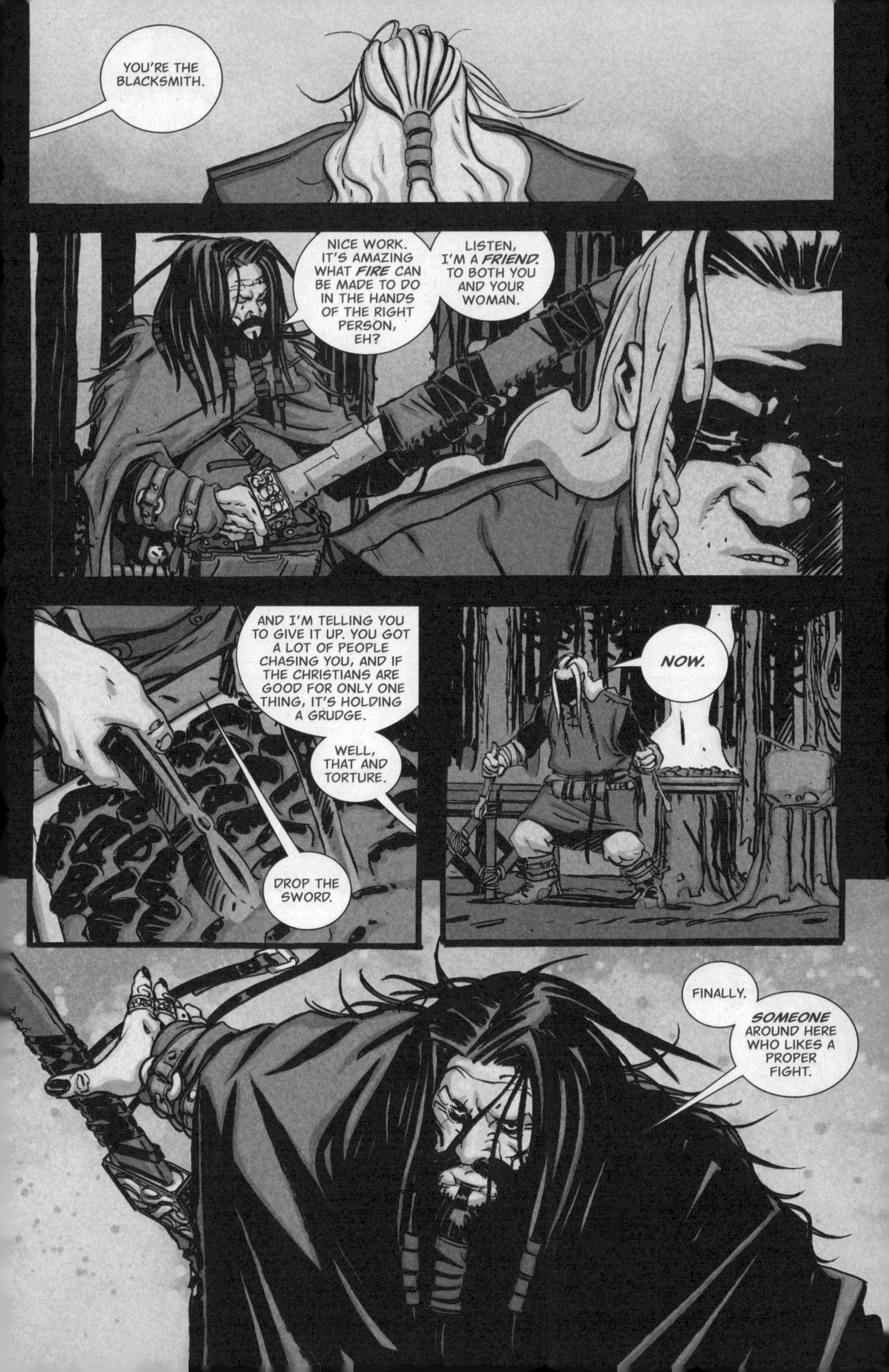
YOU'RE THE BLACKSMITH.
NICE WORK. IT'S AMAZING WHAT *FIRE* CAN BE MADE TO DO IN THE HANDS OF THE RIGHT PERSON, EH?
LISTEN, I'M A *FRIEND.* TO BOTH YOU AND YOUR WOMAN.
AND I'M TELLING YOU TO GIVE IT UP. YOU GOT A LOT OF PEOPLE CHASING YOU, AND IF THE CHRISTIANS ARE GOOD FOR ONLY ONE THING, IT'S HOLDING A GRUDGE.
WELL, THAT AND TORTURE.
DROP THE SWORD.
NOW.
FINALLY.
SOMEONE AROUND HERE WHO LIKES A PROPER FIGHT.

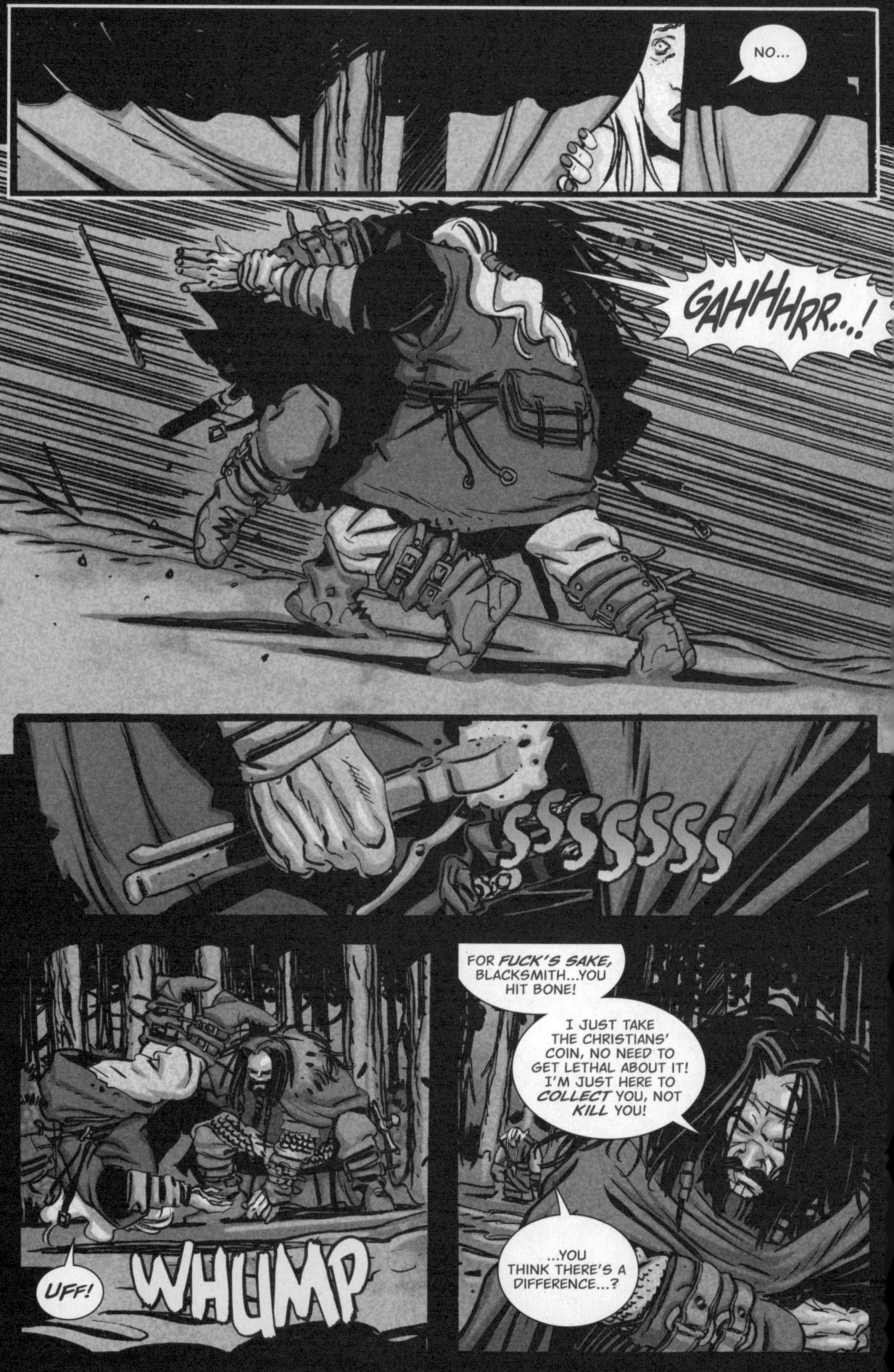

NO...
GAHHHRR...!
SSSSSSS
UFF!
WHUMP
FOR FUCK'S SAKE, BLACKSMITH...YOU HIT BONE!
I JUST TAKE THE CHRISTIANS' COIN, NO NEED TO GET LETHAL ABOUT IT! I'M JUST HERE TO COLLECT YOU, NOT KILL YOU!
...YOU THINK THERE'S A DIFFERENCE...?

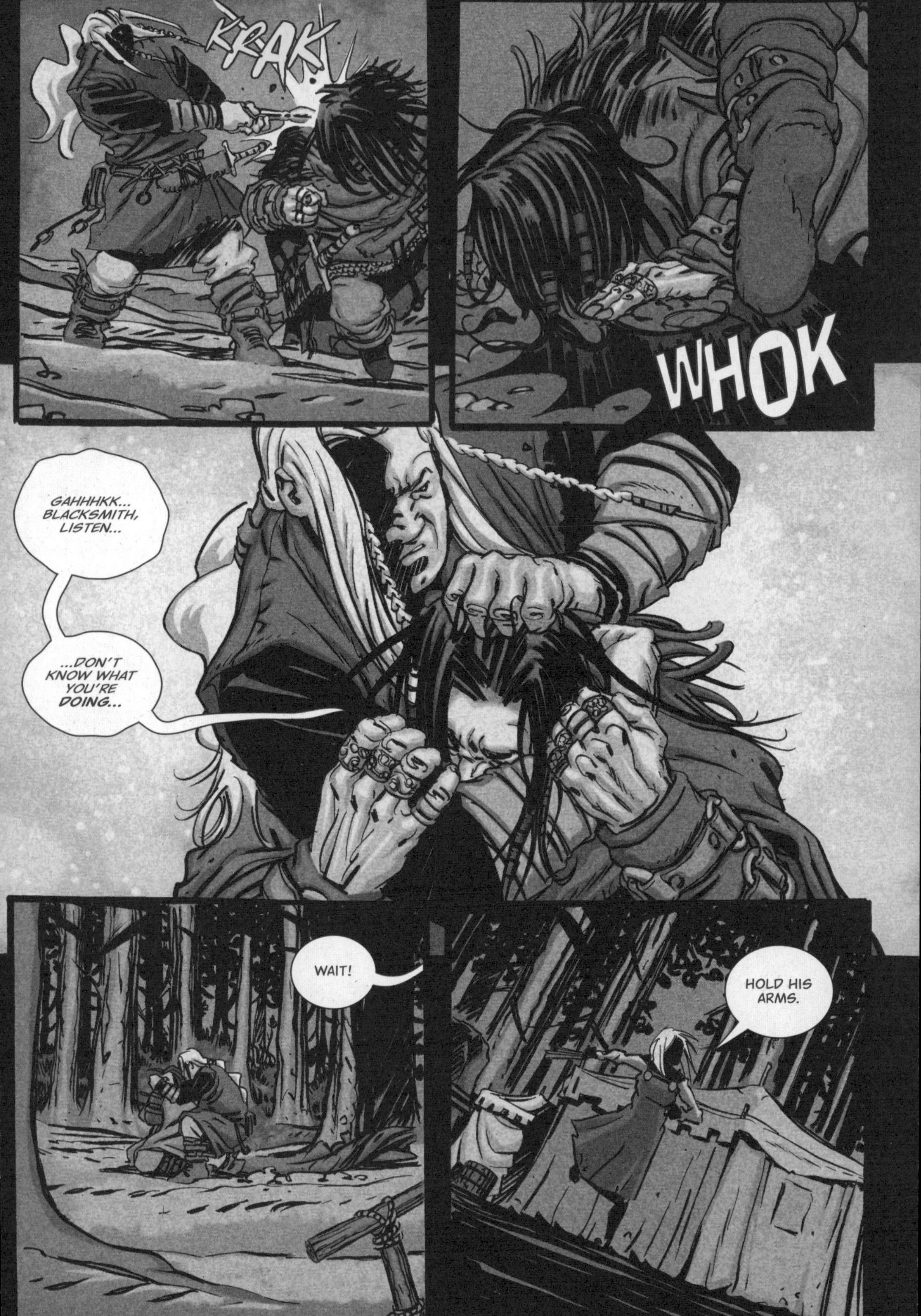
KRAK
WHOK
GAHHHKK... BLACKSMITH, LISTEN...
...DON'T KNOW WHAT YOU'RE DOING...
WAIT!
HOLD HIS ARMS.

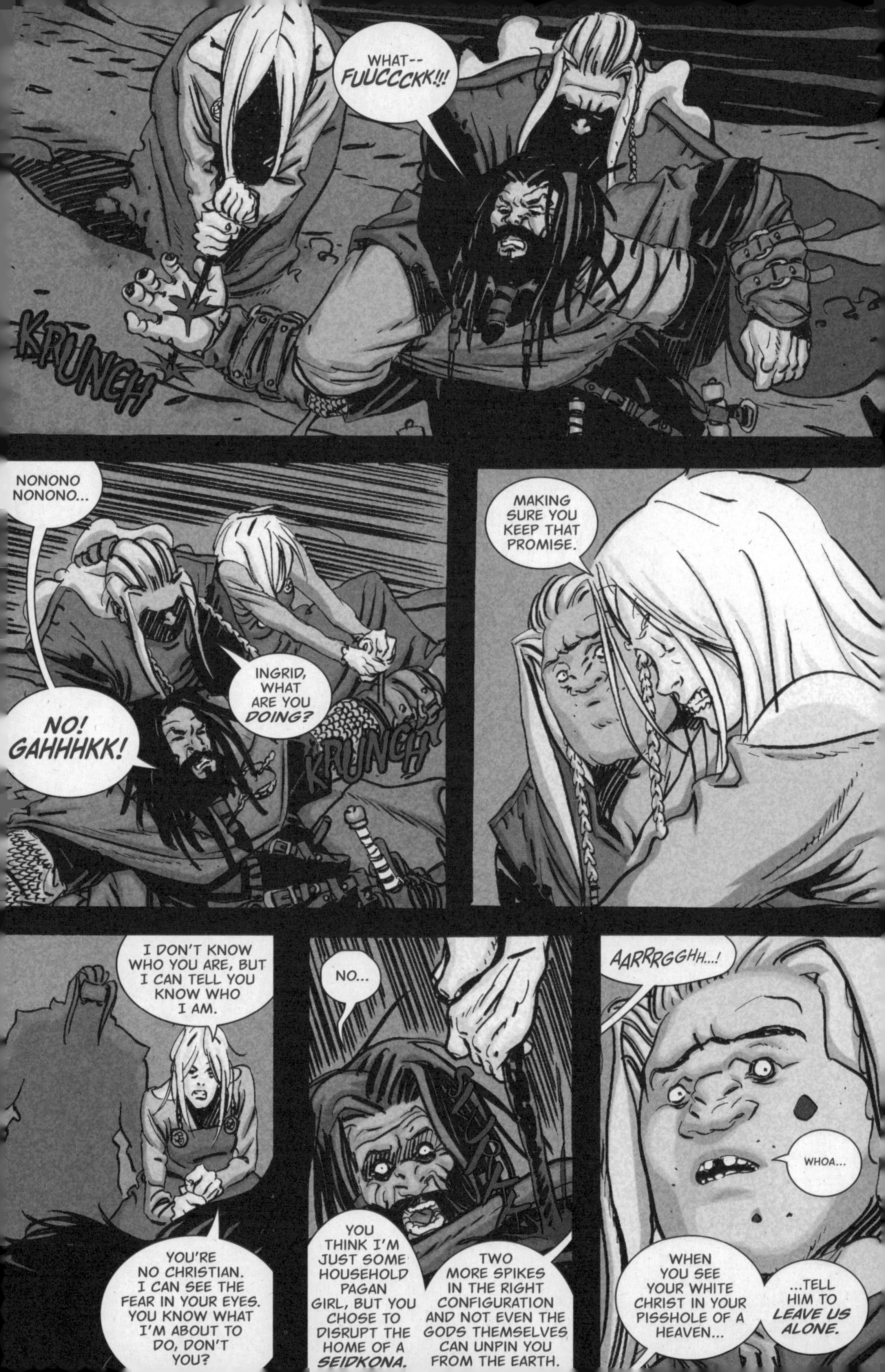
WHAT-- FUUCCCKK!!!
KRUNCH
NONONO NONONO...
INGRID, WHAT ARE YOU DOING?
NO! GAHHHKK!
KRUNCH
MAKING SURE YOU KEEP THAT PROMISE.
I DON'T KNOW WHO YOU ARE, BUT I CAN TELL YOU KNOW WHO I AM.
YOU'RE NO CHRISTIAN. I CAN SEE THE FEAR IN YOUR EYES. YOU KNOW WHAT I'M ABOUT TO DO, DON'T YOU?
NO...
YOU THINK I'M JUST SOME HOUSEHOLD PAGAN GIRL, BUT YOU CHOSE TO DISRUPT THE HOME OF A SEIDKONA.
TWO MORE SPIKES IN THE RIGHT CONFIGURATION AND NOT EVEN THE GODS THEMSELVES CAN UNPIN YOU FROM THE EARTH.
AARRRGGHH...!
WHOA...
WHEN YOU SEE YOUR WHITE CHRIST IN YOUR PISSHOLE OF A HEAVEN...
...TELL HIM TO LEAVE US ALONE.

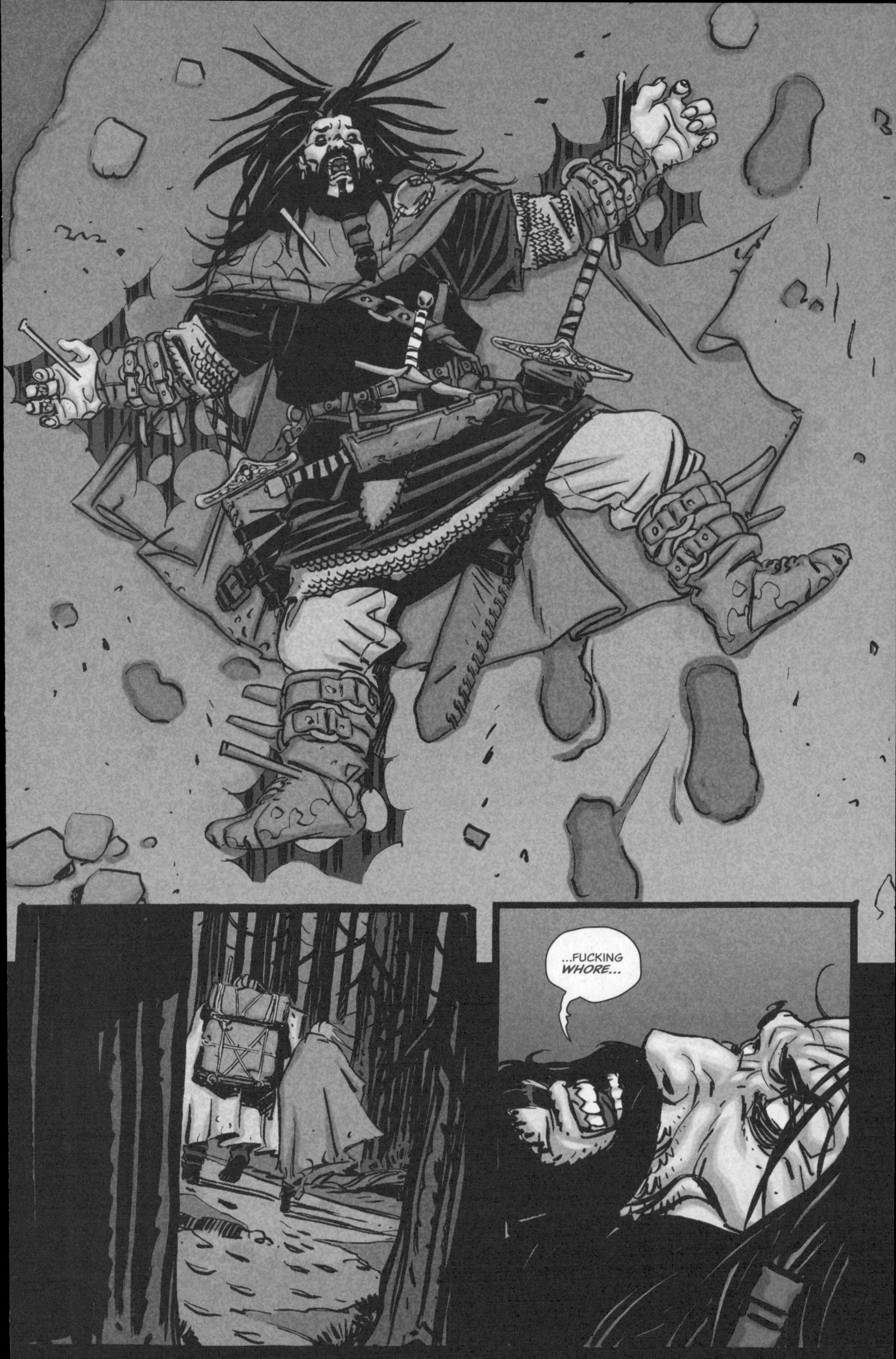
...FUCKING WHORE...

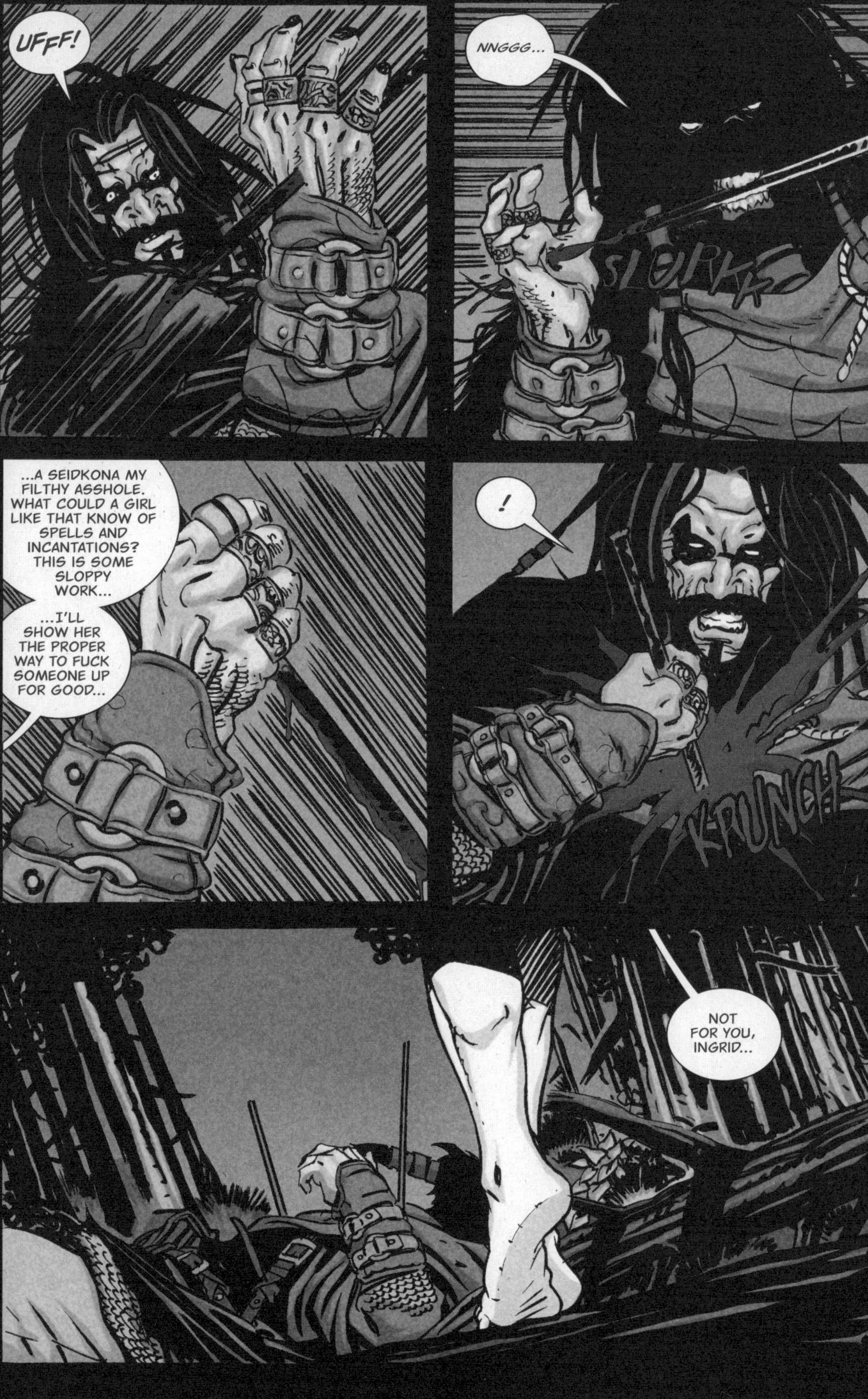
UFFF!
NNGGG...
SLORKK
...A SEIDKONA MY FILTHY ASSHOLE. WHAT COULD A GIRL LIKE THAT KNOW OF SPELLS AND INCANTATIONS? THIS IS SOME SLOPPY WORK...
...I'LL SHOW HER THE PROPER WAY TO FUCK SOMEONE UP FOR GOOD...
!
KRUNCH
NOT FOR YOU, INGRID...

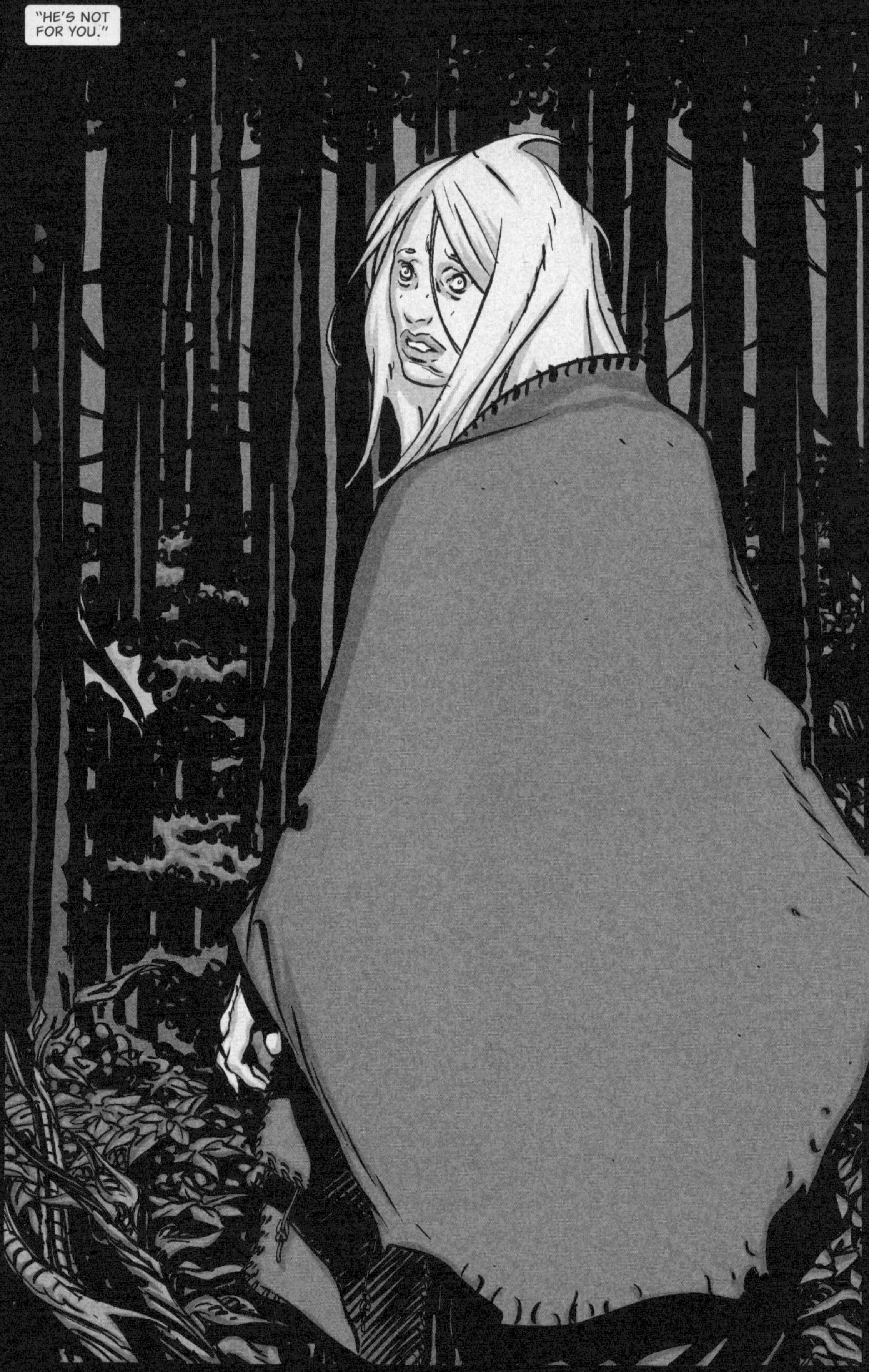
"HE'S NOT FOR YOU."

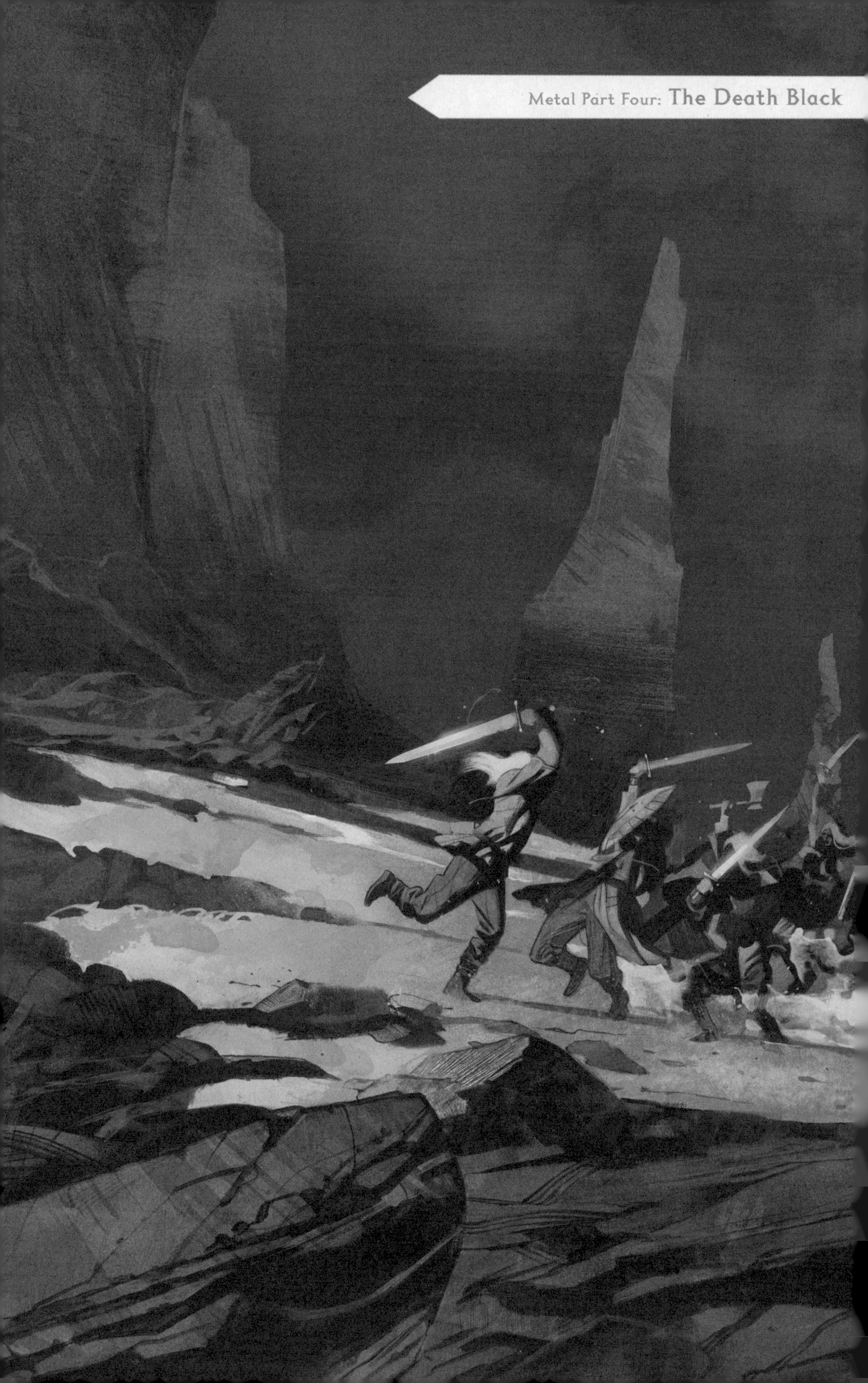

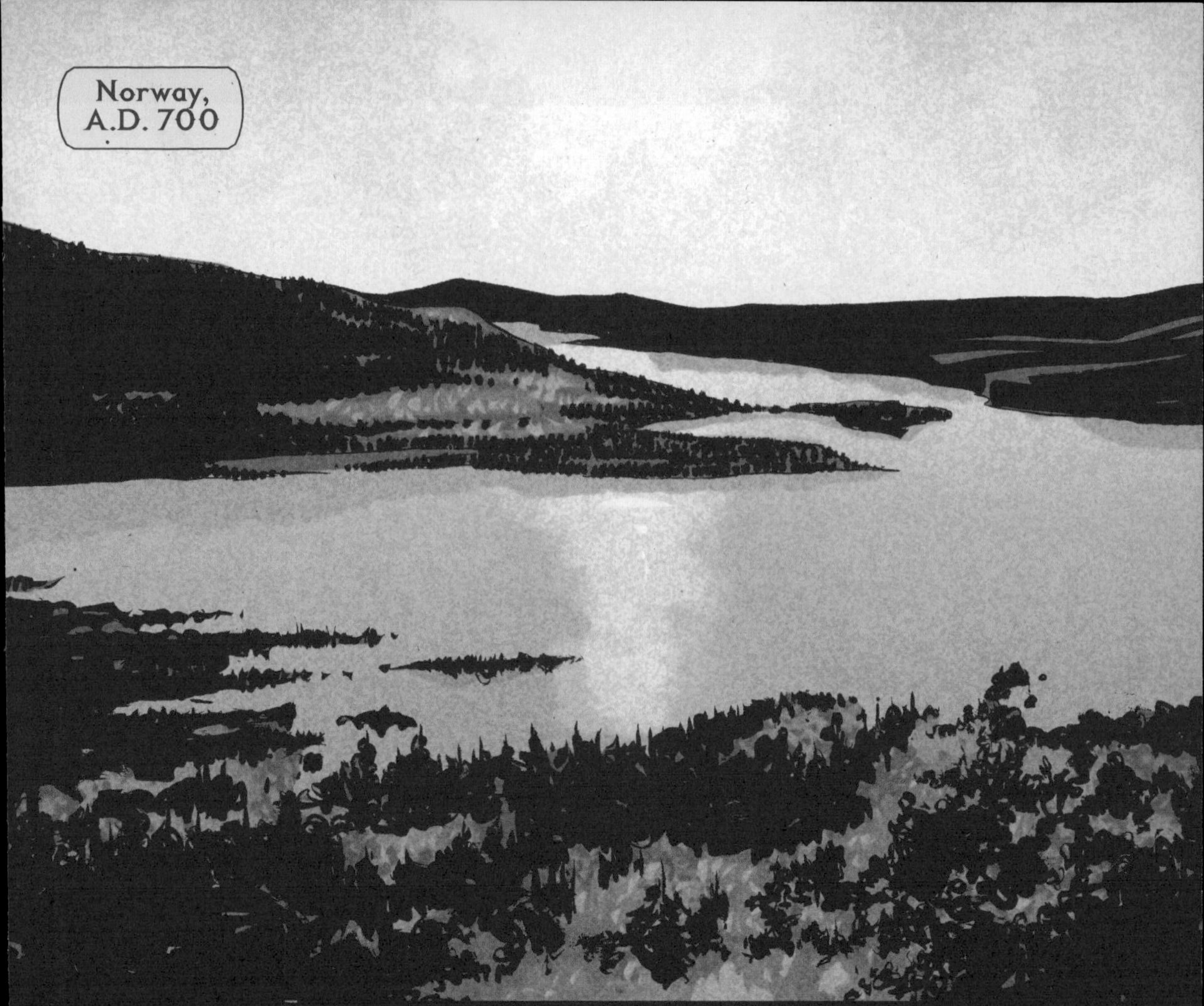
Norway, A.D. 700

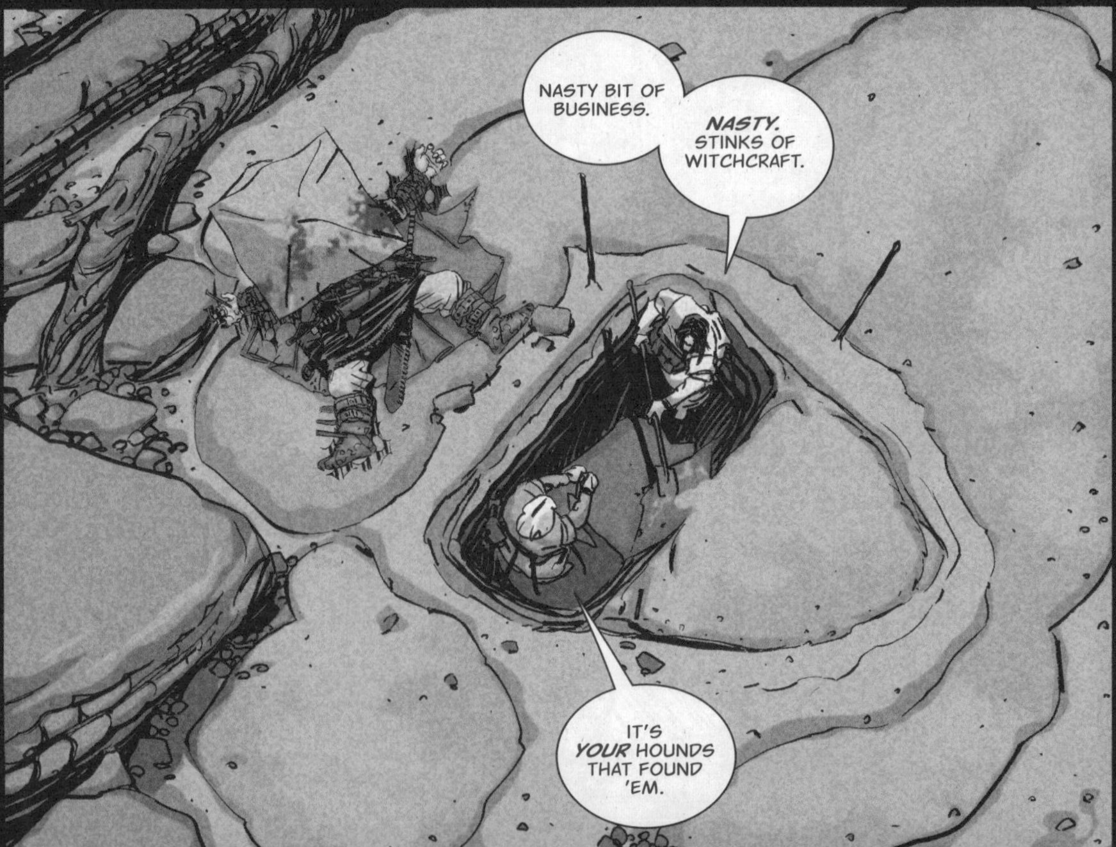
NASTY BIT OF BUSINESS.
NASTY. STINKS OF WITCHCRAFT.
IT'S YOUR HOUNDS THAT FOUND 'EM.

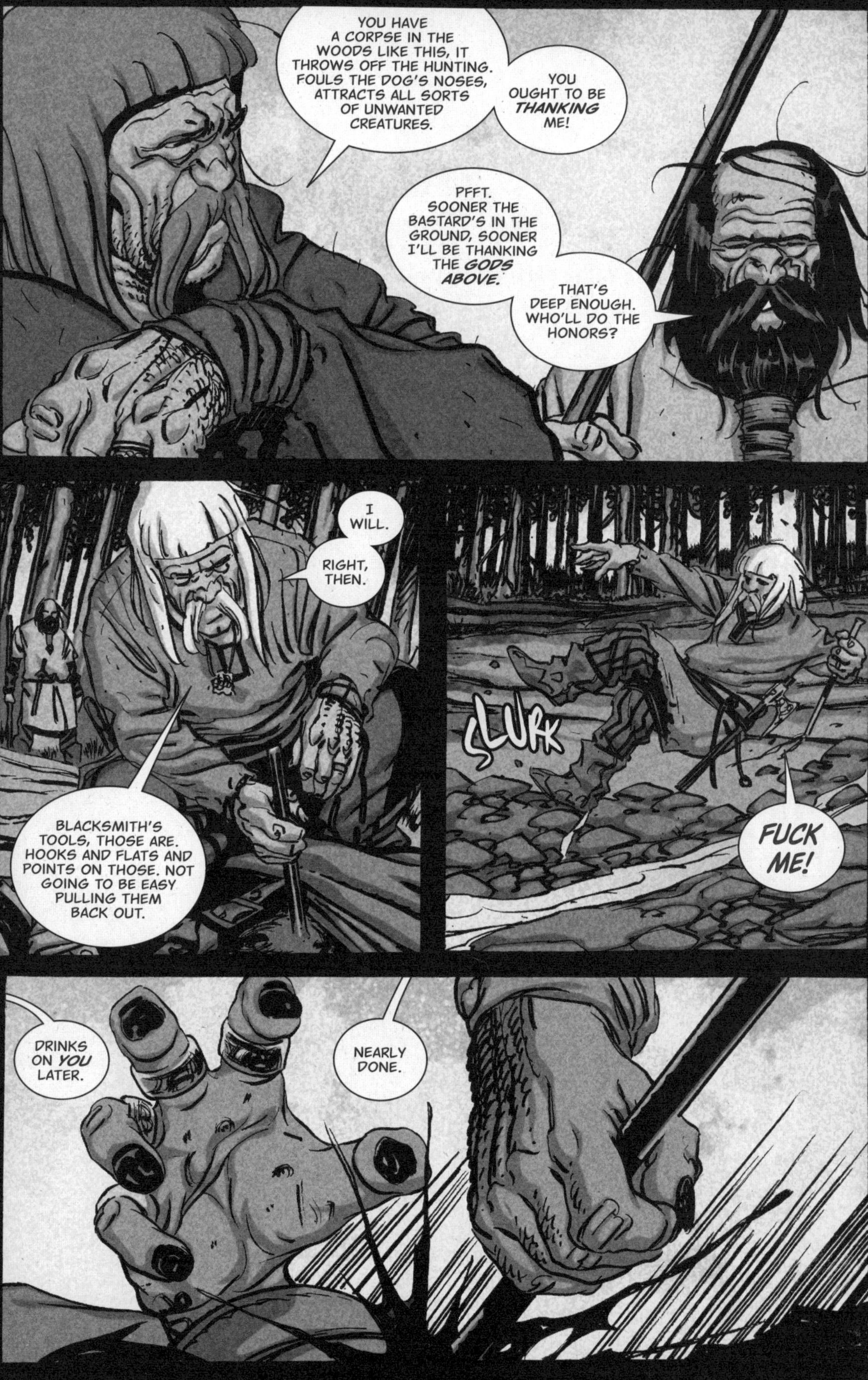
YOU HAVE A CORPSE IN THE WOODS LIKE THIS, IT THROWS OFF THE HUNTING. FOULS THE DOG'S NOSES, ATTRACTS ALL SORTS OF UNWANTED CREATURES.
YOU OUGHT TO BE *THANKING* ME!
PFFT. SOONER THE BASTARD'S IN THE GROUND, SOONER I'LL BE THANKING THE *GODS ABOVE.*
THAT'S DEEP ENOUGH. WHO'LL DO THE HONORS?
I WILL.
RIGHT, THEN.
BLACKSMITH'S TOOLS, THOSE ARE. HOOKS AND FLATS AND POINTS ON THOSE. NOT GOING TO BE EASY PULLING THEM BACK OUT.
SLURK
FUCK ME!
DRINKS ON *YOU* LATER.
NEARLY DONE.

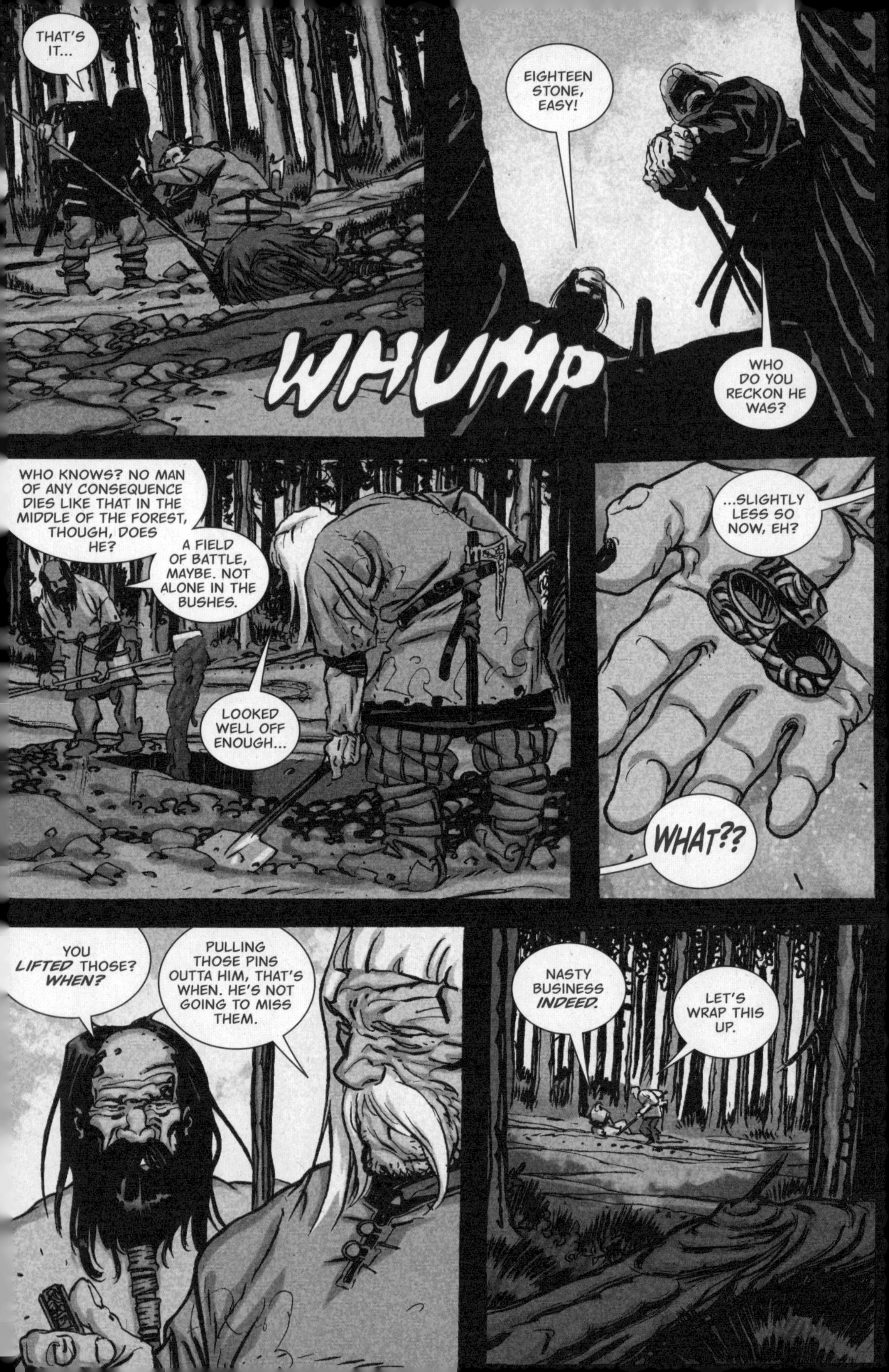
THAT'S IT...
EIGHTEEN STONE, EASY!
WHUMP
WHO DO YOU RECKON HE WAS?
WHO KNOWS? NO MAN OF ANY CONSEQUENCE DIES LIKE THAT IN THE MIDDLE OF THE FOREST, THOUGH, DOES HE?
A FIELD OF BATTLE, MAYBE. NOT ALONE IN THE BUSHES.
LOOKED WELL OFF ENOUGH...
...SLIGHTLY LESS SO NOW, EH?
WHAT??
YOU *LIFTED* THOSE? *WHEN?*
PULLING THOSE PINS OUTTA HIM, THAT'S WHEN. HE'S NOT GOING TO MISS THEM.
NASTY BUSINESS *INDEED.*
LET'S WRAP THIS UP.

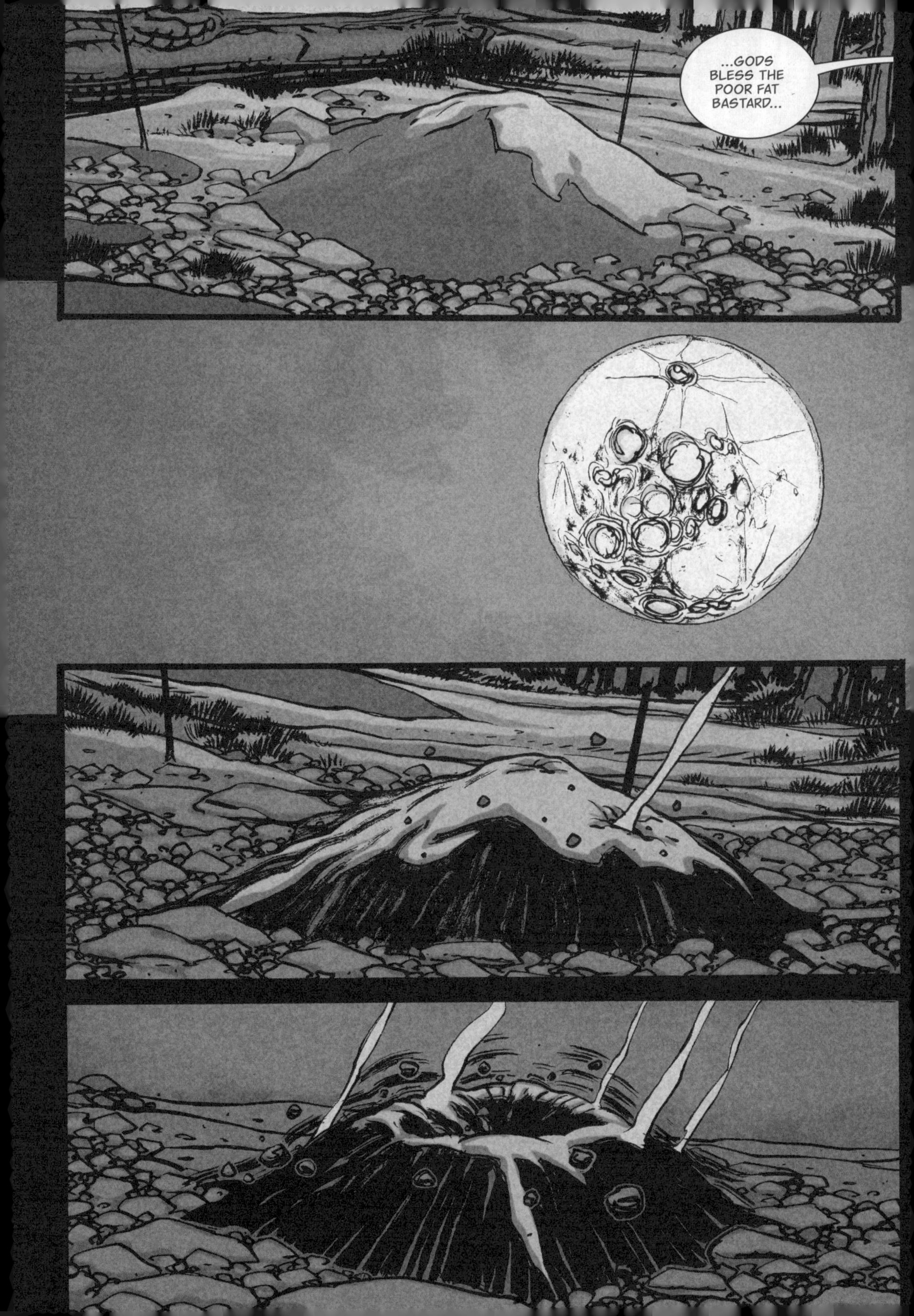
...GODS BLESS THE POOR FAT BASTARD...

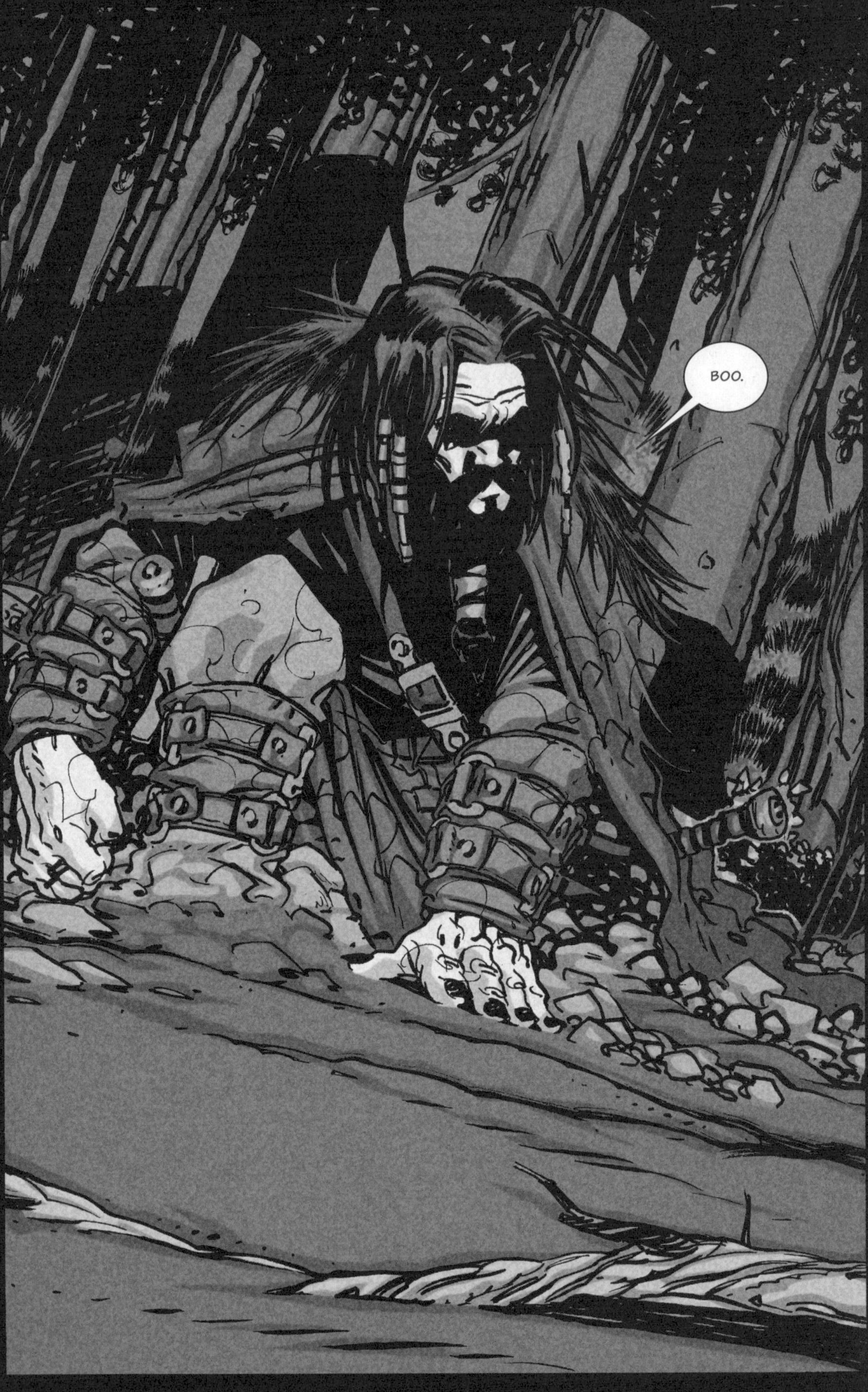
BOO.

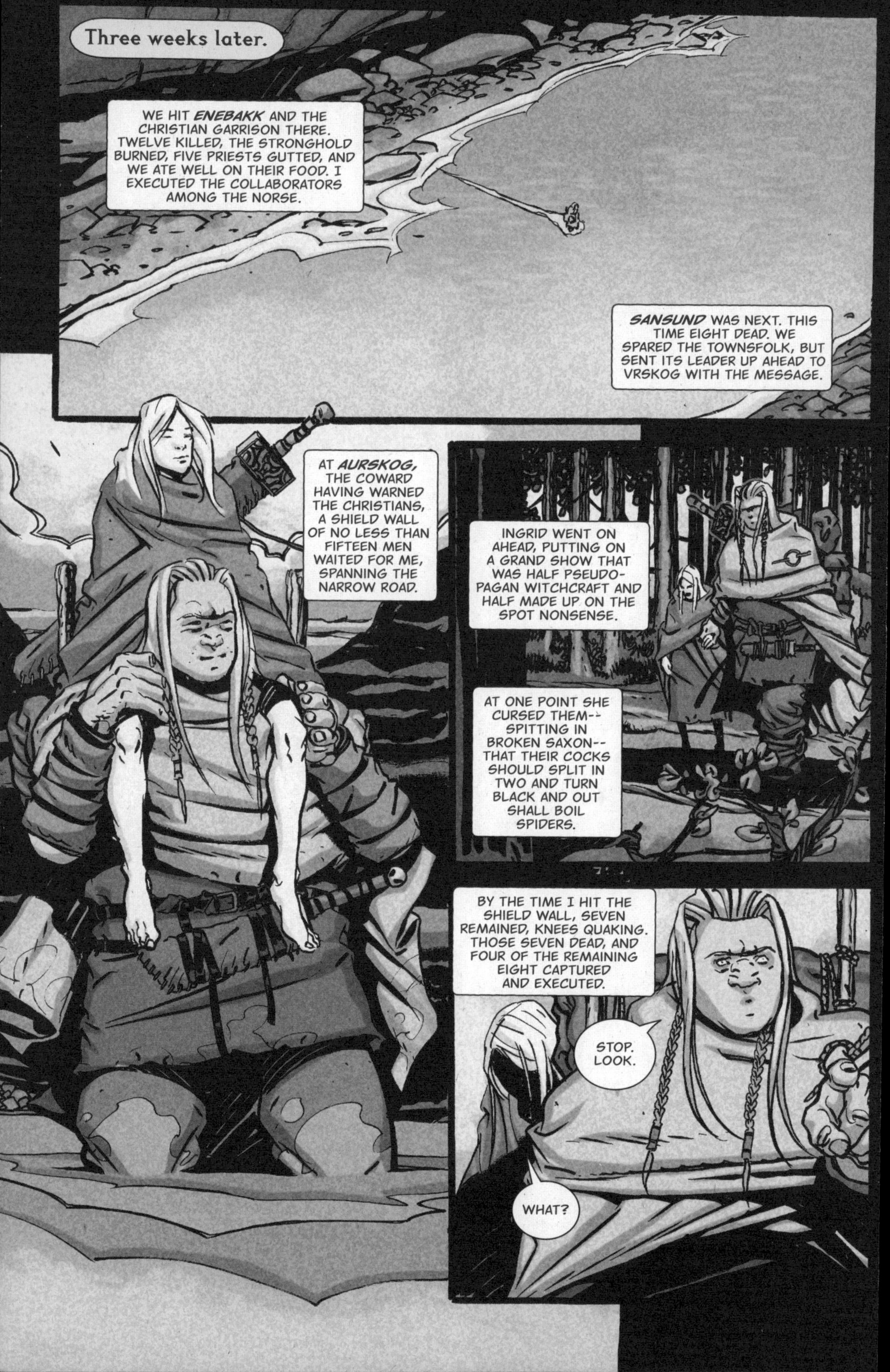
Three weeks later.
WE HIT ENEBAKK AND THE CHRISTIAN GARRISON THERE. TWELVE KILLED, THE STRONGHOLD BURNED, FIVE PRIESTS GUTTED, AND WE ATE WELL ON THEIR FOOD. I EXECUTED THE COLLABORATORS AMONG THE NORSE.
SANSUND WAS NEXT. THIS TIME EIGHT DEAD. WE SPARED THE TOWNSFOLK, BUT SENT ITS LEADER UP AHEAD TO VRSKOG WITH THE MESSAGE.
AT AURSKOG, THE COWARD HAVING WARNED THE CHRISTIANS, A SHIELD WALL OF NO LESS THAN FIFTEEN MEN WAITED FOR ME, SPANNING THE NARROW ROAD.
INGRID WENT ON AHEAD, PUTTING ON A GRAND SHOW THAT WAS HALF PSEUDO-PAGAN WITCHCRAFT AND HALF MADE UP ON THE SPOT NONSENSE.
AT ONE POINT SHE CURSED THEM--SPITTING IN BROKEN SAXON--THAT THEIR COCKS SHOULD SPLIT IN TWO AND TURN BLACK AND OUT SHALL BOIL SPIDERS.
BY THE TIME I HIT THE SHIELD WALL, SEVEN REMAINED, KNEES QUAKING. THOSE SEVEN DEAD, AND FOUR OF THE REMAINING EIGHT CAPTURED AND EXECUTED.
STOP. LOOK.
WHAT?

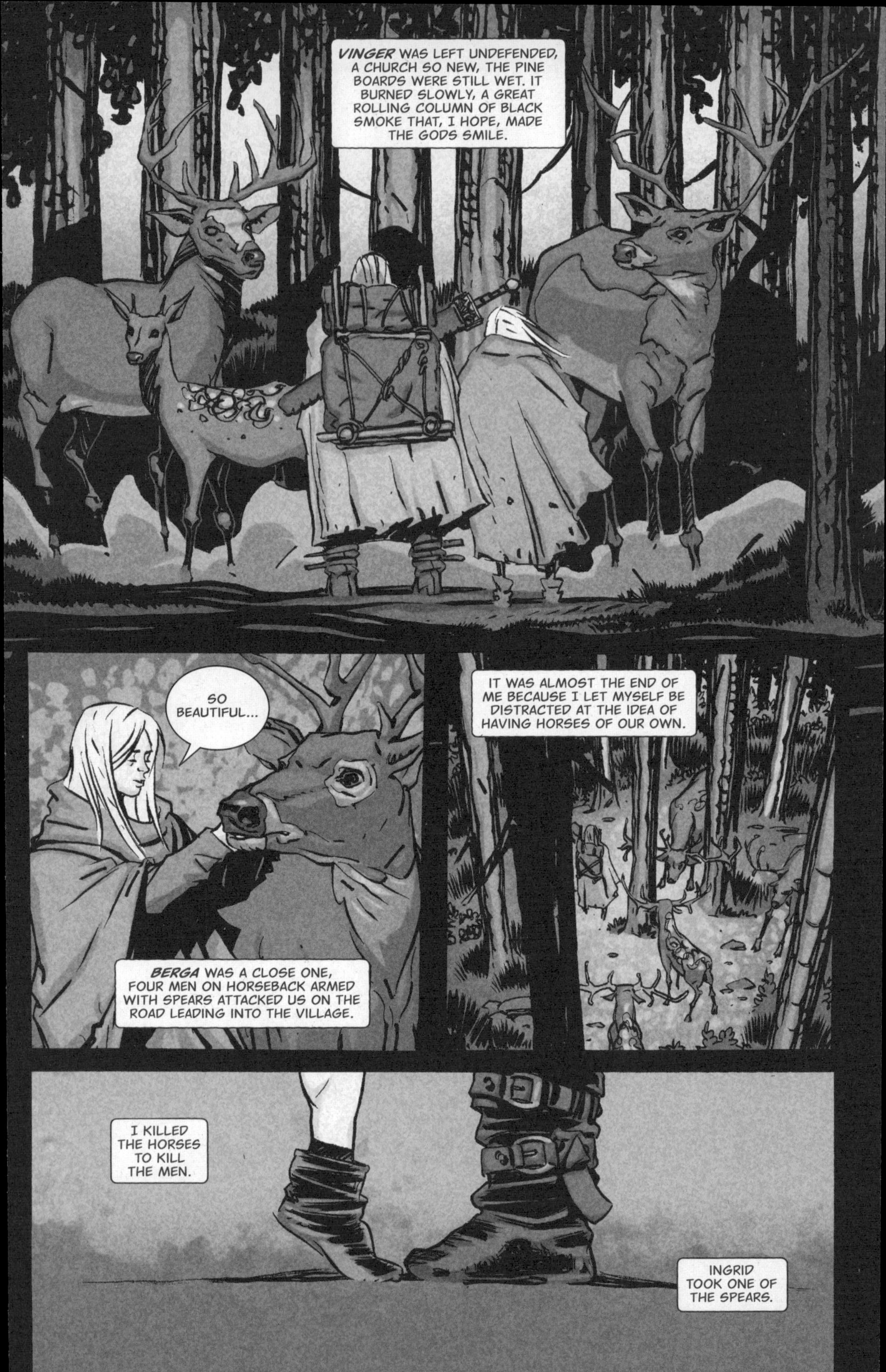
VINGER WAS LEFT UNDEFENDED, A CHURCH SO NEW, THE PINE BOARDS WERE STILL WET. IT BURNED SLOWLY, A GREAT ROLLING COLUMN OF BLACK SMOKE THAT, I HOPE, MADE THE GODS SMILE.
SO BEAUTIFUL...
BERGA WAS A CLOSE ONE, FOUR MEN ON HORSEBACK ARMED WITH SPEARS ATTACKED US ON THE ROAD LEADING INTO THE VILLAGE.
IT WAS ALMOST THE END OF ME BECAUSE I LET MYSELF BE DISTRACTED AT THE IDEA OF HAVING HORSES OF OUR OWN.
I KILLED THE HORSES TO KILL THE MEN.
INGRID TOOK ONE OF THE SPEARS.

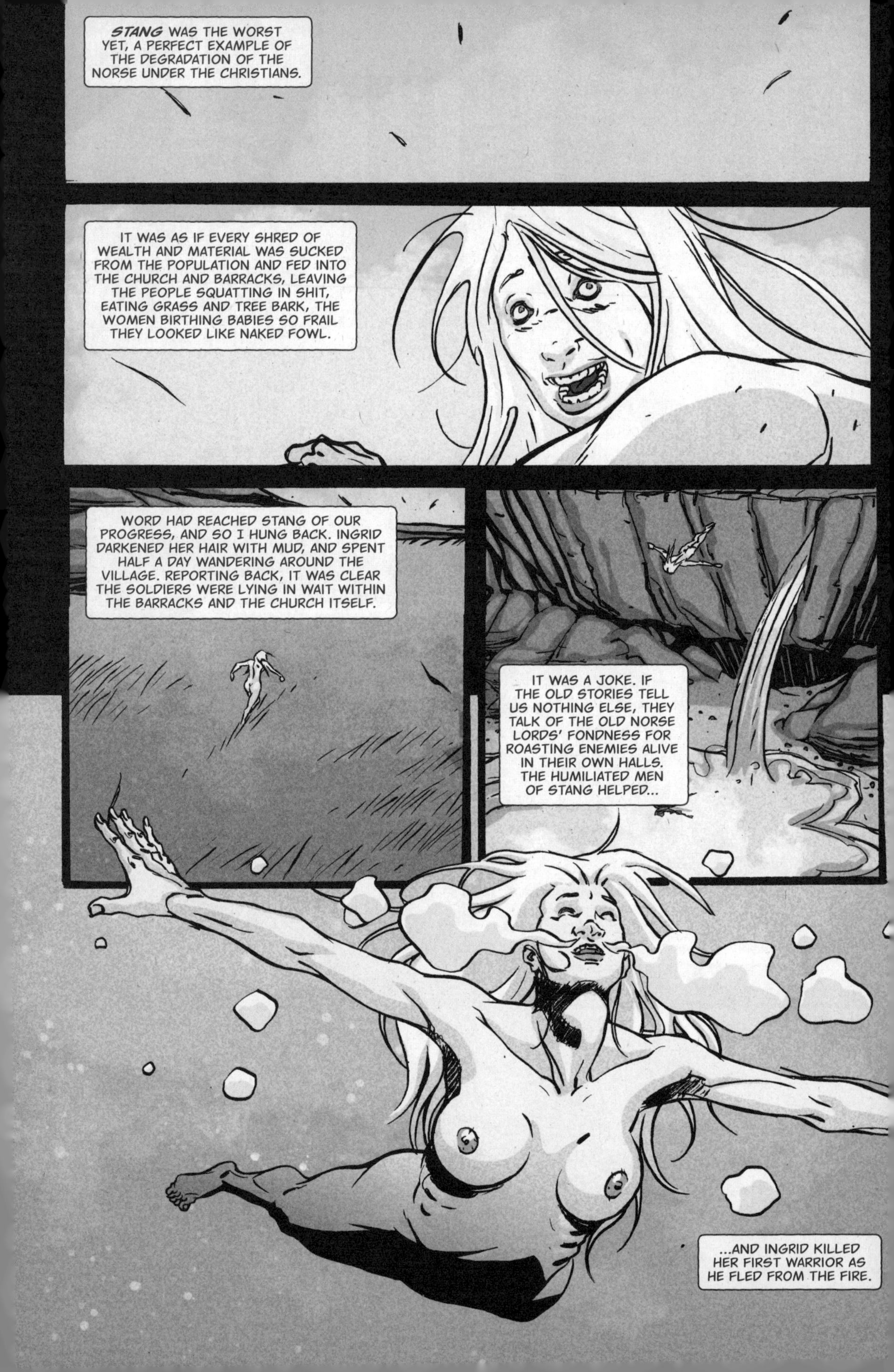
STANG WAS THE WORST YET, A PERFECT EXAMPLE OF THE DEGRADATION OF THE NORSE UNDER THE CHRISTIANS.
IT WAS AS IF EVERY SHRED OF WEALTH AND MATERIAL WAS SUCKED FROM THE POPULATION AND FED INTO THE CHURCH AND BARRACKS, LEAVING THE PEOPLE SQUATTING IN SHIT, EATING GRASS AND TREE BARK, THE WOMEN BIRTHING BABIES SO FRAIL THEY LOOKED LIKE NAKED FOWL.
WORD HAD REACHED STANG OF OUR PROGRESS, AND SO I HUNG BACK. INGRID DARKENED HER HAIR WITH MUD, AND SPENT HALF A DAY WANDERING AROUND THE VILLAGE. REPORTING BACK, IT WAS CLEAR THE SOLDIERS WERE LYING IN WAIT WITHIN THE BARRACKS AND THE CHURCH ITSELF.
IT WAS A JOKE. IF THE OLD STORIES TELL US NOTHING ELSE, THEY TALK OF THE OLD NORSE LORDS' FONDNESS FOR ROASTING ENEMIES ALIVE IN THEIR OWN HALLS. THE HUMILIATED MEN OF STANG HELPED...
...AND INGRID KILLED HER FIRST WARRIOR AS HE FLED FROM THE FIRE.

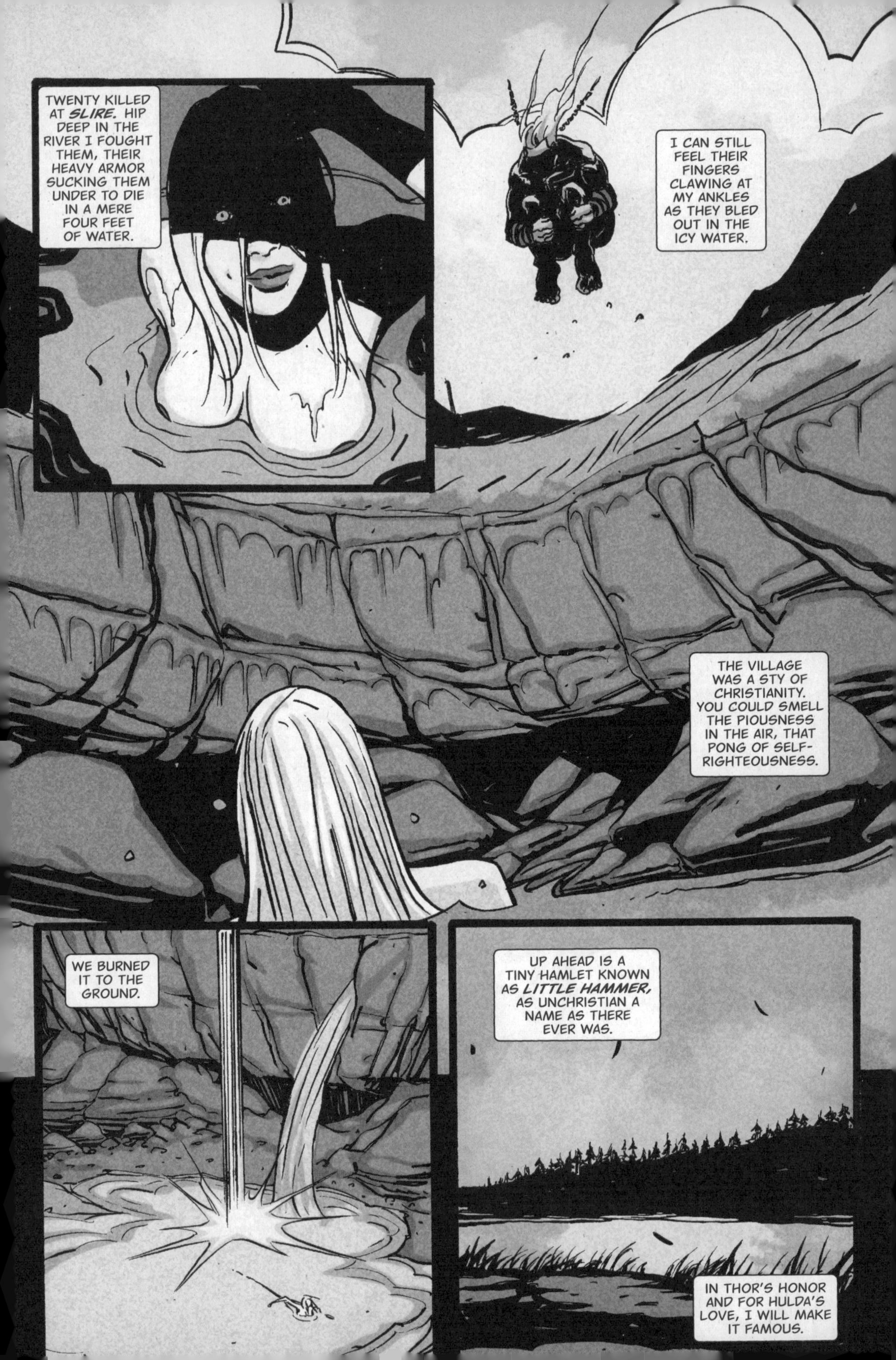
TWENTY KILLED AT SLIRE. HIP DEEP IN THE RIVER I FOUGHT THEM, THEIR HEAVY ARMOR SUCKING THEM UNDER TO DIE IN A MERE FOUR FEET OF WATER.
I CAN STILL FEEL THEIR FINGERS CLAWING AT MY ANKLES AS THEY BLED OUT IN THE ICY WATER.
THE VILLAGE WAS A STY OF CHRISTIANITY. YOU COULD SMELL THE PIOUSNESS IN THE AIR, THAT PONG OF SELF-RIGHTEOUSNESS.
WE BURNED IT TO THE GROUND.
UP AHEAD IS A TINY HAMLET KNOWN AS LITTLE HAMMER, AS UNCHRISTIAN A NAME AS THERE EVER WAS.
IN THOR'S HONOR AND FOR HULDA'S LOVE, I WILL MAKE IT FAMOUS.

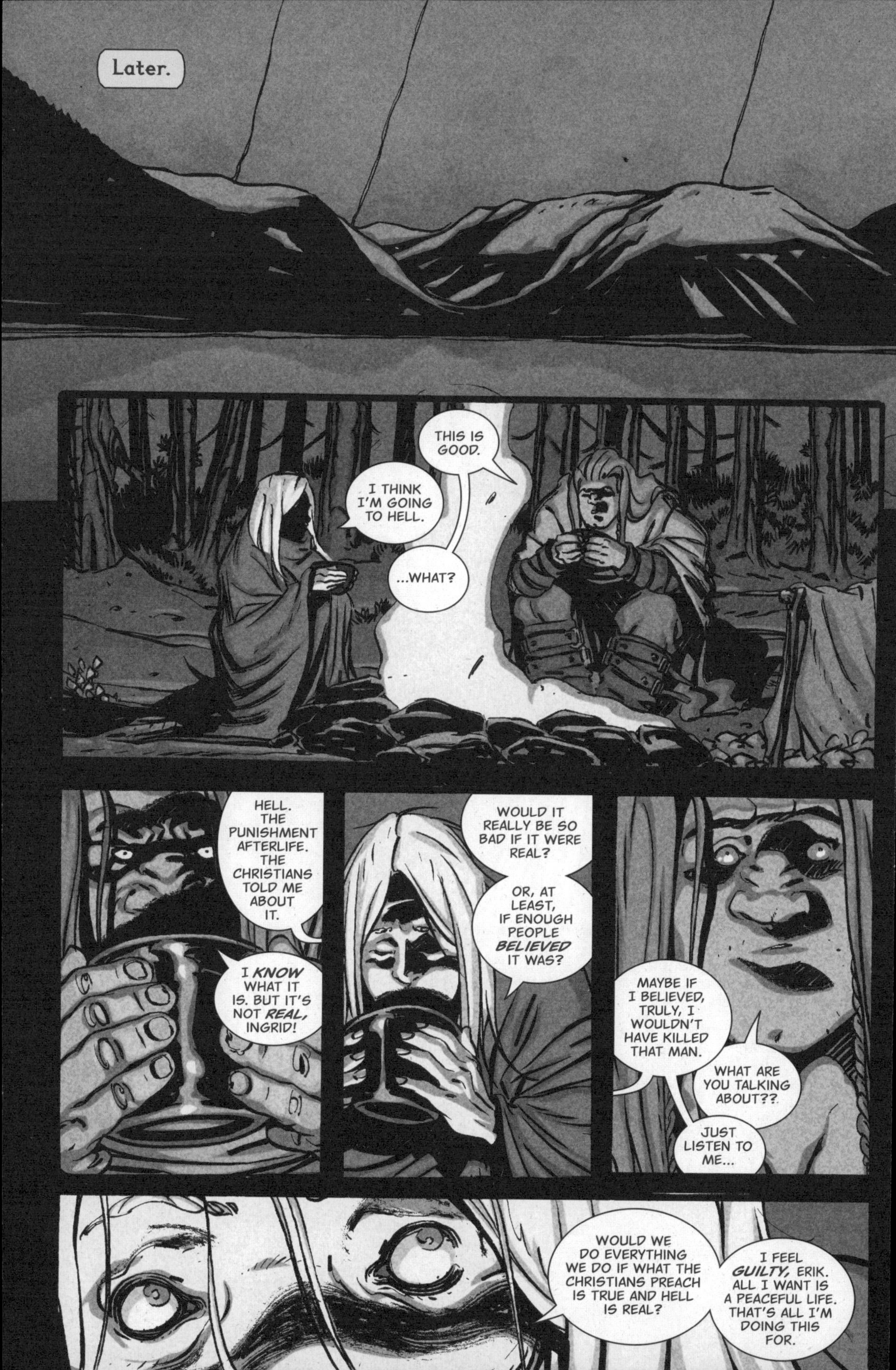
Later.
THIS IS GOOD.
I THINK I'M GOING TO HELL.
...WHAT?
HELL. THE PUNISHMENT AFTERLIFE. THE CHRISTIANS TOLD ME ABOUT IT.
I *KNOW* WHAT IT IS. BUT IT'S NOT *REAL,* INGRID!
WOULD IT REALLY BE SO BAD IF IT WERE REAL?
OR, AT LEAST, IF ENOUGH PEOPLE *BELIEVED* IT WAS?
MAYBE IF I BELIEVED, TRULY, I WOULDN'T HAVE KILLED THAT MAN.
WHAT ARE YOU TALKING ABOUT??
JUST LISTEN TO ME...
WOULD WE DO EVERYTHING WE DO IF WHAT THE CHRISTIANS PREACH IS TRUE AND HELL IS REAL?
I FEEL *GUILTY,* ERIK. ALL I WANT IS A PEACEFUL LIFE. THAT'S ALL I'M DOING THIS FOR.

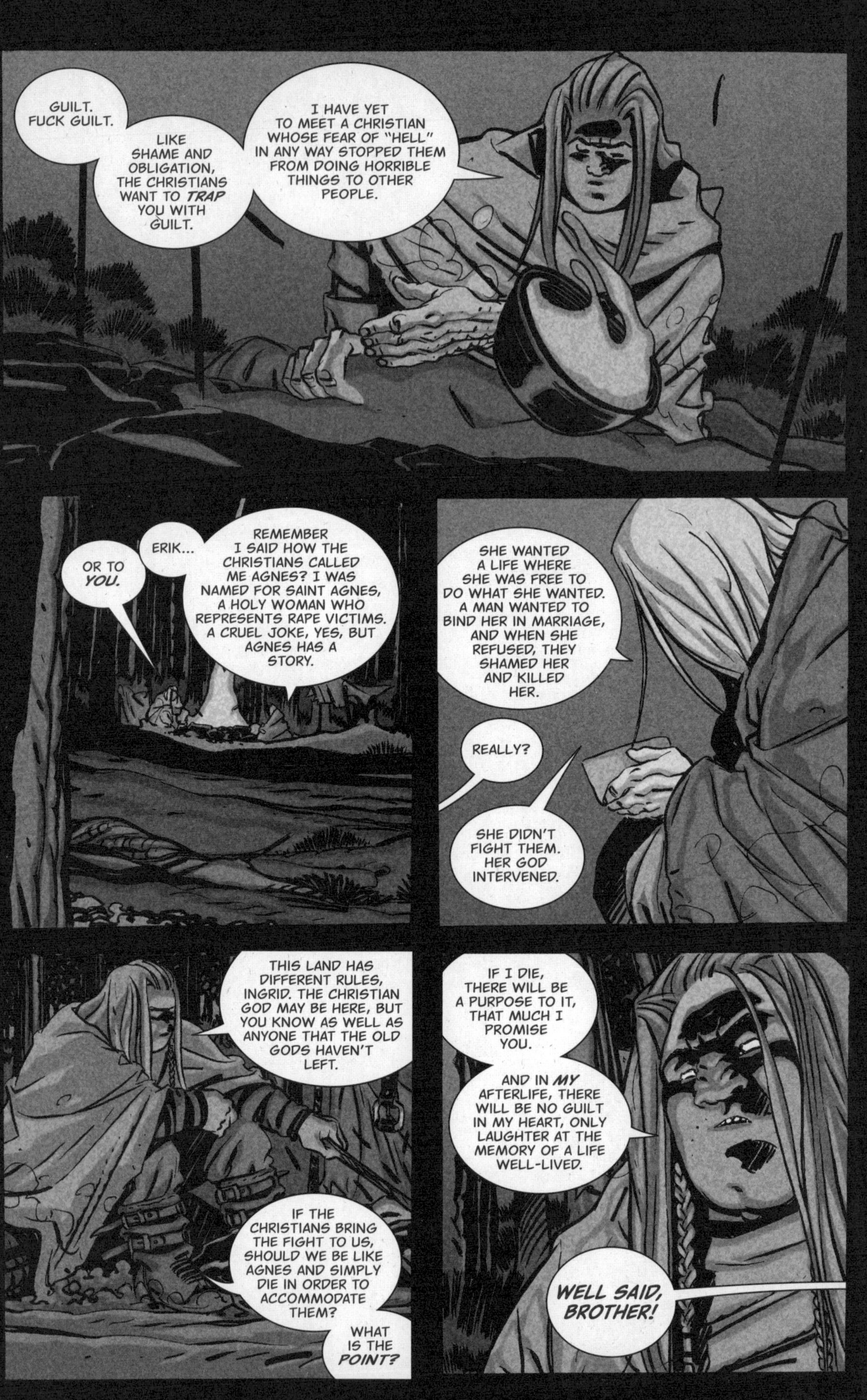
GUILT. FUCK GUILT.
LIKE SHAME AND OBLIGATION, THE CHRISTIANS WANT TO *TRAP* YOU WITH GUILT.
I HAVE YET TO MEET A CHRISTIAN WHOSE FEAR OF "HELL" IN ANY WAY STOPPED THEM FROM DOING HORRIBLE THINGS TO OTHER PEOPLE.
OR TO *YOU.*
ERIK...
REMEMBER I SAID HOW THE CHRISTIANS CALLED ME AGNES? I WAS NAMED FOR SAINT AGNES, A HOLY WOMAN WHO REPRESENTS RAPE VICTIMS. A CRUEL JOKE, YES, BUT AGNES HAS A STORY.
SHE WANTED A LIFE WHERE SHE WAS FREE TO DO WHAT SHE WANTED. A MAN WANTED TO BIND HER IN MARRIAGE, AND WHEN SHE REFUSED, THEY SHAMED HER AND KILLED HER.
REALLY?
SHE DIDN'T FIGHT THEM. HER GOD INTERVENED.
THIS LAND HAS DIFFERENT RULES, INGRID. THE CHRISTIAN GOD MAY BE HERE, BUT YOU KNOW AS WELL AS ANYONE THAT THE OLD GODS HAVEN'T LEFT.
IF THE CHRISTIANS BRING THE FIGHT TO US, SHOULD WE BE LIKE AGNES AND SIMPLY DIE IN ORDER TO ACCOMMODATE THEM?
WHAT IS THE *POINT?*
IF I DIE, THERE WILL BE A PURPOSE TO IT, THAT MUCH I PROMISE YOU.
AND IN *MY* AFTERLIFE, THERE WILL BE NO GUILT IN MY HEART, ONLY LAUGHTER AT THE MEMORY OF A LIFE WELL-LIVED.
WELL SAID, BROTHER!

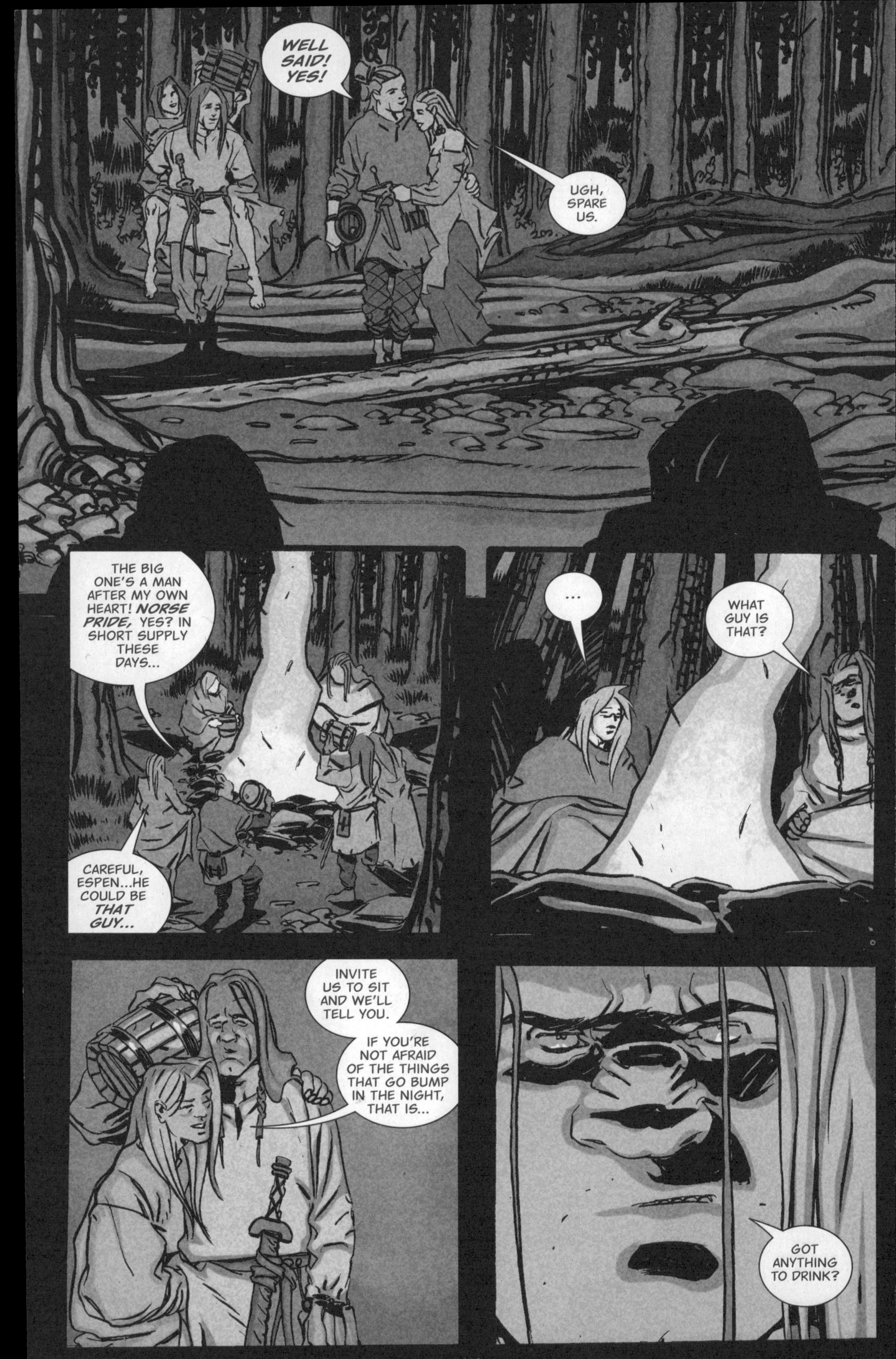
WELL SAID! YES!
UGH, SPARE US.
THE BIG ONE'S A MAN AFTER MY OWN HEART! NORSE PRIDE, YES? IN SHORT SUPPLY THESE DAYS...
CAREFUL, ESPEN...HE COULD BE THAT GUY...
...
WHAT GUY IS THAT?
INVITE US TO SIT AND WE'LL TELL YOU.
IF YOU'RE NOT AFRAID OF THE THINGS THAT GO BUMP IN THE NIGHT, THAT IS...
GOT ANYTHING TO DRINK?

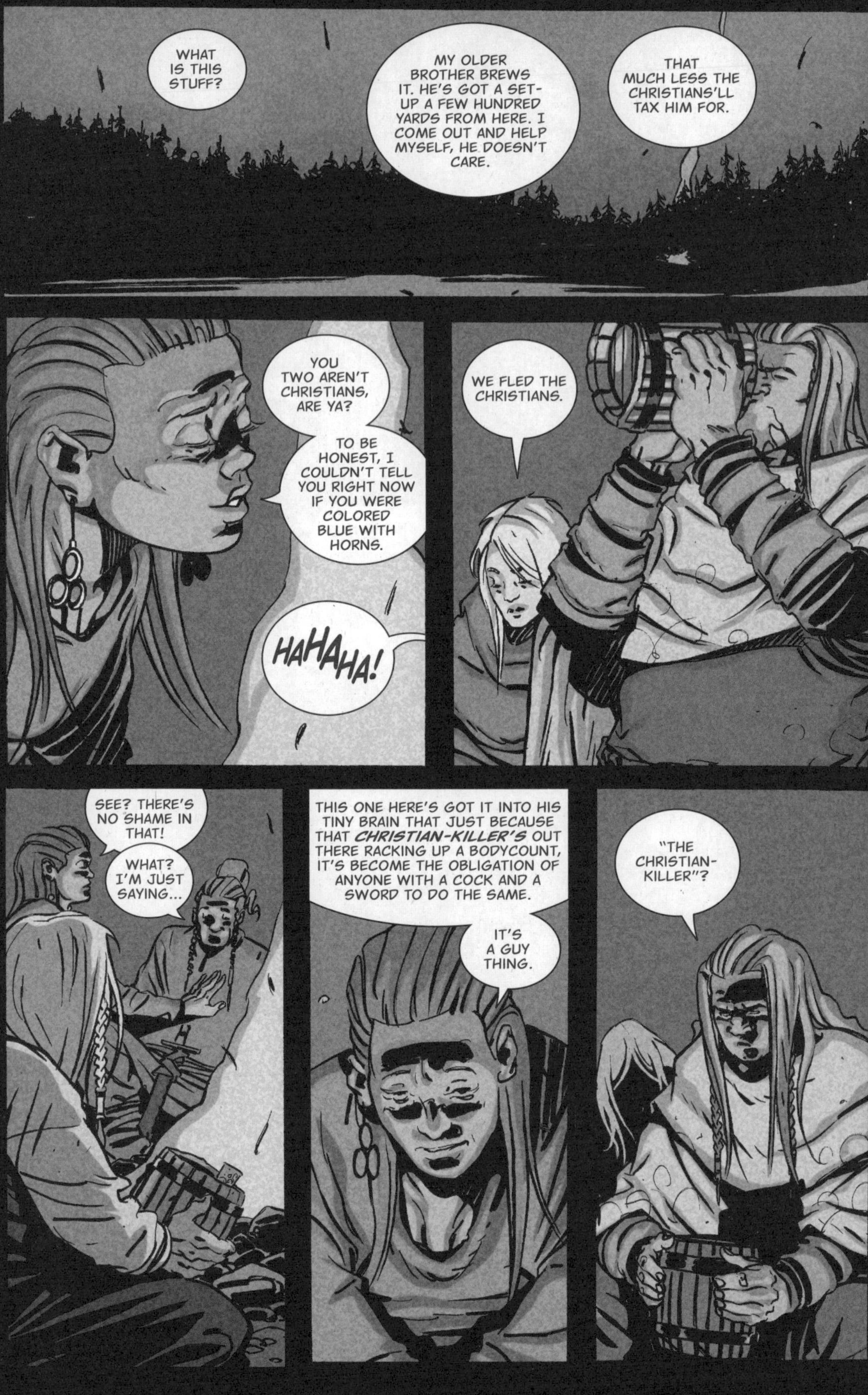
WHAT IS THIS STUFF?
MY OLDER BROTHER BREWS IT. HE'S GOT A SET-UP A FEW HUNDRED YARDS FROM HERE. I COME OUT AND HELP MYSELF, HE DOESN'T CARE.
THAT MUCH LESS THE CHRISTIANS'LL TAX HIM FOR.
YOU TWO AREN'T CHRISTIANS, ARE YA?
TO BE HONEST, I COULDN'T TELL YOU RIGHT NOW IF YOU WERE COLORED BLUE WITH HORNS.
HAHAHA!
WE FLED THE CHRISTIANS.
SEE? THERE'S NO SHAME IN THAT!
WHAT? I'M JUST SAYING...
THIS ONE HERE'S GOT IT INTO HIS TINY BRAIN THAT JUST BECAUSE THAT *CHRISTIAN-KILLER'S* OUT THERE RACKING UP A BODYCOUNT, IT'S BECOME THE OBLIGATION OF ANYONE WITH A COCK AND A SWORD TO DO THE SAME.
IT'S A GUY THING.
"THE CHRISTIAN-KILLER"?

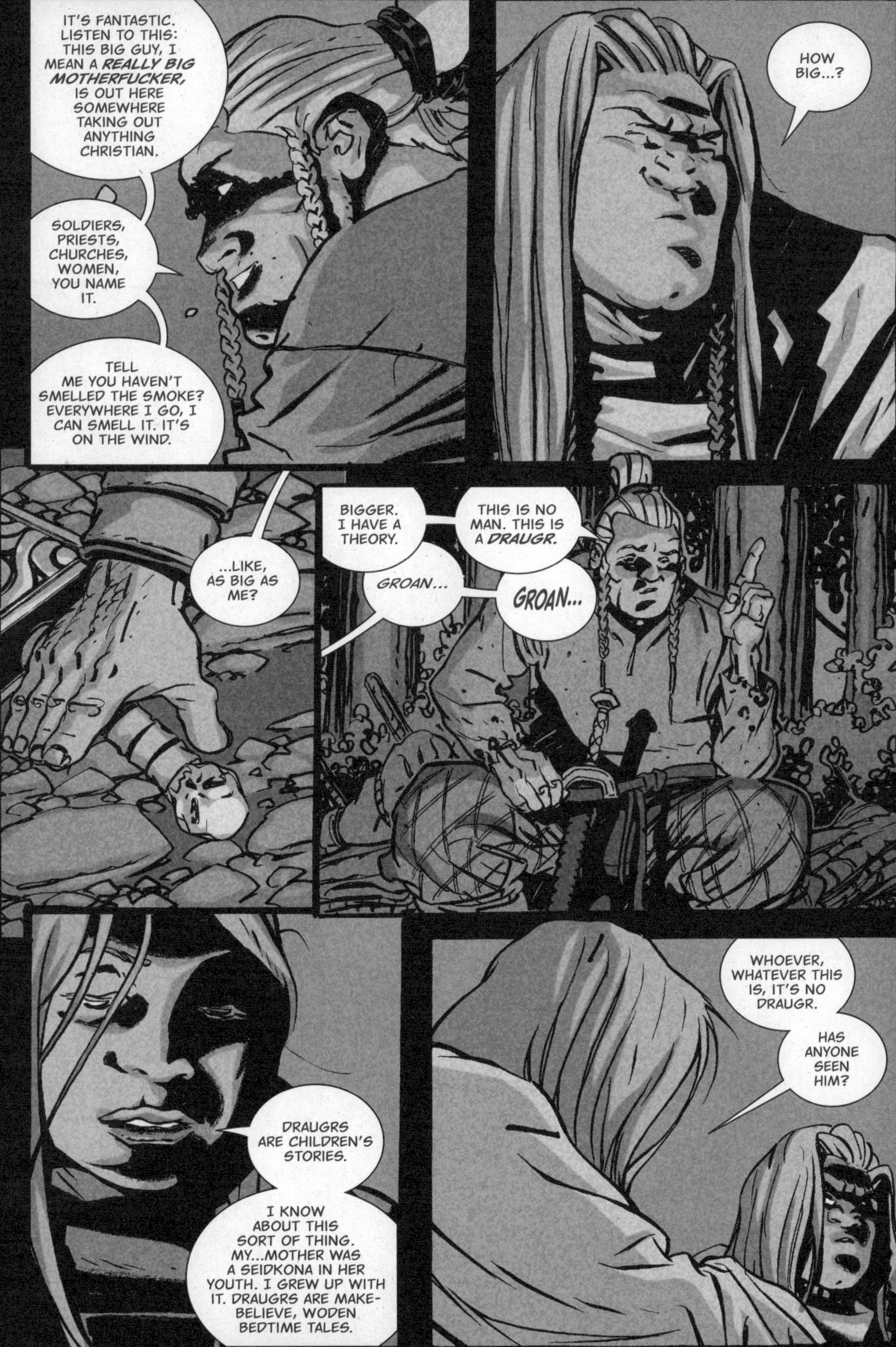
IT'S FANTASTIC. LISTEN TO THIS: THIS BIG GUY, I MEAN A *REALLY BIG MOTHERFUCKER,* IS OUT HERE SOMEWHERE TAKING OUT ANYTHING CHRISTIAN.
SOLDIERS, PRIESTS, CHURCHES, WOMEN, YOU NAME IT.
TELL ME YOU HAVEN'T SMELLED THE SMOKE? EVERYWHERE I GO, I CAN SMELL IT. IT'S ON THE WIND.
HOW BIG...?
...LIKE, AS BIG AS ME?
BIGGER. I HAVE A THEORY.
THIS IS NO MAN. THIS IS A *DRAUGR.*
GROAN...
GROAN...
DRAUGRS ARE CHILDREN'S STORIES.
I KNOW ABOUT THIS SORT OF THING. MY...MOTHER WAS A SEIDKONA IN HER YOUTH. I GREW UP WITH IT. DRAUGRS ARE MAKE-BELIEVE, WODEN BEDTIME TALES.
WHOEVER, WHATEVER THIS IS, IT'S NO DRAUGR.
HAS ANYONE SEEN HIM?

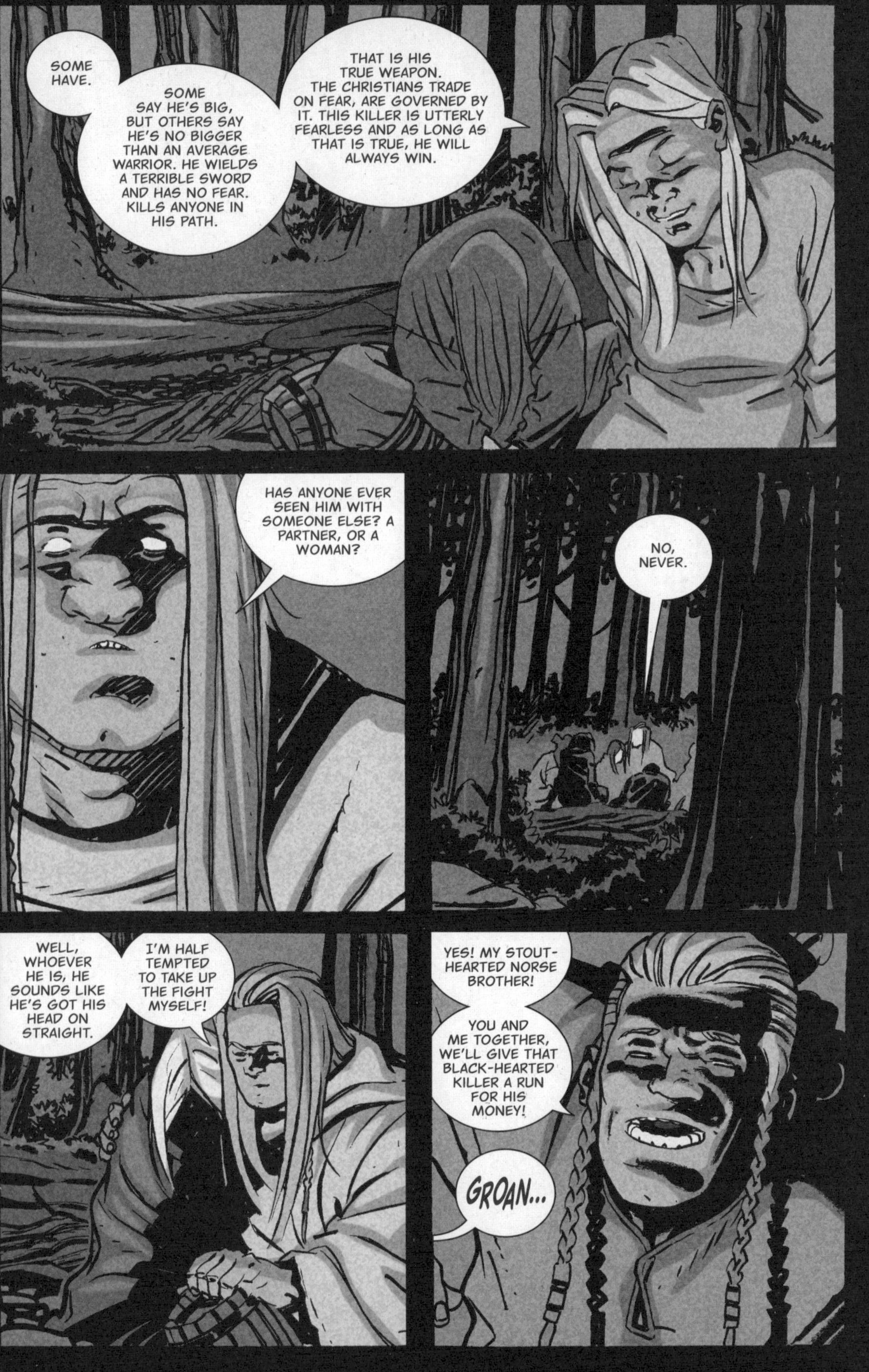
SOME HAVE.
SOME SAY HE'S BIG, BUT OTHERS SAY HE'S NO BIGGER THAN AN AVERAGE WARRIOR. HE WIELDS A TERRIBLE SWORD AND HAS NO FEAR. KILLS ANYONE IN HIS PATH.
THAT IS HIS TRUE WEAPON. THE CHRISTIANS TRADE ON FEAR, ARE GOVERNED BY IT. THIS KILLER IS UTTERLY FEARLESS AND AS LONG AS THAT IS TRUE, HE WILL ALWAYS WIN.
HAS ANYONE EVER SEEN HIM WITH SOMEONE ELSE? A PARTNER, OR A WOMAN?
NO, NEVER.
WELL, WHOEVER HE IS, HE SOUNDS LIKE HE'S GOT HIS HEAD ON STRAIGHT.
I'M HALF TEMPTED TO TAKE UP THE FIGHT MYSELF!
YES! MY STOUT-HEARTED NORSE BROTHER!
YOU AND ME TOGETHER, WE'LL GIVE THAT BLACK-HEARTED KILLER A RUN FOR HIS MONEY!
GROAN...

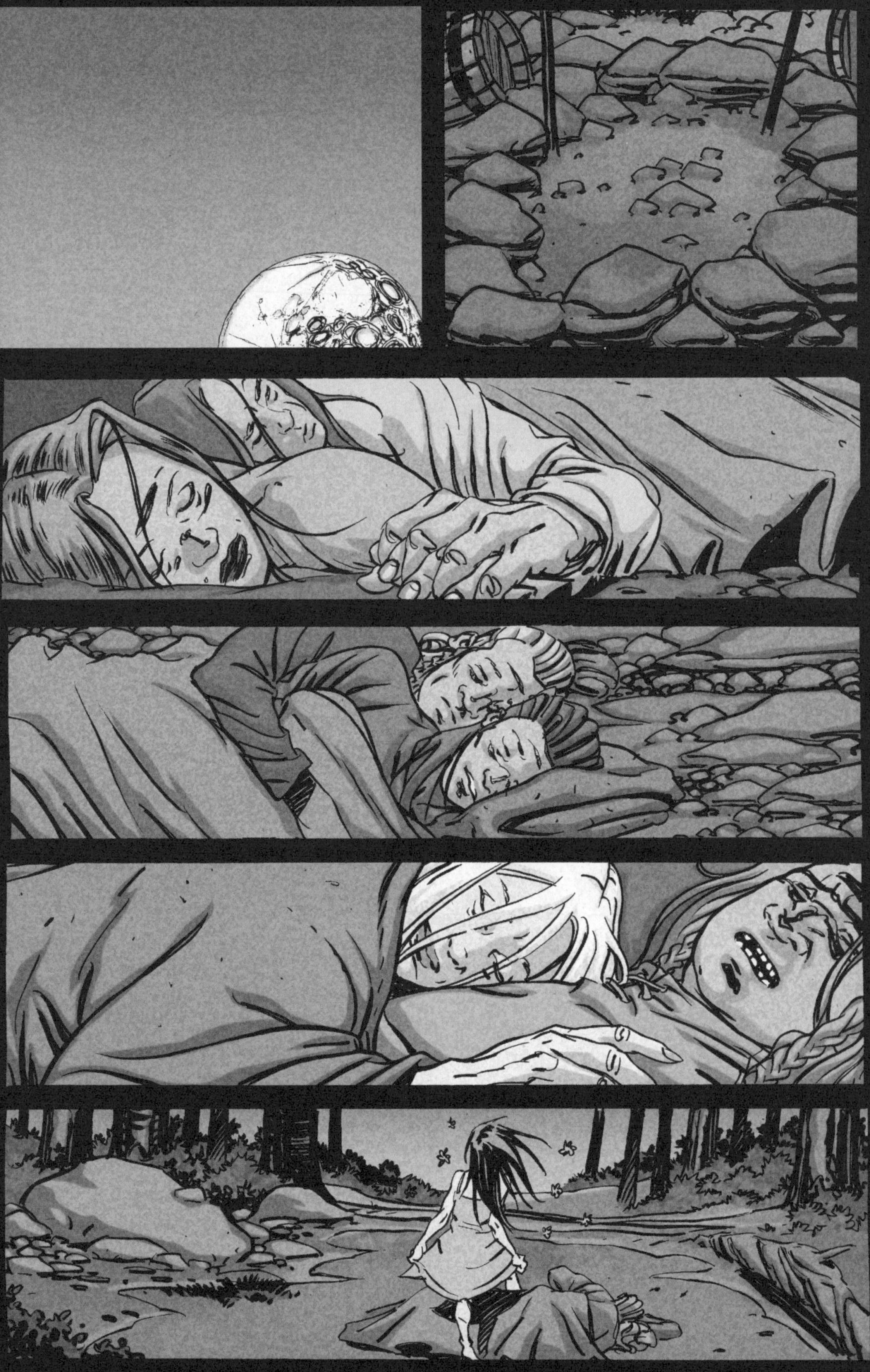

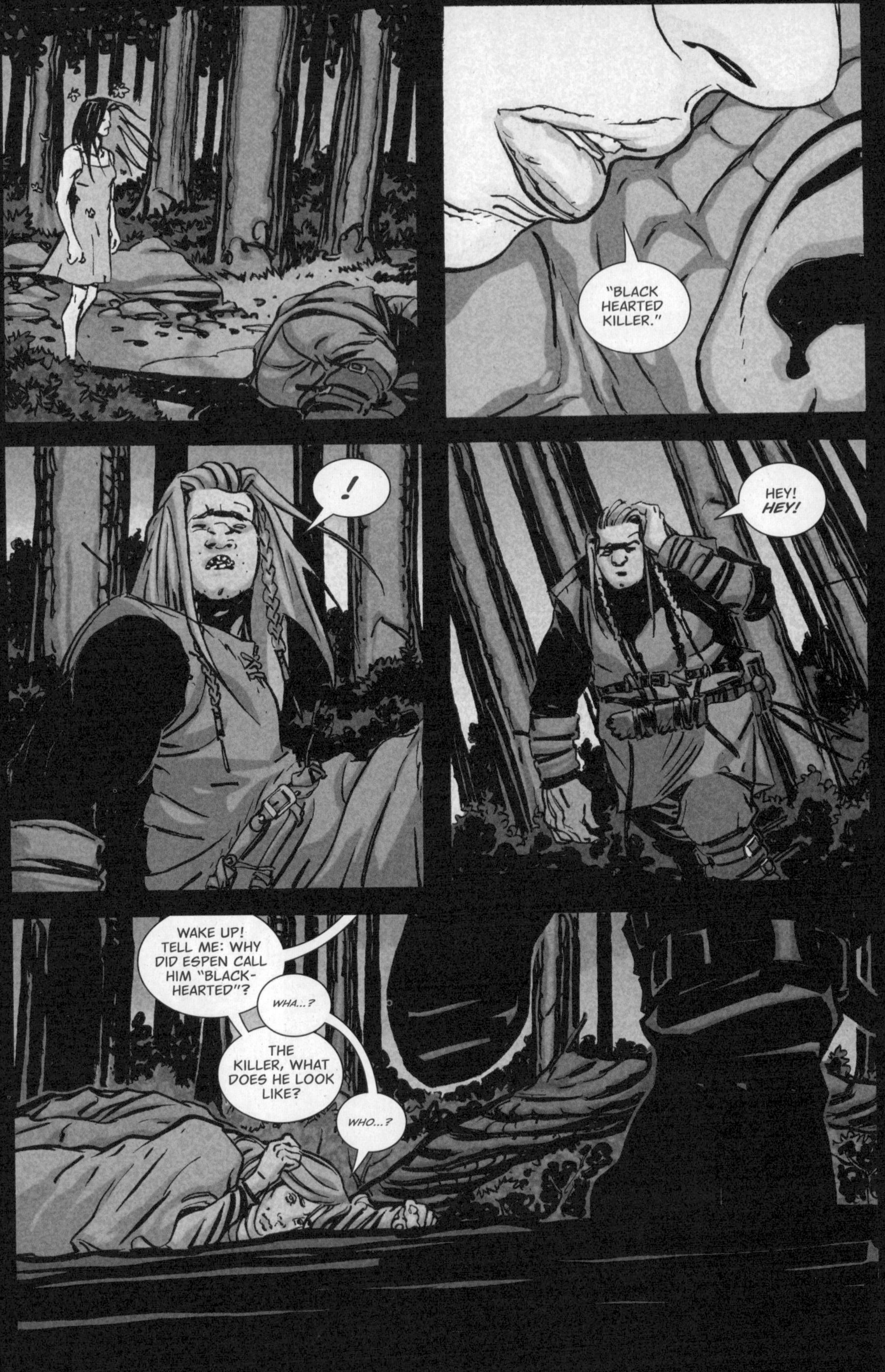
"BLACK HEARTED KILLER."
!
HEY! HEY!
WAKE UP! TELL ME: WHY DID ESPEN CALL HIM "BLACK-HEARTED"?
WHA...?
THE KILLER, WHAT DOES HE LOOK LIKE?
WHO...?

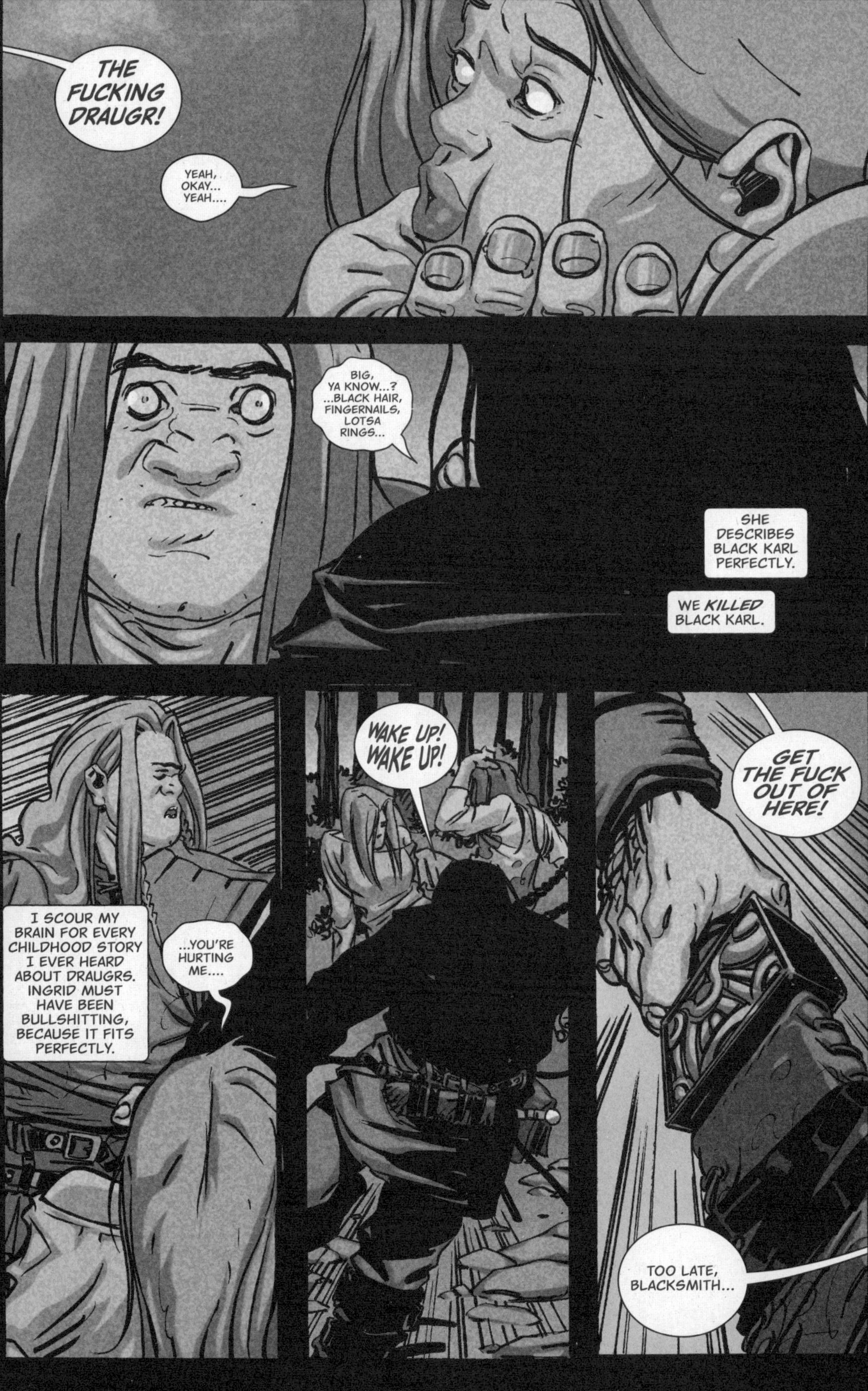
THE FUCKING DRAUGR!
YEAH, OKAY... YEAH....
BIG, YA KNOW...? ...BLACK HAIR, FINGERNAILS, LOTSA RINGS...
SHE DESCRIBES BLACK KARL PERFECTLY.
WE *KILLED* BLACK KARL.
I SCOUR MY BRAIN FOR EVERY CHILDHOOD STORY I EVER HEARD ABOUT DRAUGRS. INGRID MUST HAVE BEEN BULLSHITTING, BECAUSE IT FITS PERFECTLY.
...YOU'RE HURTING ME....
WAKE UP! WAKE UP!
GET THE FUCK OUT OF HERE!
TOO LATE, BLACKSMITH...

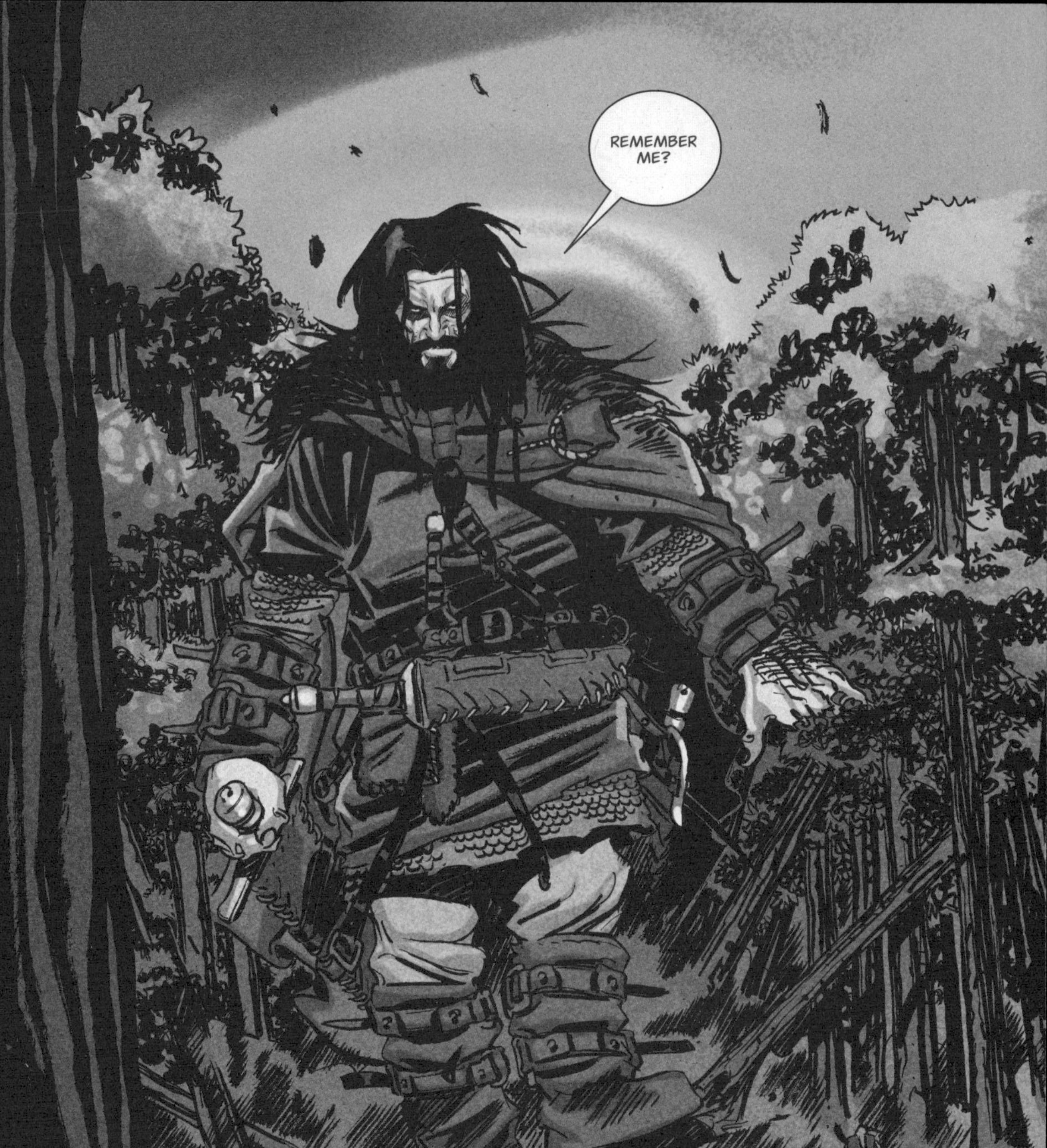
REMEMBER ME?

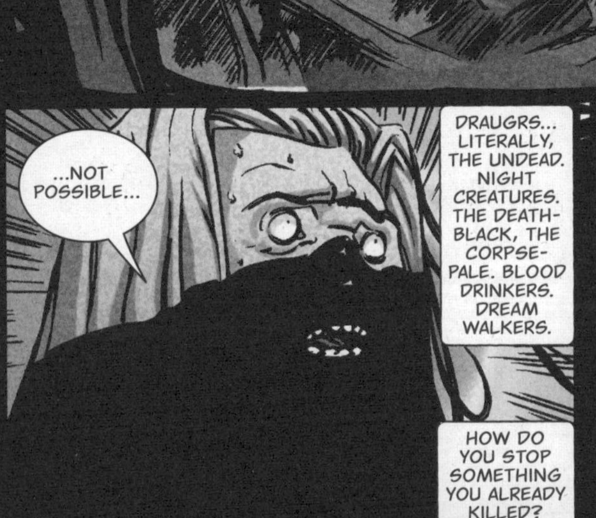
...NOT POSSIBLE...
DRAUGRS... LITERALLY, THE UNDEAD. NIGHT CREATURES. THE DEATH-BLACK, THE CORPSE-PALE. BLOOD DRINKERS. DREAM WALKERS.
HOW DO YOU STOP SOMETHING YOU ALREADY KILLED?

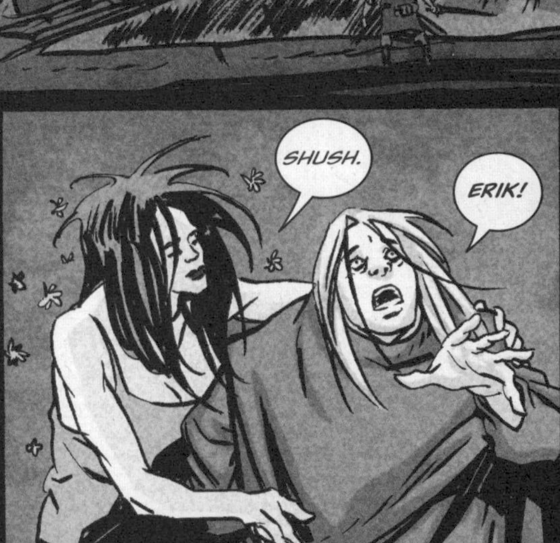
SHUSH.
ERIK!

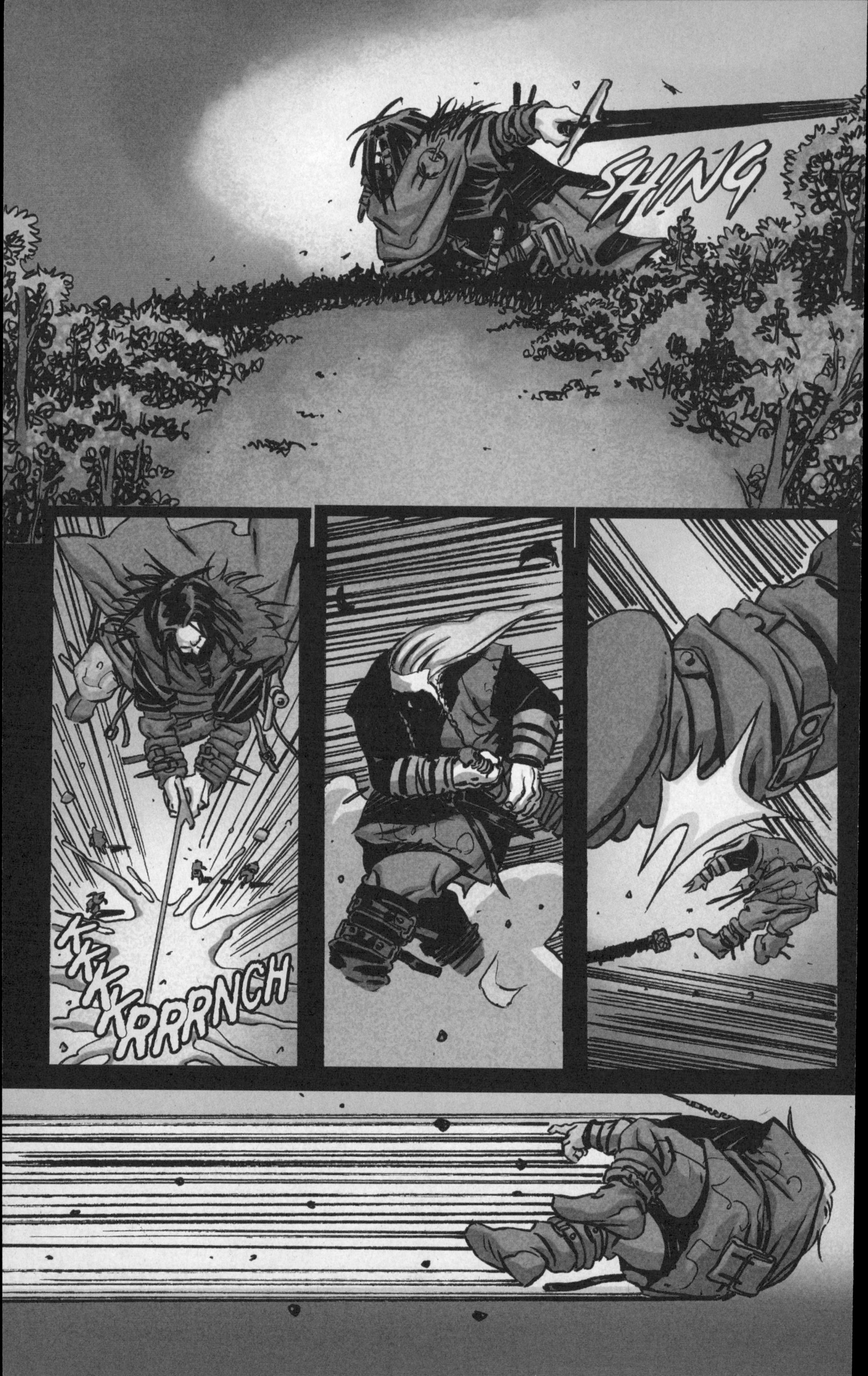
SHING
KKKKRRRRNCH

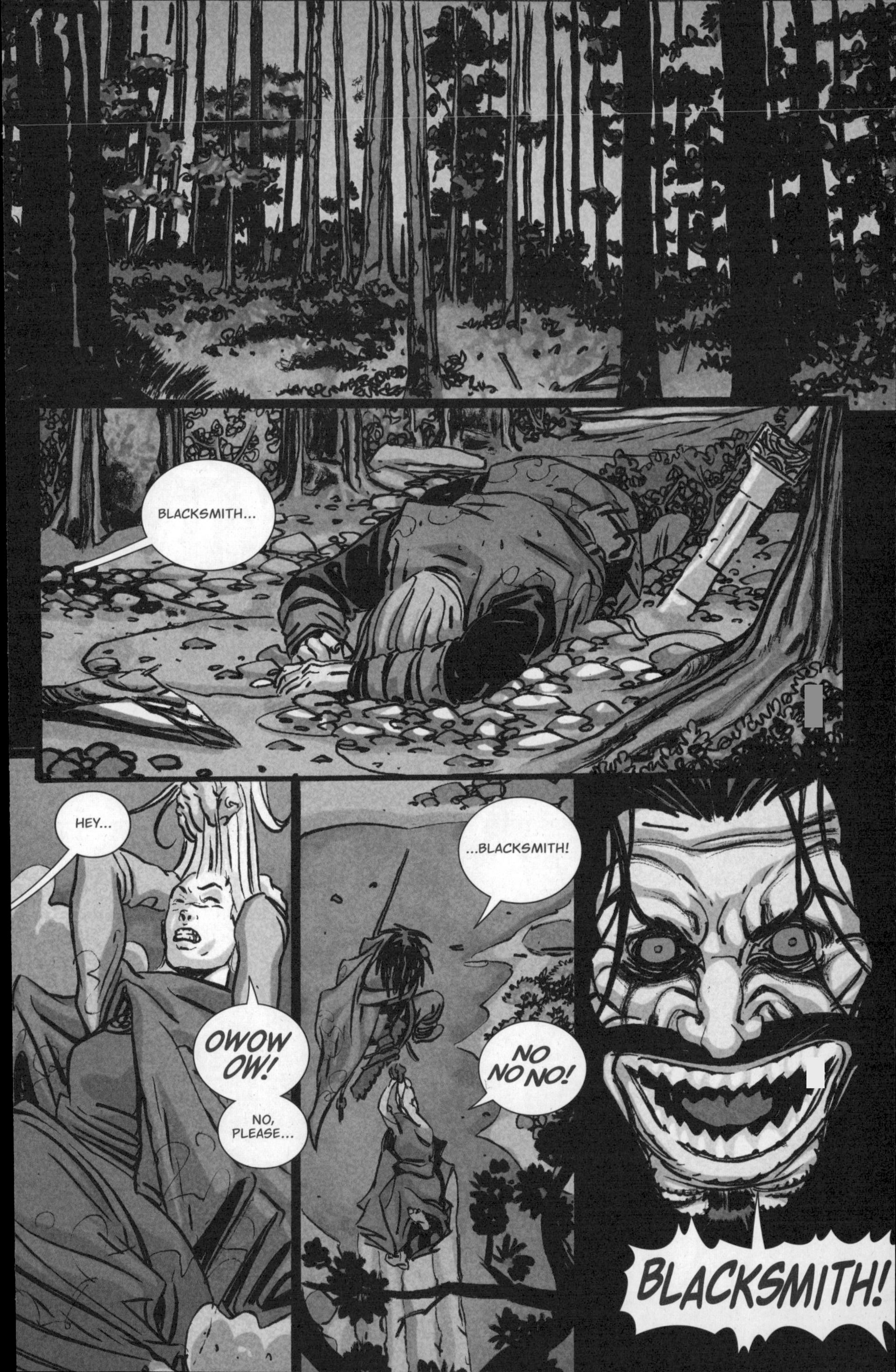
BLACKSMITH...
HEY...
OWOW OW!
NO, PLEASE...
...BLACKSMITH!
NO NO NO!
BLACKSMITH!

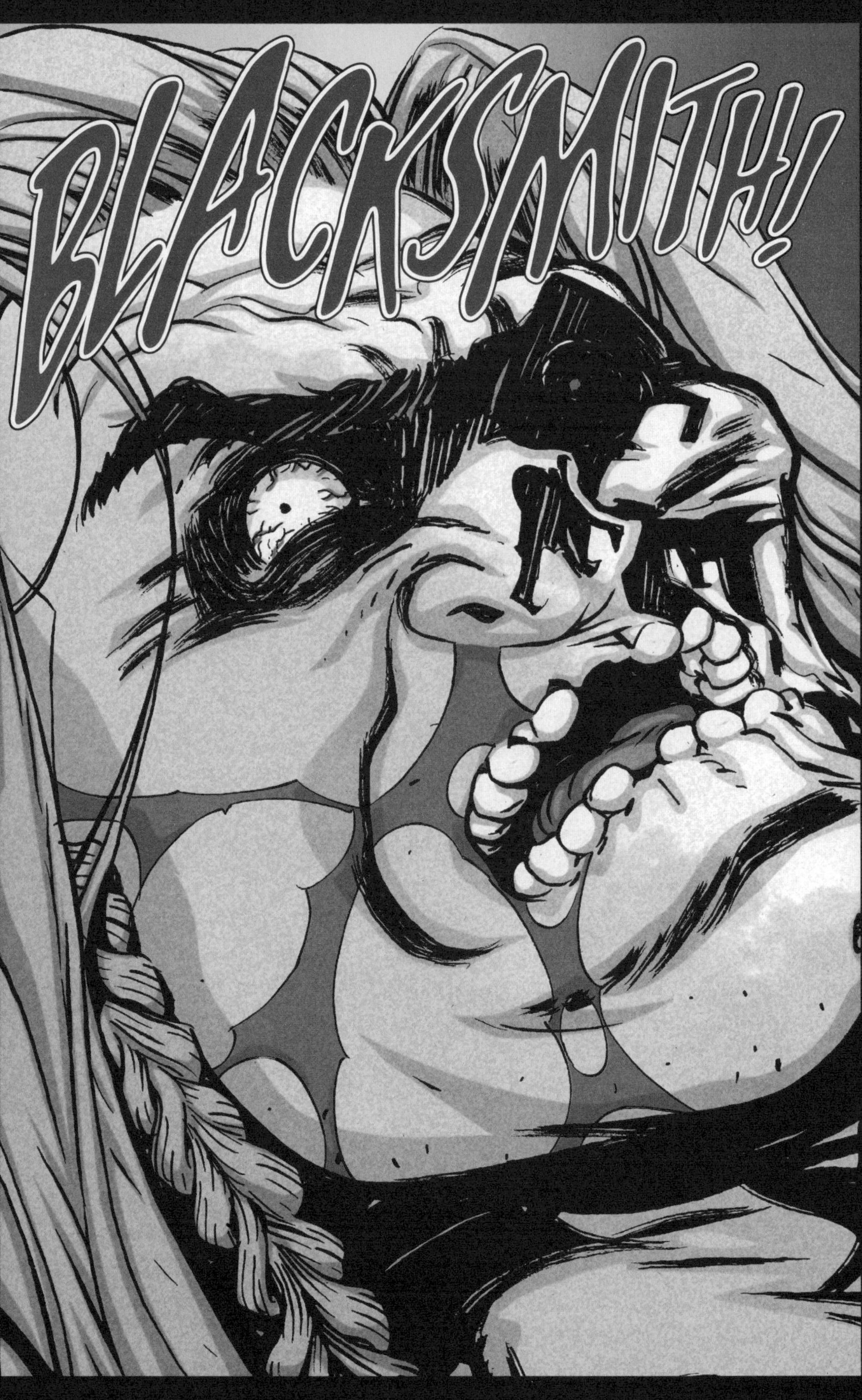
BLACKSMITH!

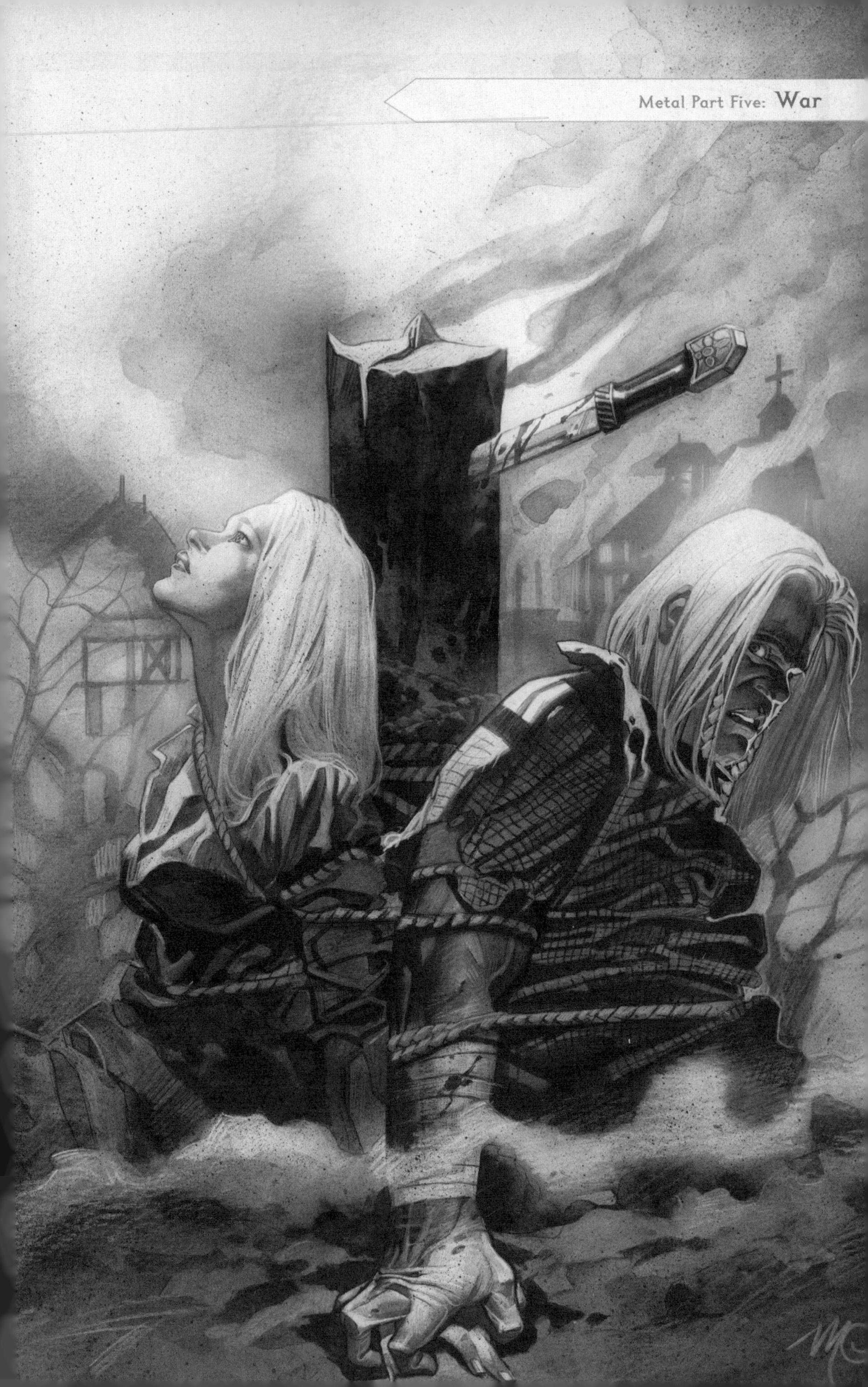

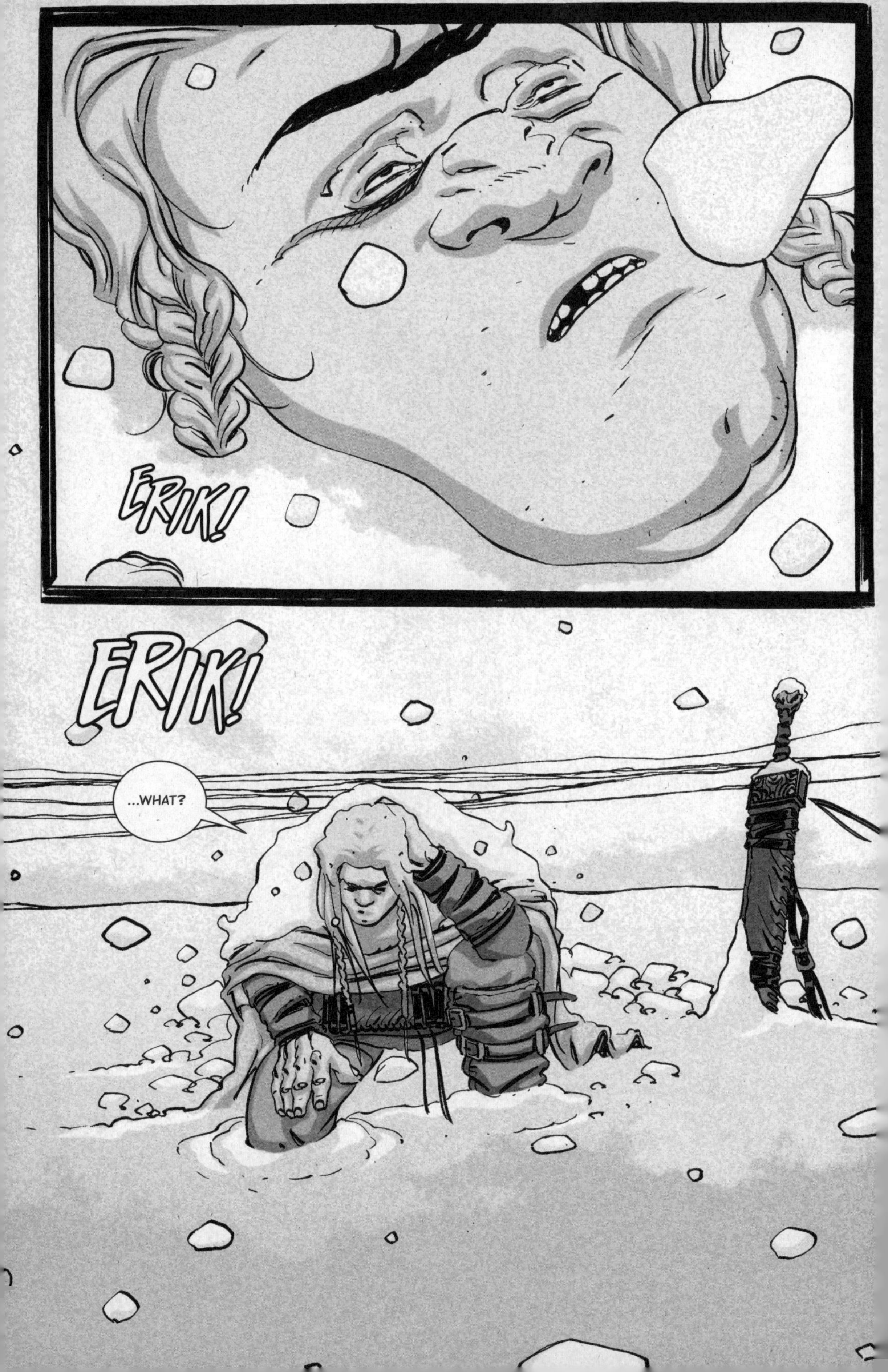
ERIK!
ERIK!
...WHAT?

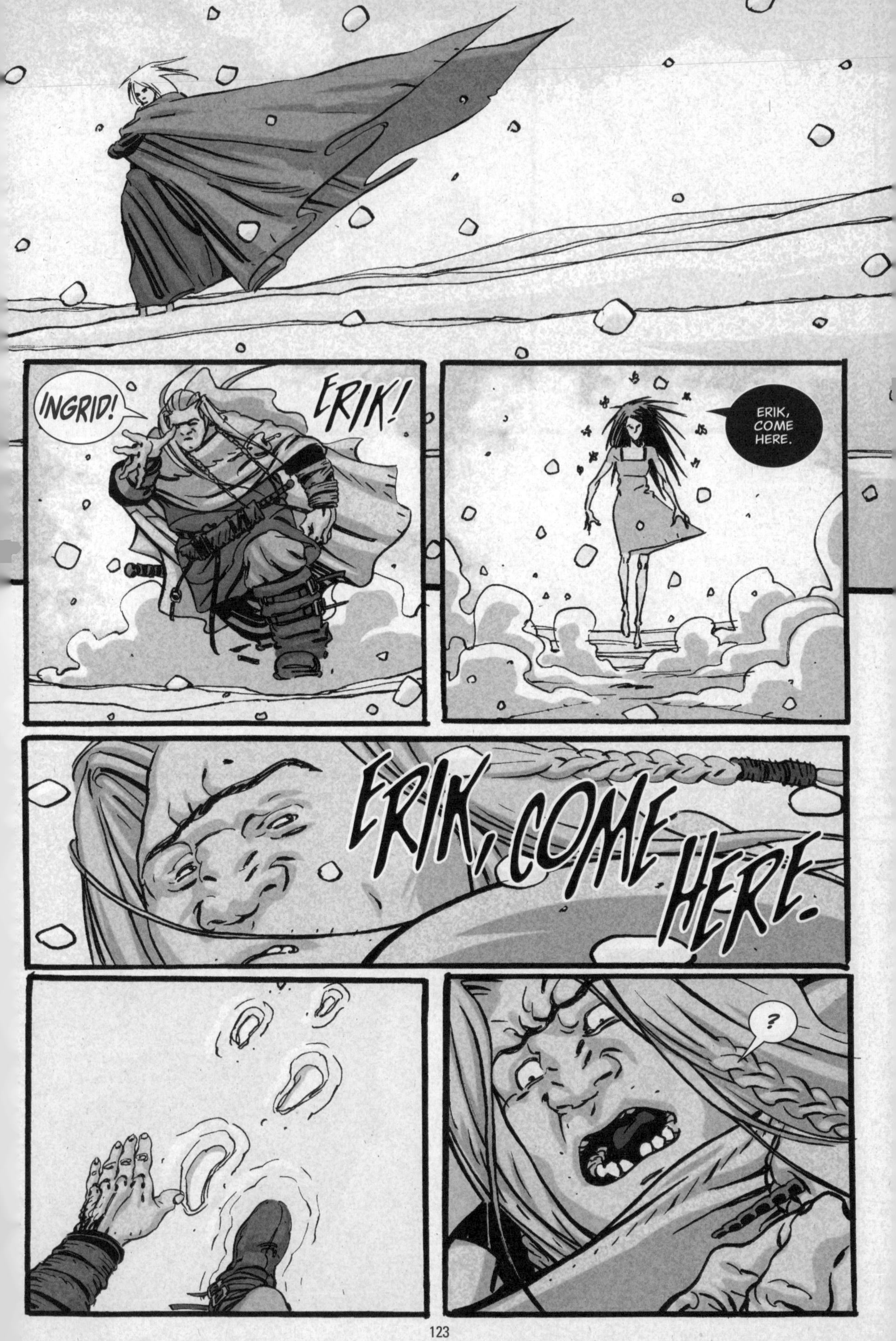
INGRID!
ERIK!
ERIK, COME HERE.
ERIK, COME HERE.
?

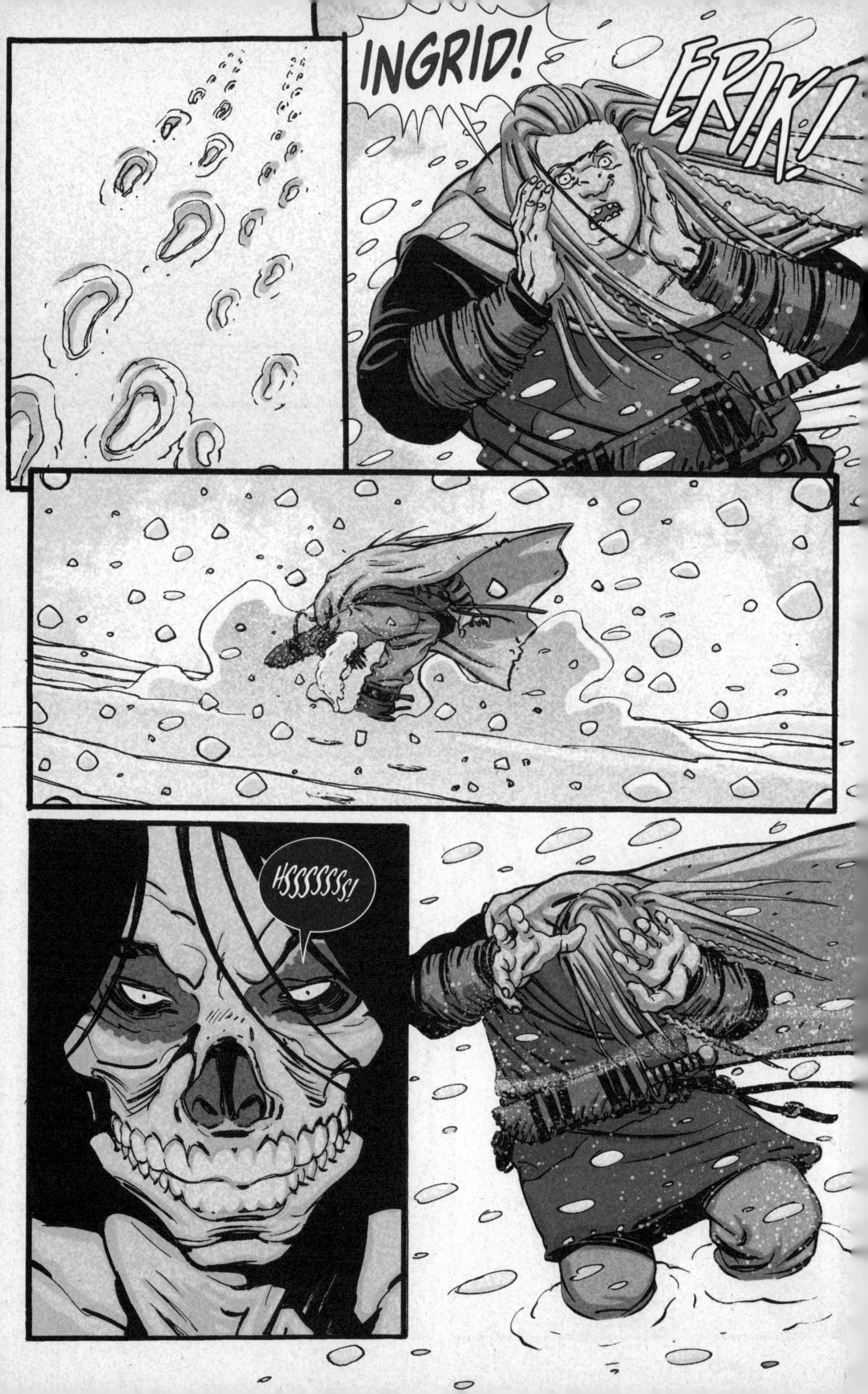
INGRID!
ERIK!
HSSSSSSSS!

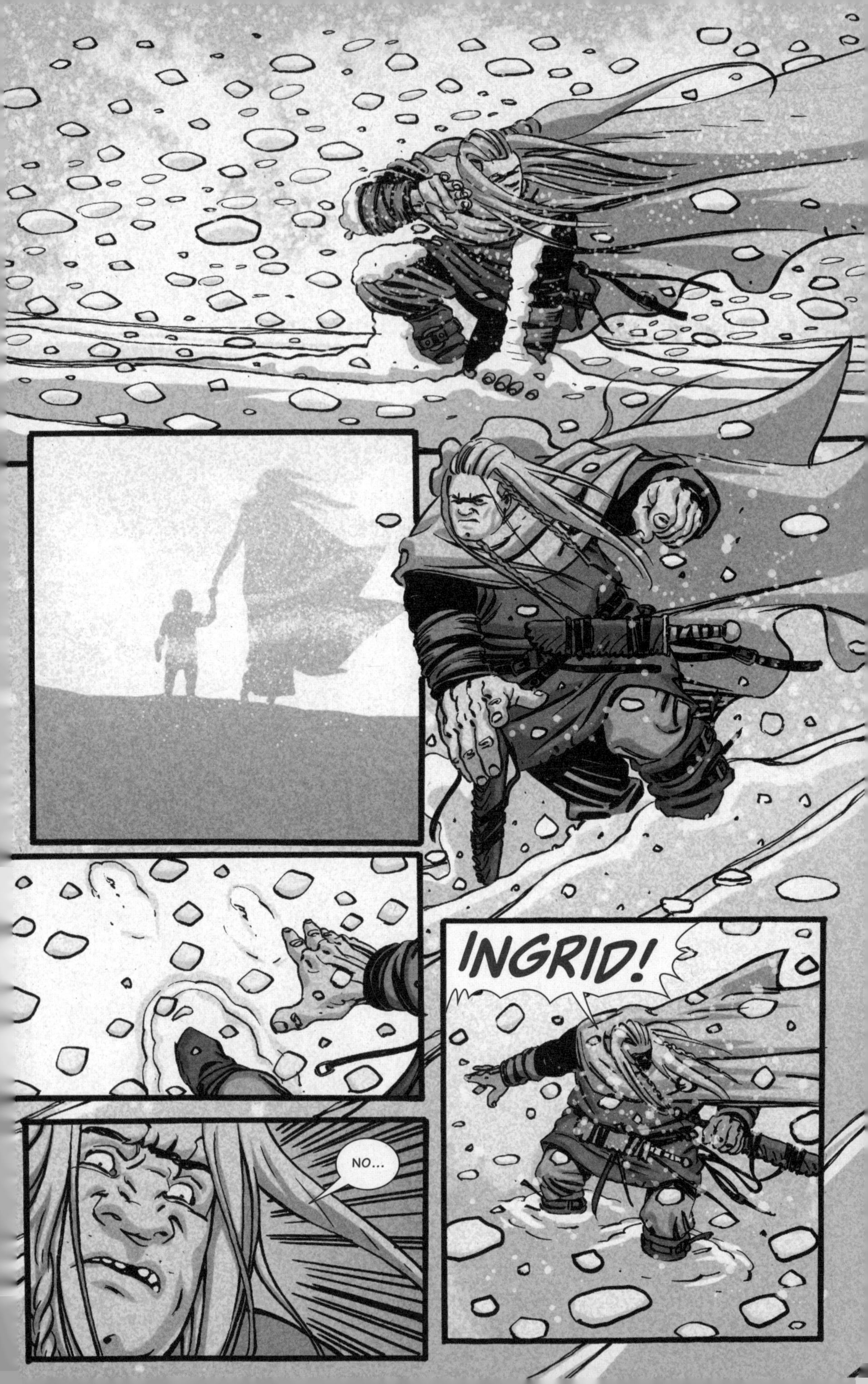
INGRID!
NO...

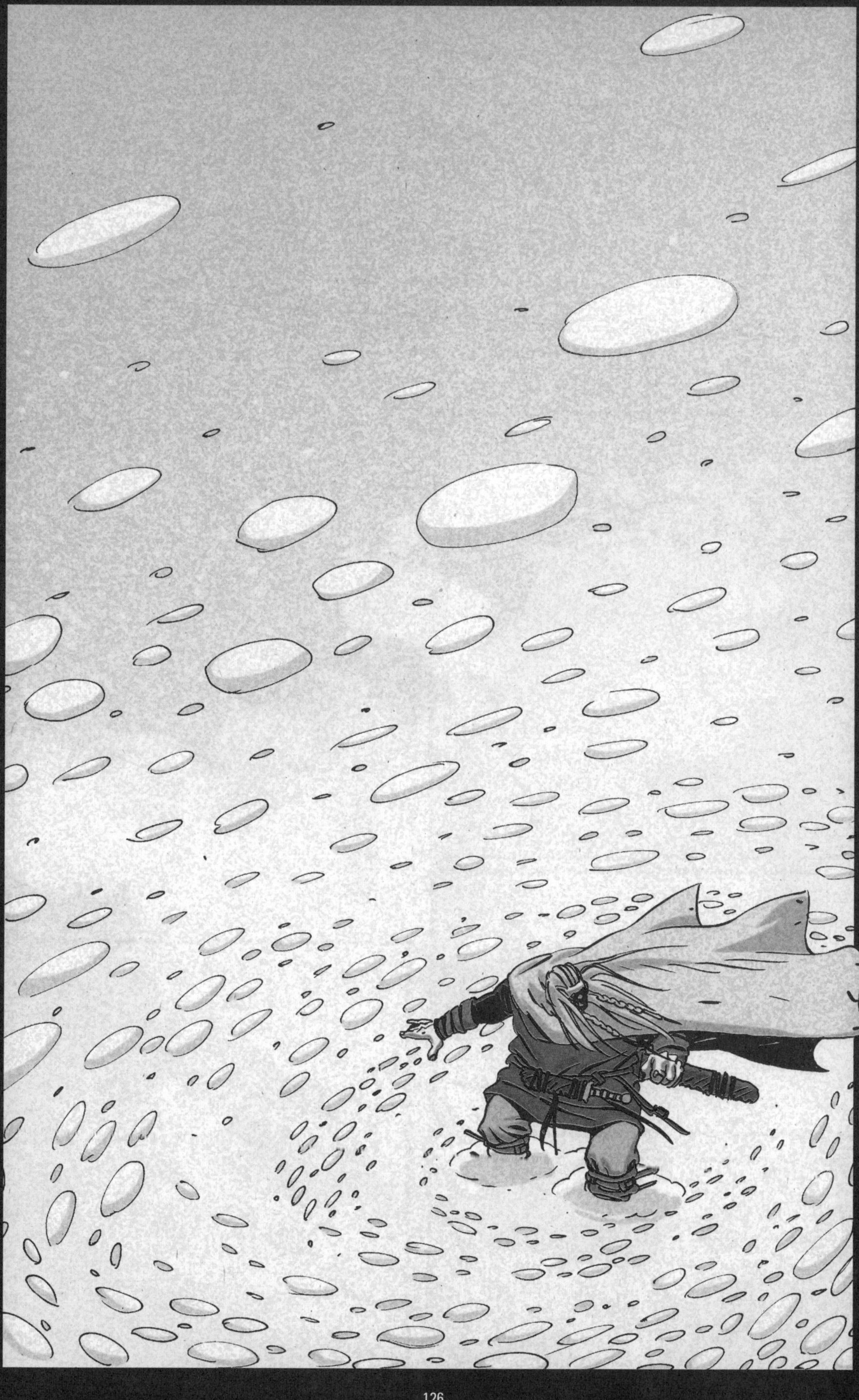

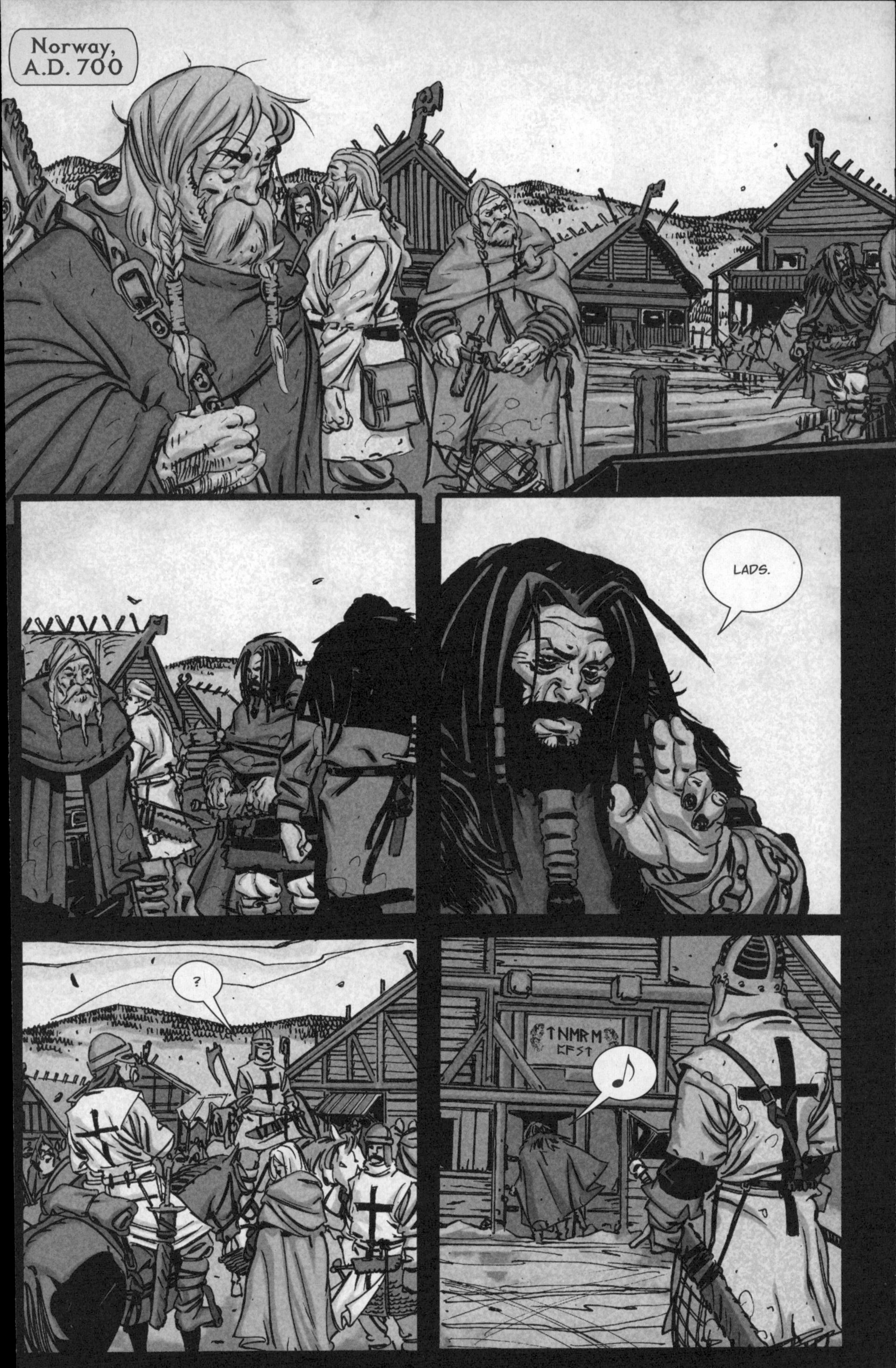
Norway,
A.D. 700
LADS.
?
♪

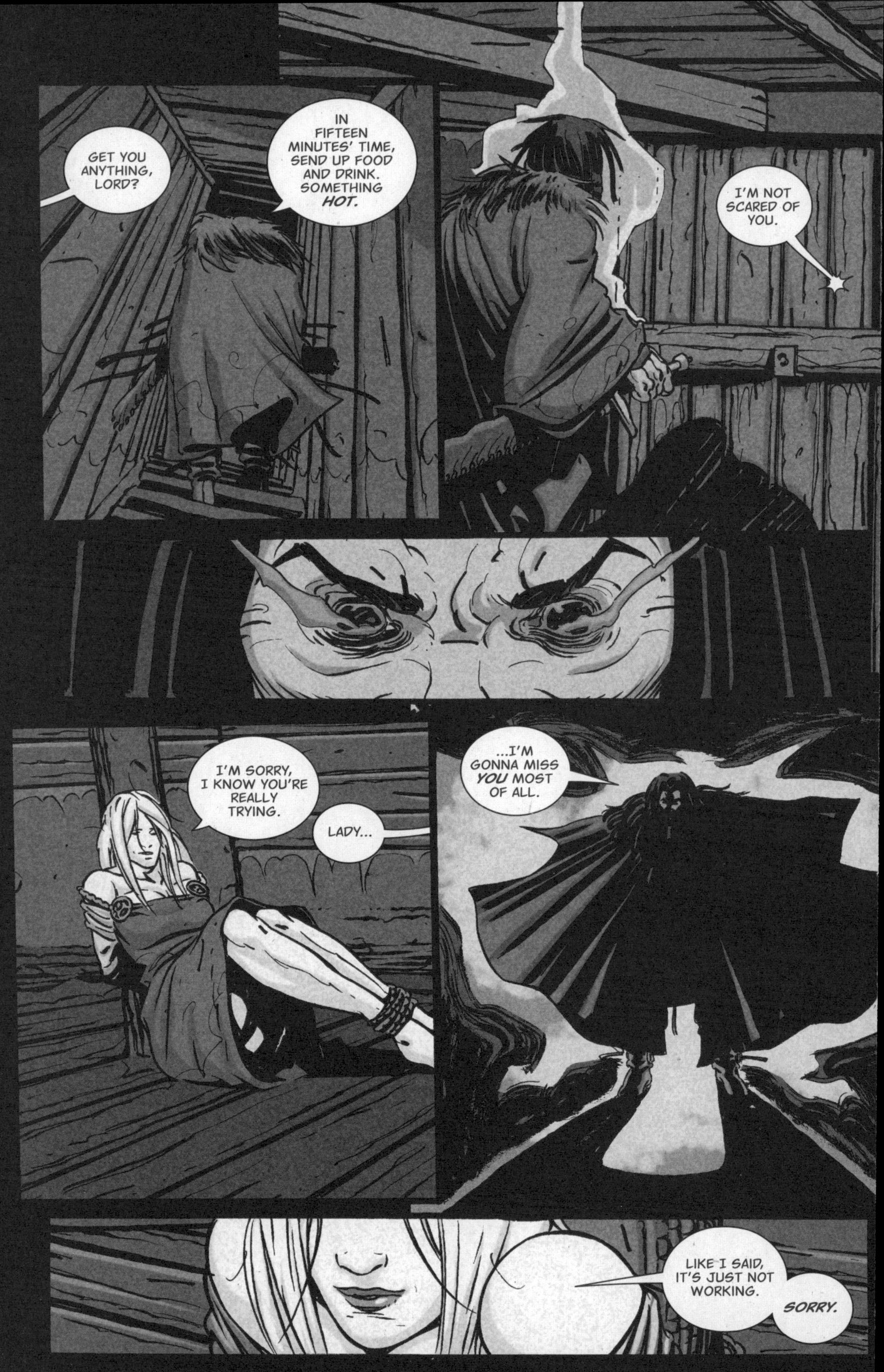

GET YOU ANYTHING, LORD?
IN FIFTEEN MINUTES' TIME, SEND UP FOOD AND DRINK. SOMETHING *HOT.*
I'M NOT SCARED OF YOU.
I'M SORRY, I KNOW YOU'RE REALLY TRYING.
LADY...
...I'M GONNA MISS *YOU* MOST OF ALL.
LIKE I SAID, IT'S JUST NOT WORKING.
SORRY.

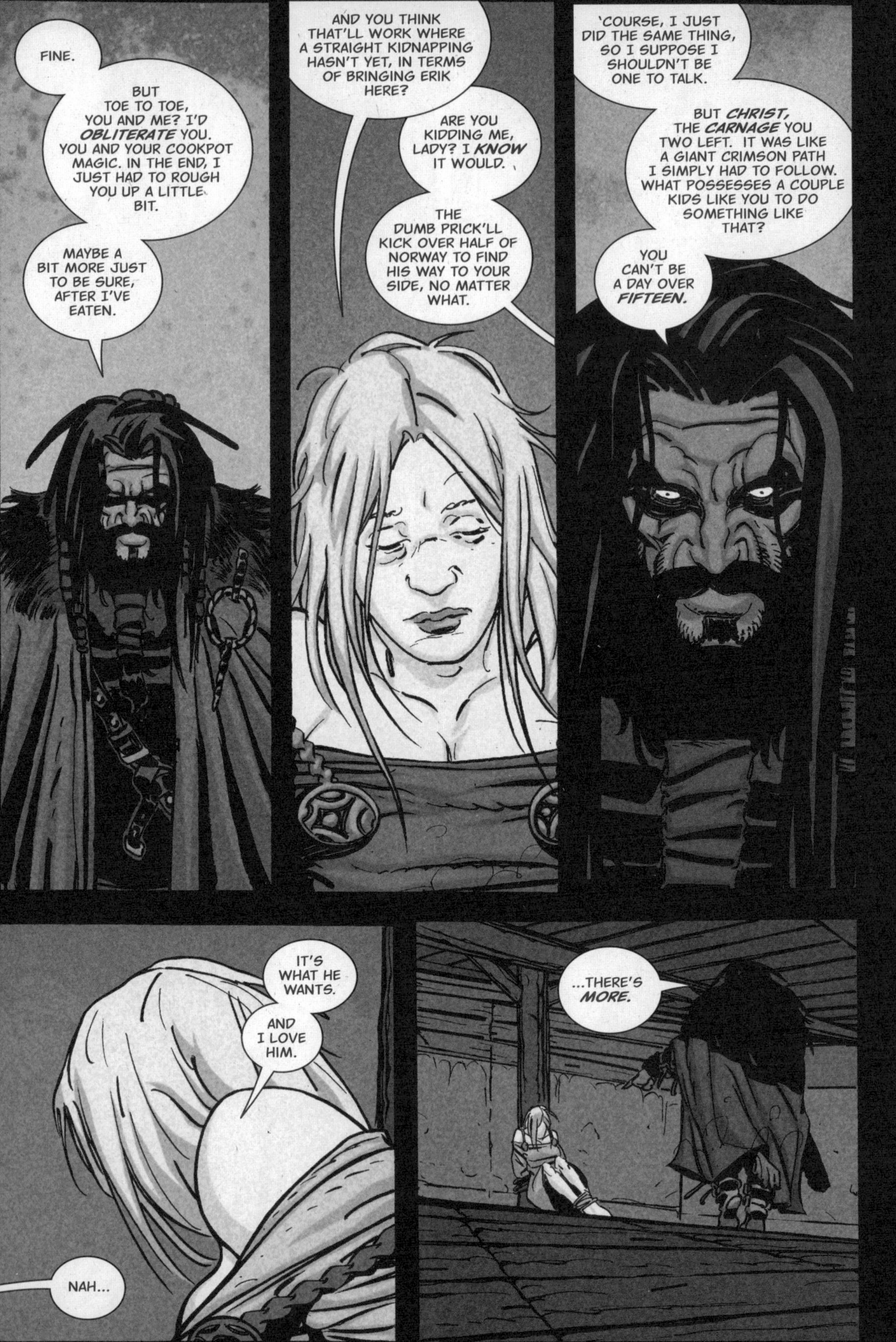
FINE.
BUT TOE TO TOE, YOU AND ME? I'D OBLITERATE YOU. YOU AND YOUR COOKPOT MAGIC. IN THE END, I JUST HAD TO ROUGH YOU UP A LITTLE BIT.
MAYBE A BIT MORE JUST TO BE SURE, AFTER I'VE EATEN.
AND YOU THINK THAT'LL WORK WHERE A STRAIGHT KIDNAPPING HASN'T YET, IN TERMS OF BRINGING ERIK HERE?
ARE YOU KIDDING ME, LADY? I KNOW IT WOULD.
THE DUMB PRICK'LL KICK OVER HALF OF NORWAY TO FIND HIS WAY TO YOUR SIDE, NO MATTER WHAT.
'COURSE, I JUST DID THE SAME THING, SO I SUPPOSE I SHOULDN'T BE ONE TO TALK.
BUT CHRIST, THE CARNAGE YOU TWO LEFT. IT WAS LIKE A GIANT CRIMSON PATH I SIMPLY HAD TO FOLLOW. WHAT POSSESSES A COUPLE KIDS LIKE YOU TO DO SOMETHING LIKE THAT?
YOU CAN'T BE A DAY OVER FIFTEEN.
IT'S WHAT HE WANTS.
AND I LOVE HIM.
NAH...
...THERE'S MORE.

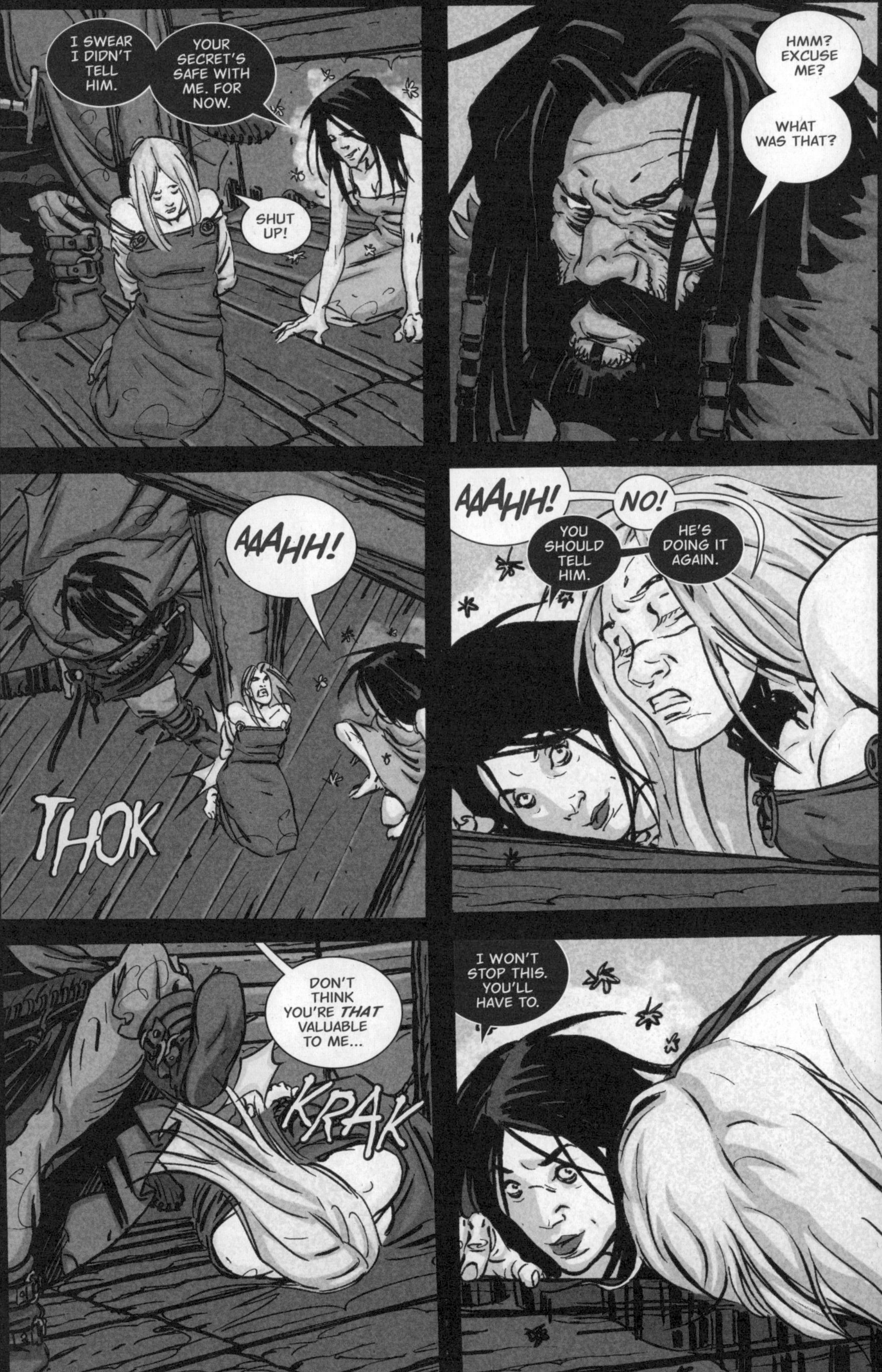
I SWEAR I DIDN'T TELL HIM.
YOUR SECRET'S SAFE WITH ME. FOR NOW.
SHUT UP!
HMM? EXCUSE ME?
WHAT WAS THAT?
AAAHH!
THOK
AAAHH!
NO!
YOU SHOULD TELL HIM.
HE'S DOING IT AGAIN.
DON'T THINK YOU'RE *THAT* VALUABLE TO ME...
KRAK
I WON'T STOP THIS. YOU'LL HAVE TO.

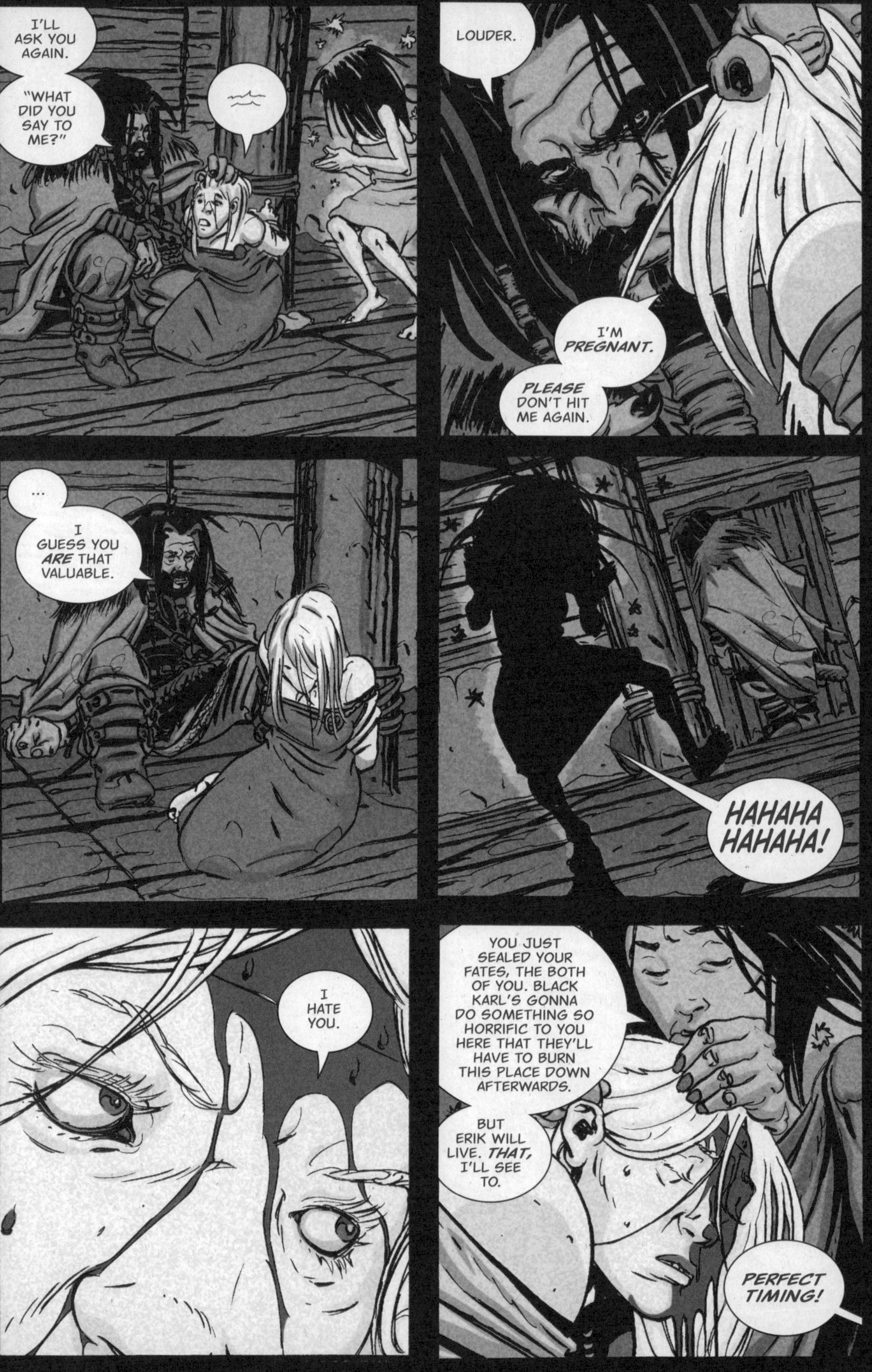
I'LL ASK YOU AGAIN.
"WHAT DID YOU SAY TO ME?"
LOUDER.
I'M *PREGNANT.*
PLEASE DON'T HIT ME AGAIN.
...
I GUESS YOU *ARE* THAT VALUABLE.
HAHAHA HAHAHA!
I HATE YOU.
YOU JUST SEALED YOUR FATES, THE BOTH OF YOU. BLACK KARL'S GONNA DO SOMETHING SO HORRIFIC TO YOU HERE THAT THEY'LL HAVE TO BURN THIS PLACE DOWN AFTERWARDS.
BUT ERIK WILL LIVE. *THAT,* I'LL SEE TO.
PERFECT TIMING!

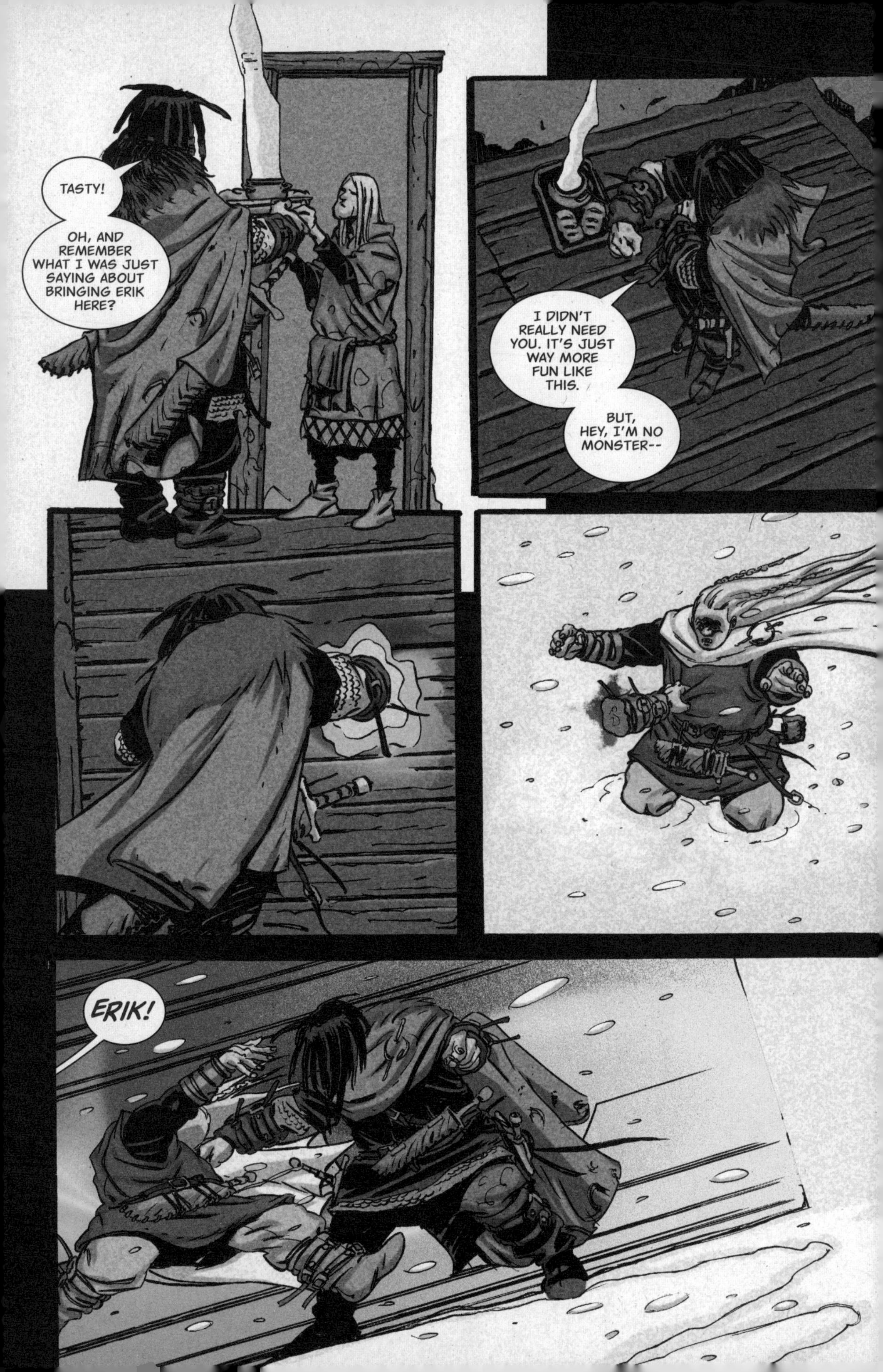
TASTY!
OH, AND REMEMBER WHAT I WAS JUST SAYING ABOUT BRINGING ERIK HERE?
I DIDN'T REALLY NEED YOU. IT'S JUST WAY MORE FUN LIKE THIS.
BUT, HEY, I'M NO MONSTER--
ERIK!

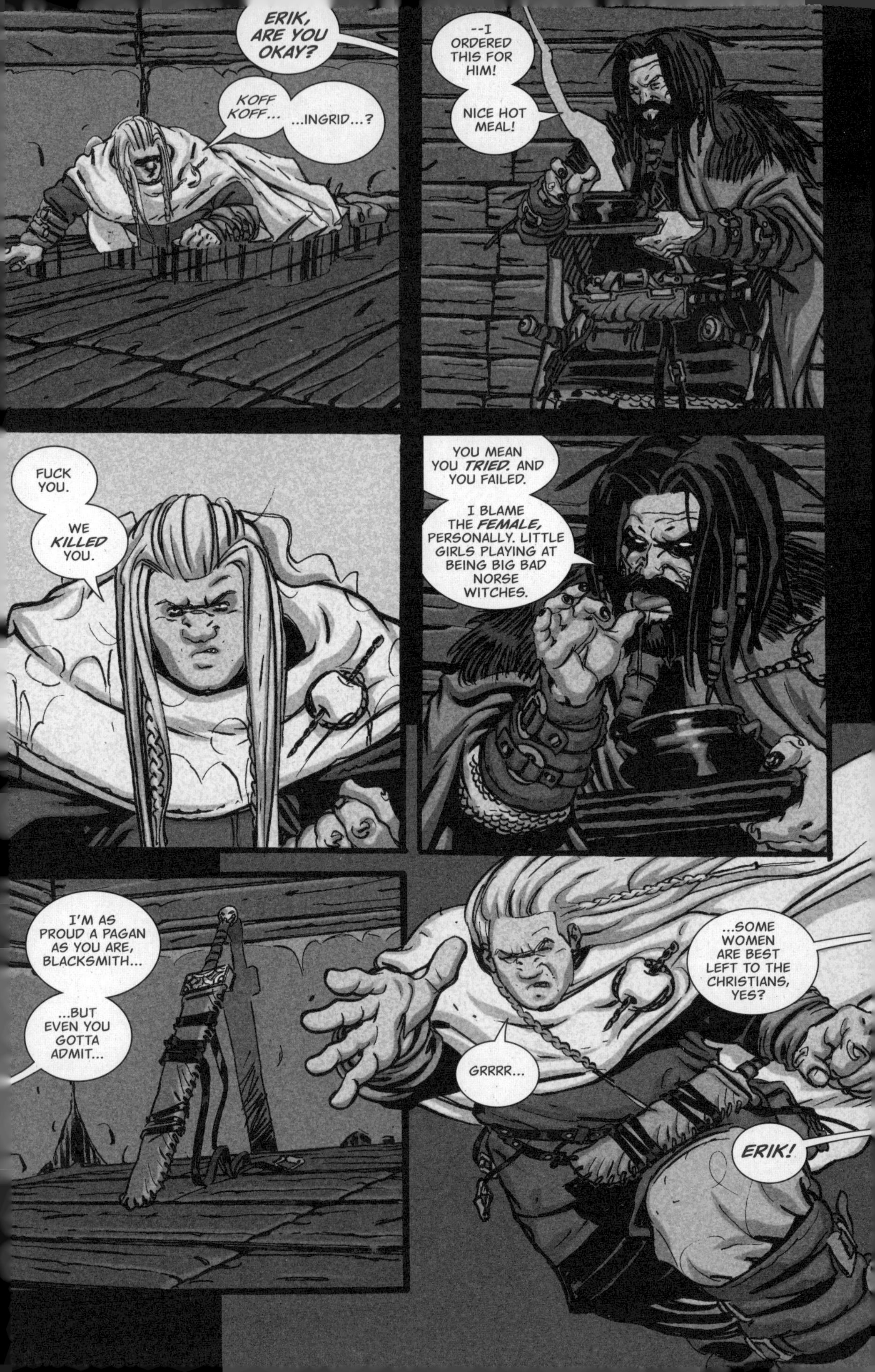
ERIK, ARE YOU OKAY?
KOFF KOFF...
...INGRID...?
--I ORDERED THIS FOR HIM!
NICE HOT MEAL!
FUCK YOU.
WE KILLED YOU.
YOU MEAN YOU TRIED. AND YOU FAILED.
I BLAME THE FEMALE, PERSONALLY. LITTLE GIRLS PLAYING AT BEING BIG BAD NORSE WITCHES.
I'M AS PROUD A PAGAN AS YOU ARE, BLACKSMITH...
...BUT EVEN YOU GOTTA ADMIT...
...SOME WOMEN ARE BEST LEFT TO THE CHRISTIANS, YES?
GRRRR...
ERIK!

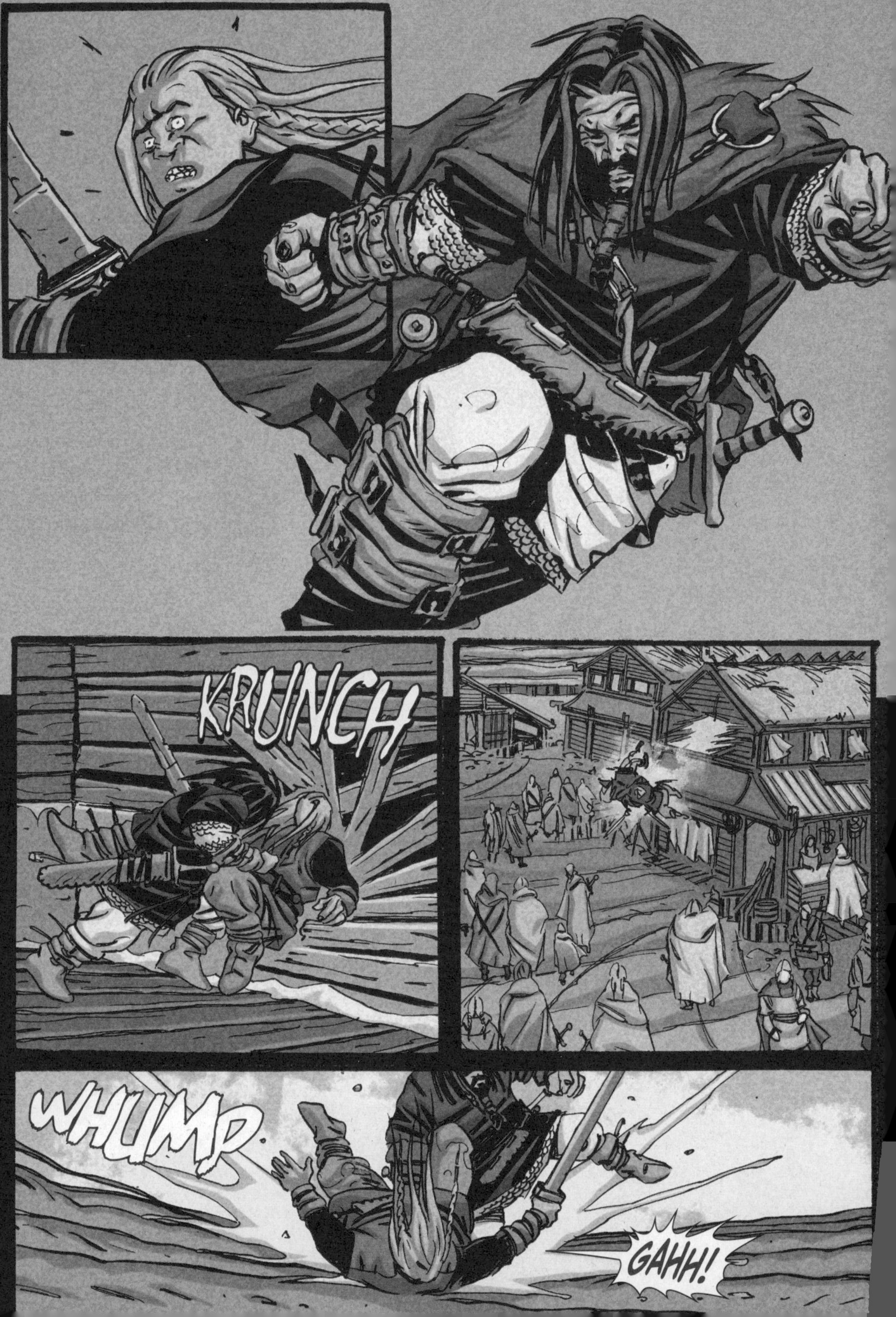
KRUNCH
WHUMP
GAHH!

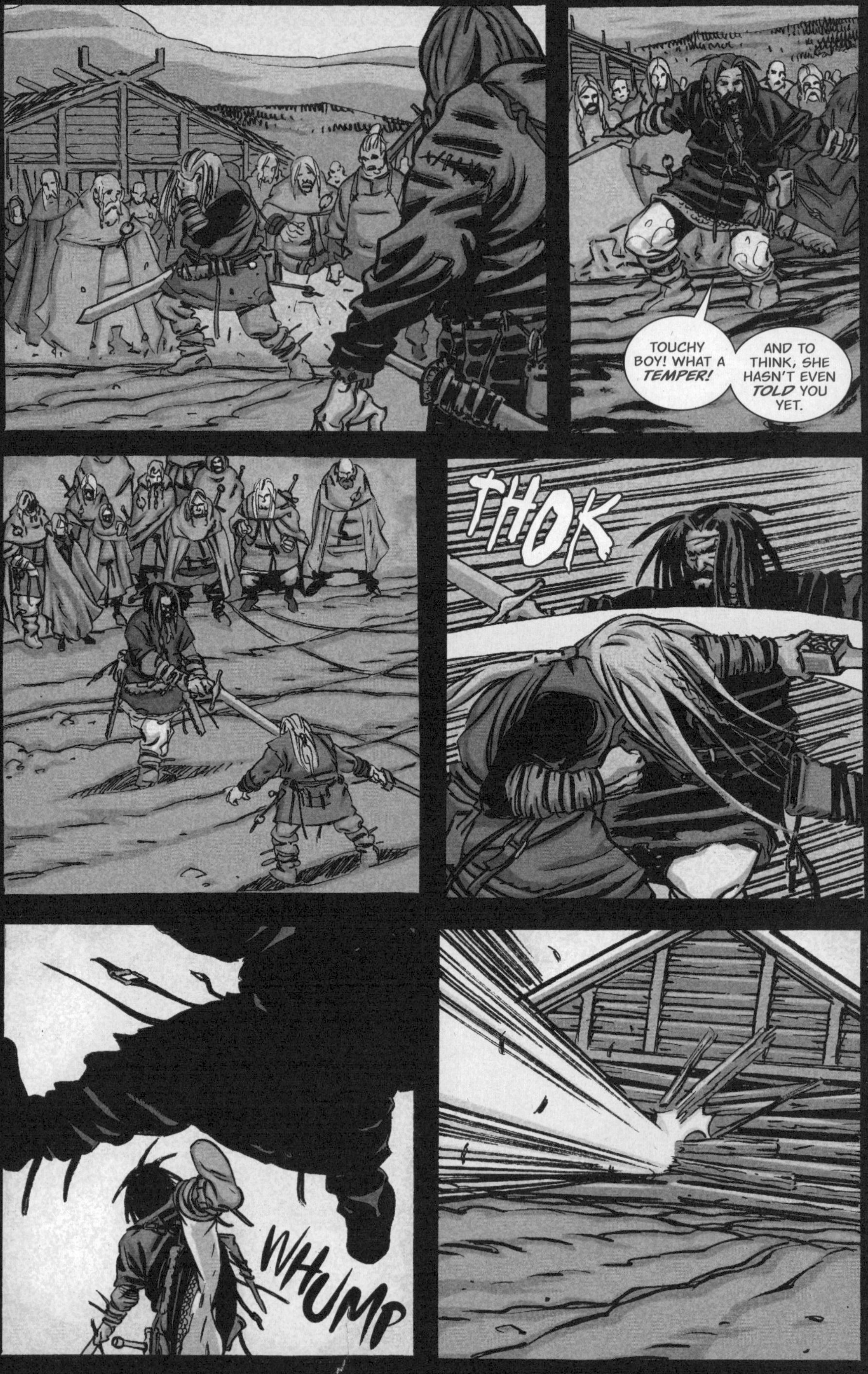

TOUCHY BOY! WHAT A TEMPER!
AND TO THINK, SHE HASN'T EVEN TOLD YOU YET.
THOK
WHUMP

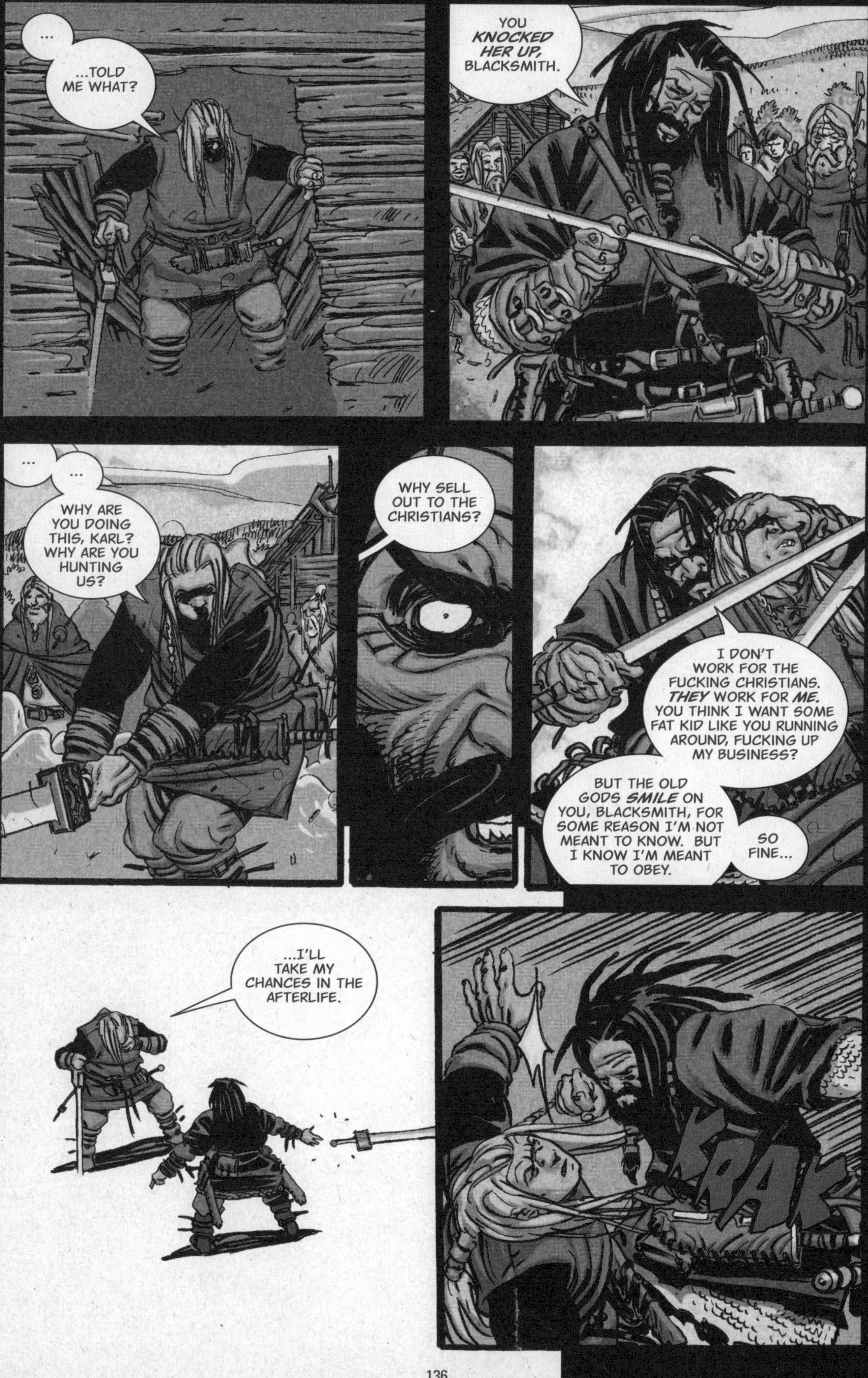
...
...TOLD ME WHAT?
YOU KNOCKED HER UP, BLACKSMITH.
...
...
WHY ARE YOU DOING THIS, KARL? WHY ARE YOU HUNTING US?
WHY SELL OUT TO THE CHRISTIANS?
I DON'T WORK FOR THE FUCKING CHRISTIANS. THEY WORK FOR ME. YOU THINK I WANT SOME FAT KID LIKE YOU RUNNING AROUND, FUCKING UP MY BUSINESS?
BUT THE OLD GODS SMILE ON YOU, BLACKSMITH, FOR SOME REASON I'M NOT MEANT TO KNOW. BUT I KNOW I'M MEANT TO OBEY.
SO FINE...
...I'LL TAKE MY CHANCES IN THE AFTERLIFE.
KRAK

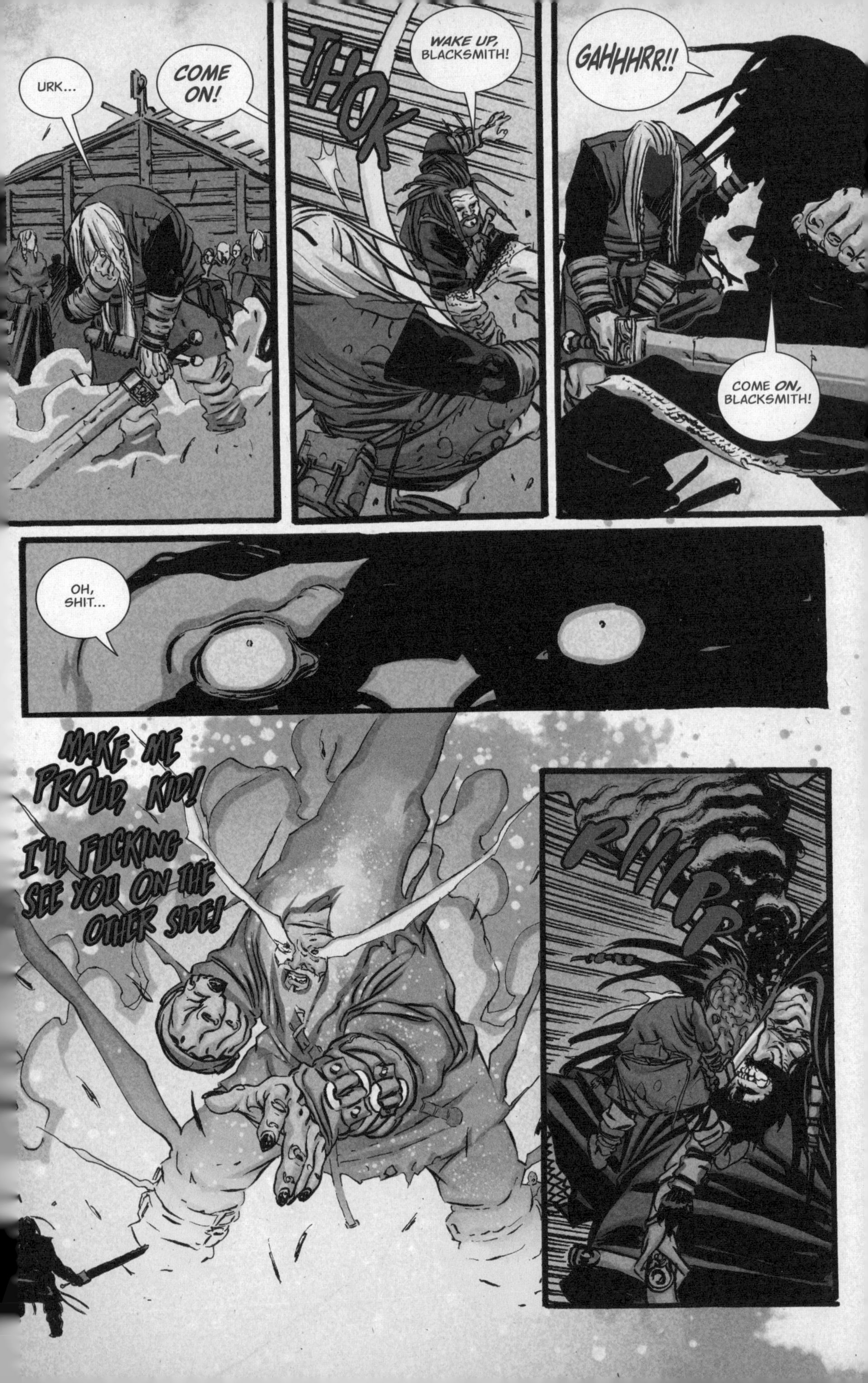
URK...
COME ON!
THOK
WAKE UP, BLACKSMITH!
GAHHHRR!!
COME ON, BLACKSMITH!
OH, SHIT...
MAKE ME PROUD, KID!
I'LL FUCKING SEE YOU ON THE OTHER SIDE!
RIIIPP

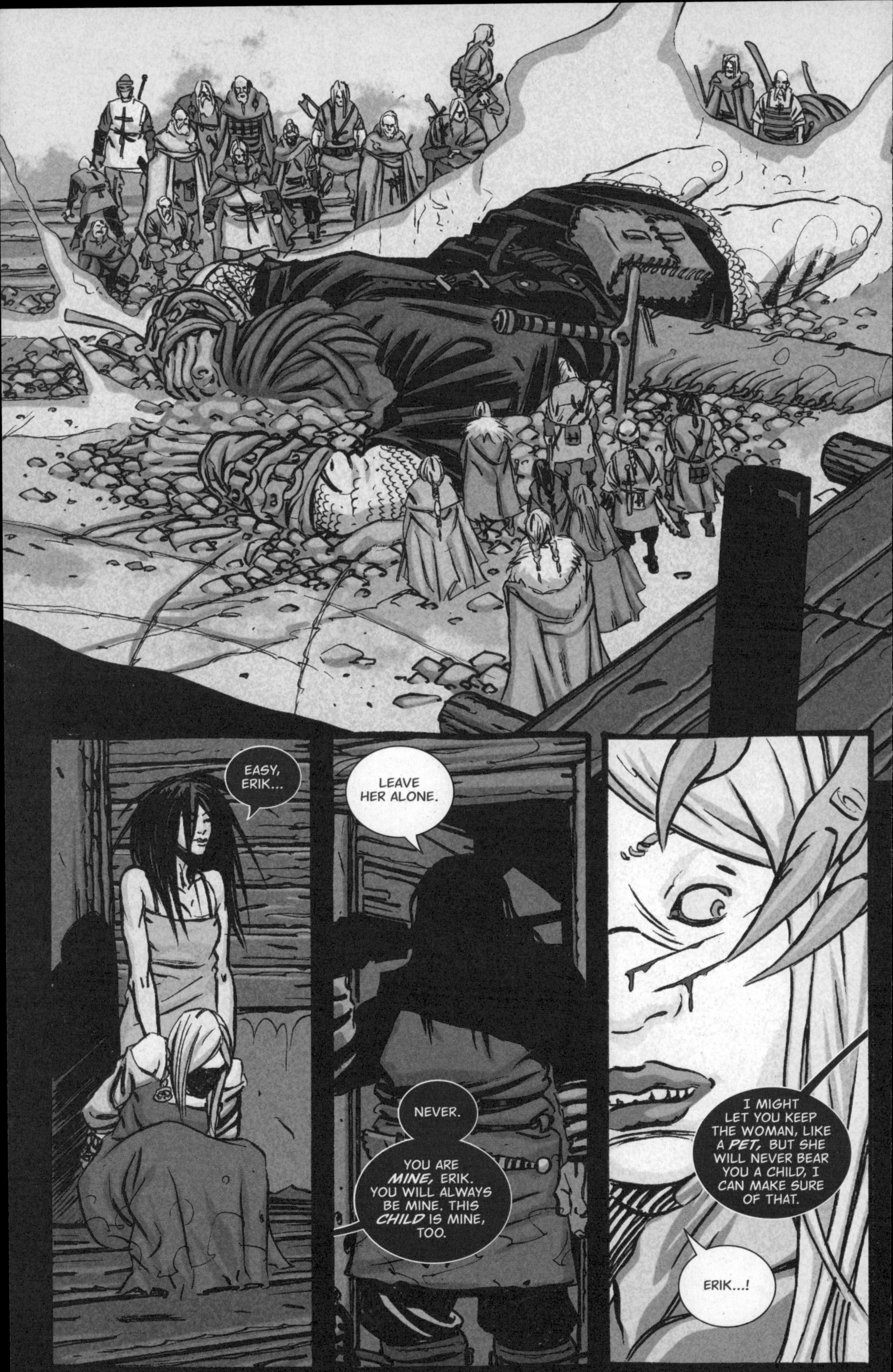
EASY, ERIK...
LEAVE HER ALONE.
NEVER.
YOU ARE MINE, ERIK. YOU WILL ALWAYS BE MINE. THIS CHILD IS MINE, TOO.
I MIGHT LET YOU KEEP THE WOMAN, LIKE A PET, BUT SHE WILL NEVER BEAR YOU A CHILD, I CAN MAKE SURE OF THAT.
ERIK...!

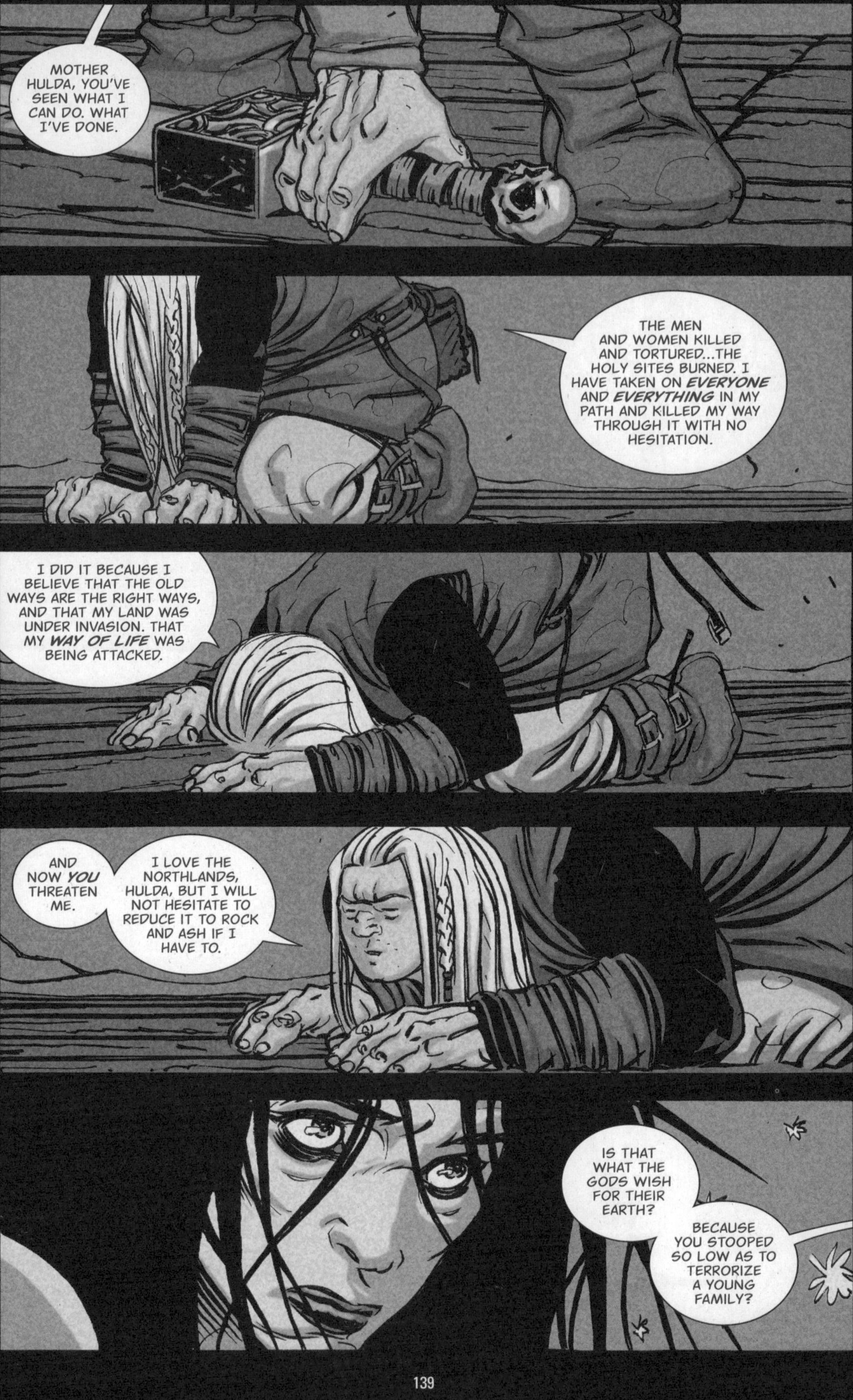
MOTHER HULDA, YOU'VE SEEN WHAT I CAN DO. WHAT I'VE DONE.
THE MEN AND WOMEN KILLED AND TORTURED...THE HOLY SITES BURNED. I HAVE TAKEN ON *EVERYONE* AND *EVERYTHING* IN MY PATH AND KILLED MY WAY THROUGH IT WITH NO HESITATION.
I DID IT BECAUSE I BELIEVE THAT THE OLD WAYS ARE THE RIGHT WAYS, AND THAT MY LAND WAS UNDER INVASION. THAT MY *WAY OF LIFE* WAS BEING ATTACKED.
AND NOW *YOU* THREATEN ME.
I LOVE THE NORTHLANDS, HULDA, BUT I WILL NOT HESITATE TO REDUCE IT TO ROCK AND ASH IF I HAVE TO.
IS THAT WHAT THE GODS WISH FOR THEIR EARTH?
BECAUSE YOU STOOPED SO LOW AS TO TERRORIZE A YOUNG FAMILY?

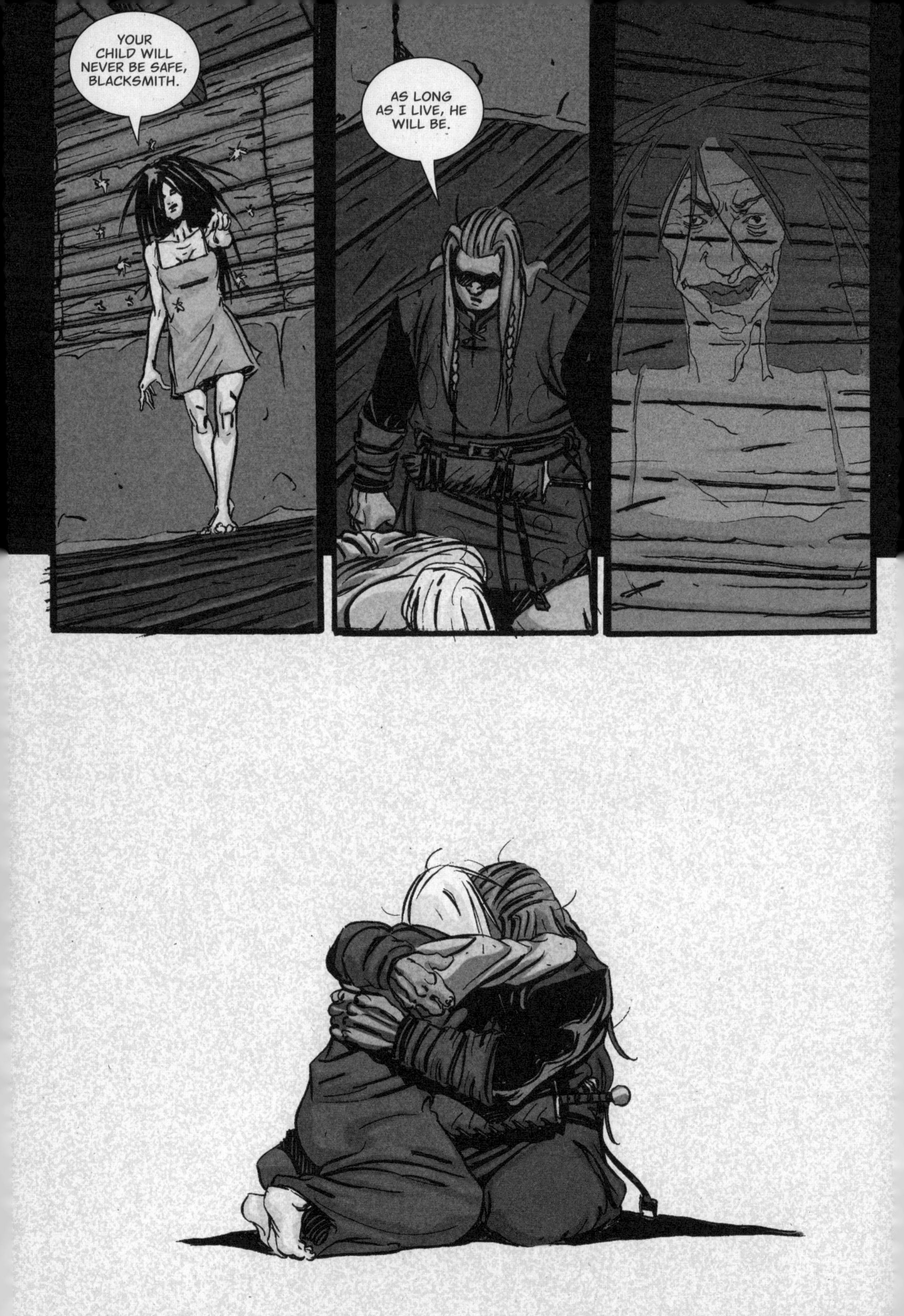
YOUR CHILD WILL NEVER BE SAFE, BLACKSMITH.
AS LONG AS I LIVE, HE WILL BE.

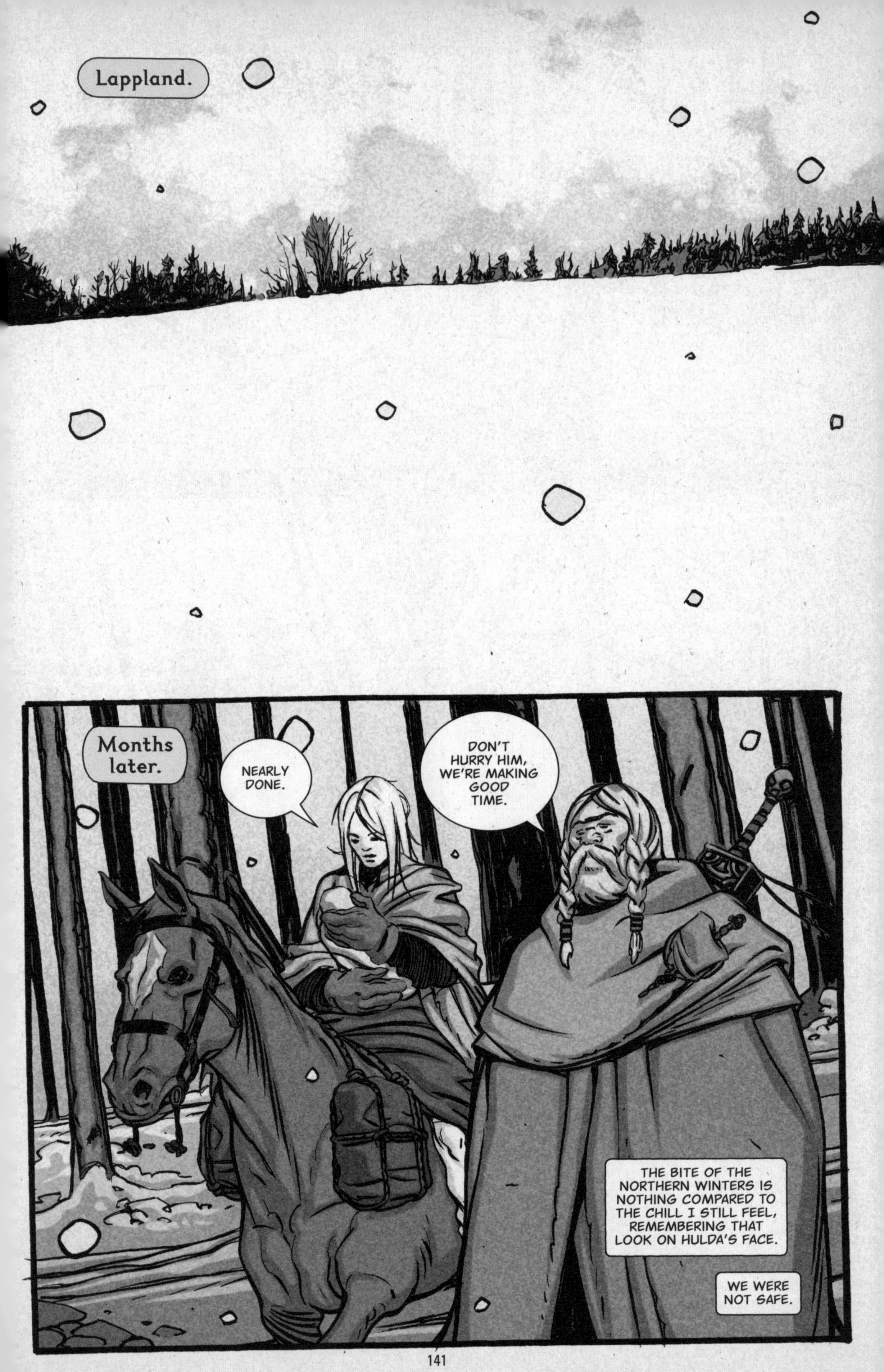
Lappland.
Months later.
NEARLY DONE.
DON'T HURRY HIM, WE'RE MAKING GOOD TIME.
THE BITE OF THE NORTHERN WINTERS IS NOTHING COMPARED TO THE CHILL I STILL FEEL, REMEMBERING THAT LOOK ON HULDA'S FACE.
WE WERE NOT SAFE.

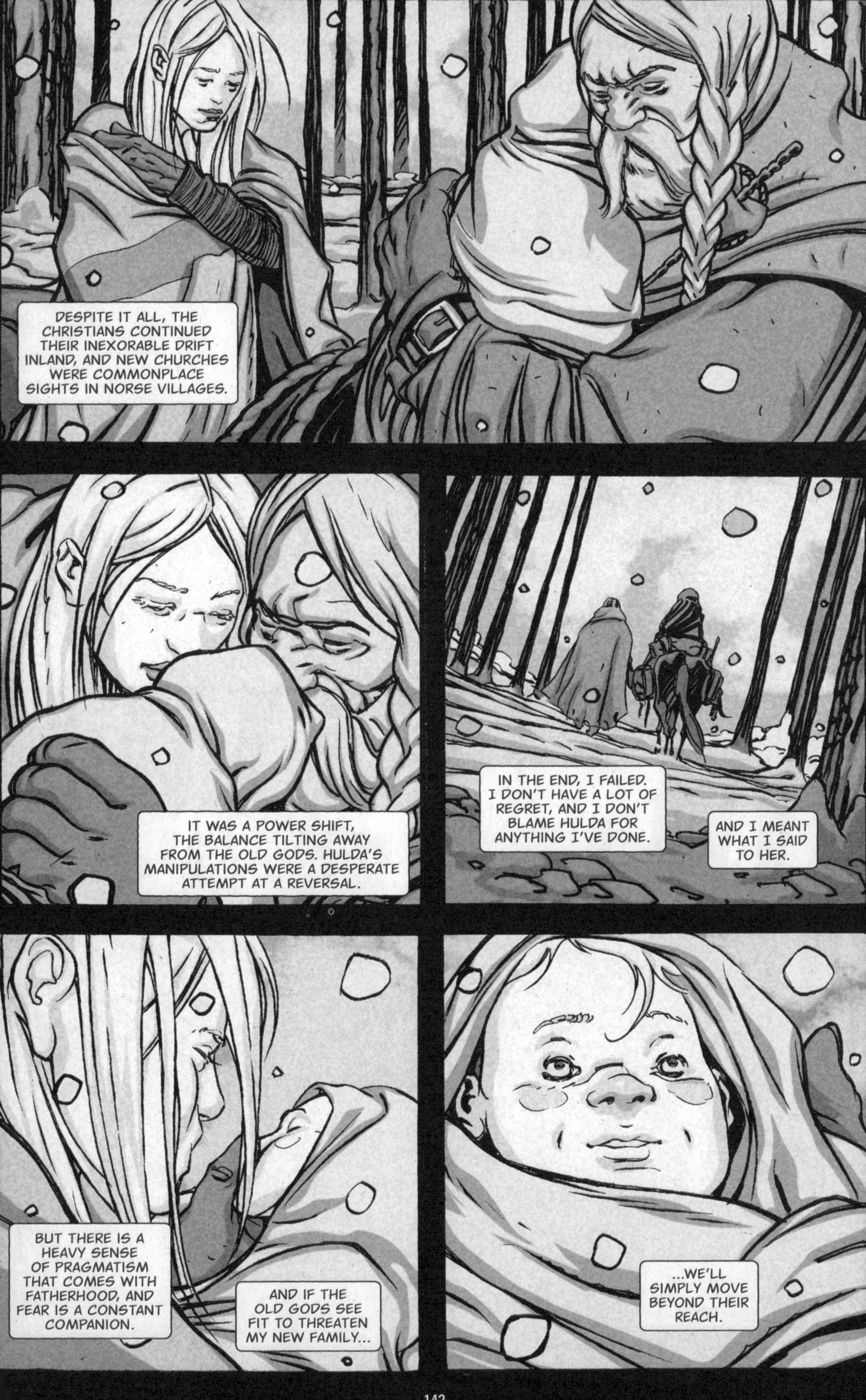
DESPITE IT ALL, THE CHRISTIANS CONTINUED THEIR INEXORABLE DRIFT INLAND, AND NEW CHURCHES WERE COMMONPLACE SIGHTS IN NORSE VILLAGES.
IT WAS A POWER SHIFT, THE BALANCE TILTING AWAY FROM THE OLD GODS. HULDA'S MANIPULATIONS WERE A DESPERATE ATTEMPT AT A REVERSAL.
IN THE END, I FAILED. I DON'T HAVE A LOT OF REGRET, AND I DON'T BLAME HULDA FOR ANYTHING I'VE DONE.
AND I MEANT WHAT I SAID TO HER.
BUT THERE IS A HEAVY SENSE OF PRAGMATISM THAT COMES WITH FATHERHOOD, AND FEAR IS A CONSTANT COMPANION.
AND IF THE OLD GODS SEE FIT TO THREATEN MY NEW FAMILY...
...WE'LL SIMPLY MOVE BEYOND THEIR REACH.

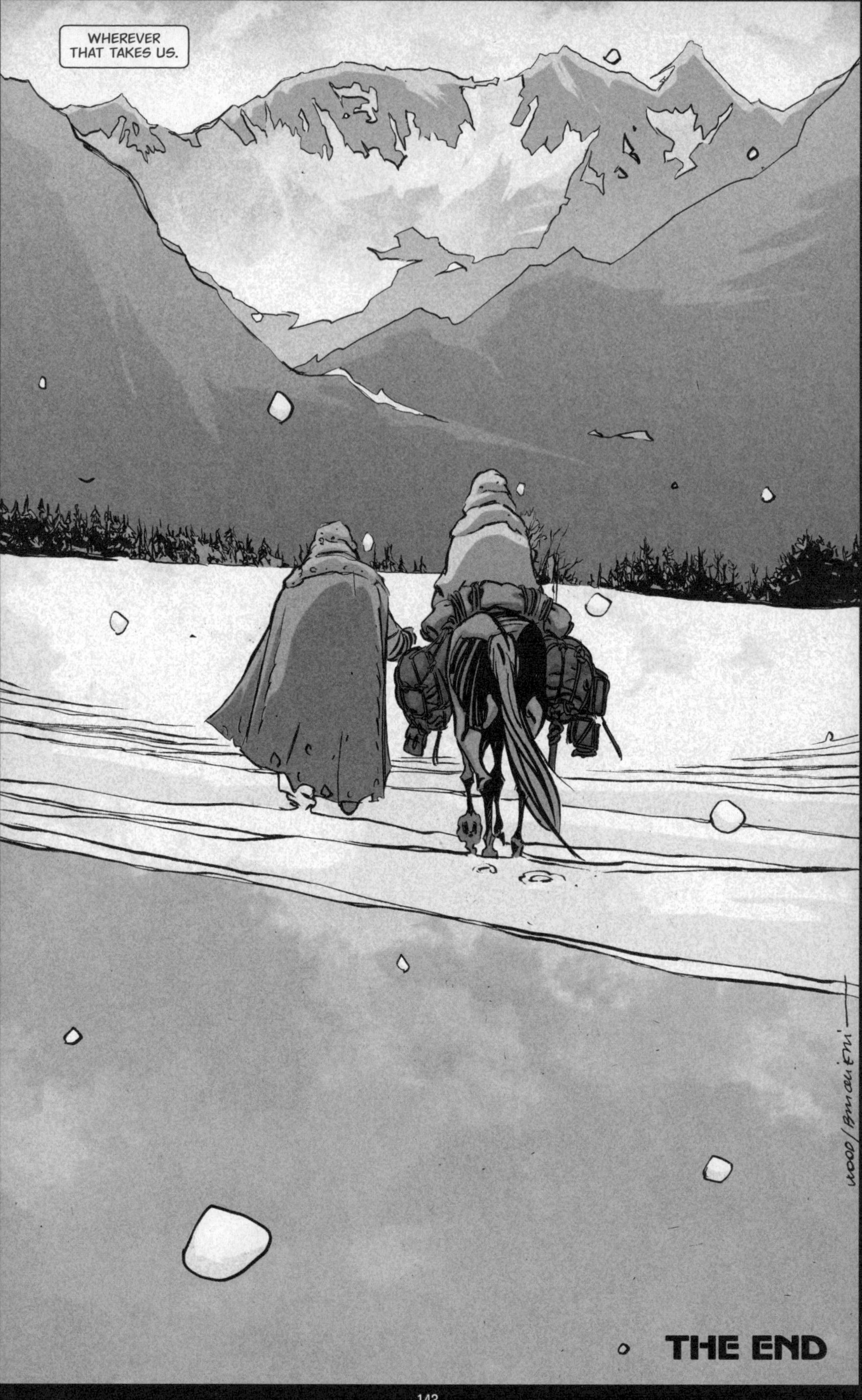
WHEREVER THAT TAKES US.
THE END

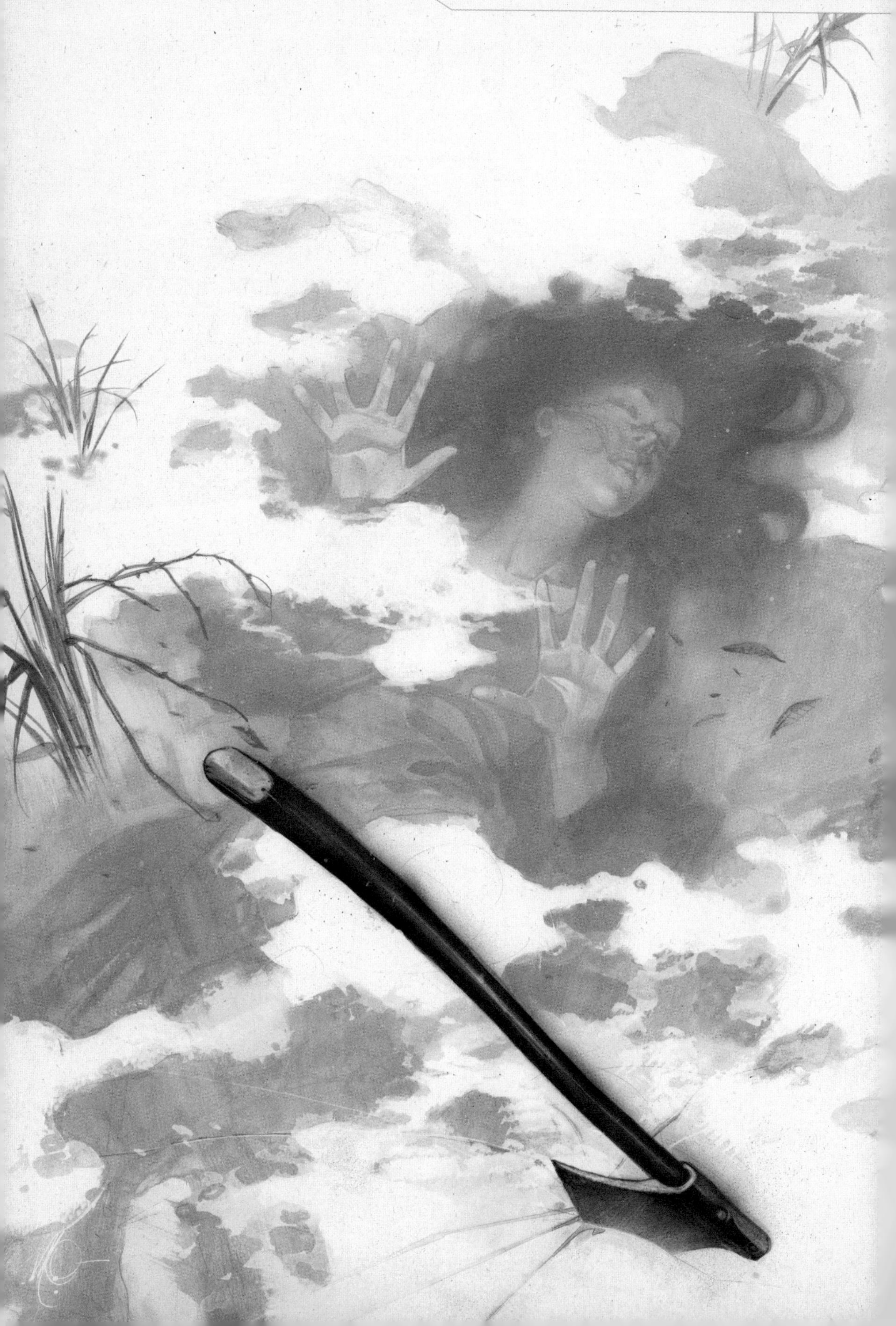

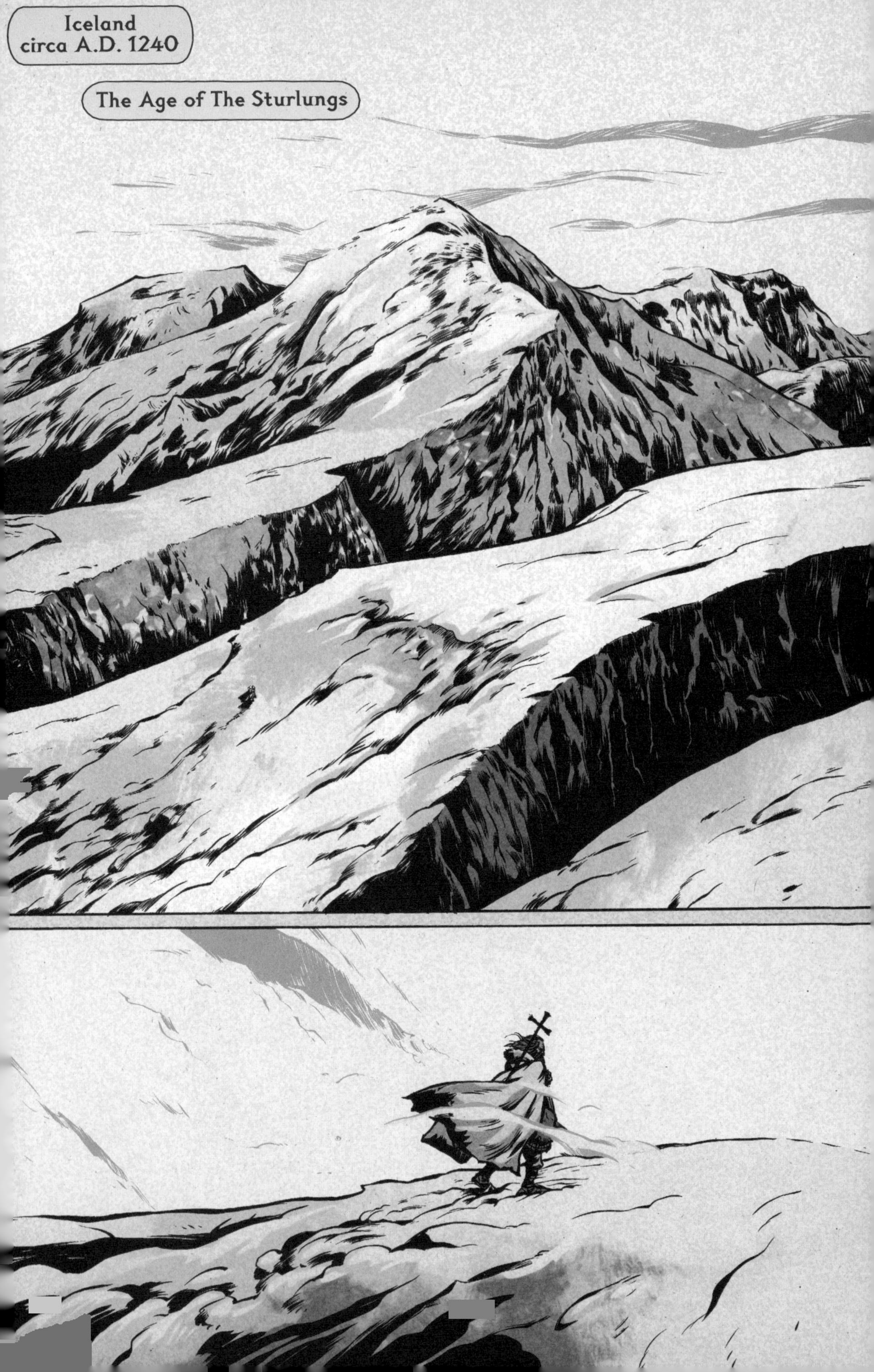
Iceland
circa A.D. 1240
The Age of The Sturlungs

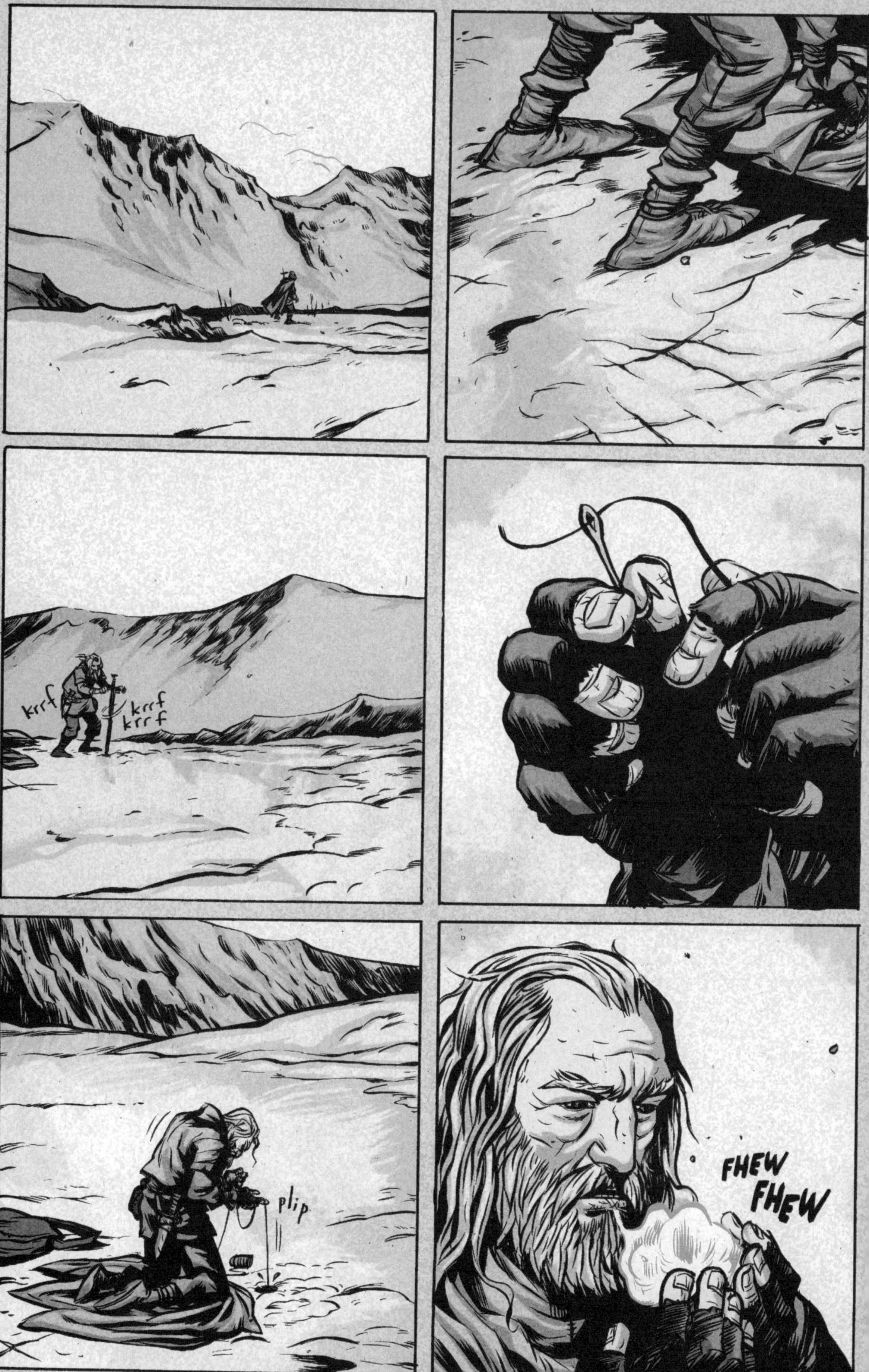
krrf
krrf
krrf
plip
FHEW
FHEW

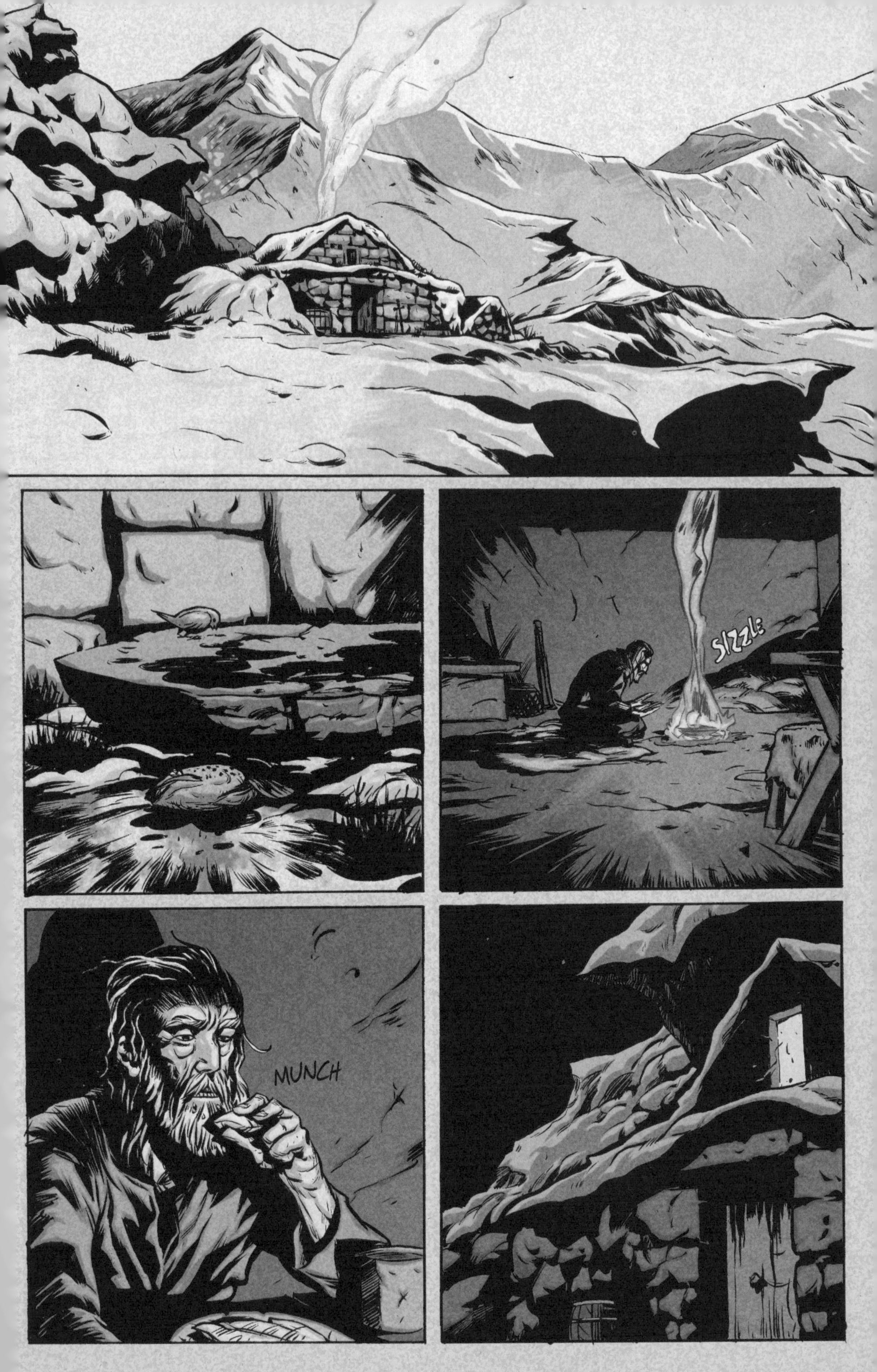
SIZZLE
MUNCH

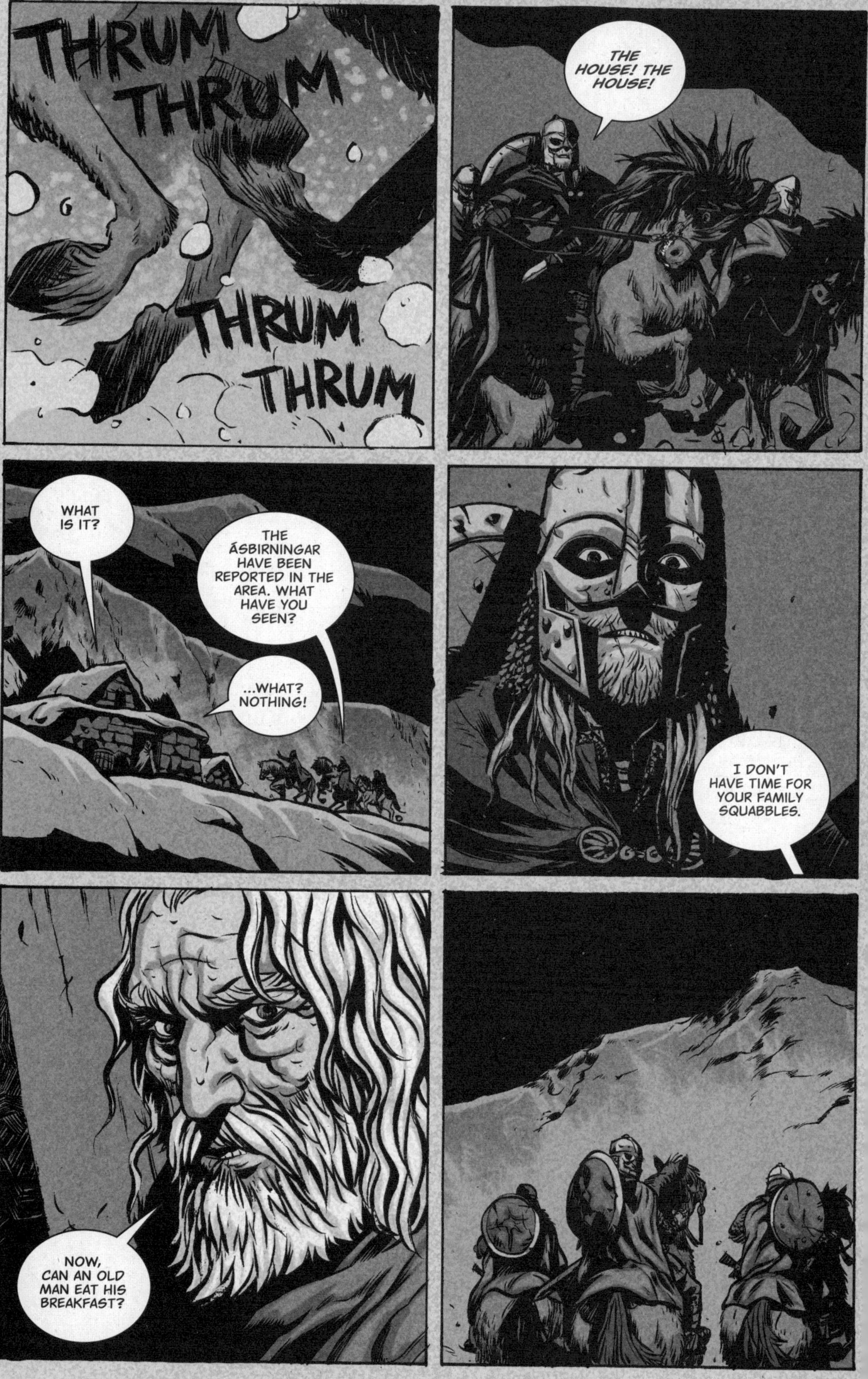
THRUM
THRUM
THRUM
THRUM
THE HOUSE! THE HOUSE!
WHAT IS IT?
THE ÁSBIRNINGAR HAVE BEEN REPORTED IN THE AREA. WHAT HAVE YOU SEEN?
...WHAT? NOTHING!
I DON'T HAVE TIME FOR YOUR FAMILY SQUABBLES.
NOW, CAN AN OLD MAN EAT HIS BREAKFAST?

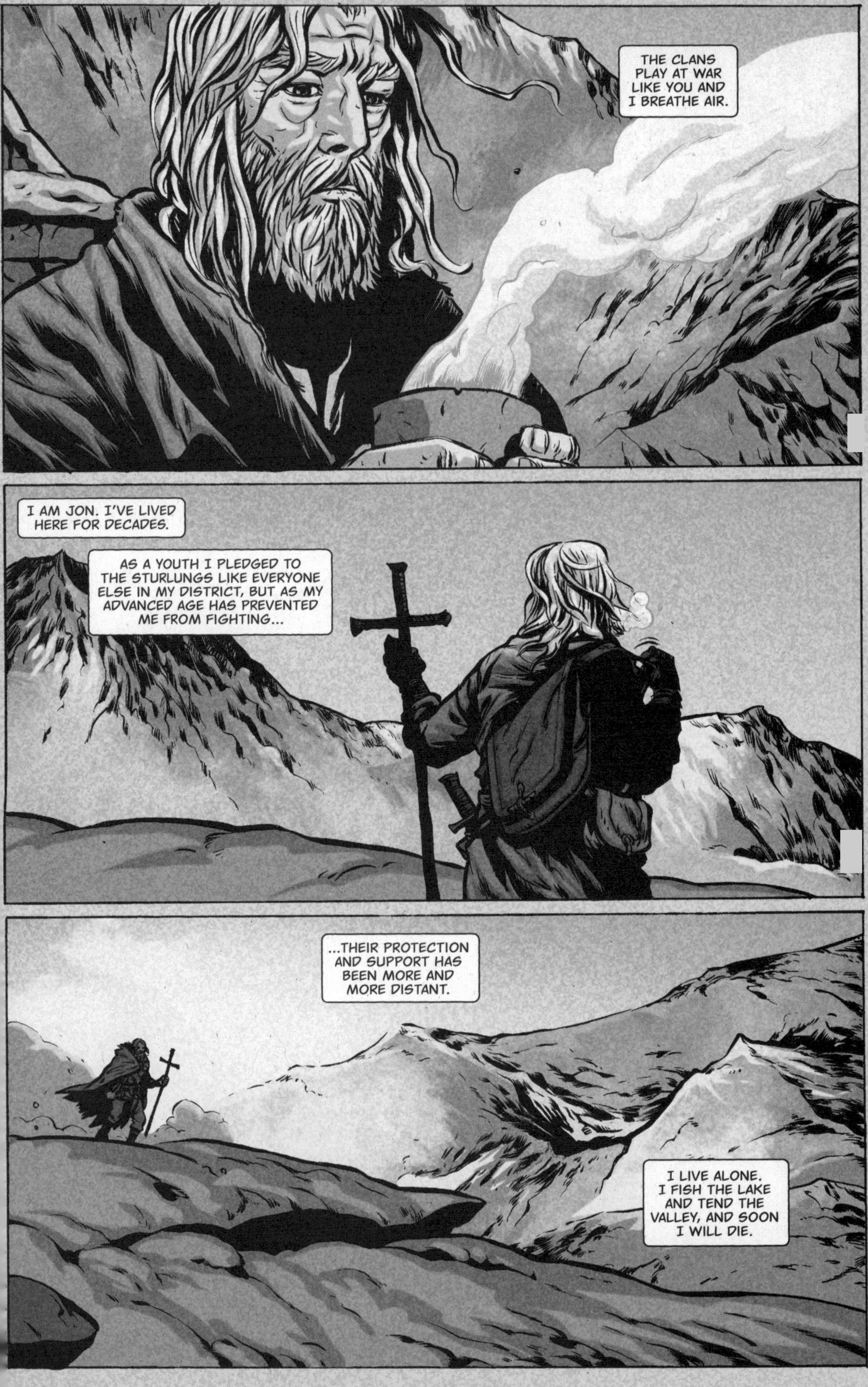
THE CLANS PLAY AT WAR LIKE YOU AND I BREATHE AIR.
I AM JON. I'VE LIVED HERE FOR DECADES.
AS A YOUTH I PLEDGED TO THE STURLUNGS LIKE EVERYONE ELSE IN MY DISTRICT, BUT AS MY ADVANCED AGE HAS PREVENTED ME FROM FIGHTING...
...THEIR PROTECTION AND SUPPORT HAS BEEN MORE AND MORE DISTANT.
I LIVE ALONE. I FISH THE LAKE AND TEND THE VALLEY, AND SOON I WILL DIE.

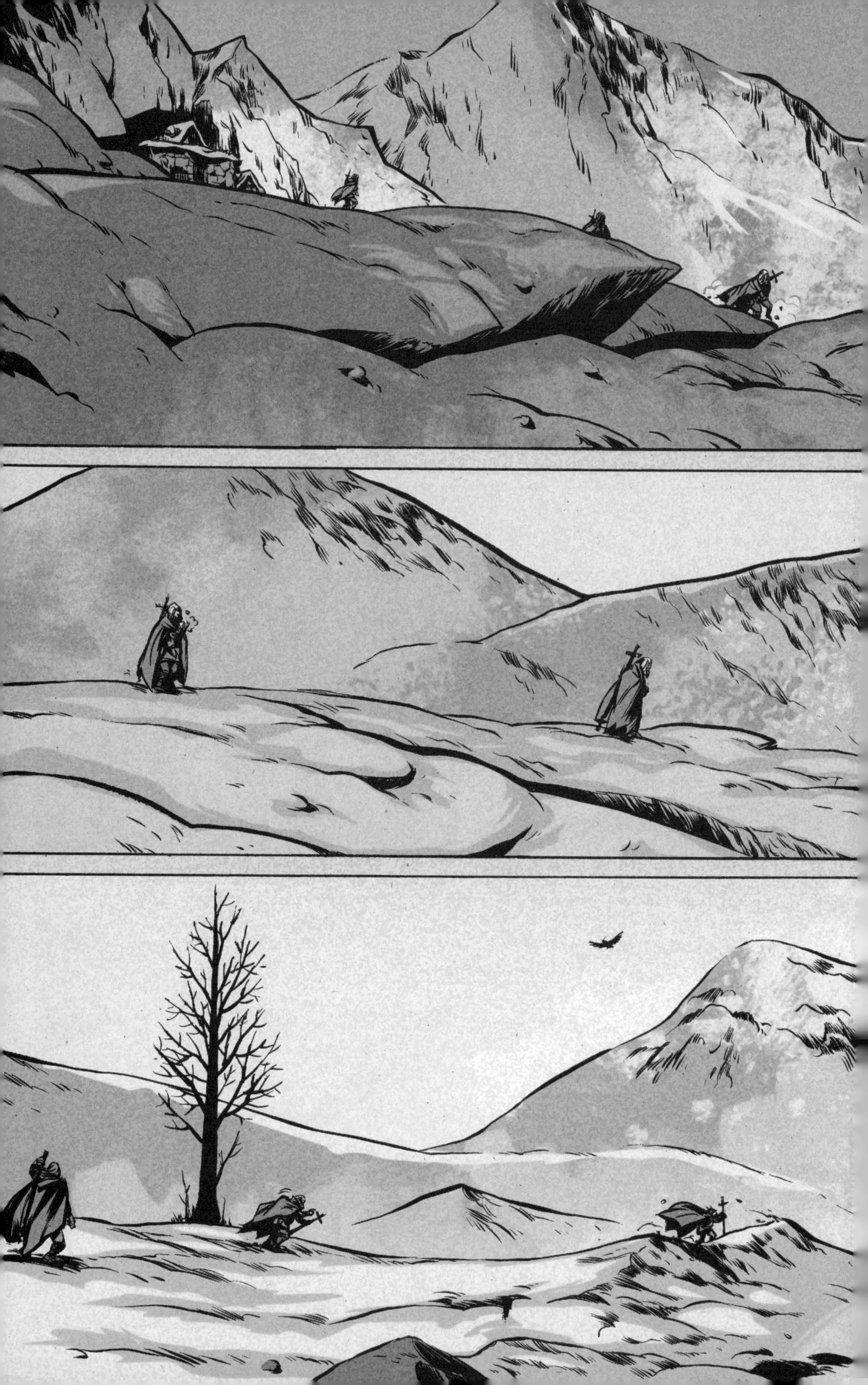

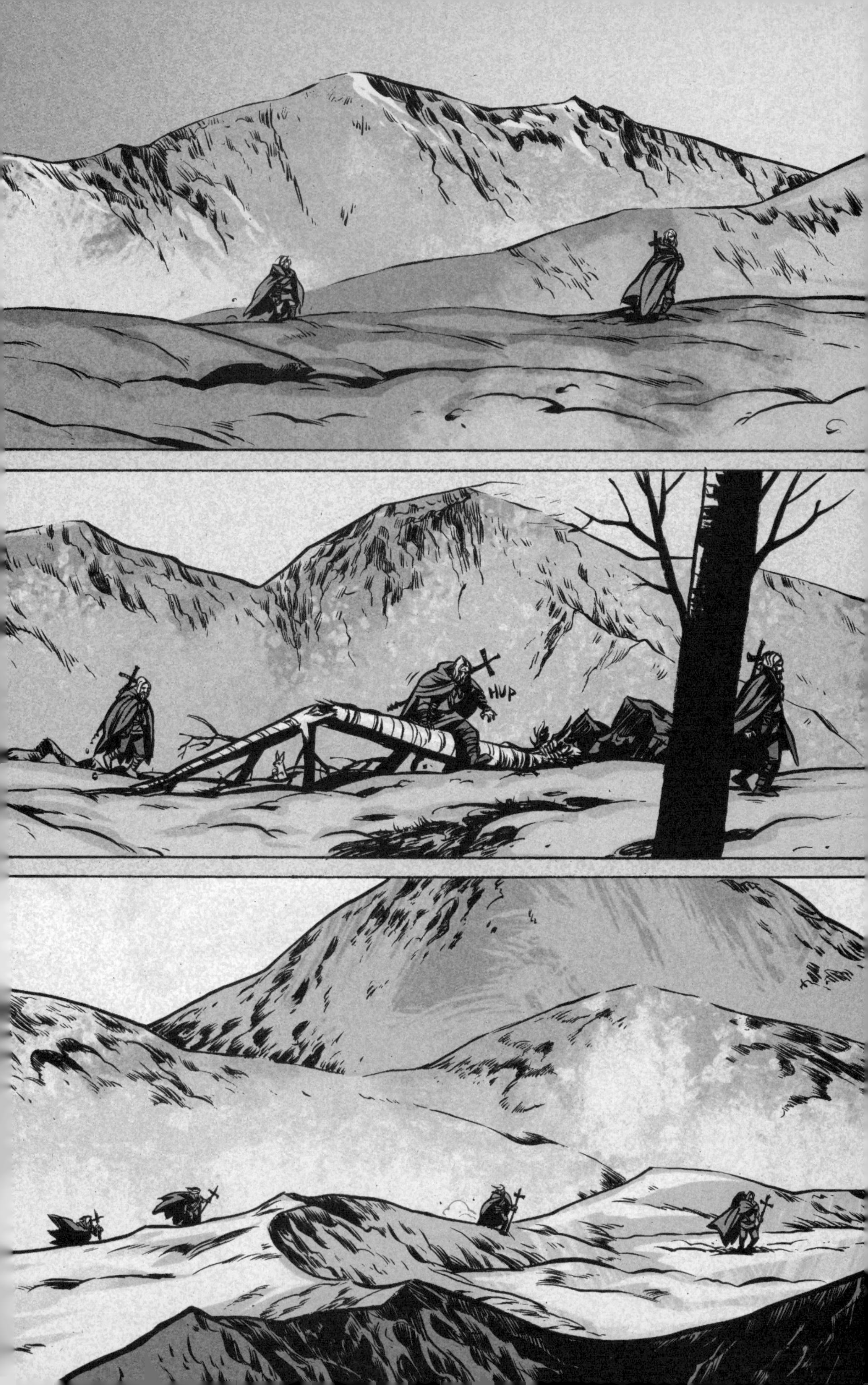
HUP

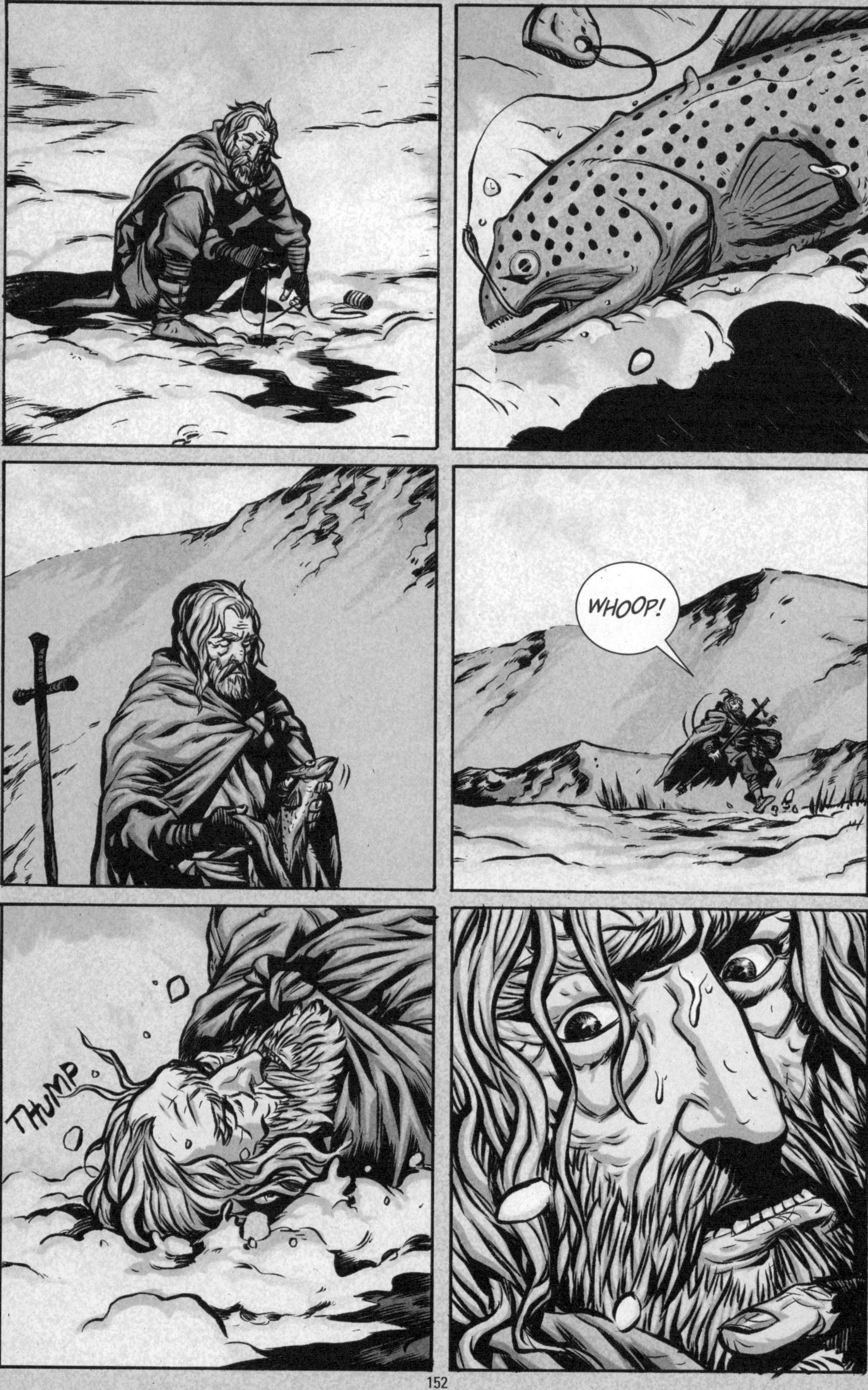
WHOOP!
THUMP

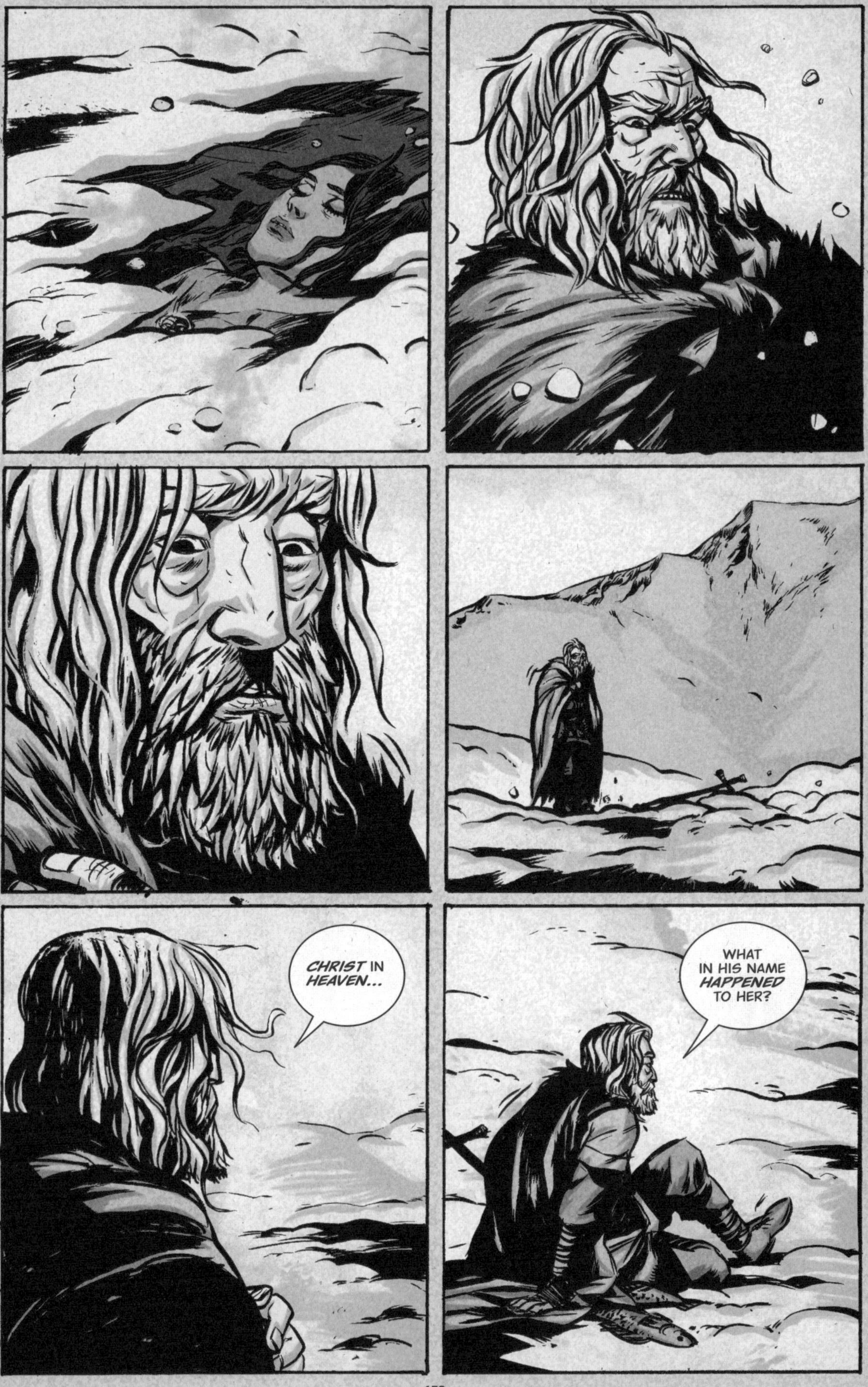
CHRIST IN HEAVEN...
WHAT IN HIS NAME HAPPENED TO HER?

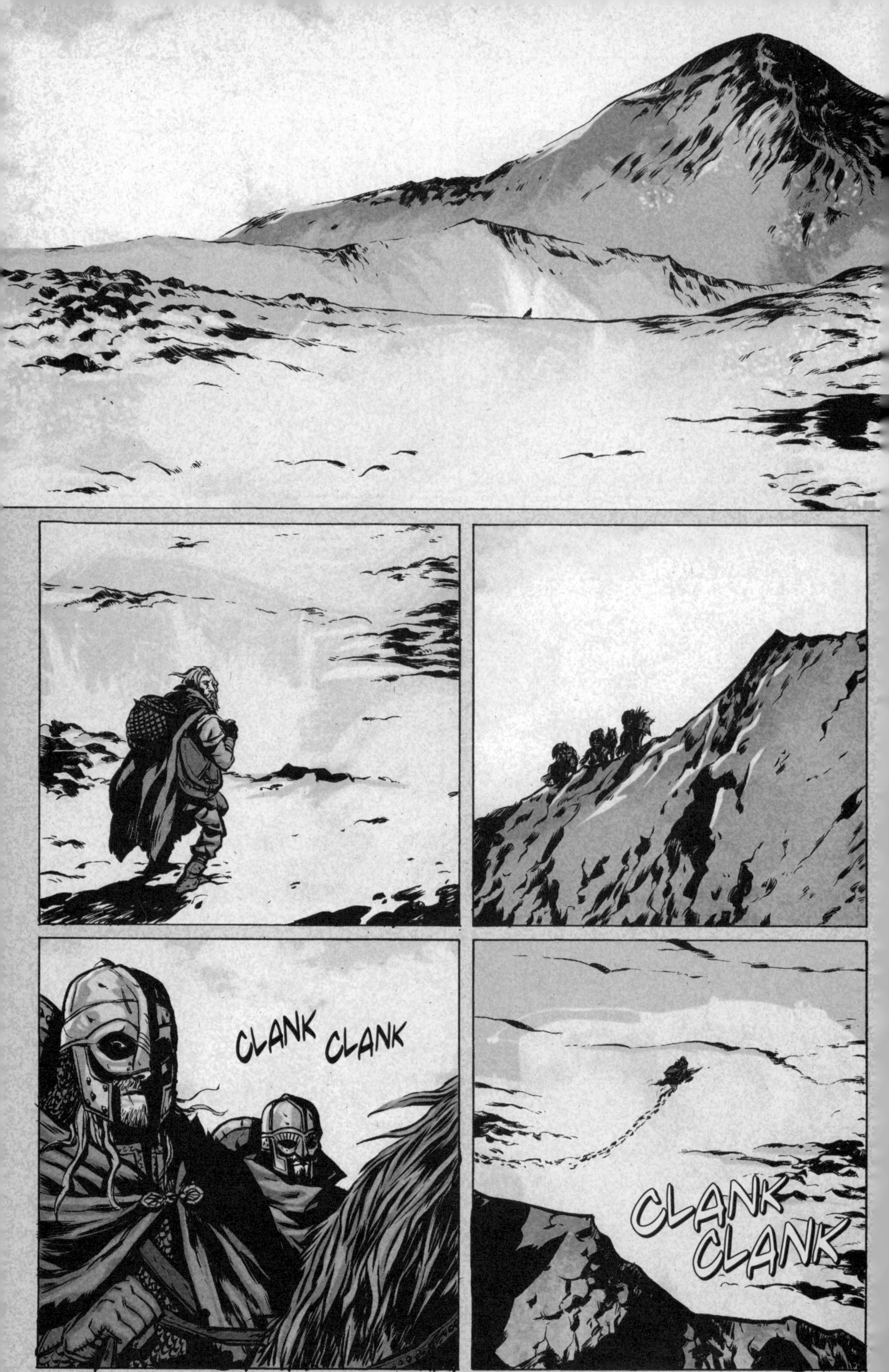
CLANK CLANK
CLANK CLANK

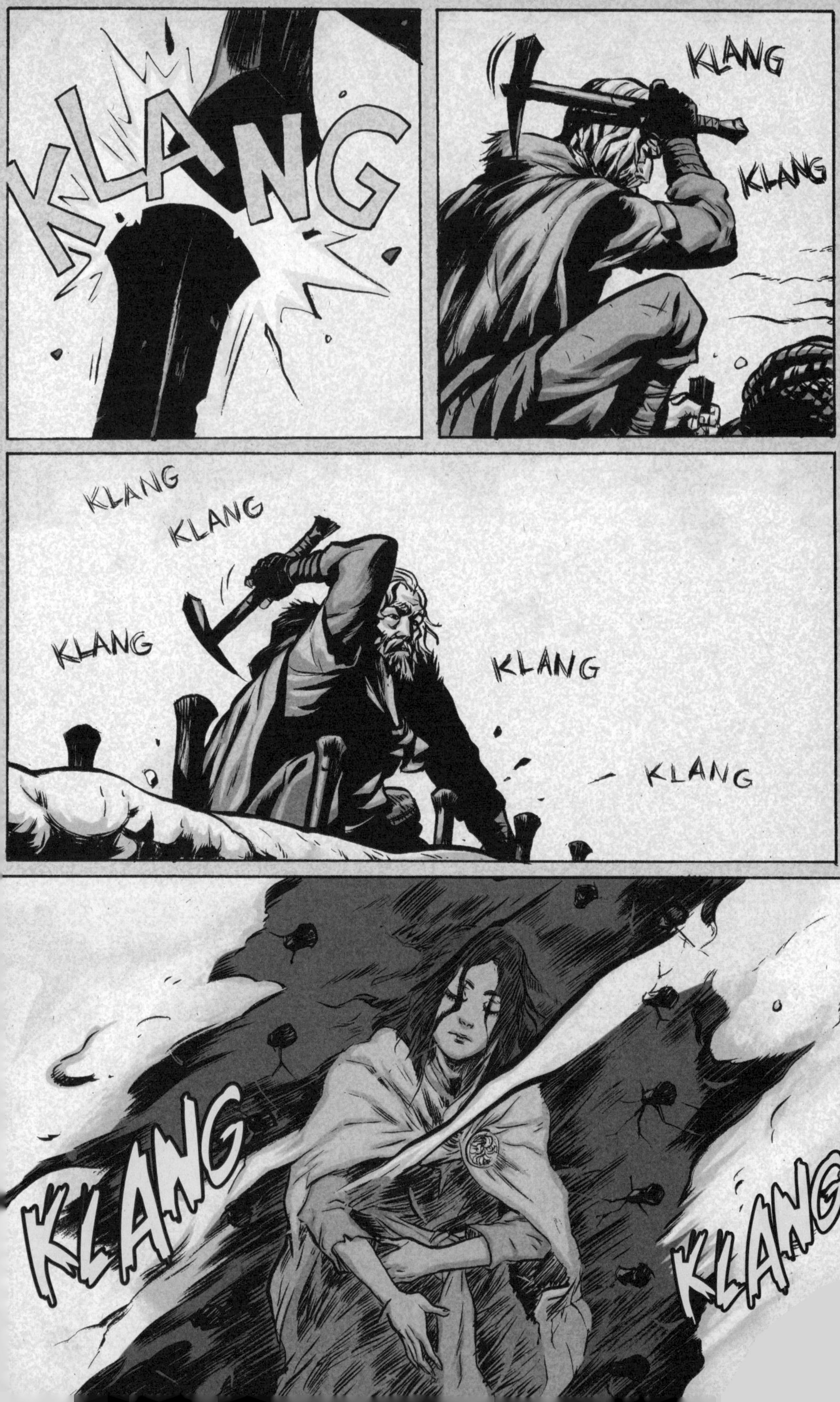
KLANG
KLANG
KLANG
KLANG
KLANG
KLANG
KLANG
KLANG
KLANG
KLANG

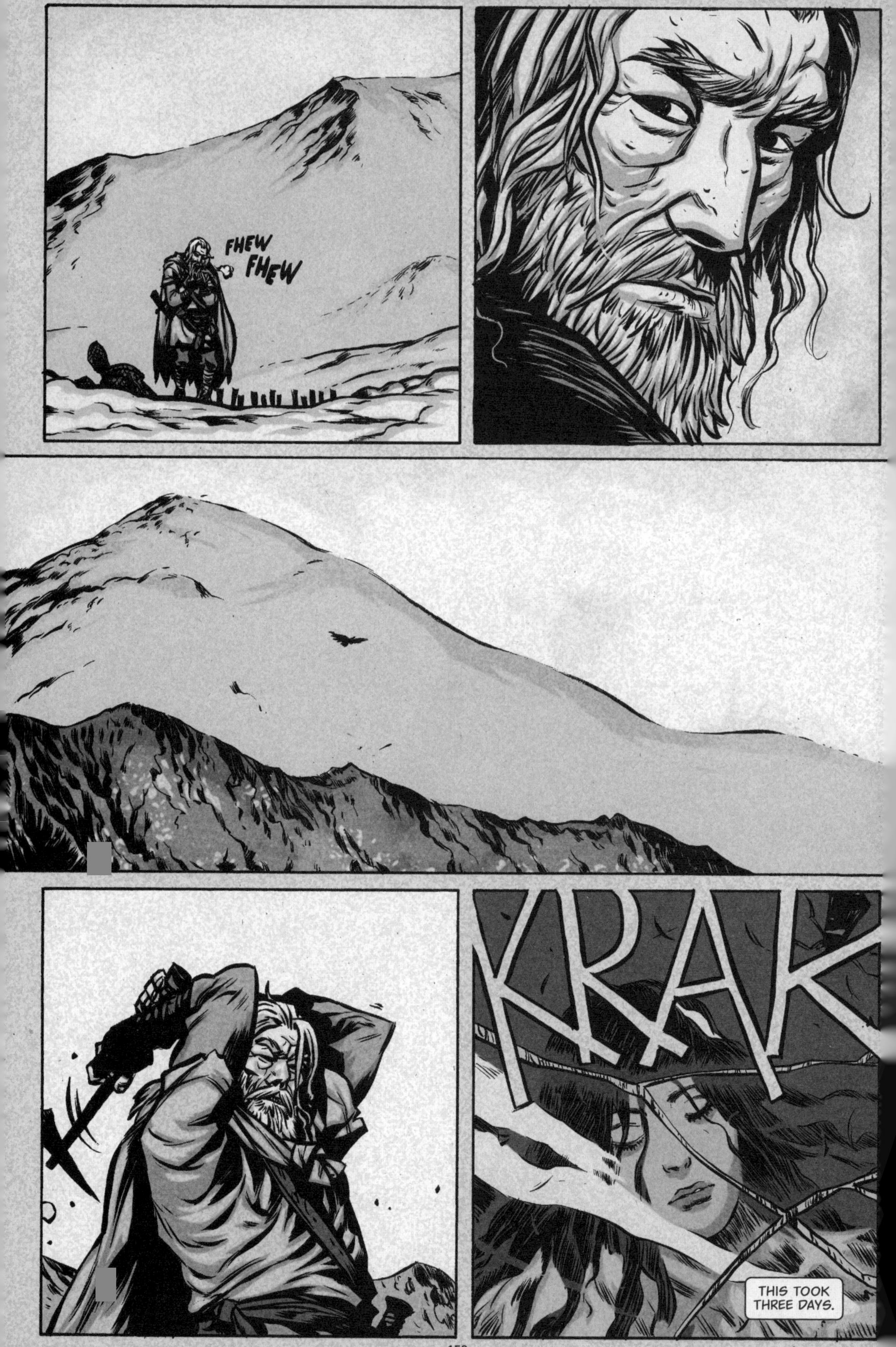
FHEW
FHEW
KRAK
THIS TOOK THREE DAYS.

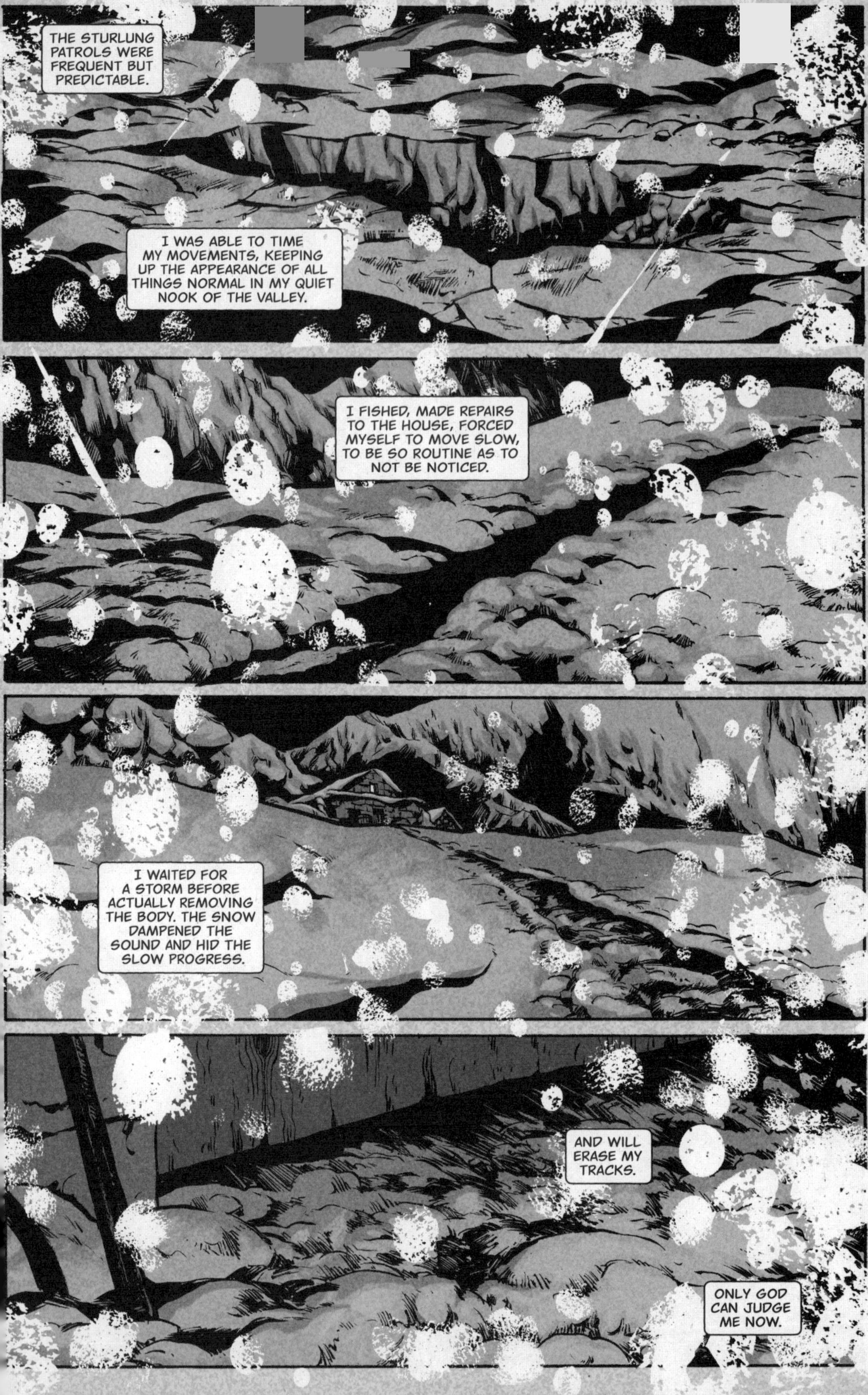
THE STURLUNG PATROLS WERE FREQUENT BUT PREDICTABLE.
I WAS ABLE TO TIME MY MOVEMENTS, KEEPING UP THE APPEARANCE OF ALL THINGS NORMAL IN MY QUIET NOOK OF THE VALLEY.
I FISHED, MADE REPAIRS TO THE HOUSE, FORCED MYSELF TO MOVE SLOW, TO BE SO ROUTINE AS TO NOT BE NOTICED.
I WAITED FOR A STORM BEFORE ACTUALLY REMOVING THE BODY. THE SNOW DAMPENED THE SOUND AND HID THE SLOW PROGRESS.
AND WILL ERASE MY TRACKS.
ONLY GOD CAN JUDGE ME NOW.

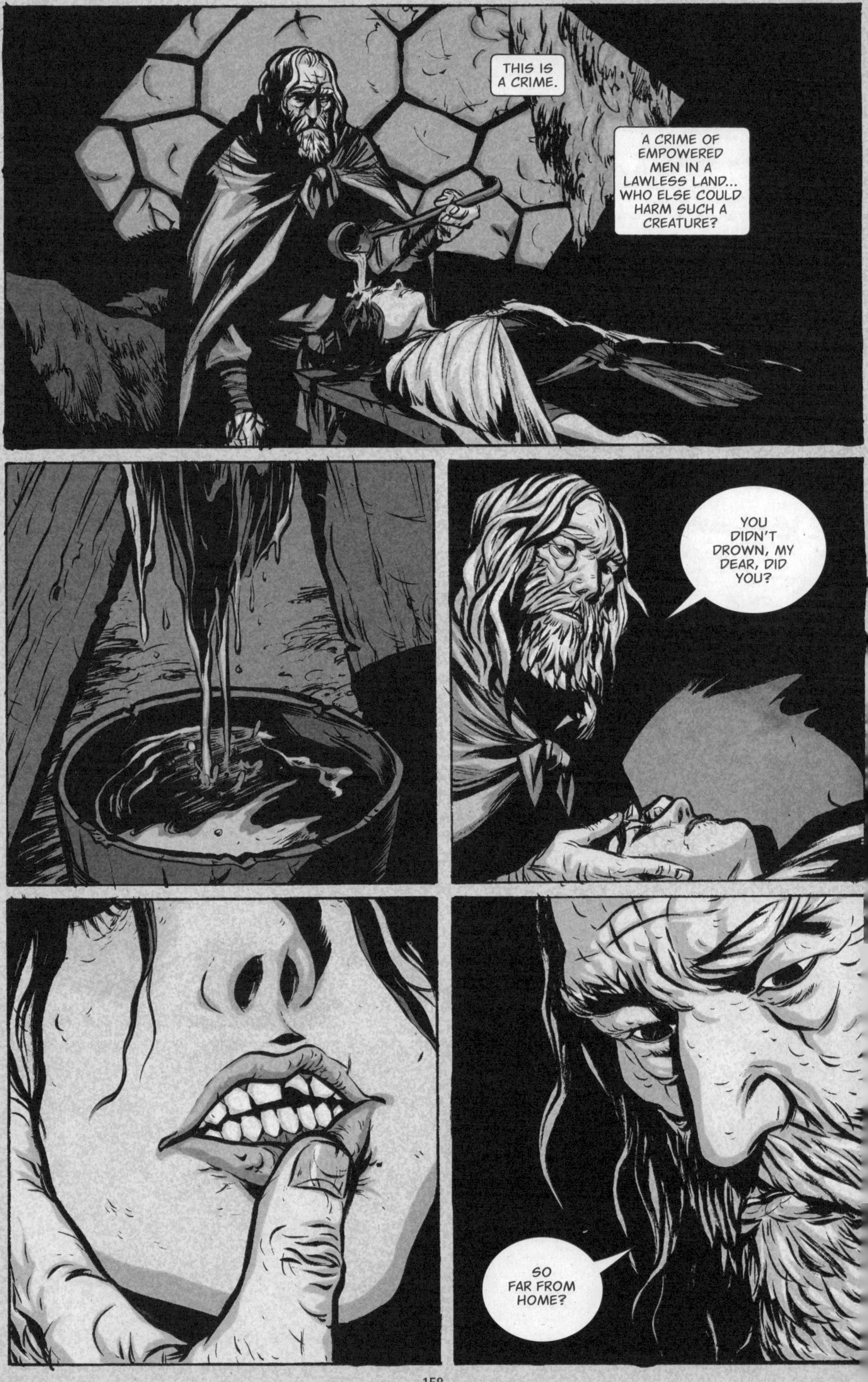
THIS IS A CRIME.
A CRIME OF EMPOWERED MEN IN A LAWLESS LAND... WHO ELSE COULD HARM SUCH A CREATURE?
YOU DIDN'T DROWN, MY DEAR, DID YOU?
SO FAR FROM HOME?

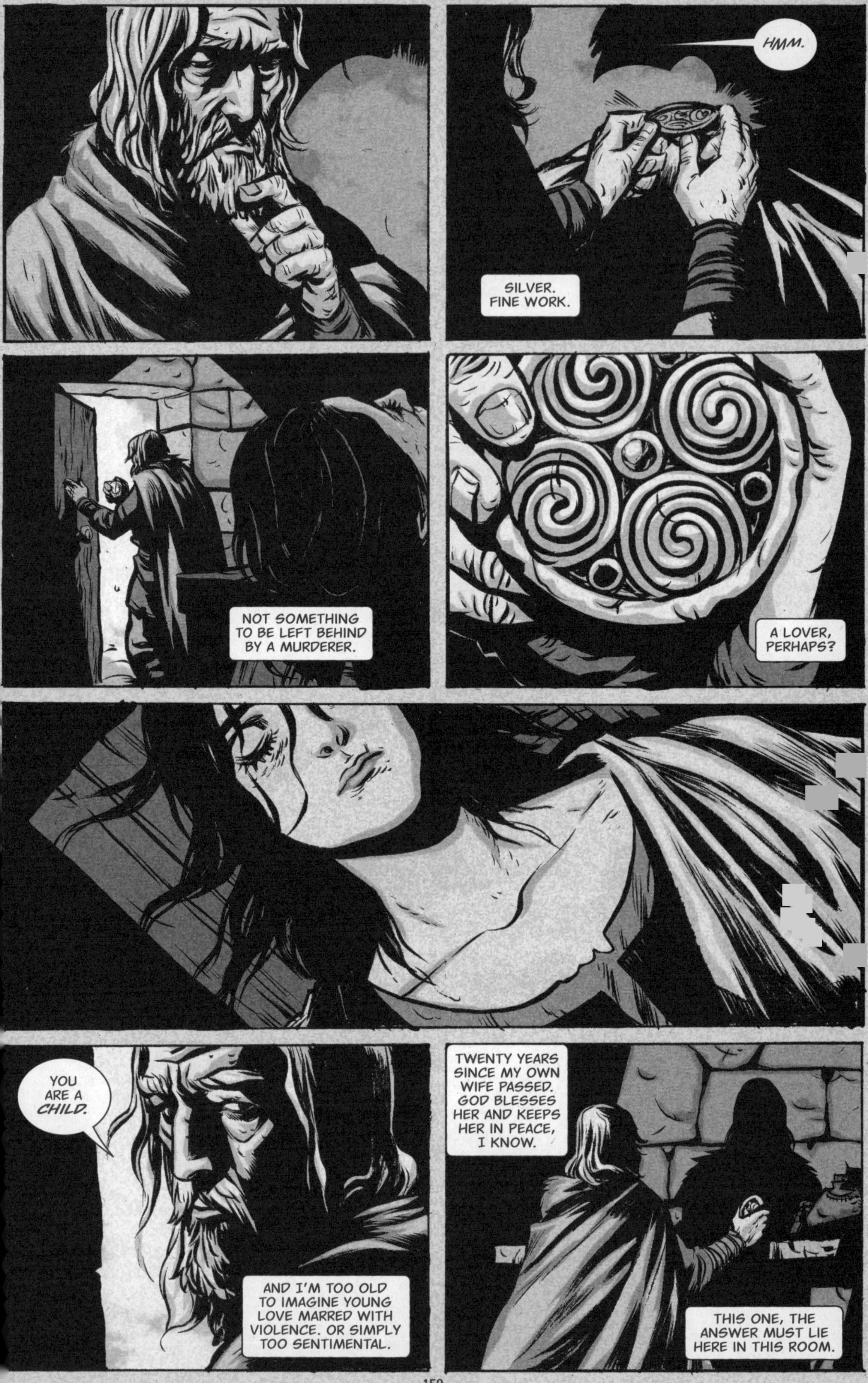
HMM.
SILVER. FINE WORK.
NOT SOMETHING TO BE LEFT BEHIND BY A MURDERER.
A LOVER, PERHAPS?
YOU ARE A CHILD.
AND I'M TOO OLD TO IMAGINE YOUNG LOVE MARRED WITH VIOLENCE. OR SIMPLY TOO SENTIMENTAL.
TWENTY YEARS SINCE MY OWN WIFE PASSED. GOD BLESSES HER AND KEEPS HER IN PEACE, I KNOW.
THIS ONE, THE ANSWER MUST LIE HERE IN THIS ROOM.

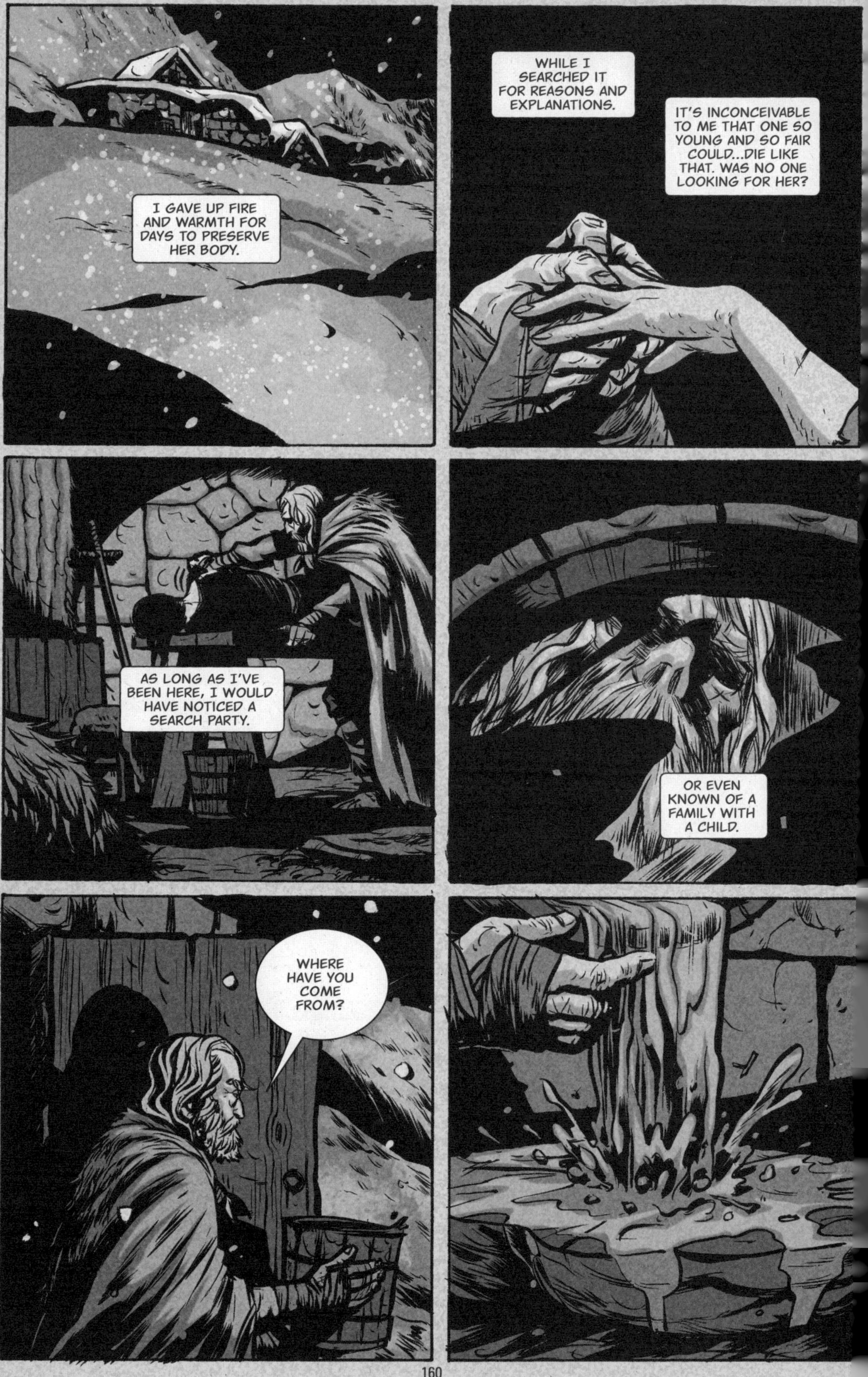
I GAVE UP FIRE AND WARMTH FOR DAYS TO PRESERVE HER BODY.
WHILE I SEARCHED IT FOR REASONS AND EXPLANATIONS.
IT'S INCONCEIVABLE TO ME THAT ONE SO YOUNG AND SO FAIR COULD...DIE LIKE THAT. WAS NO ONE LOOKING FOR HER?
AS LONG AS I'VE BEEN HERE, I WOULD HAVE NOTICED A SEARCH PARTY.
OR EVEN KNOWN OF A FAMILY WITH A CHILD.
WHERE HAVE YOU COME FROM?

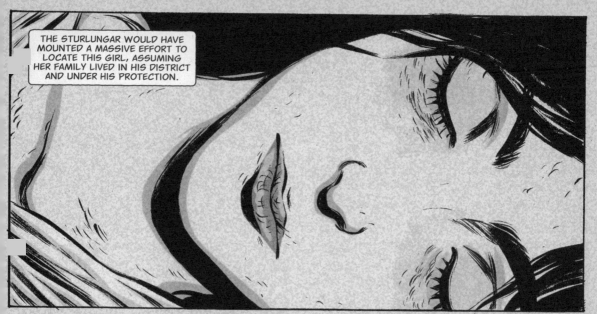

THE STURLUNGAR WOULD HAVE MOUNTED A MASSIVE EFFORT TO LOCATE THIS GIRL, ASSUMING HER FAMILY LIVED IN HIS DISTRICT AND UNDER HIS PROTECTION.

NOT TO DO SO WOULD BE AN UNTHINKABLE LAPSE IN RESPONSIBILITY.

HE WOULD NOT SURVIVE IT, POLITICALLY. ALL HIS ALLIES WOULD INSTANTLY LOSE FAITH. GOES AGAINST THE VERY FABRIC OF COMMONWEATH SOCIETY.

SO...THE GIRL IS EITHER FROM ANOTHER DISTRICT--WOULD HAVE TO BE QUITE FAR NOT TO CAUSE EVEN A MURMUR HERE--OR HER DEATH WAS KNOWN TO THE STURLUNGS.

AND... ALLOWED?

ORDERED?

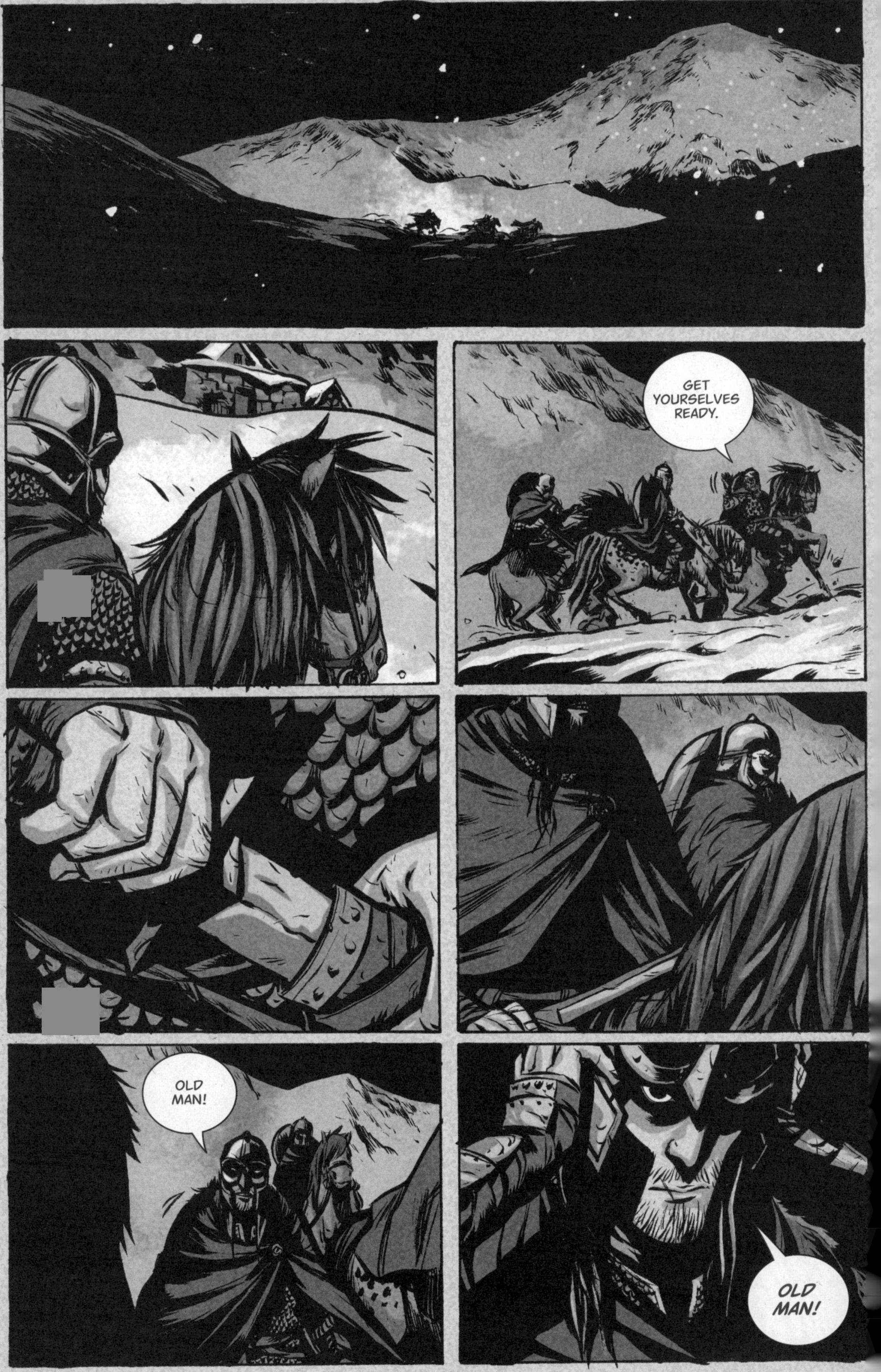
GET YOURSELVES READY.
OLD MAN!
OLD MAN!

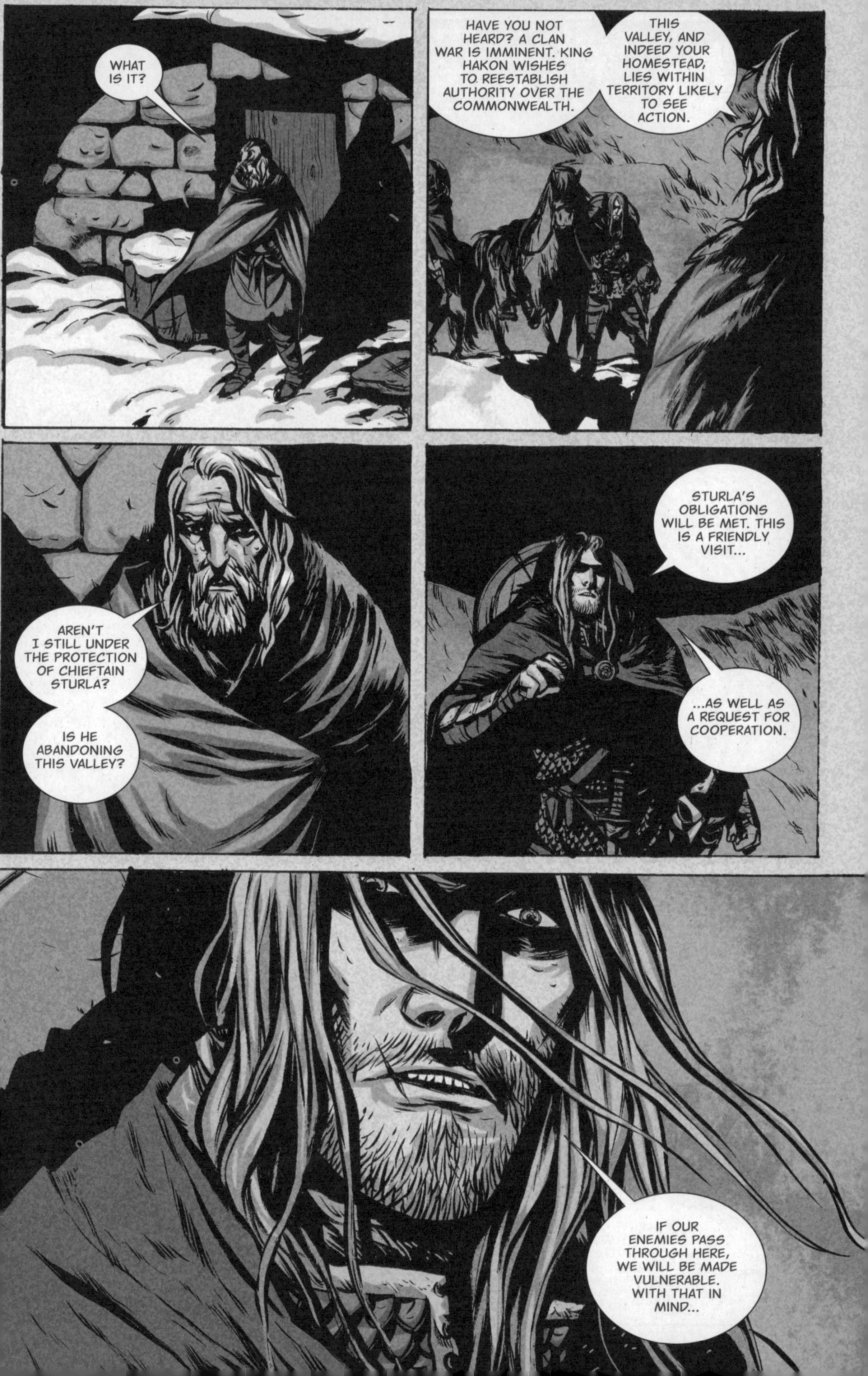
WHAT IS IT?
HAVE YOU NOT HEARD? A CLAN WAR IS IMMINENT. KING HAKON WISHES TO REESTABLISH AUTHORITY OVER THE COMMONWEALTH.
THIS VALLEY, AND INDEED YOUR HOMESTEAD, LIES WITHIN TERRITORY LIKELY TO SEE ACTION.
AREN'T I STILL UNDER THE PROTECTION OF CHIEFTAIN STURLA?
IS HE ABANDONING THIS VALLEY?
STURLA'S OBLIGATIONS WILL BE MET. THIS IS A FRIENDLY VISIT...
...AS WELL AS A REQUEST FOR COOPERATION.
IF OUR ENEMIES PASS THROUGH HERE, WE WILL BE MADE VULNERABLE. WITH THAT IN MIND...

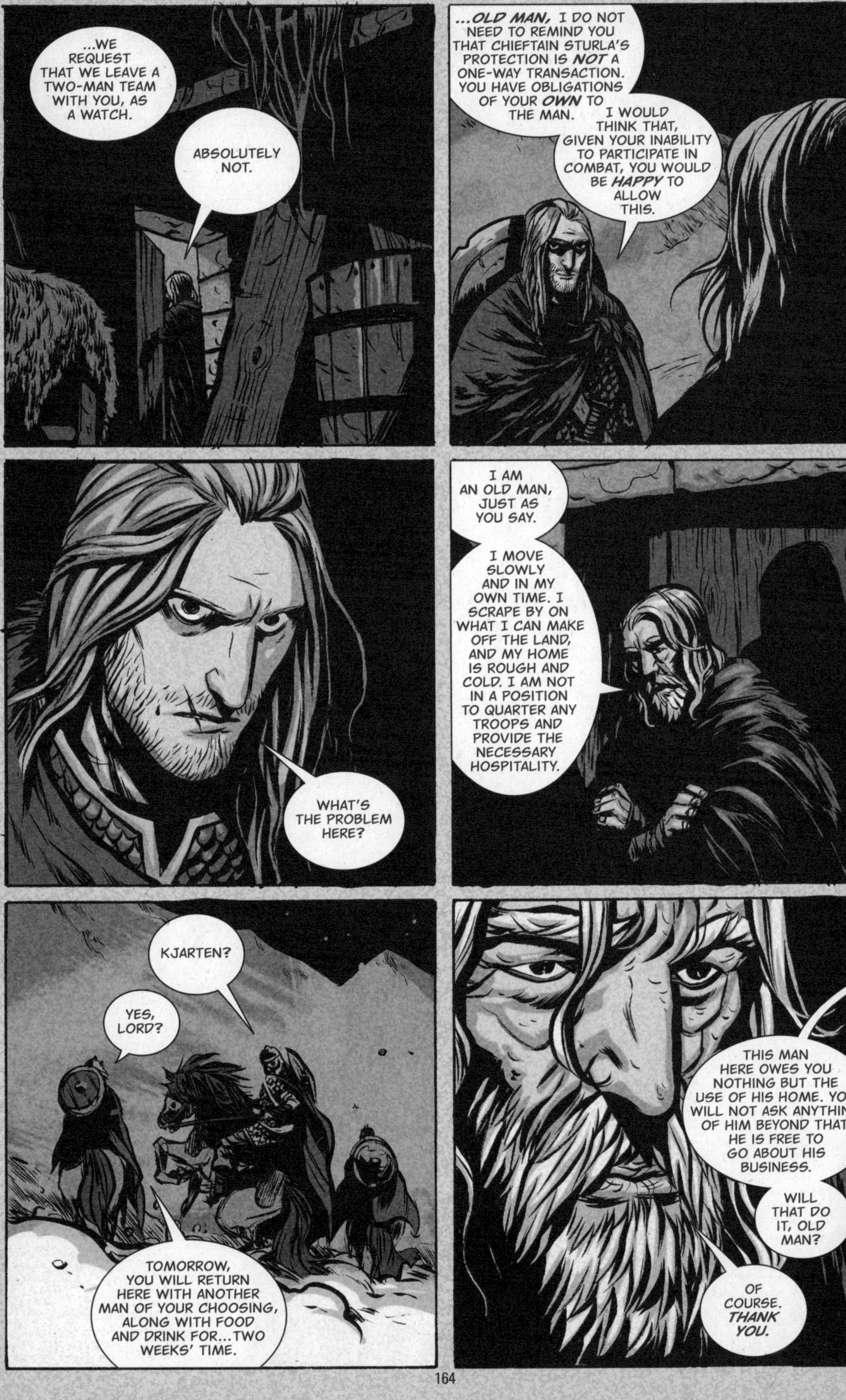
...WE REQUEST THAT WE LEAVE A TWO-MAN TEAM WITH YOU, AS A WATCH.
ABSOLUTELY NOT.
...OLD MAN, I DO NOT NEED TO REMIND YOU THAT CHIEFTAIN STURLA'S PROTECTION IS NOT A ONE-WAY TRANSACTION. YOU HAVE OBLIGATIONS OF YOUR OWN TO THE MAN.
I WOULD THINK THAT, GIVEN YOUR INABILITY TO PARTICIPATE IN COMBAT, YOU WOULD BE HAPPY TO ALLOW THIS.
WHAT'S THE PROBLEM HERE?
I AM AN OLD MAN, JUST AS YOU SAY.
I MOVE SLOWLY AND IN MY OWN TIME. I SCRAPE BY ON WHAT I CAN MAKE OFF THE LAND, AND MY HOME IS ROUGH AND COLD. I AM NOT IN A POSITION TO QUARTER ANY TROOPS AND PROVIDE THE NECESSARY HOSPITALITY.
KJARTEN?
YES, LORD?
TOMORROW, YOU WILL RETURN HERE WITH ANOTHER MAN OF YOUR CHOOSING, ALONG WITH FOOD AND DRINK FOR...TWO WEEKS' TIME.
THIS MAN HERE OWES YOU NOTHING BUT THE USE OF HIS HOME. YOU WILL NOT ASK ANYTHING OF HIM BEYOND THAT. HE IS FREE TO GO ABOUT HIS BUSINESS.
WILL THAT DO IT, OLD MAN?
OF COURSE. THANK YOU.

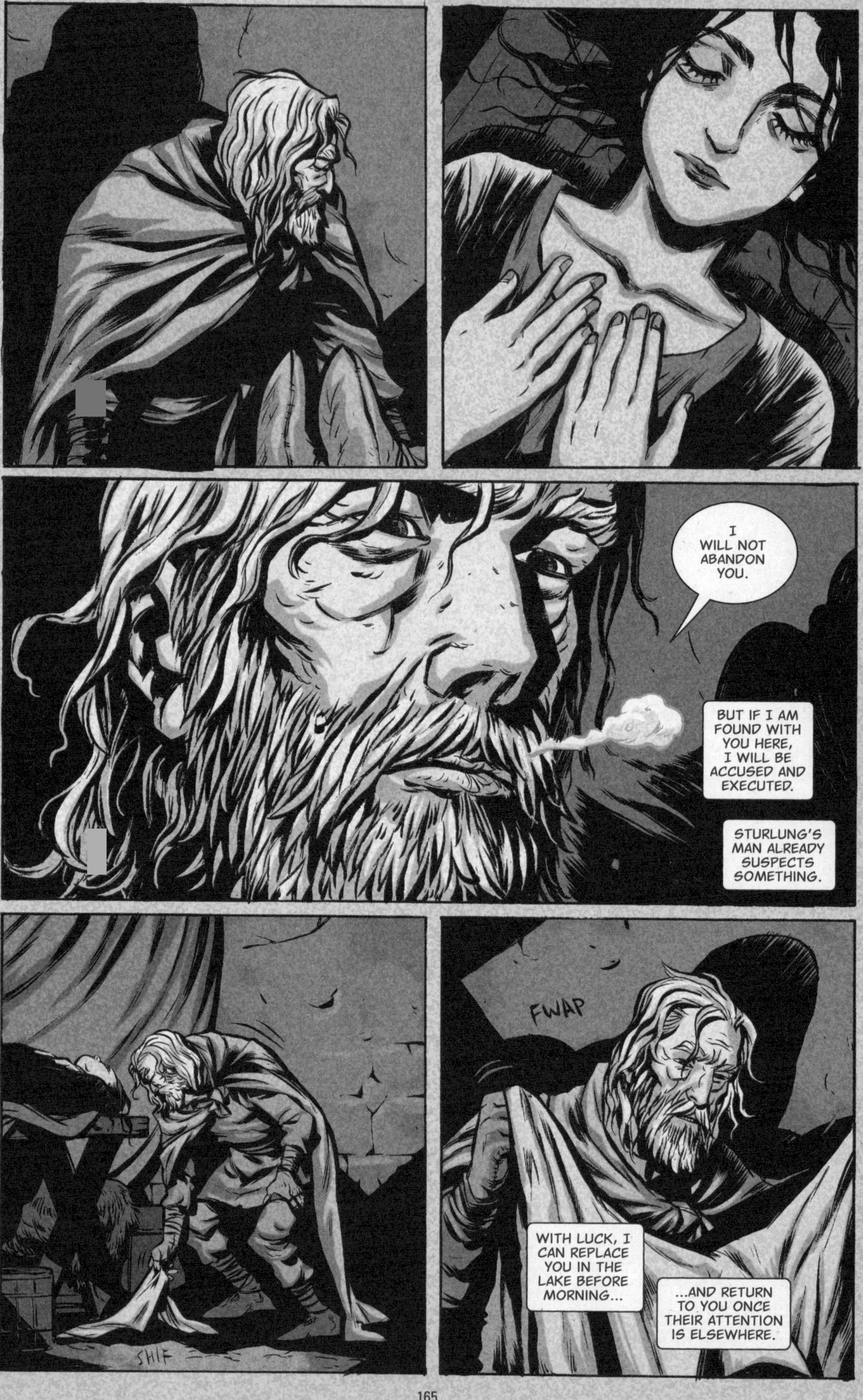
I WILL NOT ABANDON YOU.
BUT IF I AM FOUND WITH YOU HERE, I WILL BE ACCUSED AND EXECUTED.
STURLUNG'S MAN ALREADY SUSPECTS SOMETHING.
SHIF
FWAP
WITH LUCK, I CAN REPLACE YOU IN THE LAKE BEFORE MORNING...
...AND RETURN TO YOU ONCE THEIR ATTENTION IS ELSEWHERE.

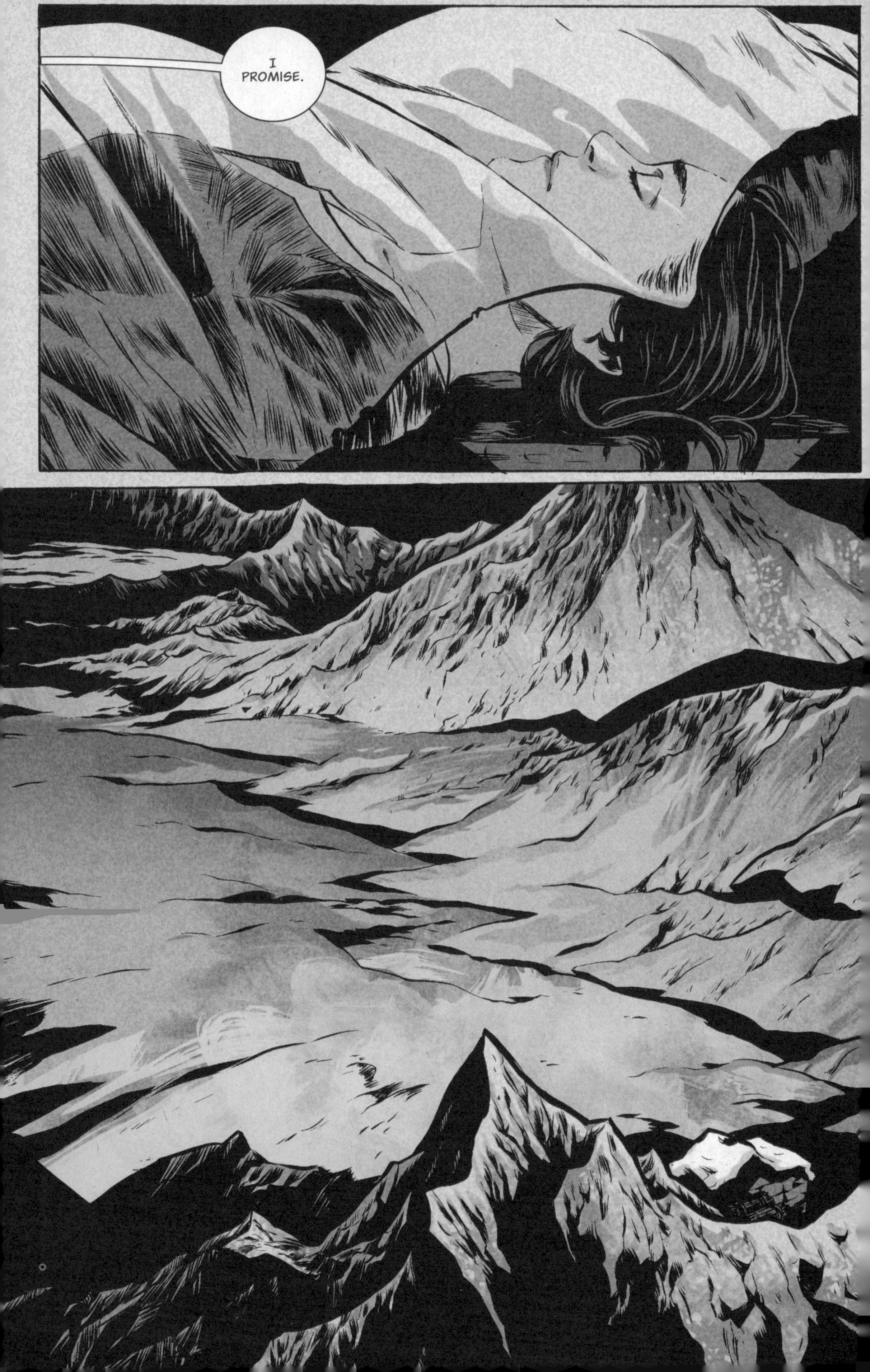
I PROMISE.

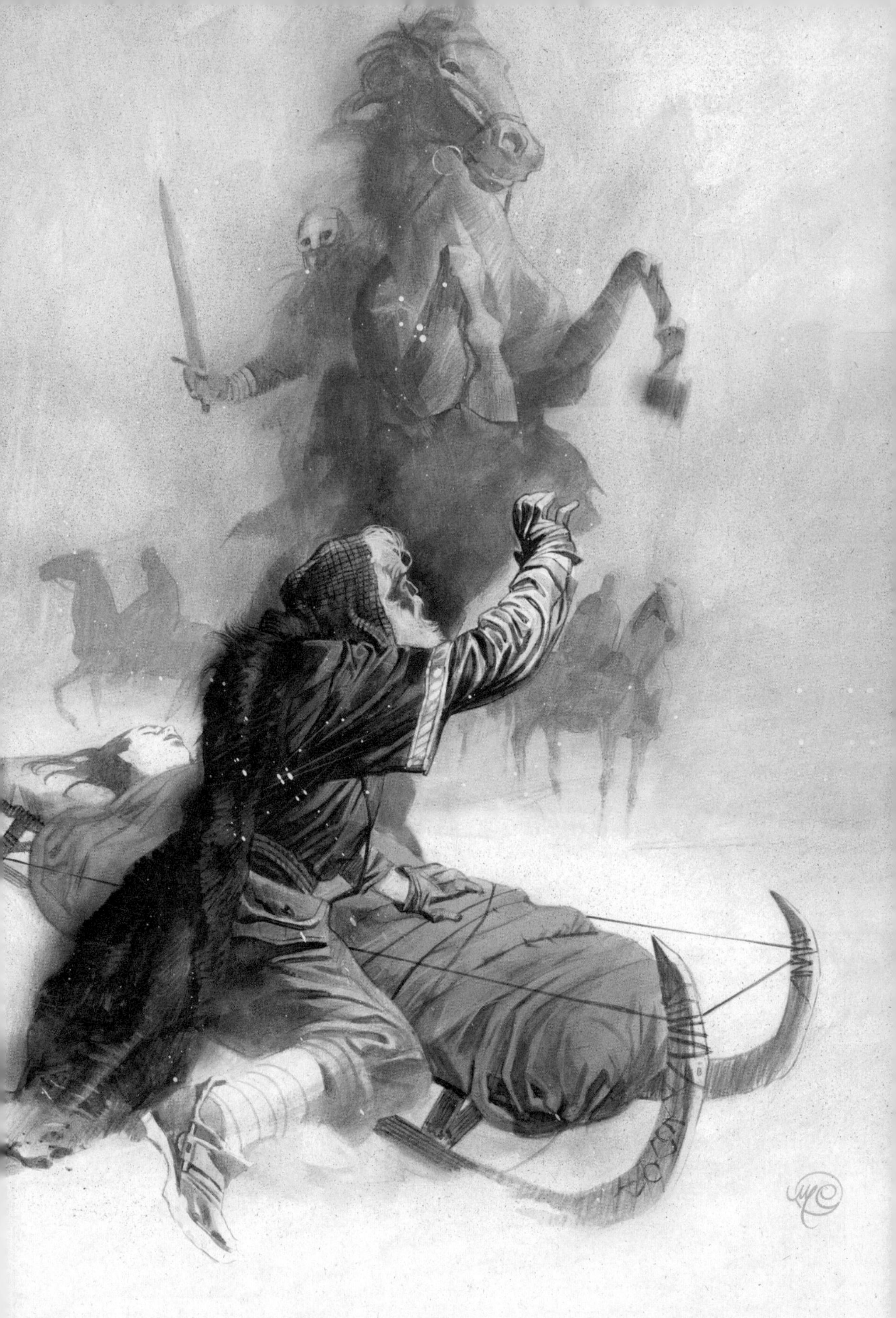

The Girl In The Ice Part Two

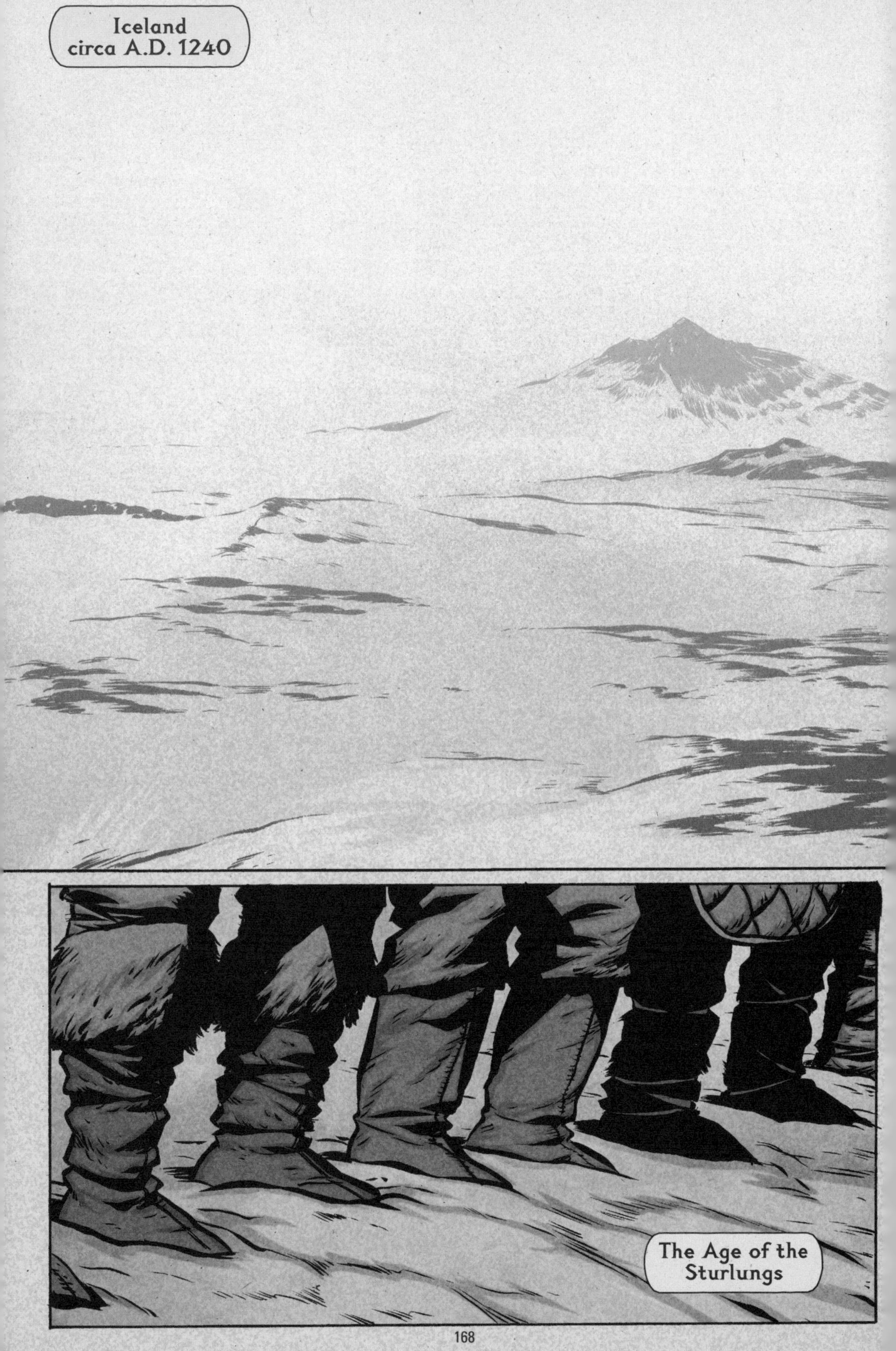
Iceland
circa A.D. 1240
The Age of the Sturlungs

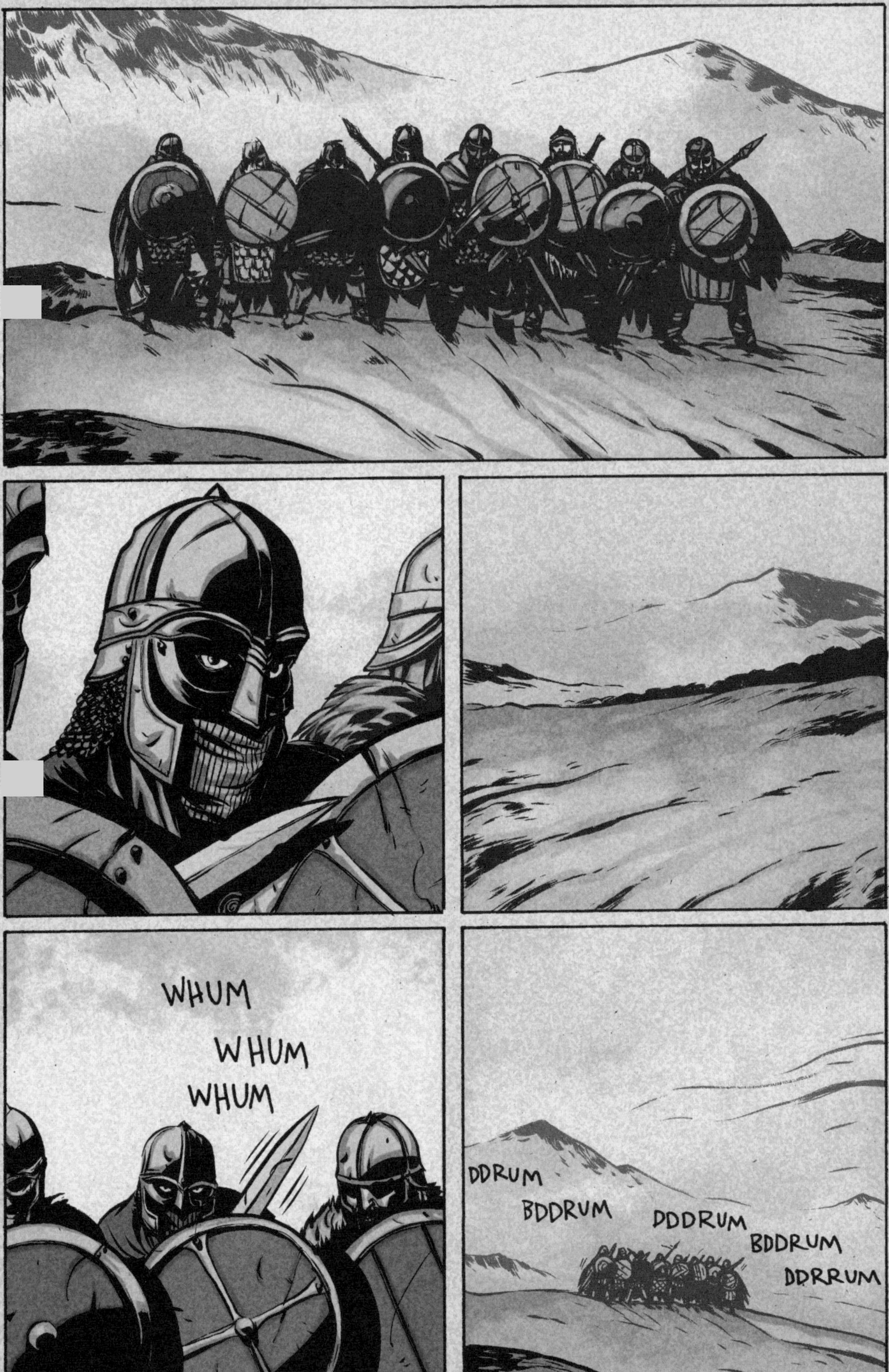
WHUM
WHUM
WHUM
DDRUM
BDDRUM
DDDRUM
BDDRUM
DDRRUM

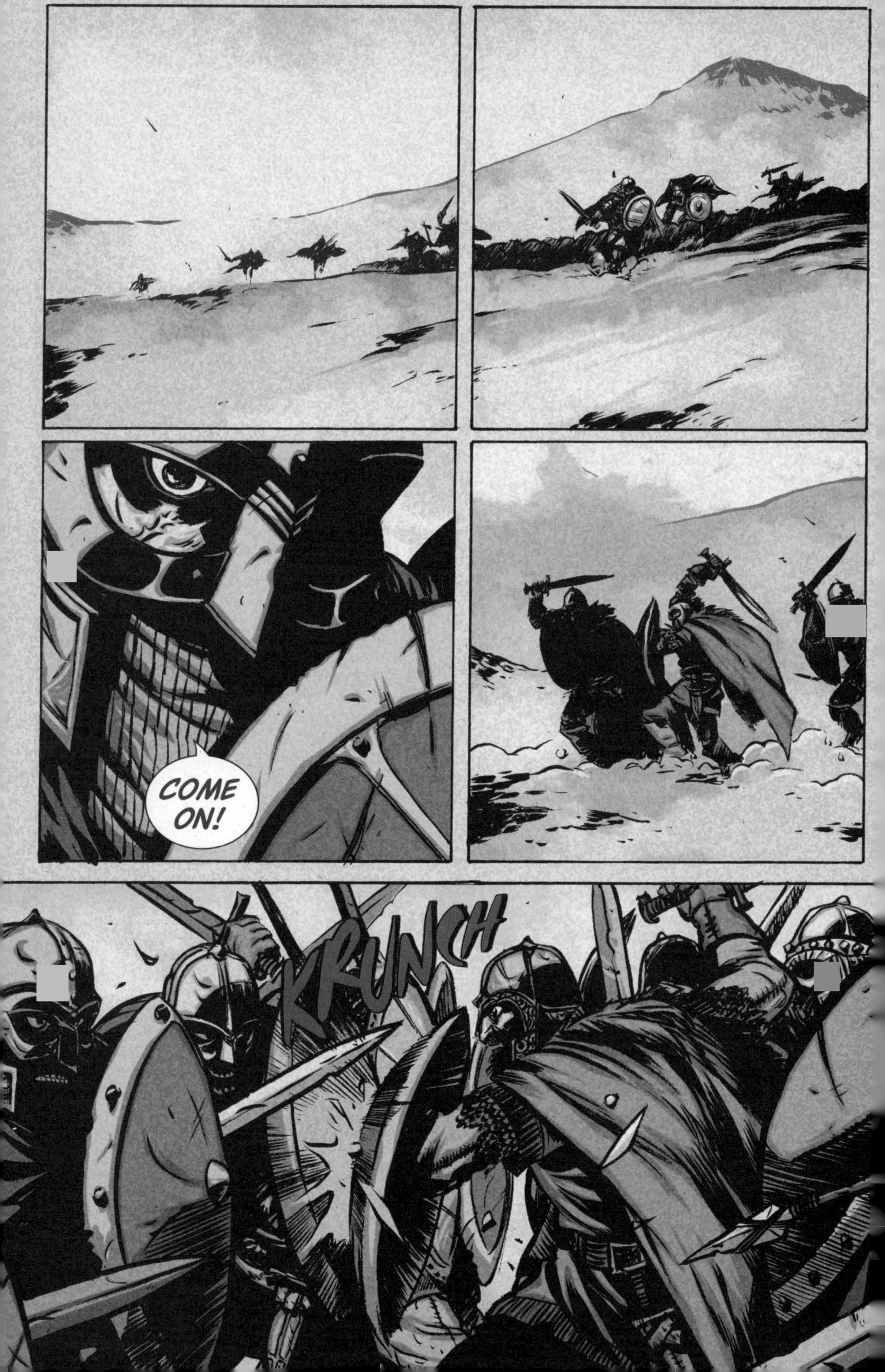
COME ON!
KRUNCH

SHLUK.

KKRSCHH

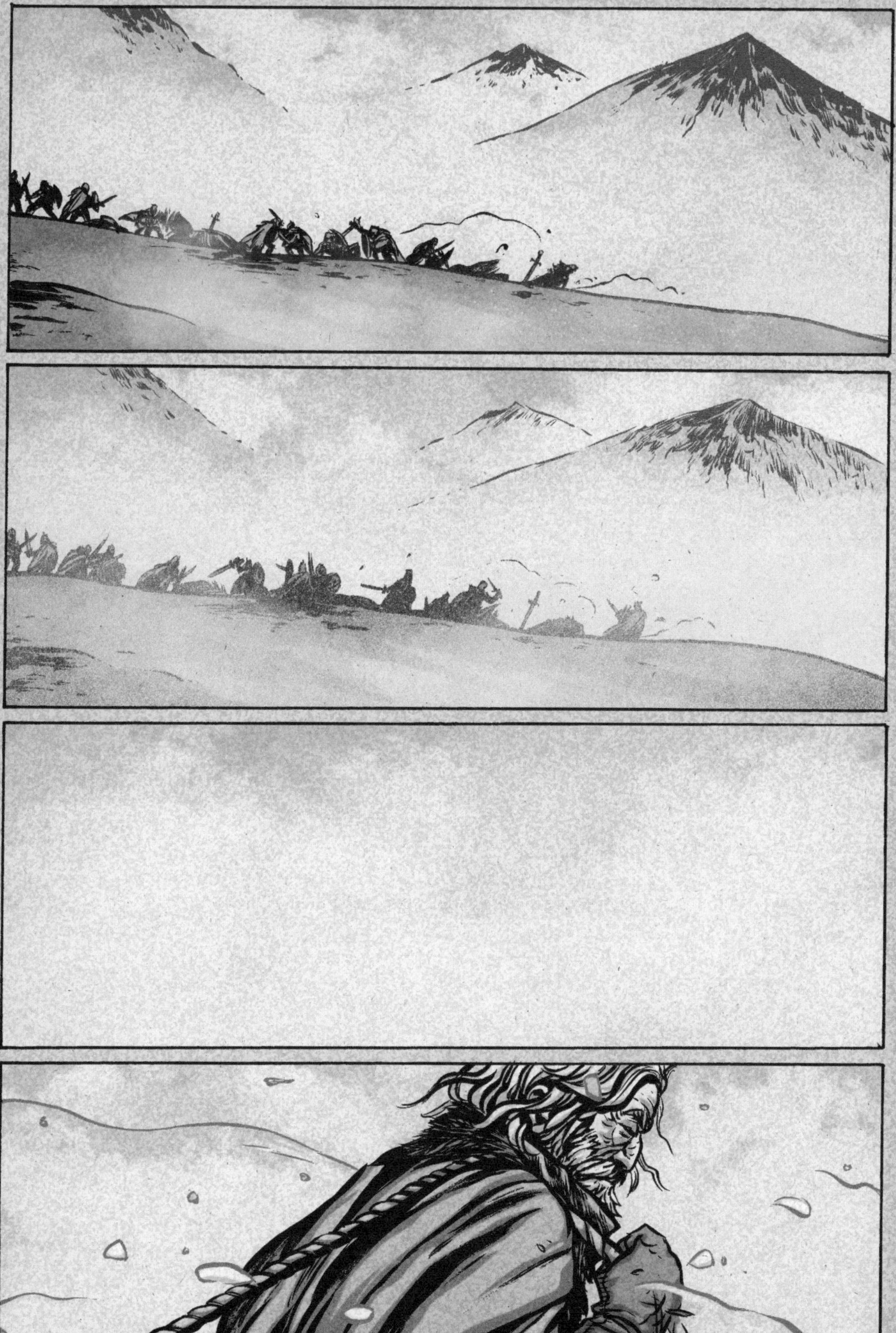

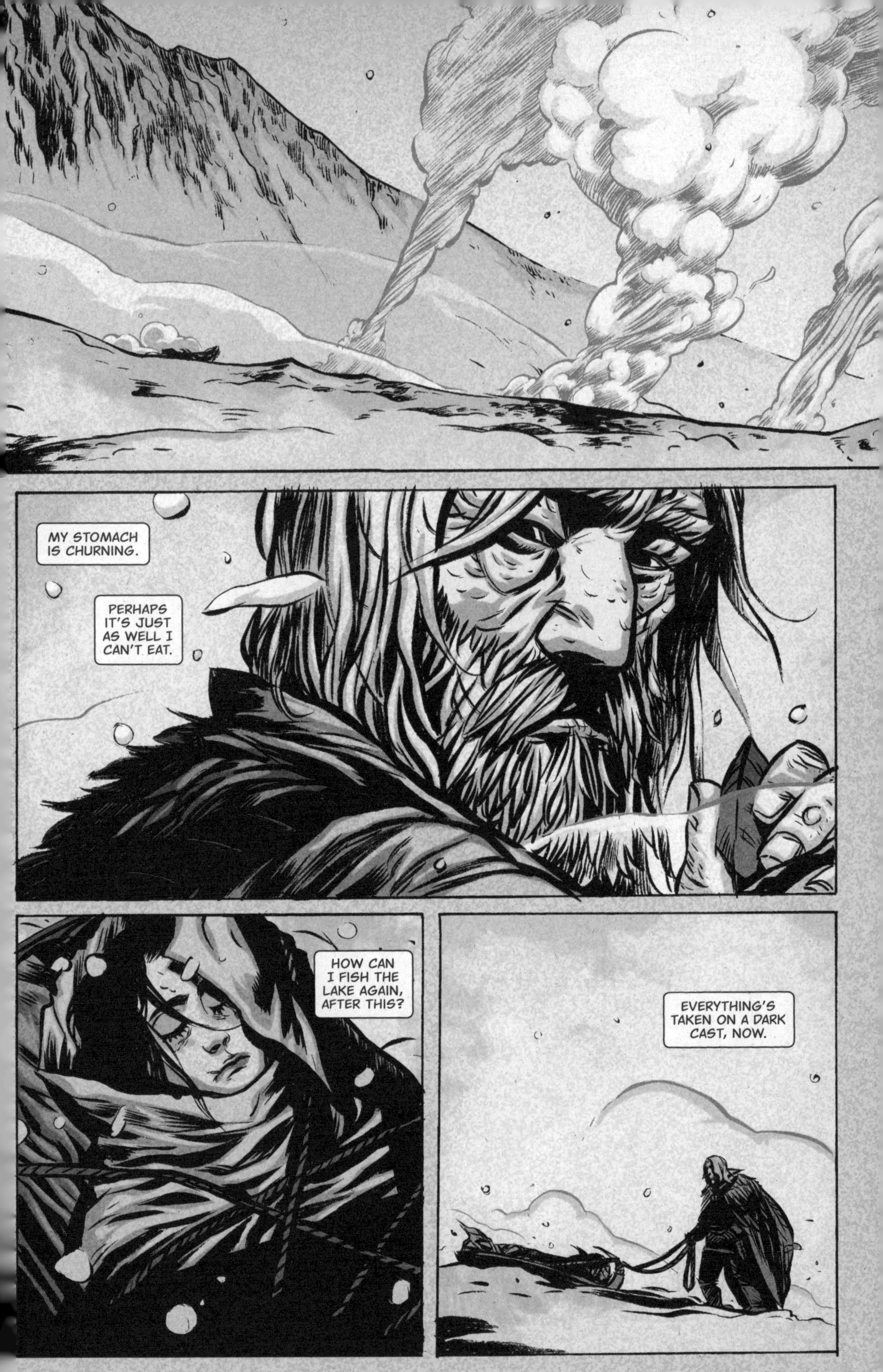
MY STOMACH IS CHURNING.
PERHAPS IT'S JUST AS WELL I CAN'T EAT.
HOW CAN I FISH THE LAKE AGAIN, AFTER THIS?
EVERYTHING'S TAKEN ON A DARK CAST, NOW.

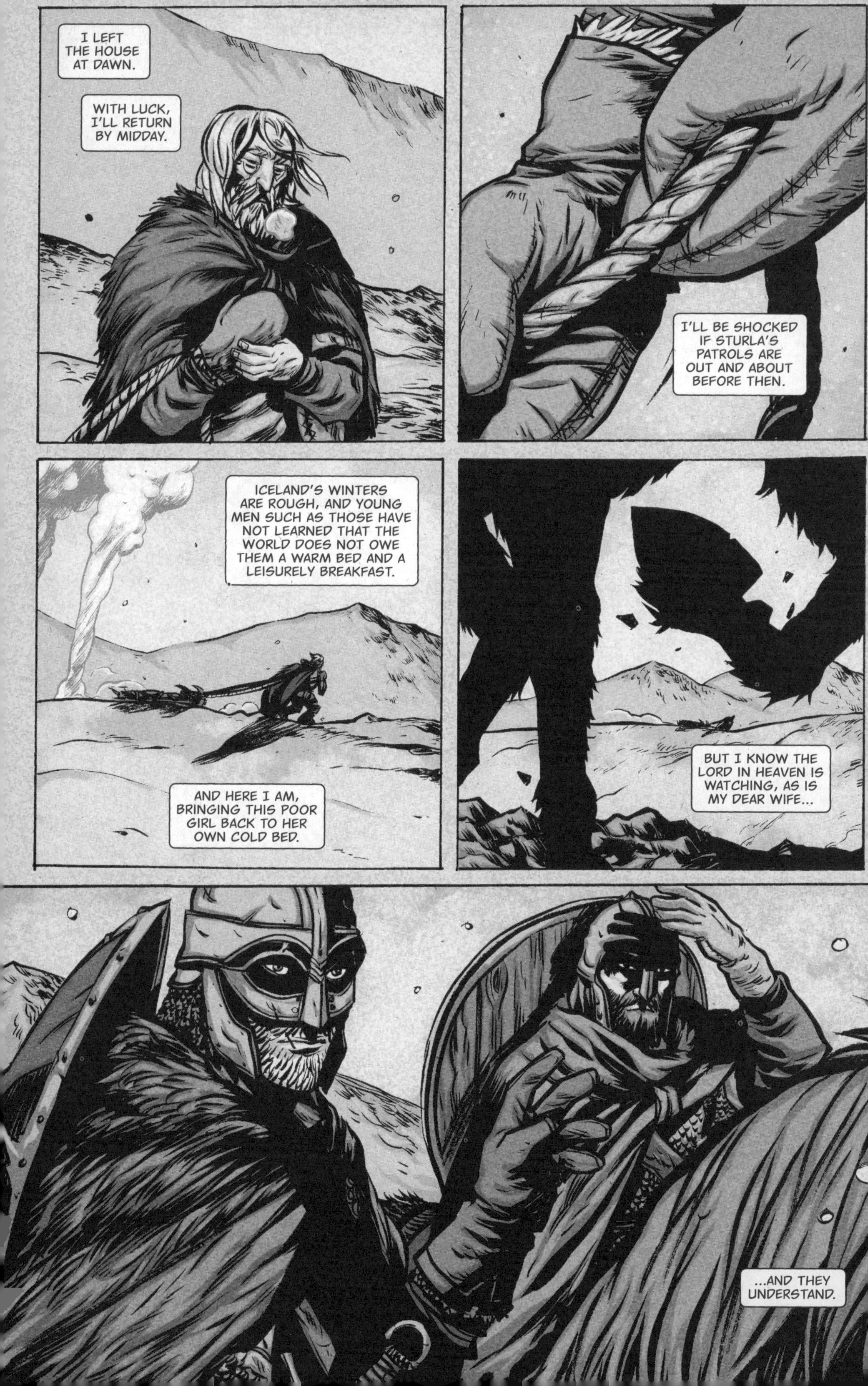
I LEFT THE HOUSE AT DAWN.
WITH LUCK, I'LL RETURN BY MIDDAY.
I'LL BE SHOCKED IF STURLA'S PATROLS ARE OUT AND ABOUT BEFORE THEN.
ICELAND'S WINTERS ARE ROUGH, AND YOUNG MEN SUCH AS THOSE HAVE NOT LEARNED THAT THE WORLD DOES NOT OWE THEM A WARM BED AND A LEISURELY BREAKFAST.
AND HERE I AM, BRINGING THIS POOR GIRL BACK TO HER OWN COLD BED.
BUT I KNOW THE LORD IN HEAVEN IS WATCHING, AS IS MY DEAR WIFE...
...AND THEY UNDERSTAND.

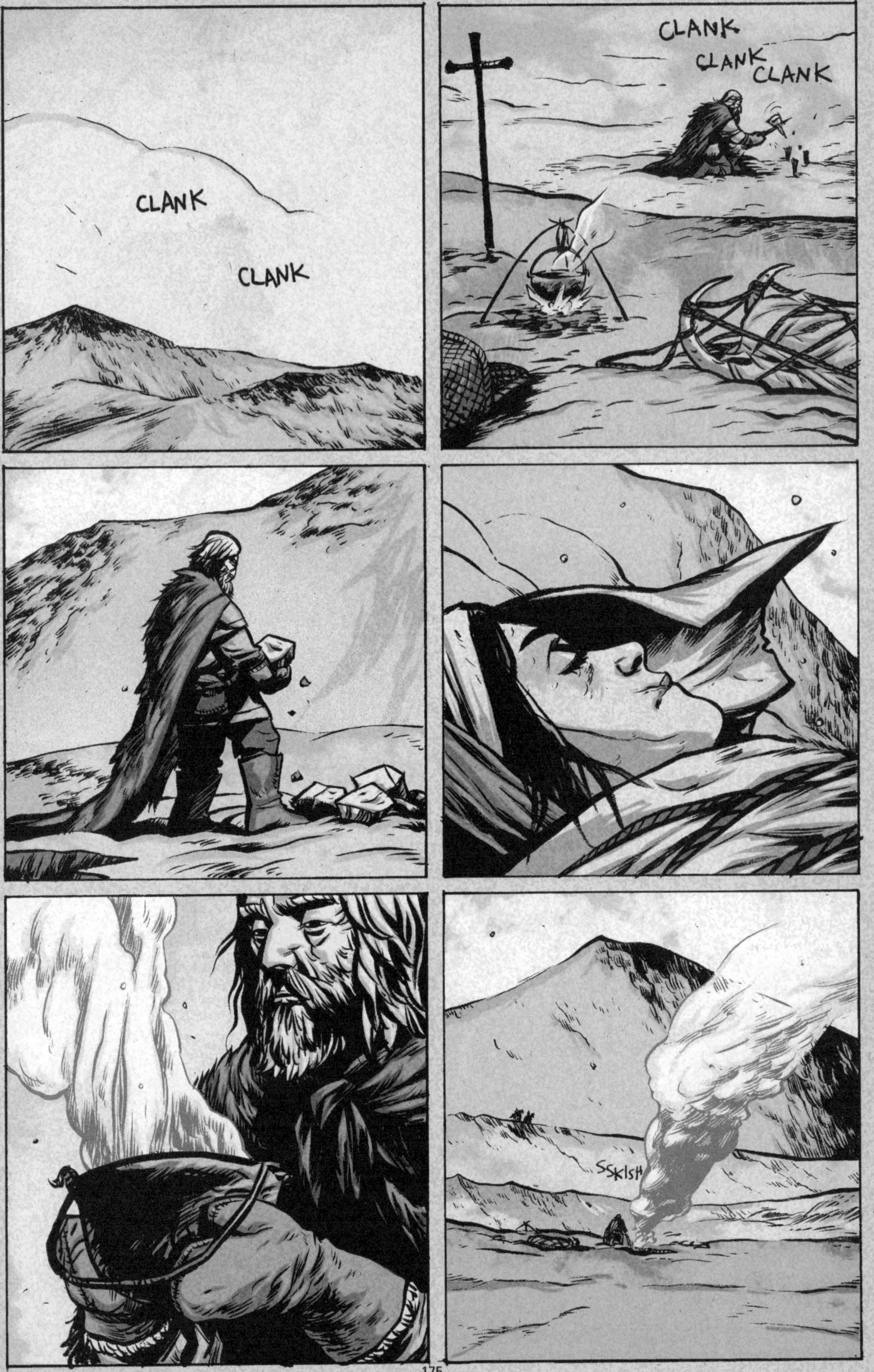
CLANK
CLANK
CLANK
CLANK
CLANK
SSKISH

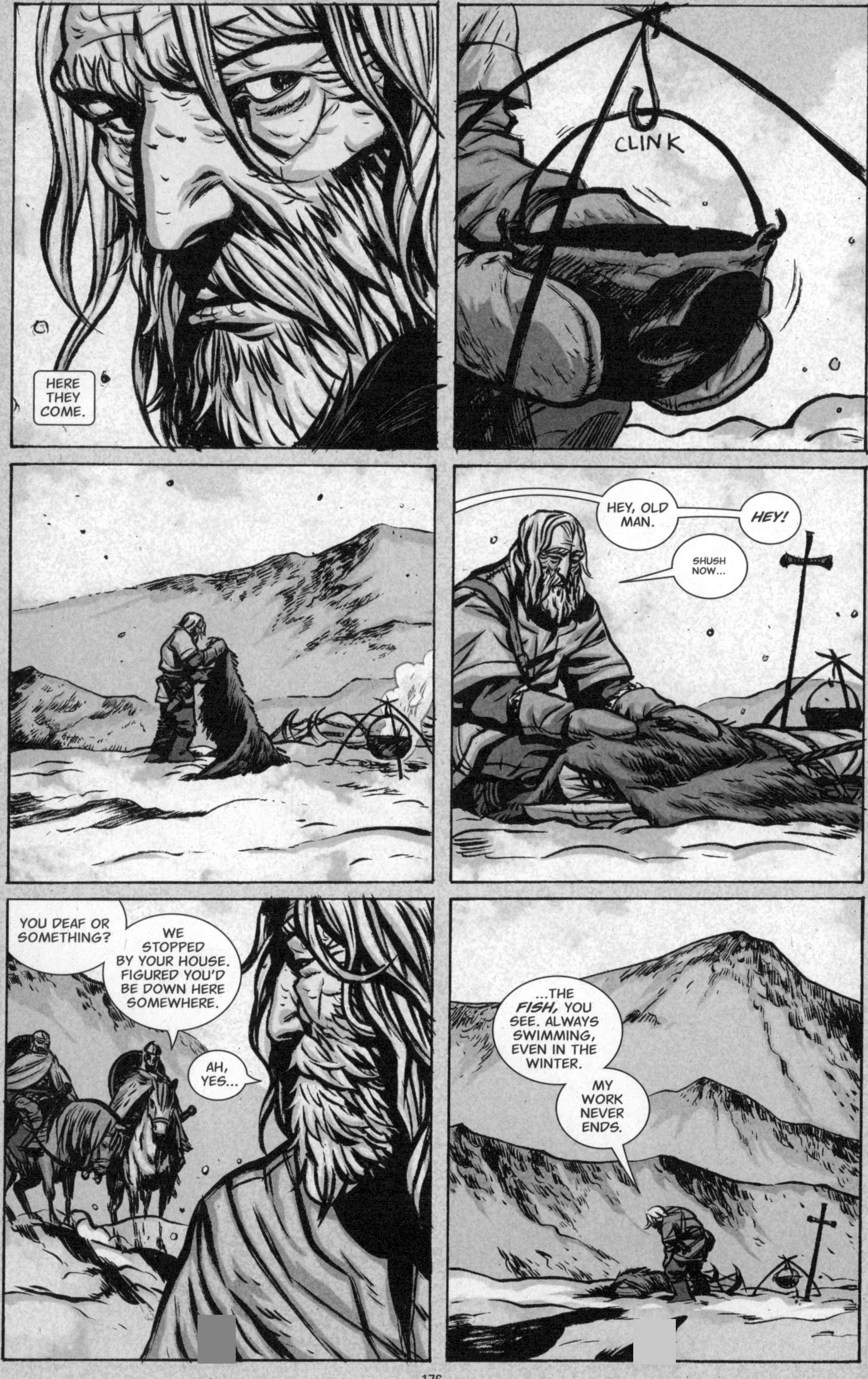
HERE THEY COME.
CLINK
HEY, OLD MAN.
HEY!
SHUSH NOW...
YOU DEAF OR SOMETHING?
WE STOPPED BY YOUR HOUSE. FIGURED YOU'D BE DOWN HERE SOMEWHERE.
AH, YES...
...THE FISH, YOU SEE. ALWAYS SWIMMING, EVEN IN THE WINTER.
MY WORK NEVER ENDS.

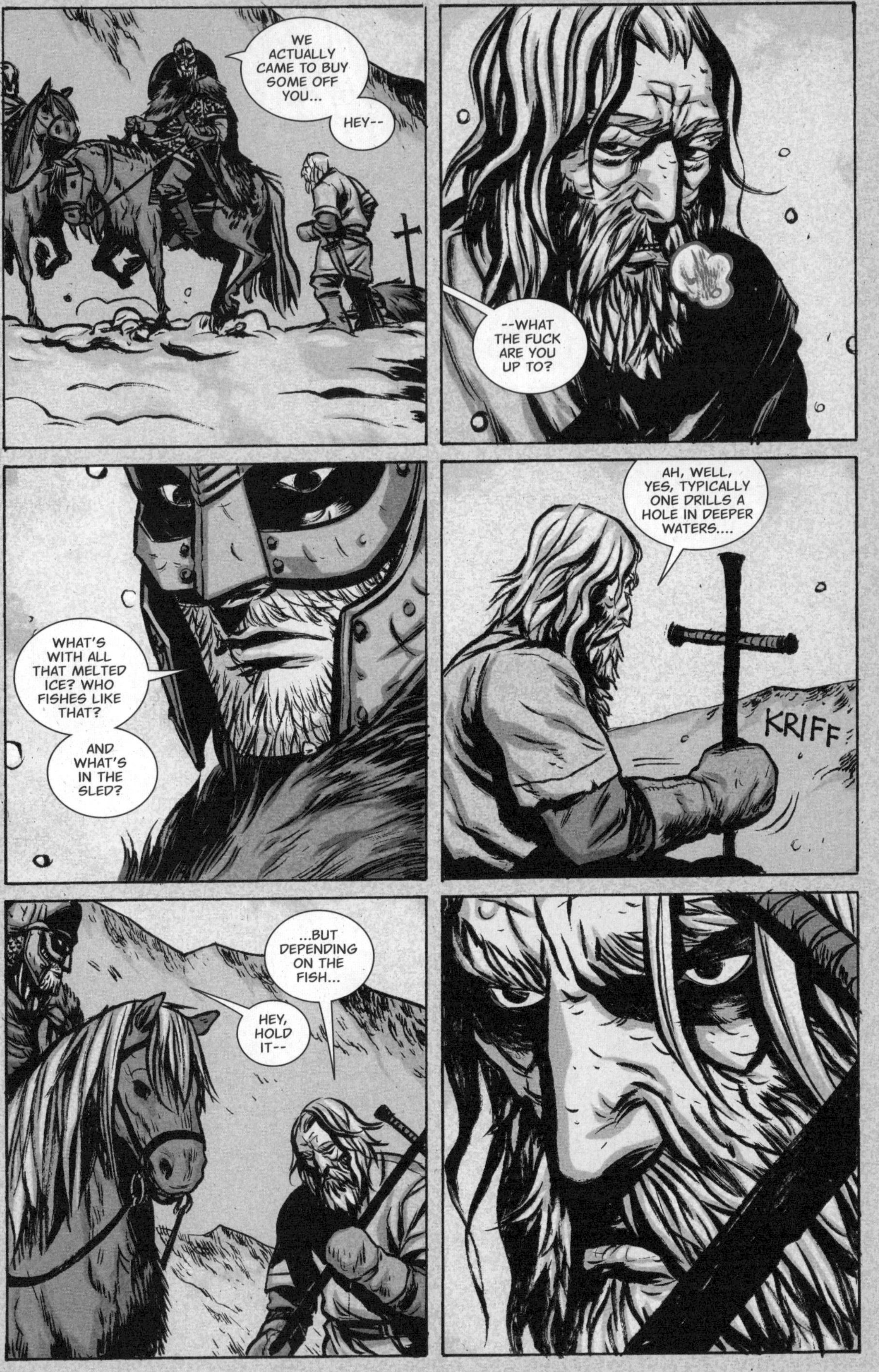
WE ACTUALLY CAME TO BUY SOME OFF YOU...
HEY--
--WHAT THE FUCK ARE YOU UP TO?
WHAT'S WITH ALL THAT MELTED ICE? WHO FISHES LIKE THAT?
AND WHAT'S IN THE SLED?
AH, WELL, YES, TYPICALLY ONE DRILLS A HOLE IN DEEPER WATERS....
KRIFF
...BUT DEPENDING ON THE FISH...
HEY, HOLD IT--

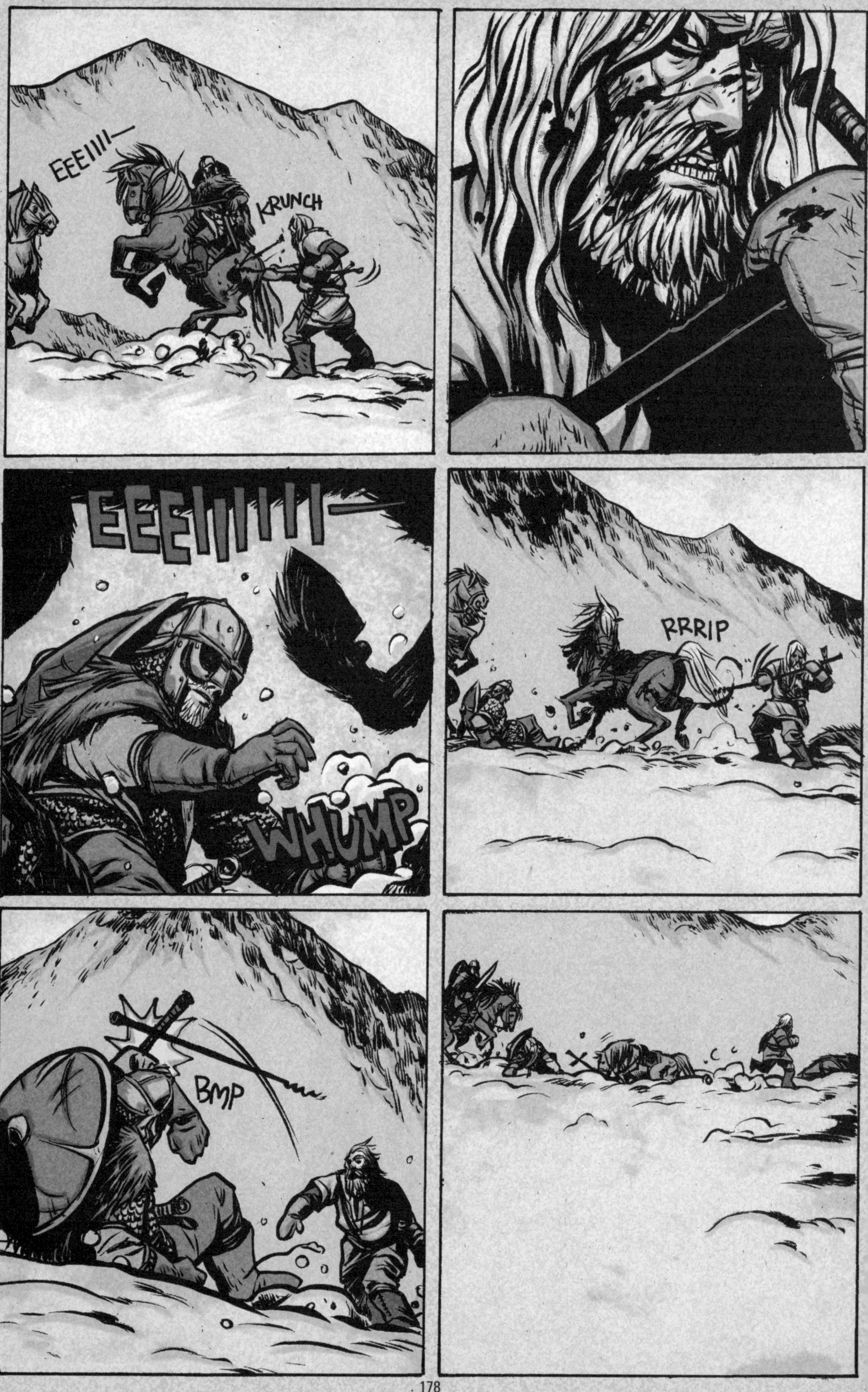
EEEIIII—
KRUNCH
EEEIIIIIIII—
WHUMP
RRRIP
BMP

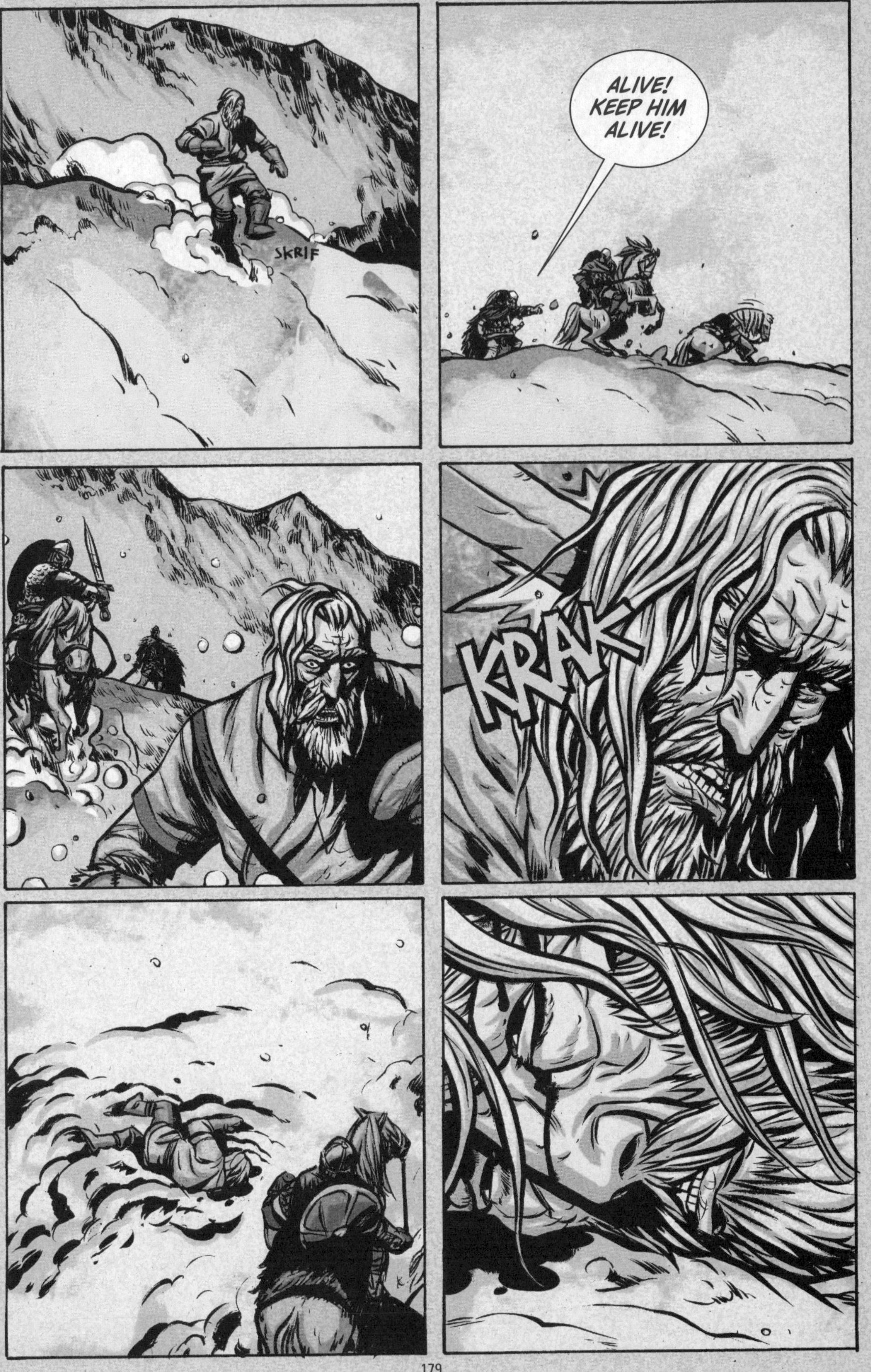
SKRIF
ALIVE! KEEP HIM ALIVE!
KRAK

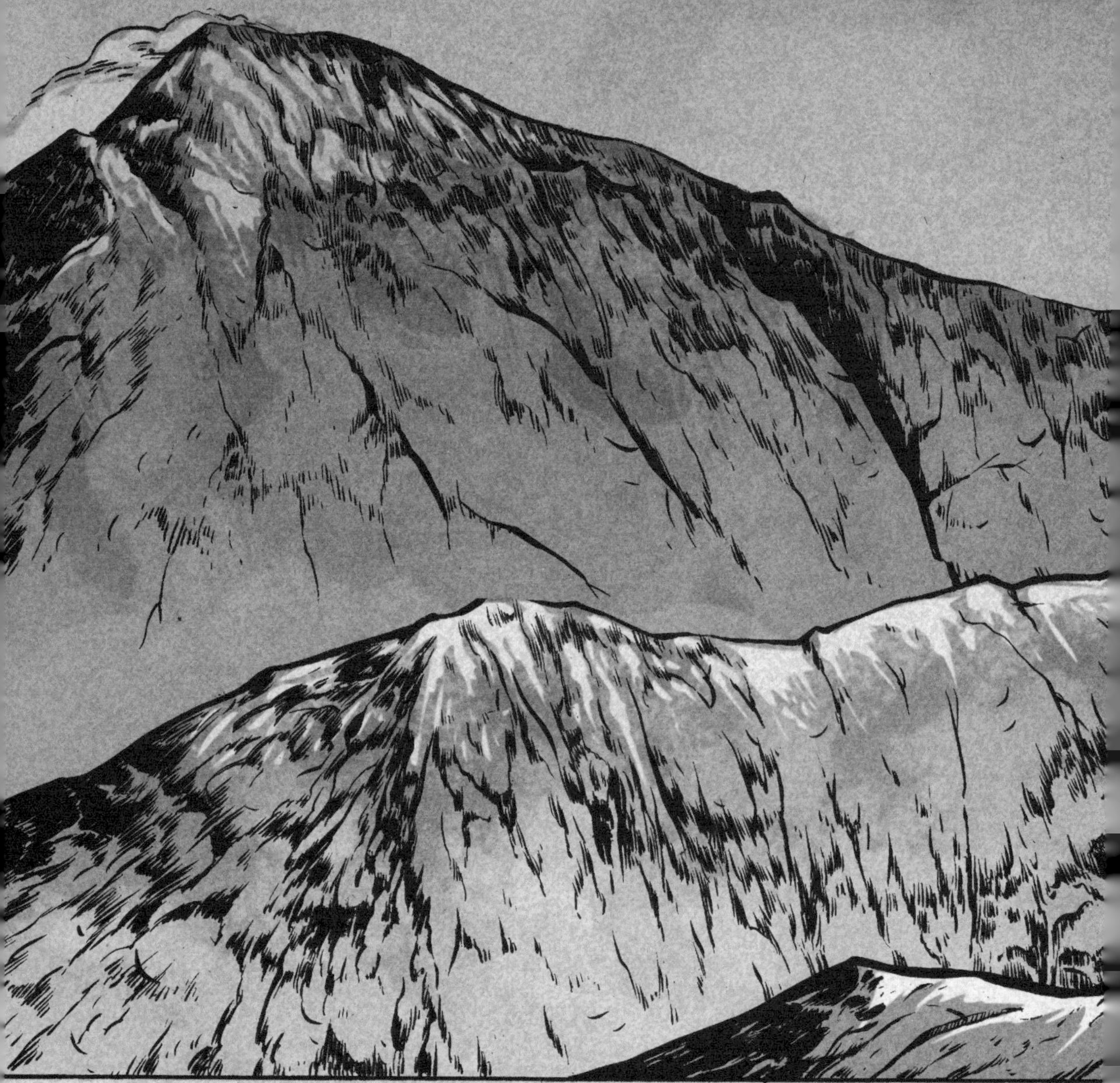

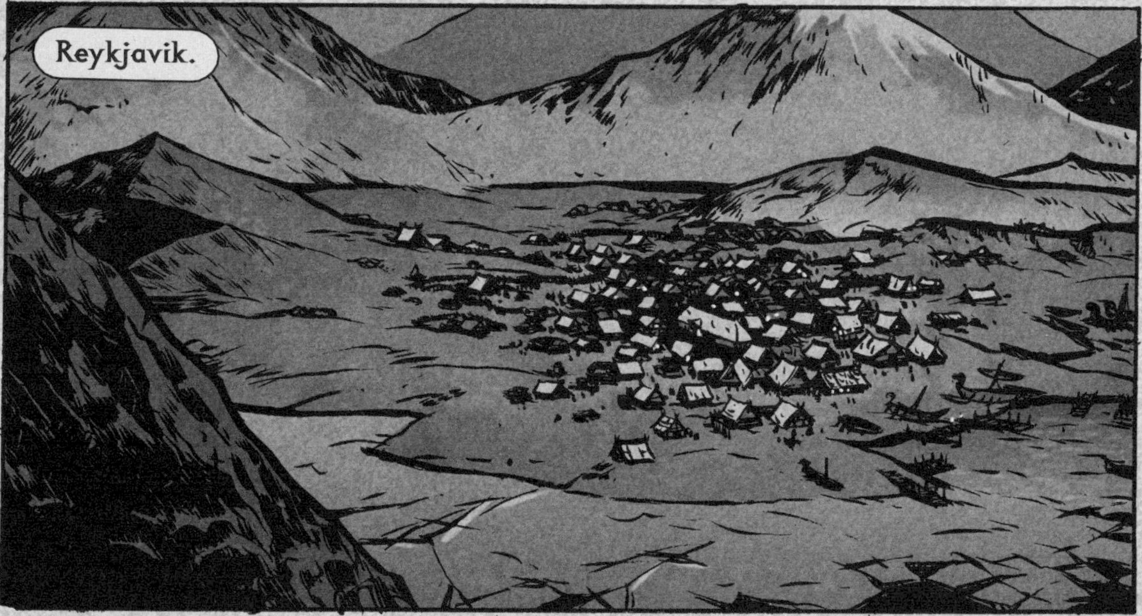
Reykjavik.

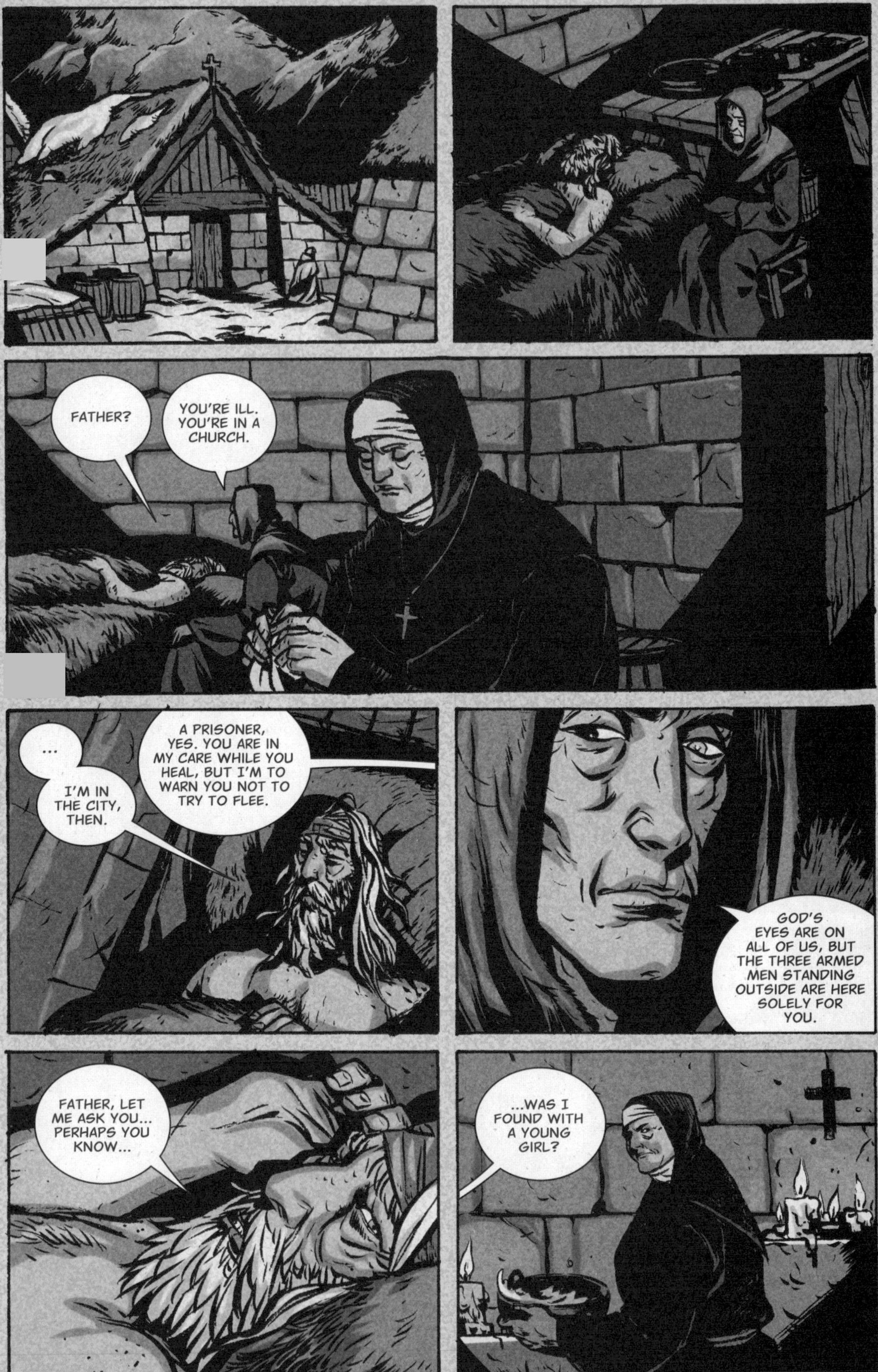
FATHER?
YOU'RE ILL. YOU'RE IN A CHURCH.
...
I'M IN THE CITY, THEN.
A PRISONER, YES. YOU ARE IN MY CARE WHILE YOU HEAL, BUT I'M TO WARN YOU NOT TO TRY TO FLEE.
GOD'S EYES ARE ON ALL OF US, BUT THE THREE ARMED MEN STANDING OUTSIDE ARE HERE SOLELY FOR YOU.
FATHER, LET ME ASK YOU... PERHAPS YOU KNOW...
...WAS I FOUND WITH A YOUNG GIRL?

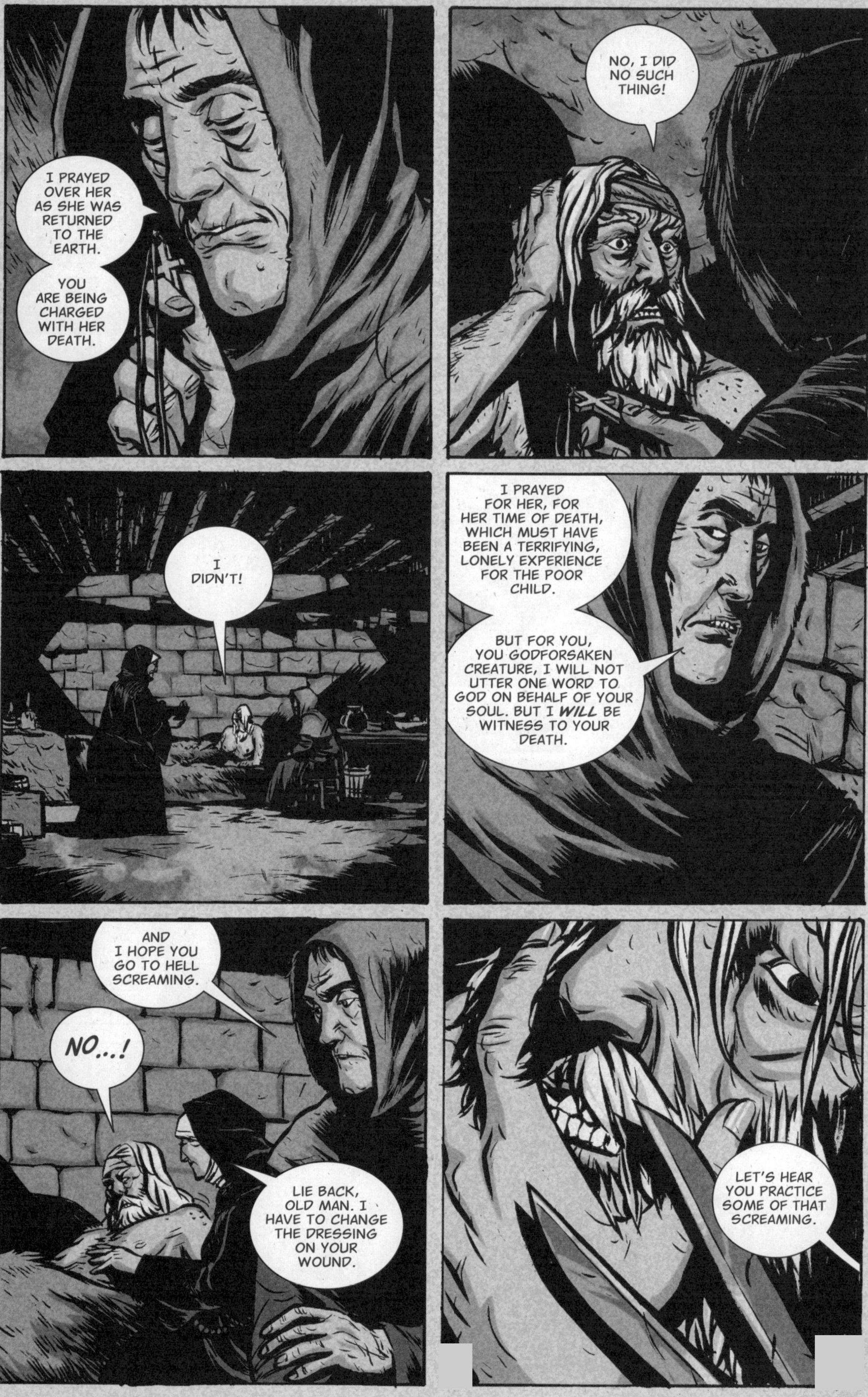
I PRAYED OVER HER AS SHE WAS RETURNED TO THE EARTH.
YOU ARE BEING CHARGED WITH HER DEATH.
NO, I DID NO SUCH THING!
I DIDN'T!
I PRAYED FOR HER, FOR HER TIME OF DEATH, WHICH MUST HAVE BEEN A TERRIFYING, LONELY EXPERIENCE FOR THE POOR CHILD.
BUT FOR YOU, YOU GODFORSAKEN CREATURE, I WILL NOT UTTER ONE WORD TO GOD ON BEHALF OF YOUR SOUL. BUT I *WILL* BE WITNESS TO YOUR DEATH.
AND I HOPE YOU GO TO HELL SCREAMING.
NO...!
LIE BACK, OLD MAN. I HAVE TO CHANGE THE DRESSING ON YOUR WOUND.
LET'S HEAR YOU PRACTICE SOME OF THAT SCREAMING.

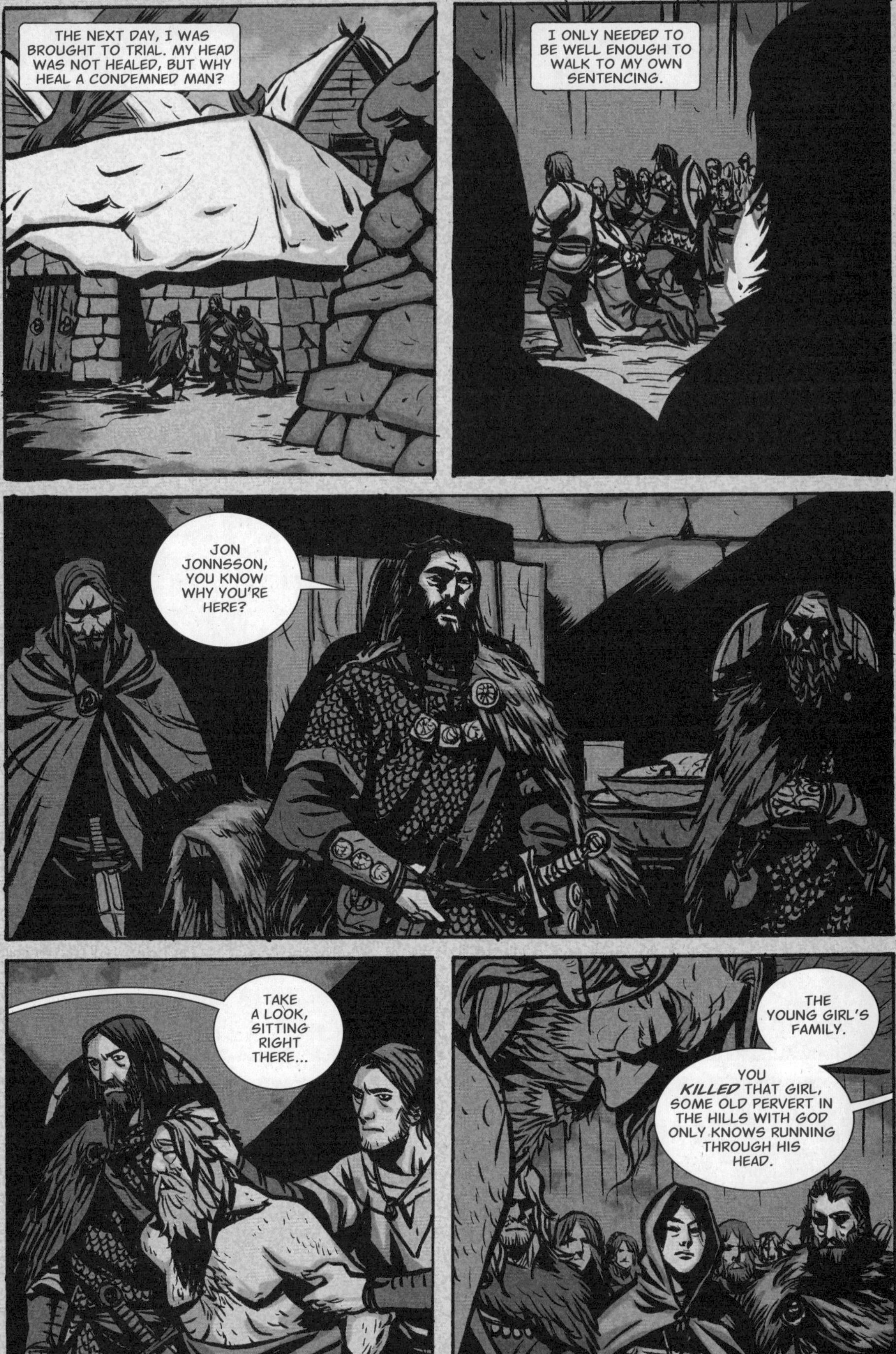
THE NEXT DAY, I WAS BROUGHT TO TRIAL. MY HEAD WAS NOT HEALED, BUT WHY HEAL A CONDEMNED MAN?
I ONLY NEEDED TO BE WELL ENOUGH TO WALK TO MY OWN SENTENCING.
JON JONNSSON, YOU KNOW WHY YOU'RE HERE?
TAKE A LOOK, SITTING RIGHT THERE...
THE YOUNG GIRL'S FAMILY.
YOU *KILLED* THAT GIRL, SOME OLD PERVERT IN THE HILLS WITH GOD ONLY KNOWS RUNNING THROUGH HIS HEAD.

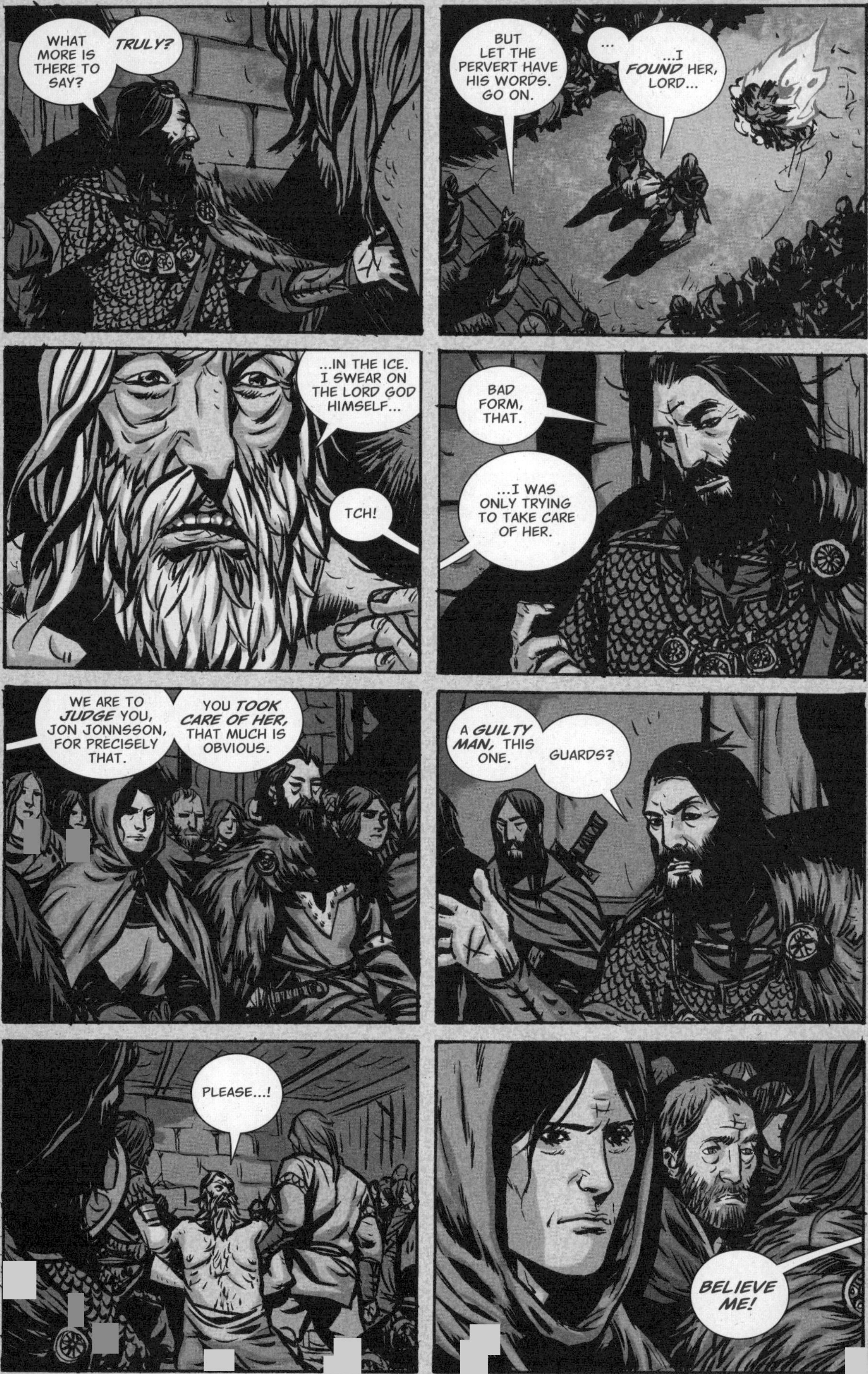
WHAT MORE IS THERE TO SAY?
TRULY?
BUT LET THE PERVERT HAVE HIS WORDS. GO ON.
...
...I FOUND HER, LORD...
...IN THE ICE. I SWEAR ON THE LORD GOD HIMSELF...
TCH!
BAD FORM, THAT.
...I WAS ONLY TRYING TO TAKE CARE OF HER.
WE ARE TO JUDGE YOU, JON JONNSSON, FOR PRECISELY THAT.
YOU TOOK CARE OF HER, THAT MUCH IS OBVIOUS.
A GUILTY MAN, THIS ONE.
GUARDS?
PLEASE...!
BELIEVE ME!

AND WHAT SHOULD I HAVE EXPECTED?

NO ONE COULD REALLY KNOW WHAT HAPPENED OUT THERE ON MY LAKE.

THIS IS A DIFFICULT TIME FOR THE PEOPLE OF ICELAND, A TIME RIFE WITH DISTRUST AND IN-FIGHTING.

THAT POOR GIRL COULD HAVE DIED FOR ANY NUMBER OF REASONS.

BUT HERE I AM, THE ONLY ONE THEY HAVE.

KNOK KNOK

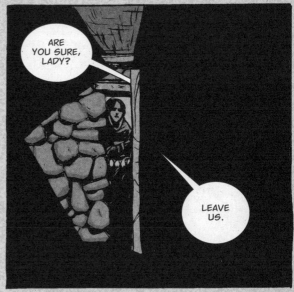
ARE YOU SURE, LADY?

LEAVE US.

...

WHY DO YOU COME HERE?

I KNOW YOU DIDN'T DO IT.

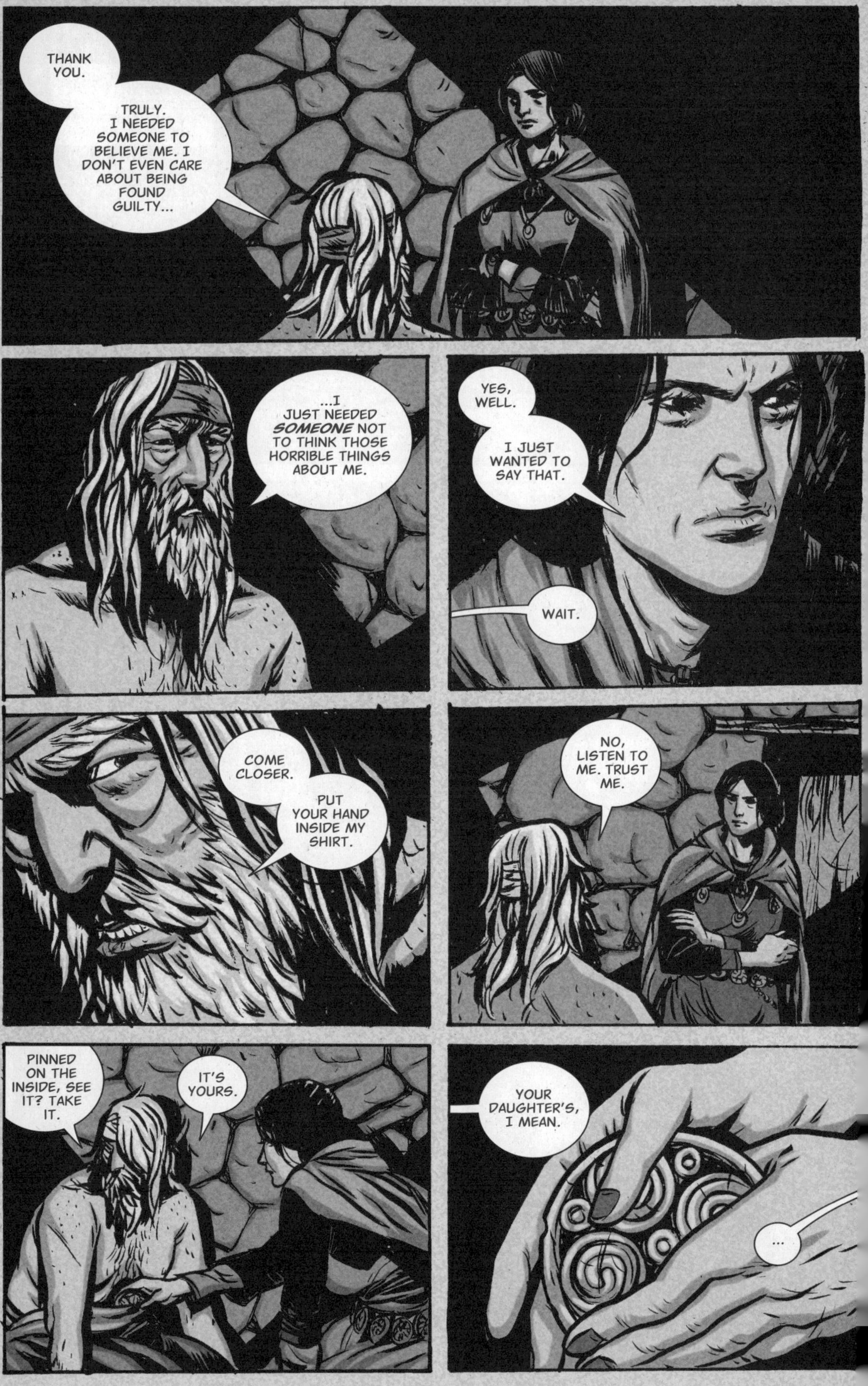
THANK YOU.
TRULY. I NEEDED SOMEONE TO BELIEVE ME. I DON'T EVEN CARE ABOUT BEING FOUND GUILTY...
...I JUST NEEDED SOMEONE NOT TO THINK THOSE HORRIBLE THINGS ABOUT ME.
YES, WELL.
I JUST WANTED TO SAY THAT.
WAIT.
COME CLOSER.
PUT YOUR HAND INSIDE MY SHIRT.
NO, LISTEN TO ME. TRUST ME.
PINNED ON THE INSIDE, SEE IT? TAKE IT.
IT'S YOURS.
YOUR DAUGHTER'S, I MEAN.
...

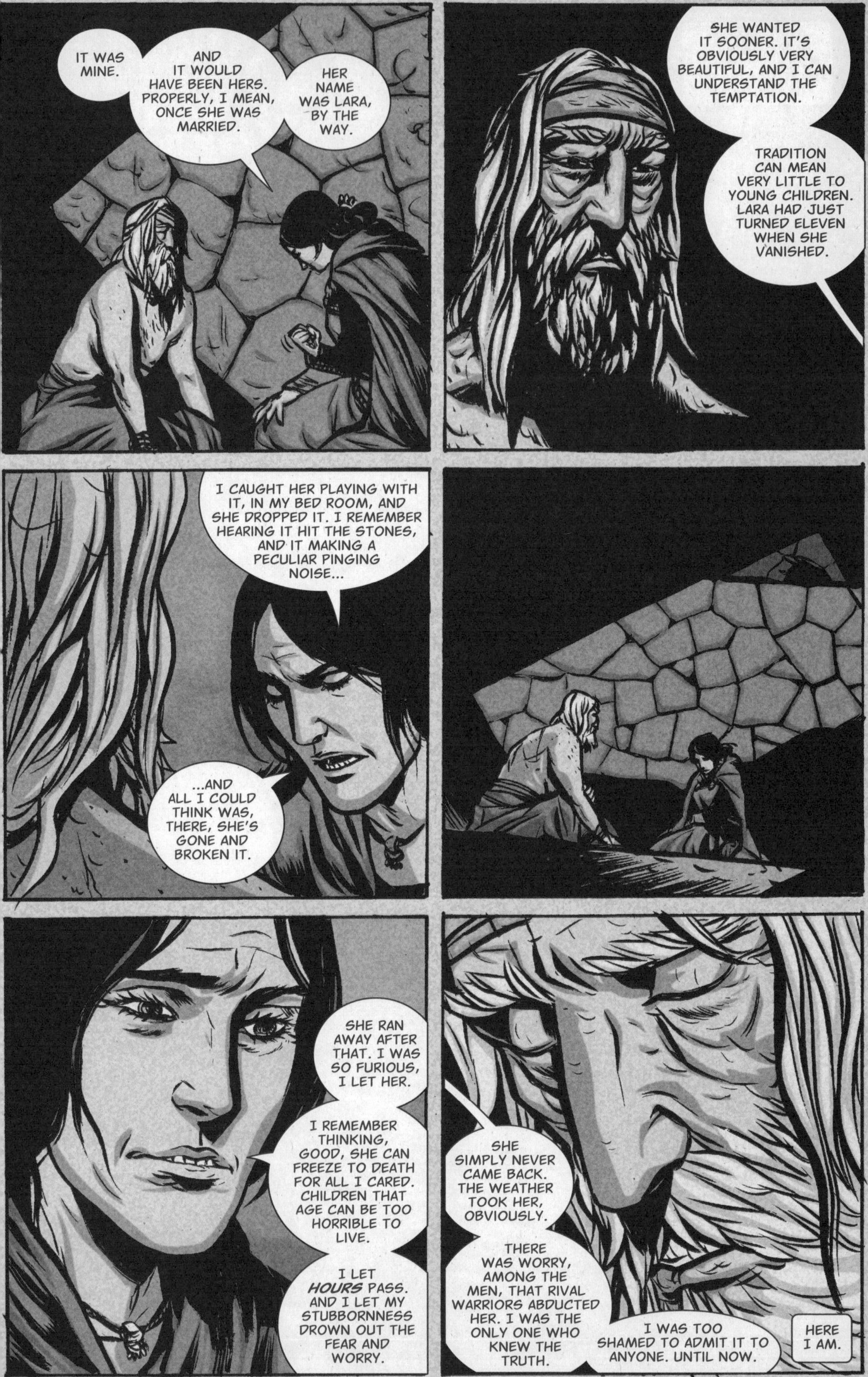
IT WAS MINE.
AND IT WOULD HAVE BEEN HERS. PROPERLY, I MEAN, ONCE SHE WAS MARRIED.
HER NAME WAS LARA, BY THE WAY.
SHE WANTED IT SOONER. IT'S OBVIOUSLY VERY BEAUTIFUL, AND I CAN UNDERSTAND THE TEMPTATION.
TRADITION CAN MEAN VERY LITTLE TO YOUNG CHILDREN. LARA HAD JUST TURNED ELEVEN WHEN SHE VANISHED.
I CAUGHT HER PLAYING WITH IT, IN MY BED ROOM, AND SHE DROPPED IT. I REMEMBER HEARING IT HIT THE STONES, AND IT MAKING A PECULIAR PINGING NOISE...
...AND ALL I COULD THINK WAS, THERE, SHE'S GONE AND BROKEN IT.
SHE RAN AWAY AFTER THAT. I WAS SO FURIOUS, I LET HER.
I REMEMBER THINKING, GOOD, SHE CAN FREEZE TO DEATH FOR ALL I CARED. CHILDREN THAT AGE CAN BE TOO HORRIBLE TO LIVE.
I LET *HOURS* PASS. AND I LET MY STUBBORNNESS DROWN OUT THE FEAR AND WORRY.
SHE SIMPLY NEVER CAME BACK. THE WEATHER TOOK HER, OBVIOUSLY.
THERE WAS WORRY, AMONG THE MEN, THAT RIVAL WARRIORS ABDUCTED HER. I WAS THE ONLY ONE WHO KNEW THE TRUTH.
I WAS TOO SHAMED TO ADMIT IT TO ANYONE. UNTIL NOW.
HERE I AM.

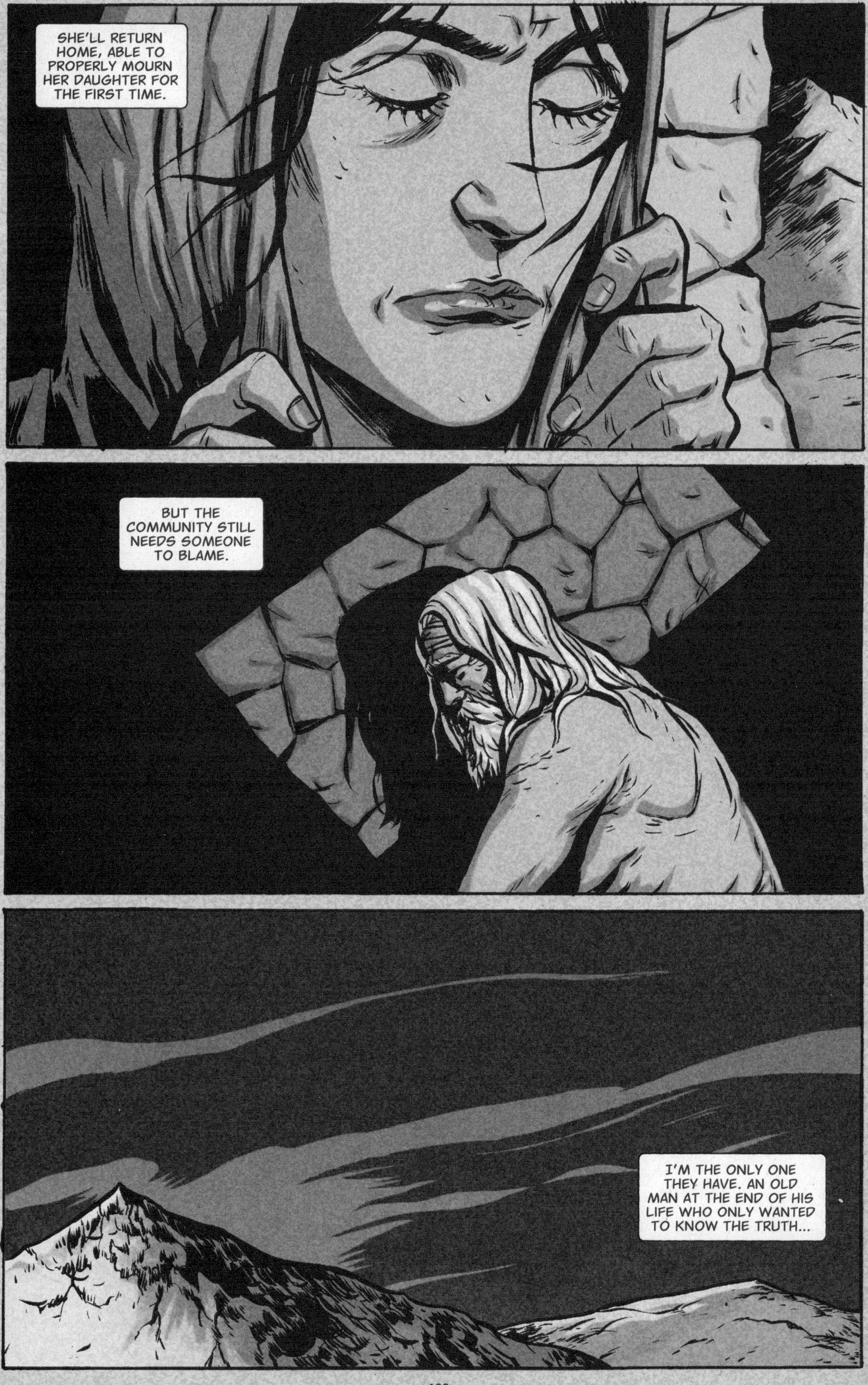
SHE'LL RETURN HOME, ABLE TO PROPERLY MOURN HER DAUGHTER FOR THE FIRST TIME.
BUT THE COMMUNITY STILL NEEDS SOMEONE TO BLAME.
I'M THE ONLY ONE THEY HAVE. AN OLD MAN AT THE END OF HIS LIFE WHO ONLY WANTED TO KNOW THE TRUTH...

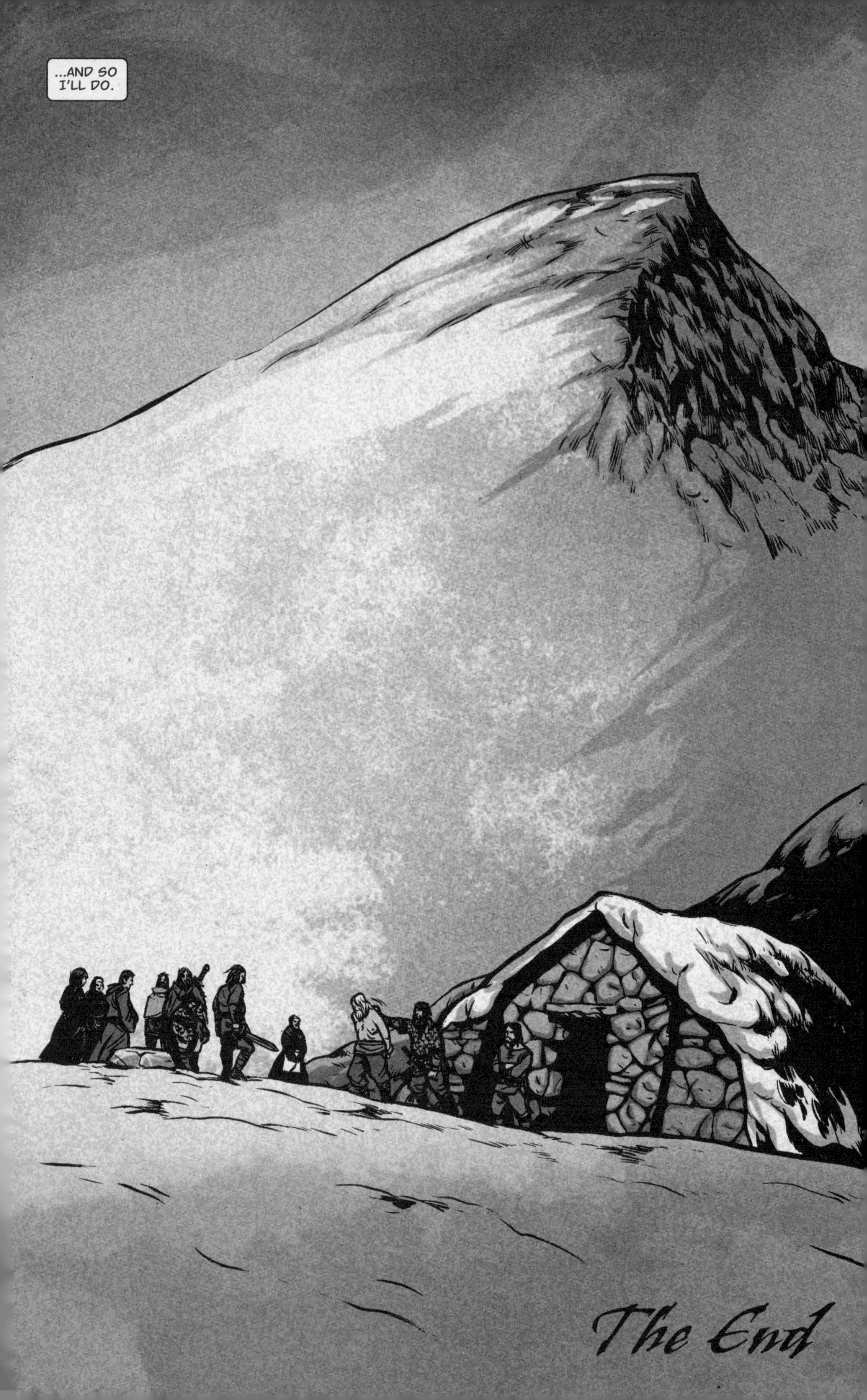
...AND SO I'LL DO.
The End

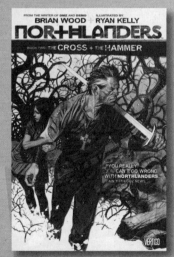

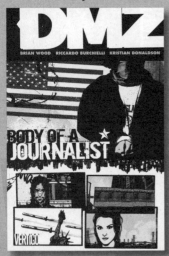

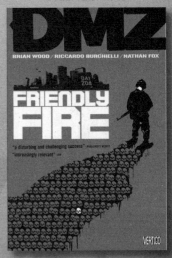

YOU'LL NEVER FORGET THE FIRST

AMERICAN VAMPIRE
VOL. I

DEMO
VOL. I

THE LOSERS
BOOK ONE

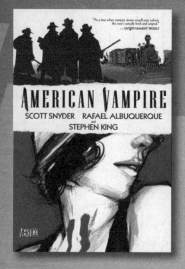

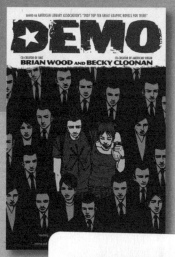

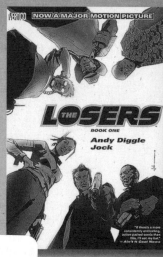

THE UNWRITTEN VOL. I:
TOMMY TAYLOR AND
THE BOGUS IDENTITY

SWEET TOOTH VOL. I:
OUT OF THE DEEP WOODS

UNKNOWN SOLDIER VOL. I:
HAUNTED HOUSE

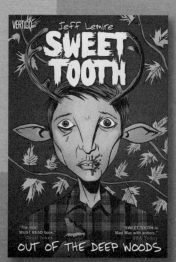

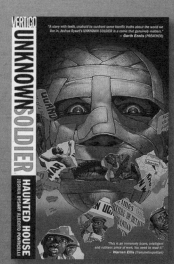

GO TO
VERTIGOBOOKS.COM
FOR FREE SAMPLES OF THE FIRST ISSUES OF OUR GRAPHIC NOVELS

Suggested for Mature Readers